Strategic Survey 2015
The Annual Review of World Affairs

published by

Routledge
Taylor & Francis Group

for

The International Institute for Strategic Studies

The International Institute for Strategic Studies

Arundel House | 13–15 Arundel Street | Temple Place | London | WC2R 3DX | UK

Strategic Survey 2015
The Annual Review of World Affairs

First published September 2015 by **Routledge**
4 Park Square, Milton Park, Abingdon, Oxon, OX14 4RN

for **The International Institute for Strategic Studies**
Arundel House, 13–15 Arundel Street, Temple Place, London, WC2R 3DX, UK

Simultaneously published in the USA and Canada by **Routledge**
270 Madison Ave., New York, NY 10016

Routledge is an imprint of Taylor & Francis, an Informa business

© 2015 The International Institute for Strategic Studies

DIRECTOR-GENERAL AND CHIEF EXECUTIVE Dr John Chipman

EDITOR Alexander Nicoll

ASSISTANT EDITOR Chris Raggett
EDITORIAL Anna Ashton, Jill Lally, Nancy Turner
MAP EDITORS Jessica Delaney, Sarah Johnstone
DESIGN/PRODUCTION John Buck
COVER Kelly Verity
ADDITIONAL MAP RESEARCH Henry Boyd, Erika Broers, Annabel Corser, Joseph Dempsey, Tilly Grove, Nicholas Payne, Alexa van Sickle, Hebatalla Taha
CARTOGRAPHY Martin J. Lubikowski

COVER IMAGES Getty Images
Top row, from left to right: Health worker holds suspected Ebola victim in Liberia; a Cuban welcomes rapprochement with the US; Iran President Hassan Rouhani announces nuclear agreement; pro-democracy protesters in Hong Kong.
Second row: Smoke rising from Syrian town of Kobane; Inglewood oilfield, Los Angeles, California; Chinese President Xi Jinping and Russian President Vladimir Putin sign agreements; Chinese land reclamation on Fiery Cross Reef, South China Sea.
Third row: Scotland's vote on independence from the UK; poster with picture of German finance minister Wolfgang Schäuble calls for 'No' vote in Greek referendum on austerity; migrants on Italian navy vessel at port of Salerno; NATO commander General John Campbell marks end of combat operations in Afghanistan.
Bottom row: After Islamist attack on French magazine *Charlie Hebdo*, Parisians hold placards saying 'I am Charlie'; fighters supporting Iraqi government hold captured ISIS flag; German Chancellor Angela Merkel and French President François Hollande hold hands after visiting crash site of a German aircraft in France.

PRINTED BY Bell & Bain Ltd, Glasgow, UK

British Library Cataloguing in Publication Data
A catalogue record for this book is available from the British Library

Library of Congress Cataloguing in Publication Data

ISBN 978-1-85743-778-2
ISSN 0459-7230

Contents

Strategic Geography (after p. 160)

Index of Regional Maps

Events at a Glance

July 2014–June 2015

July

1   **Japan:** Cabinet adopts a resolution to lift a ban on the Japanese military fighting abroad. The change to the 1947 constitution would allow Japan to take action in 'collective self-defence' if an ally were attacked.

10   **Germany:** Chancellor Angela Merkel orders the CIA's Berlin station chief to leave Germany, amid accusations the organisation spied on the German government.

15   The European Parliament approves Jean-Claude Juncker as president of the European Commission, replacing José Manuel Barroso. Juncker is the lead candidate of the centre-right European People's Party, which won the May European elections. But the appointment is opposed by the UK and Hungary due to his perceived enthusiasm for greater EU integration.

17   **Ukraine:** Malaysia Airlines flight MH17 is shot down over Ukraine, allegedly by Russian-backed separatists, killing all 298 people on board, including 193 Dutch citizens. The area of the crash is controlled by the pro-Russian rebel forces, who restrict access to the site. Ukraine releases evidence that separatists fired a Russian-supplied 9K37 *Buk* missile. Moscow denies involvement.

17   **Australia:** Parliament repeals a tax on carbon emissions two years after it was introduced by the previous government.

22   **Indonesia:** Joko Widodo, governor of Jakarta, is declared the winner of the presidential elections held on 9 July, defeating Prabowo Subianto and replacing Susilo Bambang Yudhoyono.

29   **Russia:** In response to Russian involvement in the Ukraine crisis, the United States and the European Union impose wide-ranging sanctions on Russia's

banking, energy and defence sectors. Moscow in turn bans imports of agricultural and food products from Western countries.

August

1   **Sierra Leone:** A state of emergency is declared after the death toll from an outbreak of Ebola in West Africa reaches 700. The Liberian government quarantines some areas, imposes travel bans and closes schools to contain the outbreak. Over the next ten months, at least 11,000 people die of the disease in Sierra Leone, Liberia and Guinea.

8   **Iraq:** The US begins airstrikes against the Islamic State of Iraq and al-Sham (ISIS) in Iraq, in response to territorial gains made by the group against Kurdish Peshmerga forces. In particular, the strikes are intended to reduce the threat to minorities such as the Yazidis, thousands of whom are stranded on a mountain.

10 **Turkey:** Recep Tayyip Erdogan wins Turkey's first presidential elections after 11 years as prime minister. He is succeeded by Ahmet Davutoglu, foreign minister.

11 **Iraq:** Haider al-Abadi is appointed prime minister by President Fuad Masum, ending Nuri al-Maliki's eight-year premiership. The move follows four months of political infighting, after elections in which Maliki's Dawa party won the largest number of seats but he was unable to form a government. The US, which had been lobbying for Maliki to be replaced since ISIS captured large areas of Iraq, agrees to give direct military aid to Kurdish Peshmerga forces fighting the group.

19 **Syria:** American journalist James Foley, a hostage since 2012, is beheaded by ISIS, which posts video of the event on the internet. The killing is the first in a series of high-profile executions of foreigners by the group.

27 **Israel/Palestine:** The Israeli government and Hamas agree on a long-term ceasefire, suspending a conflict reignited by the murder of three Israeli teenagers in June. More than 2,000 Palestinians and around 70 Israelis have been killed in the latest round of fighting.

31 The EU appoints Polish Prime Minister Donald Tusk and Italian Foreign Minister Federica Mogherini as council president and foreign-affairs chief respectively.

September

1   **Somalia:** Ahmed Abdi Godane, leader of Islamist militant group al-Shabaab, is killed in a US airstrike.

5   **United Kingdom:** NATO leaders meeting in Wales agree to keep a constant military presence in eastern countries of the Alliance, as well as to boost military readiness and create a new rapid-reaction force in response to Russian aggression in Ukraine.

10 **Malta:** About 500 migrants from the Middle East and North Africa are drowned off the coast of Malta when their vessel is rammed by traffickers transporting them from Egypt to Italy. A few days later, more than 200 migrants die when their vessel sinks off the coast of Libya.

14 **Sweden:** The ruling centre-right coalition is ousted in a general election, in which the leftist Swedish Social Democratic Party (SSDP) wins the largest number of seats. However, the right-wing Swedish Democrats, a populist anti-immigration party, comes third, preventing the SSDP from forming a majority government. The SSDP forms a minority coalition with the fourth-placed Greens, and Stefan Löfven becomes prime minister.

18 **United Kingdom:** Residents of Scotland vote to remain part of the United Kingdom, with unionists achieving a 55% vote on an 85% turnout. British Prime Minister David Cameron promises to devolve additional powers to the Scottish parliament. Alex Salmond resigns as Scotland's first minister and head of the Scottish National Party, to be replaced by his deputy, Nicola Sturgeon.

23 **Syria:** The US and a coalition of allies begin a campaign of airstrikes in Syria, in response to the advance of ISIS there. Al-Qaeda affiliates in Syria are also targeted.

28 **Hong Kong:** Thousands of pro-democracy protesters demonstrate in the centre of Hong Kong, angry at Beijing's proposed arrangements for the election of the territory's chief executive. Police use tear gas and pepper spray. Protests continue for two months.

29 **Afghanistan:** Ashraf Ghani becomes president, replacing Hamid Karzai after 13 years. Abdullah Abdullah, his opponent in the June election, becomes the new government's chief executive following a US-brokered deal to resolve a dispute over the election outcome. The government immediately signs security agreements with the US and NATO, enabling foreign troops to remain in Afghanistan in a non-combat role after the end of 2014.

October

2 **Vietnam:** The US partially lifts a 40-year arms embargo on Vietnam, to help it improve maritime security.

3 **India/Pakistan:** Clashes between Indian and Pakistani forces in the disputed Kashmir region begin the worst outbreak of violence between the two sides in a decade.

13 **United Kingdom:** British lawmakers vote 274–12 in favour of recognising Palestine as a state, a symbolic move that would be mirrored in the French parliament on 2 December.

22 **Canada:** A Canadian soldier is killed by a gunman, a Muslim convert with a criminal record, who then attacks parliament buildings in Ottawa before being shot dead.

26 **Ukraine:** The pro-European political bloc led by President Petro Poroshenko wins a majority in Ukraine's parliamentary elections.

27 **Brazil:** Dilma Rousseff is narrowly re-elected president of Brazil, winning 51.6% in the run-off vote against Aecio Neves.

30 **Burkina Faso:** Army seizes power when protests break out after President Blaise Compaoré proposes a parliamentary vote on allowing him to run for a fifth presidential term. On 18 November, the army hands power to Michel Kafando as transitional president, ahead of elections in 2015.

November

4 **United States:** Republican Party wins control of the Senate in mid-term elections, gaining nine seats to give it a total of 54 out of 100. It increases its majority in the House of Representatives.

7 **Iraq:** US President Barack Obama authorises the deployment of 1,500 more American troops to advise and train Iraqi and Kurdish forces battling ISIS.

18 **Israel:** Four rabbis and a policeman are killed at a synagogue in Jerusalem by two Palestinian attackers, who are also killed.

20 **United States:** President Obama offers amnesty to five million undocumented immigrants, allowing them to work legally and avoid deportation. A judge later stays his executive action.

24 **Iran:** Interim agreement with major powers on Iran's nuclear programme is extended until June 2015 to allow more time to reach a full accord.

25 **France:** President François Hollande indefinitely suspends the planned sale of two *Mistral* helicopter carriers to Russia, due to Moscow's actions in Ukraine.

27 **Mexico:** President Enrique Peña Nieto announces reforms designed to counter corruption and gang violence in Mexico, in an attempt to quell protests spurred by the suspected killing of 43 student teachers.

December

5 **Kenya:** The International Criminal Court withdraws charges of crimes against humanity levelled at Kenyan President Uhuru Kenyatta, who was accused of encouraging ethnic violence following his country's 2007 presidential election. Prosecutors say they were forced to suspend the case due to political obstruction and interference with witnesses.

6 **China:** Zhou Yongkang, once a member of the Politburo Standing Committee in charge of the country's internal security, is expelled from the Communist Party and arrested. Charged with abuse of power, bribery and intentional disclosure of state secrets, Zhou is the most prominent figure to be caught up in President

Xi Jinping's sweeping anti-corruption campaign. Zhou is later sentenced to life in prison.

14 **Japan:** Japanese Prime Minister Shinzo Abe retains a two-thirds majority in a snap election, strengthening his position to pursue an assertive foreign policy and a reflationary economic strategy.

15 **Australia:** Gunman seizes hostages in a Sydney cafe. Two hostages die as the siege is ended by security forces, and the Iranian-born attacker, a refugee who was on bail for sexual assault charges, is also killed.

16 **Pakistan:** The Pakistani Taliban attacks a school in Peshawar, killing 145 people, including 132 children. Around 1,000 people are rescued by special forces, who kill some of the gunmen.

17 **United States/Cuba:** Talks are announced on establishing diplomatic ties for the first time in 53 years, following agreement on a prisoner exchange. The move promises to end US economic sanctions on Cuba. US President Barack Obama says isolation 'has not worked'.

19 **Iraq:** Kurdish Peshmerga forces break an ISIS siege on Mount Sinjar, where thousands of Yazidis have been trapped since August.

28 **Afghanistan:** The NATO-led International Security Assistance Force (ISAF) ends its mission after 13 years, and is replaced by a new NATO-led non-combat mission, *Resolute Support*, with 12,000 troops, mainly American, advising and training Afghan forces.

January 2015

2 **North Korea:** Washington strengthens financial sanctions on North Korea following a cyber attack on the US entertainment company Sony Pictures.

7 **Nigeria:** Hundreds of people – some reports say more than 2,000 – are killed in a series of attacks over several days, as insurgent group Boko Haram conducts an offensive against the northeastern town of Baga.

7 **France:** The office of *Charlie Hebdo*, a Paris-based magazine that published cartoons mocking Islam, is attacked by gunmen. Twelve people, including the editor and several cartoonists, are shot dead. A manhunt begins for the two attackers, Cherif and Said Kouachi, French-born brothers of Algerian descent, of whom one had previous convictions for Islamist terrorism. The next morning, a Paris policewoman is shot dead by Amedy Coulibaly, a French-born jihadist of Malian descent. On 9 January, Coulibaly attacks a kosher supermarket and takes hostages, four of whom are subsequently killed. The same evening, security forces storm both the supermarket and a printing plant outside Paris, which the Kouachi brothers had entered following a police chase. All three gunmen are killed. On 11 January, millions of people, including world leaders, march on the streets of France in a show of unity to commemorate the 17 victims.

8 **Sri Lanka:** Maithripala Sirisena is elected president, ousting Mahinda Rajapaksa by a margin of 51% to 48%. Sirisena was minister of health in Rajapaksa's government but broke from him two months before the elections and announced his candidacy with the aim of reforming government.

15 **Belgium:** Police kill two suspected Islamists in a shootout in the town of Verviers. The two men were said to have returned from Syria and to be planning an imminent attack.

18 **Argentina:** Alberto Nisman, a prosecutor who investigated the 1994 bombing of a Jewish centre in Buenos Aires, is found shot dead in his apartment. He had drafted a warrant for the arrest of President Cristina Fernández de Kirchner for allegedly covering up Iranian involvement in the attack, in which 85 people were killed. Kirchner says she does not believe Nisman, who had received death threats, committed suicide. She says she will dissolve one of the country's intelligence services.

22 **Yemen:** President Abd Rabbuh Mansour Hadi resigns after Houthi rebels, who had gained control of the capital Sana'a in September 2014, captured his residence. The Houthi takeover prompts violent resistance.

22 The European Central Bank announces a plan to inject €60 billion per month into the eurozone economy through purchases of bonds. The programme of 'quantitative easing', similar to those undertaken by the central banks of the US, UK and Japan, is intended to ward off severe deflation amidst near-zero inflation and growth.

23 **Saudi Arabia:** King Abdullah dies at the age of 90 and is succeeded by his half-brother, Salman bin Abdulaziz al-Saud, aged 79.

25 **Philippines:** A raid to capture two militants sheltered by the Moro Islamic Liberation Front results in the deaths of 44 police commandos and 18 rebels. The operation casts doubt on the peace process between the insurgent group and the government.

25 **Greece:** The leftist Syriza party wins the general elections and forms a government led by Alexis Tsipras. It seeks a radical revision of the austerity measures that were part of its bailout from fellow members of the eurozone, as well as the EU and IMF. After difficult talks, it agrees a temporary extension of the bailout while a longer-term arrangement is discussed.

February

1 **Hungary:** Several thousand people take part in the latest of a series of protests against Prime Minister Viktor Orbán's perceived authoritarianism and support for Russia.

4 **Brazil:** Top managers of Petrobras, including chief executive Maria das Graças Foster, resign as the state-controlled oil company is engulfed by a corruption scandal. The chief prosecutor later initiates investigations and arrests of dozens

of people, including senior politicians and business executives, over alleged kickbacks.

5 **Jordan:** Jordan's military launches 56 airstrikes against ISIS in three days, shortly after the government confirms the murder of Jordanian pilot Moaz al-Kasasbeh at the hands of the group.

12 **Ukraine:** Russia and Ukraine agree a ceasefire from 15 February in the conflict in the east of the country, after diplomatic efforts by the leaders of France and Germany. Government and separatist forces are to remove heavy weapons from the front line. Following local elections, Ukraine is to regain control of the eastern border by the end of 2015 and to undertake constitutional reform giving special status to Donetsk and Lugansk. However, fighting continues in the town of Debaltsevo, a railway hub, which falls to the separatists on 18 February.

14 **Denmark:** A gunman opens fire on an event at a Copenhagen cultural centre attended by a Danish cartoonist who drew the Prophet Mohammad. One man, a film director, is killed. Later, the gunman attacks a synagogue, killing a Jewish man on security duty. The attacker, Danish-born of Jordanian/Palestinian parentage, is killed by police.

15 **Libya:** ISIS releases video showing the beheading of 21 Egyptians, all Coptic Christian fishermen, who had previously been kidnapped. Next day, Egyptian aircraft carry out airstrikes on ISIS facilities in Libya.

19 **Venezuela:** The mayor of Caracas, Antonio Ledezma, is arrested and later charged with attempting to organise a US-funded coup against President Nicolás Maduro. His lawyers and the US deny the charges.

27 **Mexico:** Federal police capture Servando Gómez, head of the Knights Templar cartel. The arrest is followed on 4 March by the capture of Los Zetas leader Miguel Angel Trevino.

27 **Russia:** Gunmen murder liberal politician Boris Nemtsov, a former deputy prime minister and an outspoken critic of Russian involvement in the Ukraine conflict. Nemtsov is the latest of several prominent opposition figures to be killed during the presidency of Vladimir Putin. Five men from Chechnya are later arrested.

March

3 **United States/Israel:** Israeli Prime Minister Benjamin Netanyahu, invited to address the US Congress by Republican House speaker John Boehner, strongly criticises international efforts to strike a nuclear deal with Iran. The speech is boycotted by many Democrats but receives 26 standing ovations from Republicans.

6 **Philippines:** A military offensive against rebel group the Bangsamoro Islamic Freedom Fighters results in the displacement of around 70,000 people, raising

new concerns about the peace process between the government and the Moro Islamic Liberation Front.

13 **China/Myanmar:** An alleged aistrike by Myanmar forces results in the deaths of four Chinese civilians in Yunnan Province, on China's southern border. The incident occurs amid a conflict between Myanmar forces and ethnic Chinese rebels in the neighbouring Kokang region of Myanmar. The deaths prompt a diplomatic spat between Beijing and Naypyidaw.

15 **Brazil:** One million people participate in demonstrations against corruption and economic downturn, calling for the impeachment of President Dilma Rousseff.

17 **Israel:** The Likud party narrowly wins national elections. Coalition negotiations begin, resulting in the formation of a government on 6 May, with Benjamin Netanyahu remaining prime minister.

18 **Tunisia:** Gunmen attack foreign tourists at the Bardo Museum in Tunis, resulting in the deaths of 22 people. ISIS claims responsibility.

19 **Japan/China:** Beijing and Tokyo hold their first high-level security talks in four years, amid territorial disputes over the East China Sea and persistent historical tensions.

20 **Yemen:** Four suicide bombers attack two mosques in Sana'a, killing 142 people. On 25 March, a Saudi-led coalition begins airstrikes in Yemen, targeting Houthi rebels who have seized control of much of the country. The Saudis are supporting the government of deposed President Hadi, who has fled to Riyadh. The US provides logistical and intelligence support to the operation against the insurgents, whom Riyadh regards as Iranian proxies.

23 **Singapore:** Lee Kuan Yew, founder of modern Singapore and international statesman, dies aged 91.

24 **France:** An airliner operated by Germanwings crashes in the French Alps on a flight from Barcelona to Düsseldorf, killing all 150 people on board. Evidence suggests the co-pilot was suffering from mental illness and deliberately flew the aircraft into the ground.

31 **Nigeria:** Opposition leader Muhammadu Buhari wins the presidential elections, defeating the incumbent Goodluck Jonathan, who concedes defeat. The vote results in Nigeria's first democratic transfer of power to an opposition party.

April

2 **Iran:** The EU and the E3+3 (China, France, Germany, Russia, the United Kingdom and the US) reach a preliminary agreement with Iran on the country's nuclear programme, with a deadline of 30 June for completing a deal.

2   **Kenya:** Al-Shabaab kills 147 people during a 15-hour siege at Kenya's Garissa University, singling out Christians in the most deadly attack yet by the Somali jihadist group.

19   More than 700 migrants travelling to Europe from the Middle East and North Africa are killed while attempting to cross the Mediterranean Sea from Libya. The EU later agrees to triple the funding of its maritime rescue mission in the region.

25   **Nepal:** Nearly 9,000 people are killed by an earthquake measuring 7.8 on the Richter scale.

May

3   **United States:** Police in Dallas shoot dead two gunmen who opened fire on an exhibition of cartoons depicting the Prophet Mohammad.

7   **United Kingdom:** The Conservative Party, led by Prime Minister David Cameron, unexpectedly wins a narrow parliamentary majority in a general election, enabling it to govern without its former coalition partner, the Liberal Democrats. Ed Miliband, Labour Party leader, resigns. The Scottish National Party, which wants independence, wins almost all the seats in Scotland and becomes the third-largest party at Westminster.

13   **North Korea:** South Korean intelligence-agency officials are quoted as saying that the North's defence minister, Hyon Yong-chol, was executed by anti-aircraft fire in late April, allegedly for disloyalty to leader Kim Jong-un and for falling asleep in meetings.

17   **Iraq:** Ramadi, the capital of Anbar province, falls to ISIS insurgents as Iraqi army soldiers flee the city. ISIS also captures the Syrian town of Palmyra, a major archaeological site.

20   **Indonesia/Malaysia:** The two countries agree to take in thousands of migrants stranded at sea, mostly Bangladeshis or ethnic Rohingya from Myanmar, until they can be resettled or sent home.

26   **Iran:** Jason Rezaian, an American-Iranian reporter for the *Washington Post* who was arrested in July 2014, goes on trial on espionage charges.

29   **United States/Cuba:** The US removes Cuba from a list of countries categorised as state sponsors of terrorism, a step towards restoration of full relations.

June

1   **China:** More than 400 people are killed when a cruise ship capsizes on the Yangtze River, leaving only 14 survivors.

2   **United States:** Congress passes legislation restricting the bulk interception of telecommunications data by the National Security Agency.

7   **Turkey:** The ruling Justice and Development Party (AKP) loses its parliamentary majority in a general election, dealing a serious blow to the ambitions of President Erdogan to change the constitution to create an executive presidency. The pro-Kurdish HDP party wins seats for the first time by securing more than 10% of the vote. With the AKP holding 46% of seats and three other parties the remainder, it is unclear whether a government can be formed.

10   **Iraq:** US says it will deploy 450 more troops to Iraq to train and advise Iraqi forces fighting against ISIS. This will bring the number of American troops in Iraq to more than 3,500.

12   **Yemen:** The leader of al-Qaeda in the Arabian Peninsula, Nassir al-Wuhayshi, is killed by a US drone strike.

15   **Chad:** More than 20 people are killed in a bomb attack in N'Djamena, the capital, believed to be carried out by Boko Haram. In response, Chad launches airstrikes against the group's bases.

26   **Kuwait:** A suicide bomber, identified as a Saudi citizen, kills 27 people, mostly Kuwaitis, at a mosque during Friday prayers.

26   **Tunisia:** A gunman attacks tourists at a beach resort hotel in Sousse, killing 38 people, of whom 30 are British. He is shot dead by police.

26   **France:** A delivery driver with Islamist connections beheads his boss and sets off an explosion at a chemicals factory near Lyon. He is arrested.

29   **Greece:** Government closes banks for a week, imposes capital controls and calls a referendum for 5 July on whether to accept terms of a potential deal with creditors. Prime Minister Alexis Tsipras urges voters to reject the draft deal. On 30 June, the existing €240bn bailout package for Greece expires without renewal and a deadline passes for it to make a €1.6bn payment to the IMF.

Chapter 1

Perspectives

The multiplying conflicts of the Middle East overshadowed the world in the year to mid-2015. Wars were being fought in Syria, Iraq, Yemen and Libya, with little sign of resolution. The conflicts were killing tens of thousands and displacing millions, setting in train a series of refugee crises. Jihadist groups' prominent role in the fragmentation of these countries spurred their recruitment of extremist fighters and increased the worldwide threat of terrorist attacks. Thus, the Middle East seemed bound to rise further up the agenda of world leaders, despite their fervent wishes to the contrary.

There was, however, significant progress in resolving one long-standing Middle Eastern confrontation, as global powers reached an agreement with Iran that would curtail its nuclear programme in exchange for the country's release from burdensome economic sanctions. Not only was the accord a landmark in countering nuclear proliferation, it also heralded a rebalancing of regional dynamics. This heightened concern for the future among the Israelis and the Gulf Arabs, as long-time allies of the United States. Since most wars in the Middle East are theatres, to a greater or lesser extent, for the chronic rivalry between Iran and Saudi Arabia, the partial rehabilitation of Tehran in international diplomacy could have important broader effects.

War was not exclusive to the Middle East. The conflict in eastern Ukraine appeared to be becoming 'frozen' along the lines of others in post-Soviet countries, despite mediation efforts made in particular by Germany and France. In response to Russia's annexation of Crimea in 2014 and its continued role in assisting separatist forces in eastern Ukraine, NATO made serious efforts to renew solidarity and to strengthen its ability to deal with future contingencies involving eastern member nations. After decades of decline in European spending on armed forces following the fall of the Berlin Wall, major European countries and those geographically close to Russia announced plans to increase their defence budgets. Military exercises were stepped up, readiness and rapid-reaction capacities enhanced, and equipment and troops shifted eastwards in an effort at reassurance. Meanwhile, NATO and its member governments were urgently debating how in future they could counter the so-called 'hybrid' tactics – a mix of military and non-military means – that Russia had employed in Ukraine.

These steps, combined with tough economic sanctions on Moscow, displayed a unified European – and transatlantic – response to the increased threat to Europe's security posed by Russia. However, Europe was also experiencing substantial internal challenges to its unity and integration, as a radical left-wing government in Greece took its country to the brink of an unprecedented exit from the euro, the common currency of 19 of the 28 countries in the European Union. The economic hardships suffered by the Greeks – and the government's defiance in negotiations with creditors on economic reforms and new financing – created hostility and division unseen among European countries for many years. The deal that was eventually reached to keep Greece in the euro seemed a temporary fix that satisfied nobody, and that would result in damaging animosities on all sides. Meanwhile, the United Kingdom risked stirring further intra-European antipathy, as a Conservative government with a new electoral mandate, harried by right-wing nationalist eurosceptics, sought to negotiate a new bargain with European partners that would distance Britain somewhat from Europe's path to integration. A referendum on whether to remain a member of the EU would be held by the end of 2017.

In addition to the deal with Iran, US President Barack Obama had other foreign-policy successes in the year to mid-2015. His most daring move was to end more than half a century of isolating Cuba, following months of secret negotiations in which the Argentinian Pope Francis played a part. Progress was made towards new international trade agreements, even if Washington was unable to stop other countries from joining Beijing's latest effort to expand its influence, a Chinese-led development bank to finance Asian infrastructure.

But in dealing with the troubles of the wider Middle East, Obama remained ineffectual. He failed to engineer, articulate or participate in any kind of credible international strategy to resolve the four-year-old Syrian civil war, even as the death toll rose to more than 230,000 and the resulting displacement of people affected many countries. Washington appeared unable to counter decisively the extremist group Islamic State of Iraq and al-Sham (ISIS), which kept control of vast areas of Iraq and continued to be a potent actor in the Syrian conflict. As it expanded from its strong-hold within Syria, ISIS beheaded foreign hostages and used the internet to attract thousands of recruits from abroad, including whole families. A US-led coalition campaign of airstrikes, coupled with special-forces activity, assistance to Kurdish fighters and advice to the Iraqi military, did have some effect in checking the group. But in the developing war in Iraq, the American-trained Iraqi army appeared to be in a state of collapse, and it was the former adversaries of the US who were taking the battle to ISIS: newly remobilised Shia militias, and the Quds Force of the Iran Revolutionary Guard Corps. The extent of the latter's involvement was indicated by its reported loss of several senior commanders in Iraq.

It was unsurprising that, having ended the involvement of US combat troops in the conflicts that he inherited in Iraq and Afghanistan, Obama would strongly resist sending them back into the fray. He had made his view clear that the world should not look to Washington to solve every problem. But the US still had important allies and interests in the Middle East, and the region's spiral into conflict, with its implications for global terrorism, was such that Western powers seemed bound eventually to be again drawn in more closely. Therefore, a more proactive approach to addressing the chronic splits and conflicts there seemed increasingly incumbent upon Washington – if not under the current president, then the next.

The persistent threat from extremism was underlined by the spread of the conflict between Nigerian government forces and the Islamist group Boko Haram. The election of a new president, Muhammadu Buhari, was a landmark for Africa's largest country, as the first democratic transfer of power from an incumbent party to an opposition party. Buhari was elected partly because of the lack of progress in defeating Boko Haram. But even as he took office, the war was spreading to involve several neighbouring countries. Meanwhile, other persistent conflicts – such as those in Somalia, Democratic Republic of the Congo, Sudan and South Sudan – continued to undermine the continent's economic progress.

In the Asia-Pacific, the temperature of long-running territorial disputes appeared to lower somewhat on the diplomatic front, but there was significant construction activity around some of the disputed features in the South China Sea, especially by Beijing. As China expanded its military, it also sought to build its regional economic influence through the new Asian Infrastructure Investment Bank, and through its 'One Belt, One Road' policy, designed to develop trade and investment links with Eurasia. Meanwhile, President Xi Jinping vigorously pursued an anti-corruption campaign that resulted in Zhou Yongkang, previously in charge of the country's domestic security apparatus, being sentenced to life imprisonment.

The slowdown in China's economic growth, though the pace was still healthy, continued to force adjustments both at home, where there was financial-market turbulence, and abroad. The effect was particularly apparent in reduced Chinese demand for some commodities from Latin America, where failures to reform economies were being exposed just as a number of corruption scandals came to light – most notably in Brazil. The steep fall in the oil price, moderated by only a small eventual recovery, significantly altered economic assumptions worldwide and was a boon to consumers. (See essay, pp. 37–48). Inflation in advanced economies was essentially halted for the time being, a remarkable occurrence. But fears of this trend turning into a deflationary spiral, especially in Europe, were allayed as the European Central Bank overcame its reluctance to embark on 'quantitative easing' – the type of exceptional monetary stimulus undertaken by central banks elsewhere. While there were persistent risks, the global economic outlook appeared more benign than it had for some time.

Middle East: Progress and regression

In a *New York Times* interview in April 2015, the US president made the case for the nuclear agreement that was being negotiated with Iran. In engaging with smaller countries, Obama said, there were not too many risks. Iran had done things that resulted in the deaths of Americans. 'But the truth of the matter is: Iran's defense budget is $30 billion. Our defense budget is closer to $600 billion. Iran understands that they cannot fight us.' Obama continued: 'you asked about an Obama doctrine. The doctrine is: we will engage, but we preserve all our capabilities.' A diplomatic (rather than a military) solution was more likely to last, he said, and 'who knows? Iran may change.' Even if it did not, the military superiority of the US would be preserved.

This seems a straightforward argument to put forward in international affairs. It is one that presidents of either party might make. It means dealing from the tremendous position of strength that the US still enjoys across the globe. But since al-Qaeda's 2001 attacks on the US, the waters had been muddied by the growing prominence of non-state groups that could not be engaged with diplomatically. Military efforts to defeat such groups – regardless of America's prowess, sacrifices and expenditure – could not produce clear victories. The fate of Afghanistan, the object of a massively ambitious international transformation project, remains in the balance with the Taliban undefeated. The US-led campaign in Iraq did not produce either a political system that could assure security for all Iraqis or a military capable of protecting them; and the country has slipped back into sectarian conflict. Islamic extremism, in the form of al-Qaeda as an organisation based in the mountains of Pakistan and Afghanistan, was severely degraded by US military action, but has since metamorphosed into more nimble groups in other places. The US still possesses a huge military advantage over any potential enemy, but the ways in which its forces have been used since 2001 have perhaps made the country appear weaker to its adversaries and even to itself. Certainly, no Republican candidate for the 2016 election wishes to be associated with George W. Bush – even his brother, Jeb, has disowned the invasion of Iraq. And Obama has been cast as weak even by some of his allies.

At least in Iran there was a state to be dealt with, if one with an unusual political system. The wish to engage with Tehran that Obama had expressed right from the beginning of his presidency in 2009 – backed up by a significant tightening of international sanctions and the threat of more – seemed to have been vindicated by the July 2015 agreement, which represented an extraordinary diplomatic success. The kudos, of course, would not be his alone, but also belonged to other international leaders and to Iranian negotiators.

But rapprochement with Iran, to the extent that this was likely to occur, seemed far from enough. Whether Obama liked it or not, Washington's burden continued to be onerous and complex. While promoting democracy in Iraq and Afghanistan, the US had continued to prop up old, creaking regimes with poor human-rights records across the Middle East. When some of them fell, Washington acceded to the revolutionary fervour that brought them down. But it was powerless to control the forces that were then unleashed, and the outcomes: in Egypt, which swung from a non-religious revolution to an elected Islamist government and then back into the control of the military; in Syria, where a regime retained nominal power over a destroyed country in a war with a shifting array of militia groups; in Yemen, where the state had gradually weakened to the benefit of non-state actors, and conflict had broken out; and in Libya, where attempts to rebuild the state following foreign intervention were largely abandoned amid an intensifying civil war.

These developments did not spring directly from Washington's decisions. But other changes in the region have more direct origins in US choices to act or refrain from action: for example, the invasion of Iraq and the disbanding of the Iraqi army directly shaped not only Iraq but also the surrounding region; the engagement of Iran and the abandonment of then Egyptian president Hosni Mubarak both caused huge anxiety to US-supported rulers in the Gulf; and the withholding of airstrikes against Syria, following the regime's use of chemical weapons on its citizens, also bewildered Washington's friends.

Obama's reassertion of the value of diplomacy, refraining from military action unless it was the only means of obtaining an end, was a correct approach after a decade of intervention that had high costs and only mixed success. It was simply a statement of fact that Washington could not solve every Middle East problem, especially not with military force. With China and other powers in the world rising, Washington's relative global influence was declining, and events from September 2001 onwards had contributed to this change. To some extent, Obama's effort has been to restore perspective in American policies and actions, and to avoid overreacting to events or seeking quick fixes where none existed. It was straightforward to argue that in invading Iraq in response to the 9/11 attacks, the US was acting against its own best interests. Expounding his approach to Vox website in January 2015, Obama said: 'We're going to have to have some humility in recognizing that we don't have the option of simply invading every country where disorder breaks out. And that to some degree, the people of these countries are going to have to, you know, find their own way. And we can help them but we can't do it for them.'

The argument had a lot going for it as a counterweight to the previous presidency, and even to the ambitious military strategy adopted under Obama himself after he increased the number of troops in Afghanistan. But it seemed more than unrealistic to suggest, for example, to the people of Syria that they should 'find their own way'. Few were making the case for the direct involvement of American troops on the ground in Syria. But given that the US still had important allies and interests in the Middle East, it was very much in Washington's interest that the Syrian war should move towards resolution. To be sure, the conflict was complicated and involved many non-state actors, none of whom seemed obviously aligned with the West. There was no quick fix. But substantive diplomatic activity – to explore solutions, build and shape alliances, corral international activity and deal with a profound humanitarian crisis – seemed extraordinarily absent.

Equally, Washington appeared to have a strong interest in working more effectively with Western and regional powers to address the sectarian conflict in Iraq. At times, it seemed at a loss as to how to react when the Iraqi government lost important cities to ISIS. It denied that setbacks were significant, but also lashed out at the Iraqi forces that it had fostered at great expense. In summer 2014, Obama was saying that 'we don't have a strategy yet' to combat the spread of ISIS, and in June 2015 he said: 'we don't yet have a complete strategy because it requires commitments on the part of the Iraqis as well.'

Meanwhile, the threat from jihadist groups such as ISIS seemed to be growing across the Western world. The greatest shock came from the attacks in Paris in January 2015, which were separately targeted against cartoonists and Jews. In the year to mid-2015, there were jihadist attacks in Australia, Belgium, Canada, Denmark, France, Kenya, Kuwait, Nigeria,

Pakistan, Tunisia and the US. It was not that the efforts being made to counter extremist groups, in terms of intelligence work and military action and advice, were at all negligible. Again, there could be no quick solution. But the extraordinary recruiting appeal of ISIS indicated that there were fundamental causes of concern, and not just in the Middle East.

More active diplomacy in the region would be needed – and not just by the US, but by world leaders as a whole. There was a large middle ground between invasion and inaction, and it needed to be explored more thoroughly before conflicts spread further and the global threat of terrorism became intolerable.

European insecurity

Shortly after becoming prime minister of Greece in January 2015, Alexis Tsipras visited a memorial for resistance fighters executed by the Nazis in 1944. The left-wing leader of the radical Syriza party had been elected on a promise to free Greeks from their misery after the country's economy shrank by a quarter in five years. He said he would end the bailouts that imposed austerity budget cuts and reforms, and he would reduce Greece's debt.

Tsipras was not the first Greek leader to invoke the Nazi occupation when facing international negotiations. But the plain fact was that following €240bn of financial rescues provided by European governments and the IMF after Athens' 2009 admission of gross fiscal mismanagement, Germany was Greece's biggest creditor. It was German Chancellor Angela Merkel who would ultimately decide whether EU countries would accede to Syriza's demands. This was, no doubt, an unwelcome position for her to be in. But she too had to meet the expectations of voters – and public resentment was high in Germany as well.

Tipping the balance was one further fact: Greece needed money. The election of Tsipras and the antagonistic, hectoring approach of his finance minister, Yanis Varoufakis (who later resigned), in effect cut Athens off from any potential sources of finance other than European governments and the European Central Bank. As deposits fled Greek banks, the country depended entirely on European institutions to keep it afloat. If they chose not to do so, Greeks faced years of even worse times, with bankrupt banks, exit from the euro, a massive devaluation and, potentially, serious social unrest. On the other side, the purely financial losses that Europe would suffer from a Greek collapse would be manageable.

Given these circumstances, only one side could determine the outcome. Either Greece would make undertakings that would satisfy creditors and it would be kept within the euro, or it would not. Greeks wanted to keep the euro. So in July 2015, a deal was duly reached as Tsipras promised economic reforms that he had previously rejected, and the eurozone grudgingly agreed to a third €86bn bailout package.

The common currency was thus preserved. The importance of avoiding 'Grexit' was that for one country to depart would undermine, perhaps fatally, the 16-year-old currency-union project. Previous attempts to fix European currencies to each other had fallen apart, and the establishment of the common currency in 1999 was an attempt, in effect, to lock the exit door and throw away the key – creating a sense of permanence. But if, facing a financial crisis, a country such as Greece were to leave, then the next time that a similar crisis afflicted another member country, there would be overwhelming market speculation and pressure that would lead, almost inevitably, towards another exit. The project would unravel.

In the case of Greece, this contingency was prevented, at least for the time being. But in the process, Europe was badly damaged. Currency union – although at one level a financial and technical undertaking – is above all a political project. The euro was an important step on the path to European integration that has been the overall goal since the Second World War. With 28 countries having joined the EU and more aspiring to do so, the union has had extraordinary success in building common democratic values, standards of governance and a powerful economy based on the principle of a single market. The entire project relies, however, on mutual trust and a sense of shared destiny. In the negotiations with Greece, these were not at all in evidence.

From a starting point of stirring anti-German sentiment, Tsipras and his government did not approach European governments as partners. Rather, he treated them as moneylenders who had exacted cruel terms. There was, in fact, merit in Greece's case that the terms of financial bailouts should be angled more towards the promotion of economic growth and less towards preventing creditors from suffering financial losses. But the government resorted to confrontation rather than persuasion. The response of Germany and most other eurozone governments was consequently defensive and negative. They had noted the progress that Greece had made towards restoring fiscal health under the previous government: the economy had even grown by a tiny amount in 2014, and it was regaining access to international financial markets. Creditors were well aware of the plight of the Greeks, which was the result not just of stringent bailout conditions but of decades of governmental mismanagement. From this basis, they could perhaps have been persuaded to be more accommodating. But instead, Athens harangued them and made strident demands, including for debt relief on loans that already had extended payback periods and low interest rates.

The culmination of five months of argument and growing mistrust was Tsipras's sudden decision to put a set of proposed bailout terms to a referendum within a week. It was a travesty of democracy that Greek voters should be presented with barely comprehensible technical documents and urged to reject them – as 61% of them duly did. Tsipras apparently believed this outcome would enable him to secure better terms. But in the following days he was humiliated as, in order to obtain an agreement, he was forced to accept worse terms than those that voters had rejected. The deal was agreed even though it was reported that 15 out of 18 creditor governments favoured a rejection that would have made Grexit inevitable. Tsipras's sole champion was French President François Hollande, who urged that Greece be accommodated in Europe's longer-term interests – and indeed, it would be disastrous for Europe to have Greece spiralling downwards within its midst, with all the risks and vulnerabilities involved.

The outcome, however, was one that almost nobody wanted or believed in. Having agreed to such unwelcome terms, Tsipras's own standing within his party and his government was seriously in question. The conditions seemed unlikely to be fully implemented: for example, the leftist government was expected to obtain €50bn from privatisation of state assets. Although creditors had no confidence in the deal, they would nevertheless advance the funding if Athens went through the motions of passing the necessary legislation. At mid-July 2015, the durability of the new arrangements was very much in doubt. What was left, above all, was a wealth of bad feeling on all sides.

If the common currency – and perhaps the entire European integration project – were to survive in the longer term, remedies would be needed for the serious harm that had been done. Firstly, it would be unacceptable for Europe's democracies to be set against each other in such a way that one held the other's fate in its hands. Partnership was not possible in such circumstances. It turned out that there had been a benefit in having faceless international institutions – the IMF and the World Bank – responsible for imposing the tough terms needed to restore countries when they fell into financial difficulties. How could Europe create parallel mechanisms, or – better – prevent problems from occurring in the first place?

Secondly, still unresolved was the more technical but important question of how to implement a currency union between a group of nations that had divergent economic policies and performances. Merkel had driven an agreement on a 'fiscal compact', limiting the size of budget deficits and government debts, but France and other countries obtained repeated delays in achieving the reductions in budget deficits that were required to bring fiscal policies into alignment – delays that did not sit easily with the hard line taken against Greece.

Thirdly, the economic and financial imperfections of currency union between sovereign nations meant that political will and trust among all parties were essential components. These had been fractured. Could they be restored? In several European countries, parties of the far right and left were growing in influence, and wished to challenge the European machine. In Britain, the UK Independence Party, which argues that sovereignty is being handed to an unaccountable Brussels bureaucracy, took 13% of the national vote in May 2015 elections. The wish of British Prime Minister David Cameron – absent from the Greek negotiations as the UK is not part of the euro – to negotiate a new European bargain could, paradoxically, be used to begin a more positive discussion on Europe's future. But amid the anti-European feeling within his party, this seemed an opportunity unlikely to be taken.

The growth of distrust and divisions within Europe threatened to undercut the solidarity that the continent was displaying in the face of Russia's actions in Ukraine. While there was no desire to intervene militarily in the conflict there, the NATO alliance had acted with remarkable unity to take measures intended to reassure eastern members. It could be convincingly argued that Russia had acted in Ukraine because it saw its fundamental interests being threatened, and that this did not mean it would seek to undermine other countries using similar hybrid tactics. Nevertheless, there was a sense of heightened risk across Northern and Eastern Europe, and the Alliance took steps to counter such tactics by increasing rapid-reaction capacities, readiness and military exercises – as well as considering ways to improve decision-making and strategic communications to oppose Russian propaganda and deception. Moscow's actions seemed to have created a sea change, bringing to an end a long decline in European defence spending.

Landmark events

The Greek debacle was a blot on the landscape in 2015, albeit one of which the effects were essentially confined to Europe. The conflicts and divisions of the Middle East, as argued above, were a spreading crisis that needed to be more effectively addressed by the world's major powers. The Ebola epidemic in West Africa was an important reminder of perennial global vulnerabilities.

Yet there were other, more positive events that were also reshaping the globe. Cuba is a small country, but the end of its isolation by the US – coupled with Obama's bold attempt to give an amnesty to millions of undocumented immigrants – seemed to begin a new era in intra-American relations. The withdrawal of combat troops from Afghanistan, bringing to an end a 13-year international campaign, was another landmark, even if the country's future remained uncertain. New Chinese initiatives, meanwhile, had the potential to boost and transform regional economies.

On 14 July 2015 came the historic nuclear agreement with Iran after years of negotiations in which the US, China, Russia, France, Germany and the UK had all worked together, with an important role played by the EU. If the accord could overcome political obstacles and be properly implemented, it had the potential to gradually restore mutual trust and bring Iran back within the normal orbit of international relations, giving the country the opportunity to become a more positive force. The agreement marked the beginning rather than the completion of this change, but it was a promising one. Finally, the most important meeting yet in international efforts to curb global warming was scheduled to be held in Paris in December 2015 (see essay, pp. 60–70) – an opportunity for an even more significant landmark in international diplomacy.

Chapter 2
Drivers of Strategic Change

In the following pages, IISS experts seek to highlight developments and themes that have the potential to drive strategic change in individual regions, and in the world as a whole. They do not offer forecasts of specific future events: this annual book remains a review of international affairs covering a 12-month period, in this case from mid-2014 to mid-2015. However, regional experts use their analysis of developments in this and recent years to identify strategic risk factors. This section is not a comprehensive list of risks facing the world, nor does it attempt to assess or quantify threats. World events will remain unpredictable. But we hope our analysis is useful for the identification of key drivers of strategic change.

28
North America

29
Latin America

30
Europe

31
Russia and Eurasia

32
Middle East and North Africa

33
Sub-Saharan Africa

34
South Asia and Afghanistan

35
Asia-Pacific

North America: drivers of strategic change

- Nuclear agreement with Iran could bring a convergence of US and Iranian interests, leading to greater tactical cooperation and increasing the need to reassure Gulf Arab states and Israel.

- President Barack Obama's middle-way strategies in Europe and East Asia will be difficult to sustain, with growing pressure to act decisively in favour of accommodation or deterrence vis-à-vis Russia and China.

- A Republican congress in an election year will seek confrontation with the White House over health care, tax and government borrowing. Obama's executive actions on climate change and immigration will be battlegrounds, subject to court challenges.

- Partisan tensions will overshadow foreign and security policy, with the nuclear agreement with Iran subject to hostile congressional scrutiny.

- The crowded field for the Republican presidential nomination heightens uncertainty about the 2016 election, contrasting with Hillary Clinton's heavily favoured Democratic candidacy.

Jeb Bush Ben Carson Chris Christie Ted Cruz Carly Fiorina Lindsey Graham Mike Huckabee Bobby Jindal

George Pataki Rand Paul Rick Perry Marco Rubio Rick Santorum Donald Trump Scott Walker

Republican

Lincoln Chafee Hillary Clinton Martin O'Malley Bernie Sanders Jim Webb

Democrat

Michael Vadon/Gage Skidmore/US Senate/US Dept of State/MarylandGovPics

Presidential candidates
As of mid-July 2015, there were 15 candidates for the Republican Party presidential nomination. The Democrats had five, with Hillary Clinton the clear leader

Obamacare enrolment growing
Percentage of US adults over 18 without health insurance

Source: Gallup

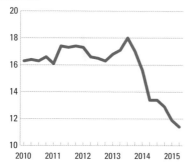

#BlackLivesMatter
Death rates for US males aged 15–29 by race/ethnicity, 2013

Source: US National Vital Statistics Report

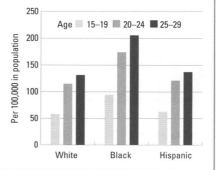

Age 15–19 20–24 25–29

Per 100,000 in population

White Black Hispanic

Latin America: drivers of strategic change

- Dampening of economic growth and competitiveness, triggered by commodity-price falls, is exposing structural weaknesses and failures to reform export-heavy economies.

- Corruption scandals – notably in Brazil, but also in Chile, Argentina, Mexico, Peru, Colombia, Bolivia, Guatemala and Panama – are leading to crises of confidence and governance.

- Resumption of links between the US and Cuba provides opportunities for a revitalised relationship between Washington and the region.

- Deterioration continues in long-standing issues of crime and insecurity, especially in Mexico and Central America, and threatens to undermine political stability and economic growth.

- Energy challenges, brought to the fore by high electricity costs, insufficient infrastructure and severe drought, create dangers for Mexico, Brazil, Central America and the Caribbean.

- Divergent policies on trade and integration between the Pacific Alliance and Mercosur countries risk polarising Latin America into 'open-regionalist' and 'closed-regionalist' blocs.

Mandel Ngan/AFP/Getty

Rapprochement between the US and Cuba
US President Barack Obama and Cuba's President Raúl Castro at the Summit of the Americas in Panama City, April 2015

Commodities-market decline
Changes in selected commodities revenues, 2013–14

Source: United Nations

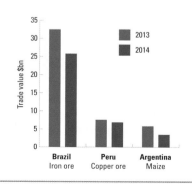

Petrobras
Consolidated net income (loss) US$million. The Brazilian state oil company registered huge losses following a corruption investigation

Source: Petrobras

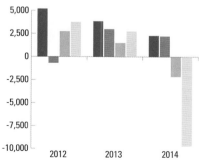

Europe: drivers of strategic change

- Greece's left-wing challenge to lending conditions imposed by eurozone governments threatens the common currency and European integration. The dispute has created mutual mistrust and animosity.

- Britain's effort to reshape its relationship with the European Union, driven by the eurosceptic right wing, poses risks for both the country and Europe.

- European defence policies are in flux as they adapt to perceived threats from Russia. The key question will be the extent to which higher spending will boost capabilities and cooperation.

- Numerous jihadist attacks indicate the growing impact on Europe of the Islamic State of Iraq and al-Sham and of Middle East/North African conflicts, but policy responses are unclear.

- Turkish politics is entering an uncertain period following an electoral setback for President Recep Tayyip Erdogan's ambitions for greater power.

Greek showdown with the EU
Customers queue at the entrance to a Eurobank Ergasias branch in Athens, 6 July 2015

Who owns Greek debt?
Official creditors of the €320-billion Greek debt
Source: Open Europe/Bloomberg

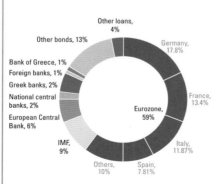

Other loans, 4%
Other bonds, 13%
Bank of Greece, 1%
Foreign banks, 1%
Greek banks, 2%
National central banks, 2%
European Central Bank, 6%
IMF, 9%
Others, 10%
Spain, 7.81%
Italy, 11.87%
Eurozone, 59%
France, 13.4%
Germany, 17.8%

Erdogan's setback
Seats (and percentage of the vote) in the Turkish National Assembly following elections on 7 June 2015
Source: Middle East Monitor

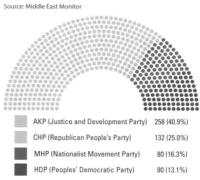

Party	Seats
AKP (Justice and Development Party)	258 (40.9%)
CHP (Republican People's Party)	132 (25.0%)
MHP (Nationalist Movement Party)	80 (16.3%)
HDP (Peoples' Democratic Party)	80 (13.1%)

Chris Ratcliffe/Bloomberg/Getty

Russia and Eurasia: drivers of strategic change

- The relationship between Russia and the West has deteriorated to levels of antagonism not seen in decades, considerably heightening risks.

- The conflict in eastern Ukraine threatens to become protracted as it persists despite two ceasefire agreements.

- The Ukraine conflict is boosting President Vladimir Putin's approval ratings to all-time highs, marginalising the opposition and creating a climate of intolerance.

- Ukraine's domestic politics remain fractious as the government tries to balance the war, economic survival and reform.

- The oil-price fall, coupled with increasingly severe Western sanctions against Russia, has hit regional economies and exposed structural weaknesses.

- EU–Russia competition for influence continues: as the Russia-led Eurasian Economic Union was launched, Ukraine, Georgia and Moldova haltingly pursued EU Association Agreements.

Anatolii Stepanov/AFP/Getty

Uneasy truce between pro-Russian forces and Ukraine
Anti-aircraft gunners from the Ukrainian armed forces take part in exercises near the southeastern city of Mariupol, Donetsk region, 7 July 2015

War in eastern Ukraine
Areas under separatist control as at December 2014

Source: UNSDC/UN

President Putin's approval ratings
'Do you approve the activities of Vladimir Putin as the President (Prime Minister) of Russia?'

Source: Levada-Center

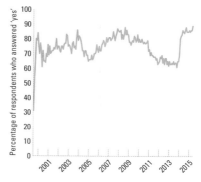

Middle East and North Africa: drivers of strategic change

▪ The Iran nuclear agreement will reshape the calculations, posture and behaviour of the region's main powers, including Saudi Arabia, Turkey and Israel.

▪ Iran's likely conduct after the deal is a significant unknown: regional escalation and detente are equally possible.

▪ The disintegration of Syria – and, to a lesser extent, Iraq – is profoundly affecting regional dynamics, upsetting demographics and boosting sectarianism.

▪ Despite tactical setbacks, the Islamic State of Iraq and al-Sham (ISIS) is resilient and adaptive, able to expand its reach and to maintain its capacity to shock.

▪ Saudi Arabia, more assertive under King Salman, has taken on significant security and political risks with its intervention in Yemen.

▪ Benjamin Netanyahu's election win further dims the limited prospect for Israeli–Palestinian progress and aggravates the troubled US–Israel relationship.

Ali Mukarrem Garip/Anadolu Agency/Getty

Battle for control of Iraq
Smoke rises after an air attack during clashes between Iraqi forces and ISIS near Kirkuk, 6 July 2015

Israeli elections, 2015
Ten larger parties are represented in the Knesset
Source: Israel Central Elections Committee

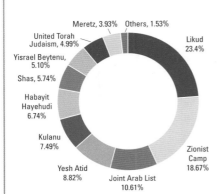

Meretz, 3.93%   Others, 1.53%
United Torah Judaism, 4.99%
Yisrael Beytenu, 5.10%
Shas, 5.74%
Habayit Hayehudi 6.74%
Kulanu 7.49%
Yesh Atid 8.82%
Joint Arab List 10.61%
Zionist Camp 18.67%
Likud 23.4%

Iran's nuclear agreement
Joint Comprehensive Plan of Action: key points
Source: IAEA

Centrifuges
Natanz will keep 6,100 less advanced IR-1 centrifuges, only 5,060 of which will be used for enrichment. There will be no enrichment at **Fordow**, although some centrifuges remain for stable isotope production

Enrichment
For 15 years, Iran will enrich uranium up to only 3.67% (the level for most nuclear fuel)

Stockpile
Iran currently has about 10,000 kilograms of low-enriched uranium; for 15 years it will keep up to 300kg

Heavy-water reprocessing
Iran will rebuild a heavy-water research reactor at Arak, re-designed so as not to produce weapons-grade plutonium

Transparency
Iran will allow expanded monitoring by the International Atomic Energy Agency anywhere in the country where there are concerns about unreported nuclear activity

Sub-Saharan Africa: drivers of strategic change

- Although economic growth continues, its fragility is underlined by commodity-price falls and, in West Africa, by the Ebola outbreak.

- The Ebola crisis illustrates capacity deficits in infrastructure and health care, and shows the future need for better community engagement and political leadership.

- Nigeria's spreading conflict with Boko Haram, and Somalia's with al-Shabaab, creates broader regional risks and highlights the dangers from jihadist groups.

- The need to create enough jobs is a major risk for the continent. According to the IMF, the proportion of Africans joining the working-age population will by 2035 'exceed that from the rest of the world combined'.

- As efforts to boost military capabilities and cooperation continue, the *Amani Africa II* exercise in late 2015 will be an important benchmark.

Daniel Berehulak/Getty

Ebola outbreak highlights deficits in regional capacity
Hospital workers spray chlorine onto pathways at a hospital in Monrovia, Liberia, December 2014

Communications infrastructure expands: key indicators
Source: ITU World Telecommunication/ICT Indicators database

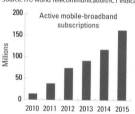
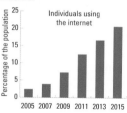
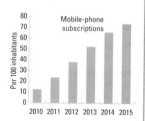

Millennium Development Goals
In 2000 world leaders adopted the UN Millennium Declaration, committing nations to reducing poverty and addressing eight Millennium Development Goals by 2015

Target 1 '*Halve, between 1990 and 2015, the proportion of people whose income is less than $1 a day.*'
Source: UN

Target 2 '*Ensure that, by 2015, children everywhere, boys and girls alike, will be able to complete a full course of primary education.*'
Source: UN

South Asia and Afghanistan: drivers of strategic change

- The government of Narendra Modi faces challenges in meeting high expectations for economic reforms as it seeks to muster sufficient political backing.

- A hardening of Indian policy towards Pakistan – as well as differing approaches to counter-terrorism – heighten regional security risks.

- Shifts in Pakistan's civil–military relations are strengthening the role of the army in government policy.

- Afghanistan's future remains in the balance, with a fractious unity government and continuing conflict with the Taliban.

- Sri Lanka's election upset was a large step in the country's transition out of a long civil war, but political tensions persist.

Graham Crouch/Bloomberg via Getty

Narendra Modi and Xi Jinping in New Delhi, September 2014

Pakistan's battle against insurgents
Fatalities in terrorist violence, 2010–14

Source: South Asia Terrorism Portal

Sri Lanka
Mahinda Rajapaksa's United People's Freedom Alliance, seeking a third term, surprisingly lost to Maithripala Sirisena's New Democratic Front

Source: Sri Lanka Department of Elections

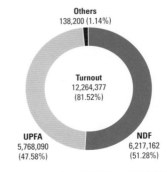

Others
138,200 (1.14%)

Turnout
12,264,377
(81.52%)

UPFA
5,768,090
(47.58%)

NDF
6,217,162
(51.28%)

Asia-Pacific: drivers of strategic change

- China's rise, and its assertiveness over maritime claims, is provoking reactions from other states and risks dividing the region into pro- and anti-Chinese blocs.

- In Southeast Asia, domestic political change is pervasive, and may significantly affect future foreign-policy and security orientations of individual states.

- Conflict related to ethnicity, religion and national identity has become more acute in parts of Southeast Asia and China. It could provoke internal security crises and displace minority populations.

- Inter-state tensions and humanitarian crises are severely challenging the credibility of regional institutions centred on the Association of Southeast Asian Nations.

- Major divergences in levels of defence spending, as well as new technologies, are contributing to growing differences in military capability across the region.

US Navy/Reuters

China's maritime claims
Chinese dredging vessels at Mischief Reef in the Spratly Islands, in the South China Sea, viewed from a US Navy surveillance aircraft, May 2015

Asia-Pacific defence spending
Defence spending in 2014 (US$billion)

Source: IISS

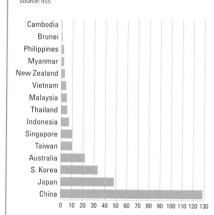

Cambodia
Brunei
Philippines
Myanmar
New Zealand
Vietnam
Malaysia
Thailand
Indonesia
Singapore
Taiwan
Australia
S. Korea
Japan
China

0 10 20 30 40 50 60 70 80 90 100 110 120 130

Irregular migration in the Indian Ocean
Rohingya people fleeing violence in Myanmar's Rakhine State; most have been heading for Malaysia

Source: UNHCR/Al-Jazeera/International Organization for Migration

In the first quarter of 2015, 25,000 migrants sailed from the Bay of Bengal, double the rate reported for the same period in 2013 and 2014. In 2014, 58,000 made the journey. Most are ethnic Rohingyas from Myanmar, others are from Bangladesh. This was the situation on 10 May 2015

6,000–8,000 were stranded on boats in the Malacca Strait

Over 1,000 landed on Langkawi, a holiday resort

THAILAND

About 500 were washed ashore in Indonesia

MALAYSIA

INDONESIA

Chapter 3

Strategic Policy Issues

A New Era in the Oil Market

The fall in the oil price of 2014–15, resulting from fundamental changes to oil supply and demand, left market forces in charge of the world's most important energy commodity for perhaps the first time in history. An important factor in the scale of the price decline was OPEC's abandonment of its role as the dominant price regulator, around 40 years after it took over from a similar cartel made up of Western oil majors.

The price for Brent crude, which runs a few dollars ahead of the US market of WTI, collapsed by around 60%, from the June 2014 high of US$115 a barrel to below US$46 in January 2015. The decline gained momentum in autumn 2014 and fell US$5 in one day, 27 November, when OPEC announced it would not follow its usual routine of cutting output to prop up a falling price. The Brent price had by mid-May 2015 slowly recovered to around US$65. There were precedents for the halving of the oil price: sharp corrections also occurred in 1986, 1998 and 2008. And there was nothing unique in the fact that the 2014–15 fall was driven by changes in both supply and demand, as this was also the case in 1986. The novel and significant aspect of the recent shift was that global oil demand fell not simply due to a cyclical drop in consumption resulting from lower economic growth or recession, but also because of a structural weakening of demand as economies became less oil-intensive.

With the development of alternative energy sources and rising concern about climate change and local pollution, many emerging countries – particularly China, the world's largest energy consumer – seemingly were making an effort to rely less on fossil fuels than had the industrialising Western states of the nineteenth and twentieth centuries. In transport, oil demand was eroded by greater vehicle efficiency; in power generation, by reductions in the cost of some renewable-electricity technologies, as well as the globalisation of the gas market.

Causes of the price drop

In hindsight, no one should have been surprised by the abrupt 2014–15 correction in the oil price. The change was necessitated by the impact on supply and demand of more than a decade of rising prices, interrupted sharply but very briefly in 2008–09. This 'scissors effect' of lower demand and higher supply was most evident in the United States, where consumption of petroleum-based fuels peaked in 2005, before declining by around two million barrels per day, or almost 10%, during the following eight years. This fall-off was all the more remarkable for having occurred in a country with a steadily rising population. At the same time, total US oil output surged from 6.8m b/d in 2008 to more than 11.6m b/d in 2014, according to BP. This was made possible by the massive increase in shale-oil production, which rose by 160,000 b/d in 2011, 850,000 b/d in 2012, 950,000 b/d in 2013 and 1.2m b/d in 2014, to reach an average of 4.2m b/d in 2014, according to the US Energy Information Administration.

The growth of US unconventional oil output caught the attention of traditional oil exporters. According to the 2011 edition of OPEC's World Oil Outlook, 'at present … shale oil should not be viewed as anything more than a source of marginal additions' to crude-oil supply. One year later, following the step change in US shale production, a new edition of the publication acknowledged that 'shale oil represents a large change to the supply picture'. However, the increase in US production was temporarily offset by growing political instability among many traditional oil exporters. Alongside the chronic production problems experienced by countries such as Nigeria and Venezuela, there was an unrelenting stream of bad news for oil production across the Middle East and North Africa. After the 2011 onset of the Arab Spring, Libya's descent into civil conflict periodically halted its oil exports, while production in the wider region was hit by successive regime changes in Egypt, Syria's intensifying civil war and the military advances in Iraq made by the Islamic State of Iraq and al-Sham. For three years, the oil market was held in a delicate balance by the tension between these two sets of developments: the steady rise in US oil output, and deteriorating security in Middle East and North African oil-exporting countries. In the end, the event that tipped the balance occurred in Libya, whose oil production had been briefly suspended in 2011 but subsequently experienced periodic revivals in exports. One of these revivals led in June 2014 to the loading of two Libyan tankers, which was enough to trigger the long-overdue price correction.

Just as OPEC producers had been caught unawares by the boom in US shale oil, so were the US and the wider oil market surprised by OPEC's passivity during the price fall. In its International Energy Outlook 2014, published in September of that year, the US Energy Information Administration expressed confidence that 'regardless of the uncertainties in oil supply projections, producers in the OPEC Middle East region are likely to continue playing a key role in balancing global demand and supply'. Yet OPEC did no such thing. In the lead-up to the organisation's meeting of 27 November 2014, Saudi Arabia tried to interest Russia and Mexico in joining OPEC in a production cut, but they would not play ball. So, against all expectations that it would reduce output, OPEC announced that it would keep production steady at 30m b/d (and by June 2015 was in fact producing more than 31m b/d). The price of Brent crude dropped from US\$77 a barrel that November to less than US\$60 during the course of the next month. The war between OPEC and American producers was on; as the *Economist* quipped in December, it was 'Sheikhs v Shale: The New Economics of Oil'.

Saudi Arabia, OPEC's dominant supplier, was outspoken about its fight against producers of high-cost oil, whom it blamed for flooding the market. In taking this course, Riyadh reversed around 30 years of OPEC policy and practice that put price before market share. Shortly after the November meeting, Saudi oil minister Ali al-Naimi asked rhetorically, 'is it reasonable for a highly efficient producer to reduce output, while the inefficient producer continues to produce?' By 'efficient', the Saudi minister meant his own country and other Gulf producers exploiting low-cost,

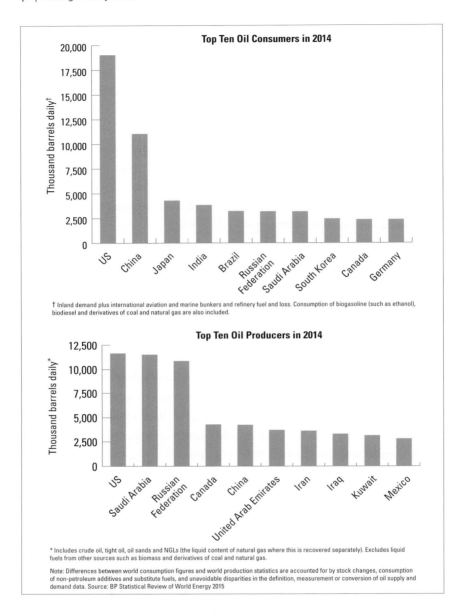

Top Ten Oil Consumers in 2014

† Inland demand plus international aviation and marine bunkers and refinery fuel and loss. Consumption of biogasoline (such as ethanol), biodiesel and derivatives of coal and natural gas are also included.

Top Ten Oil Producers in 2014

* Includes crude oil, tight oil, oil sands and NGLs (the liquid content of natural gas where this is recovered separately). Excludes liquid fuels from other sources such as biomass and derivatives of coal and natural gas.

Note: Differences between world consumption figures and world production statistics are accounted for by stock changes, consumption of non-petroleum additives and substitute fuels, and unavoidable disparities in the definition, measurement or conversion of oil supply and demand data. Source: BP Statistical Review of World Energy 2015

easy-to-extract oil, and by 'inefficient', those producers working in shale formations, the deep-water offshore and even the Arctic to extract oil that was much more expensive to produce but financeable on the back of the higher oil price. Al-Naimi correctly pointed to the economic illogicality of OPEC, especially the Gulf producers, always being the first to reduce output in times of oil gluts. Yet 'shutting-in' highly efficient Middle East production was a price that OPEC countries, especially Saudi Arabia, had often been willing to pay, as a means to support the world oil price.

Sustainability of a low oil price

Saudi Arabia seemed particularly determined to avoid repeating what it saw as its go-it-alone mistake of 1986. At that time, partly in frustration at the reluctance of other OPEC members to join in cutting production, Riyadh reduced Saudi production in the face of rising non-OPEC output, especially by the United Kingdom (in the North Sea), the US (in Alaska) and the Soviet Union. Despite drastically cutting production, Saudi Arabia was unable to force an increase in the oil price, and therefore received a double hit from lower prices and reduced output. For Riyadh, 2014 could have been a repeat of 1986. While the Saudis knew they could rely on fellow Gulf producers to carry out a coordinated production cut, they were also aware that the members making the greatest clamour for cuts, such as Venezuela and Nigeria, had every incentive to break commitments to restrain production, due to their smaller financial reserves and larger populations.

In opting not to announce production cuts, OPEC gambled that the high cost of US shale-oil production would make it unsustainable to continue to invest in this type of oil during a prolonged period of low prices. The Saudi strategy was therefore to eliminate the new competition and to reassert supremacy over the market and pricing. There was a chance that the gamble would pay off, as was suggested by data analysed by the International Energy Agency (IEA). In its Medium-Term Oil Market Report 2015, published in February, the agency concluded that the majority of US shale-oil production had a 'break-even' price higher than US$50: 'on average in 2014, about 48 per cent of total US liquids production had a breakeven price of US$50 a barrel or lower, and about 41 per cent of US crude oil and field condensate production from tight oil and shale oil had a breakeven price of US$50 or less'.

According to their published financial accounts, many US energy companies spent more money on new wells than they had generated from existing wells, and much of the new investment came from debt rather than equity. This made these firms vulnerable to lower prices. The more highly geared America's oil companies, the higher the oil price they needed to break even, covering the cost of not only operation but also capital employed. To guard against this risk, many oil companies in the US and around the world announced reductions in their capital-expenditure plans. In shale operations, such decreases were likely to have an early impact on production from wells, which tended to deplete quite rapidly (sometimes by as much as 70% in the first year). Therefore, sustained investment and drilling was often required to maintain, let alone increase, output from shale reserves.

The US Energy Information Administration recorded a small drop in US shale-oil output for May 2015 and forecasted that this slight decline might continue. At the same time, however, several US shale producers claimed that they expected to begin increasing production again, as they had sufficiently cut their production costs during the price downturn, and the oil price had recovered enough. In light of this, the IEA commented in its May oil report that 'it would thus be premature to suggest that OPEC has won the battle for market share. The battle, rather, has just started.' One sign of this came in mid-2015 with the first increase, after many months of decline, in the number of US oil rigs in operation.

US shale production could prove resilient even with an oil price lower than the break-even cost of drilling. Although the break-even cost is important to investment decisions on new wells, of more relevance to maintaining existing wells is the 'shut-in' cost: the operating expenses that had to be covered by the oil price if a well was to be profitable and not shut-in – a figure always lower than the break-even cost.

It was also possible that lower prices would take longer to revive oil demand, and be less effective at doing so, than was counted on by Saudi Arabia, Kuwait, the United Arab Emirates and Qatar. The Medium-Term Oil Market Report 2015 contended that oil-price elasticity – the degree to which changes in the oil price caused changes in oil demand – was diminishing in a rather skewed manner. Certainly, Americans purchased more gas-guzzling cars as the oil price fell. But the IEA claimed that ever-larger price drops were needed to generate increases in oil demand, while oil-price rises triggered long-lasting reductions in demand and/or gains in oil efficiency. The agency argued that this reflected 'long-run structural market changes, including steady advances in energy efficiency, increased inter-fuel competition from natural gas and renewables, and the greater share of the service industry and other non-oil-intensive sectors in the global economy'.

The weakening of this link between oil price and oil demand was to be expected in the mature Organisation for Economic Co-operation and Development (OECD) economies of North America, Europe and Japan, which in 2014 accounted for just under half of global oil consumption. More startlingly, the world's emerging economies were proving not to be the energy wastrels that OECD countries had been at a comparable stage of development. According to the IEA, many of these emerging countries were even

> cutting their own path of development and leap-frogging OECD economies in their developments. Advances in solar, wind and hydro technology have improved the competitiveness and market penetration of renewable fuels, allowing non-OECD economies to raise the share of renewables in their fuel mix at an earlier stage of development than had been possible for more advanced economies.

The generally higher rate of economic growth in emerging economies in many cases created a faster turnover of capital stock, enabling the introduction of more modern and energy-efficient equipment than in economies growing at a slower rate. The IEA stated that

> nowhere is this shift to a less oil-intensive stage of economic development more apparent than in China, a country that in recent years accounted for just under 35 per cent of aggregate oil demand growth, but whose share of incremental [global] demand is expected to drop to around one-quarter in the next few years to 2020.

Another likely dampener on oil's revival is the depressive effect of the oil-price drop on the economies of oil exporters themselves, who in recent years have led the global growth in oil demand. Moreover, several oil-exporting countries – Iran under pressure from sanctions, but also Indonesia, Kuwait, Malaysia and Egypt – sensibly used the fall-off to scale back the oil-price subsidies they offered to their citizens. Oil-importing countries such as India, Thailand and Morocco also reduced energy-price subsidies during the same period.

Due to the new supply factor of increased US shale-oil output and the changing dynamics of oil demand, the oil price seemed likely to stay relatively low for longer than it did after its preceding two drops. These were demand-driven – in 1998 following the brief Asian financial crisis, and in 2008 by the global financial crisis and subsequent recession. The 2014–15 fall more closely paralleled that which began in 1986 in that both were driven by a combination of supply and demand factors. The latest price drop will correct itself, as indicated by the 'contango' shape of the current market, with the futures price of crude for delivery in one or two years higher than that for prompt crude for early delivery. This rising price curve reflected oil oversupply in the short term, and longer-term expectations that the 2014–15 price drop would lead to reduced investment in new capacity, eventually resulting in higher prices.

Winners and losers

The fall in the oil price has had widespread effects on economies, budgets and politics. In general, oil-exporting countries and oil-producing companies lost out from the drop in price, while oil-importing states and oil-intensive industries gained – with some exceptions. The 12 members of OPEC (Algeria, Angola, Ecuador, Iran, Iraq, Kuwait, Libya, Nigeria, Qatar, Saudi Arabia, the United Arab Emirates and Venezuela) covered a wide spectrum. Gulf producers had sufficient financial reserves to withstand a prolonged price slump without experiencing serious economic pain; Saudi Arabia, for instance, had foreign-exchange reserves of around US$700 billion and net debt of only US$20bn at the end of 2013. This was not the case for OPEC countries with large populations and acute financial problems, such as Venezuela, Nigeria and Angola. Beyond OPEC, Russia was under the additional strain of Western sanctions relating to the conflict in Ukraine.

Oil-importing countries, meanwhile, were benefiting from extra disposable income, but the effect of the oil-price fall was blunted by the rise in the exchange rate for the US dollar (in which oil is priced). In Japan and Europe, there was the additional problem that falling oil prices fed deflationary expectations, which potentially encouraged people to save rather than spend, thereby depressing economic activity.

The US was in a curious position. Its shale revolution may have been a primary cause of the oil-price slump, but the development had also improved the energy security of the country and its allies, according to the Obama administration's 2015 National Security Strategy (the first such document in five years). Launching the paper, US National Security Advisor Susan Rice stated that 'we've unlocked a domestic energy boom that has made us the world's number one producer of oil and gas, strengthening our energy security – with huge ripple effects for global markets and geopolitics'. The document claimed the US energy revival 'offers new buffers against the coercive use of energy', in a clear reference to the Ukraine crisis and the possibility that US exports of liquefied natural gas could act as a counter to Russia's energy leverage over Europe.

From Washington's perspective, the oil-price fall also put extra pressure on two other countries with which it had particularly difficult relations: Iran and Venezuela. The drop in price was so politically useful for the US that there was speculation Washington had somehow engineered the development with Riyadh. Yet there was no evidence for this. The Saudis might have had few qualms about making life harder for Tehran, but the fact remained that their main economic target was US shale-oil producers (although their actions, or inaction, affected all other high-cost producers, such as those in the North Sea). By allowing the market to set the oil price, the Saudis left the role of swing producer vacant. For decades, Saudi Arabia played this role, expanding or reducing oil output to balance the market, sometimes at the high cost of keeping capacity idle. The question was whether US shale producers could take over from the Saudis, with the oil price determined by the marginal cost of shale oil. This would have meant US producers shutting-in wells to put a floor under the price at times of market glut, and bringing wells back into production to put a ceiling on the price in a tight market. But although shale production was characterised by its price elasticity, US producers could not hope to control the oil price as neatly as Saudi Arabia. Riyadh only had to adjust the single tap of the Saudi Aramco national oil company, whereas the varying production costs of US shale producers meant that they would always come to differing conclusions on when to shut-in or expand production. It seemed impossible, therefore, that such a disparate and uncoordinated group of private-sector companies could ever effectively become the world's swing producer. This is quite apart from the fact that any concerted attempt to influence the price would expose US producers to the accusation of illegal price-fixing, under US anti-trust law. The US government itself has a Strategic Petroleum Reserve on the Gulf of Mexico coast, in which it could probably store some 'excess' oil. But US presidents have only ever used the reserve to put oil on the market in order to lower prices, not to take it off the market to raise prices – and whenever the White House has drawn on the reserve, it has been criticised for manipulating the market rather than reserving stocks for genuine supply emergencies.

There were costs to taking on the role of swing producer. Saudi Arabia had a declared policy of keeping between 1.5m and 2m b/d of spare capacity on hand to deal with shortages or regain market share. By April 2015, the Saudis had raised output to an average of 10.15m b/d, up from 9.7m b/d in the second half of 2014. Using spare capacity could theoretically have increased production to 12m b/d, although this was unlikely to happen. However, US shale producers could not indulge in the expensive luxury of deliberately keeping capacity idle.

Elsewhere, the oil-price fall not only reduced exporters' revenues, but limited their ability to expand their output and revenues in the future. It exacerbated political problems in Venezuela, which remained South America's biggest producer (2.7m b/d in 2014), ahead of Brazil (2.3m b/d in 2014), but had little spare cash to fund capacity expansion. Caracas was forced to depend more heavily on China: seeking to develop oil-for-financing agreements, Venezuelan President Nicolás Maduro stated in January 2015 that he had secured more than US$20bn of new investment from Beijing, which had already lent Venezuela around US$50bn since 2007.

It appeared that a new chapter was opening for Iran, and for the oil market, with the international agreement on Tehran's nuclear programme. The deal promised to remove international sanctions that had reduced Iran's output to around 2.8m b/d, although it would take some time to raise production up towards its capacity level of 3.6m b/d, and it would put considerable financial strain on the country to do so at a time of depressed oil prices.

Russia faced, in the words of the IEA, 'a perfect storm of collapsing prices, international sanctions and currency depreciation' and would 'likely emerge as the industry's top loser'. Although the slight recovery of the oil price in spring 2015 restored some of the rouble's value against the dollar, the devaluation contributed to the general depression of Russia's economy, and was compounded by Western sanctions, which focused particularly on the oil industry (sparing the Russian gas exports crucial to Europe). Likely to remain in place due to continued political deadlock with Russia over Ukraine, the sanctions prevented Russian firms from purchasing key technology for offshore exploration and shale production, while blocking access to foreign financing for leading state-controlled oil company Rosneft. As a result, ExxonMobil suspended its joint work with Rosneft in the Kara Sea and the Bazhenov shale reserve, and Total postponed its tight-oil joint venture with Lukoil in western Siberia. Russia needed to develop these resources to offset declines in its brownfield oil sites, and the rupture with international oil firms had the potential to depress output for some time to come. According to a forecast by the IEA, Russia's oil and liquids (associated with natural gas) would slide from 10.9m b/d in 2014 to 10.4m b/d in 2020.

Lessons for the oil market

The events of the year to mid-2015 shattered any illusion of a permanent high, or indeed low, in the oil price, and underscored the essential volatility of the market. They emphasised the wisdom of constant cost control in oil and gas projects, particularly the deep-water and Arctic ventures undertaken by non-OPEC countries. To some extent, production costs were being brought down in order to follow the downward path of the oil price, but cost reduction was a painful process, especially for the many countries seeking to spur their industrialisation by imposing 'local content' rules on international oil companies. The aim of these rules, which require a set share of construction and equipment contracts to be allocated to local companies, was understandable in terms of domestic economic and social development. But if pushed too far, such rules contributed to cost increases, project delays and even corruption – as appeared to be the case in Brazil's Petrobras scandal. It was possible that heightened competition between host governments for a smaller pool of investment capital would lead to a relaxation of rules on local content.

The developments of the year also highlighted the need for oil-exporting countries to diversify their economies. Nowhere was this requirement more acute than in Middle East and North African states. Yet diversification had never been harder in these countries, where chronic political unrest and war discouraged foreign investment.

The fall in the oil price created something of a buyers' market. The US shale revolution partly closed off the American market to traditional oil suppliers such as Nigeria, which had to reorient its export focus towards Asia. For a long time, Middle East oil exporters had charged their customers in Asia what became known as the 'Asian premium', a few extra dollars demanded because Asian states, unlike the US and European countries, had few other potential suppliers. (In the same way, Russia's Gazprom used a similar market dominance and logic to charge extra to Eastern European countries.) However, after oil began to reach China and the rest of Asia from Venezuela, Africa, Kazakhstan and Russia, the Saudis began to reduce the Asian premium.

Above all, the events of the year increased uncertainty in the oil market because the main players had abandoned their traditional roles. As the IEA put it,

> the clear distribution of roles between OPEC and non-OPEC countries that governed the oil market for the last 30 years has been suspended, at least for now. Non-OPEC producers cannot, for now, count on OPEC to act as swing supplier and cut output in the event of a price drop. OPEC cannot be confident that non-OPEC supply is maxed out and incapable of being scaled up quickly.

Eventually, non-OPEC countries' supply would 'max out' due to the fact that so many of their oil reserves were hard to access and expensive to produce. Conversely, although OPEC's share of global output dropped from 42% in 2008 to 39% in 2014, it appeared set to regain market share because such a large proportion of its oil was relatively accessible and cheap to produce. Nonetheless, there was no guarantee that OPEC would regain its dominance of the market.

Reforming the Russian Military

The fall of the Soviet Union in 1991 hastened the long-term deterioration of Moscow's military. The wars in Chechnya later that decade starkly illustrated the decline of Russia's armed services, while even their 2008 victory in Georgia exposed serious failings. There are indications, however, that the trend has begun to reverse, with the military's proficient intervention in Crimea in 2014 and the launch of an undeclared campaign in eastern Ukraine.

Moscow's latest modernisation, reform and restructuring efforts were made public in late 2008, following the short Russo-Georgian war. These initiatives have been broadly successful but remain a fragile work in progress, containing elements that are vulnerable to economic developments. Western sanctions imposed as a result of Russia's actions in Ukraine and a wider weakness in the Russian economy have constrained Moscow's defence-spending plans. Finance Minister Anton Siluanov cautioned in October 2014 that the State Armament Programme (GPV), which allocated 20 trillion roubles (around US$395 billion, at the exchange rate of May 2015) to new and upgraded equipment between 2011 and 2020, was no longer affordable and that there was a need for more realism.

Despite the straitened times, Moscow was attempting to sustain the core of its defence programme. This partly reflected rising tension in its relations with Europe and the United States. Although some procurement projects were slowed and savings were planned in areas such as training, President Vladimir Putin insisted that the GPV would be completed 'in full', albeit with possible changes to the timing of deliveries. This maintained the prospect that, as a result of changes begun over the past decade, Russia could again become a formidable military power in the years to come.

The progress, nature and aims of Russia's military overhaul have taken on greater significance for the West. As a result of Russia's actions in Ukraine, Western governments have had to rethink the view that Moscow is a strategic partner – a view that led to the NATO–Russia treaty signed in 1997 and heavily influenced European threat perceptions and defence policies, as well as decisions on spending and capabilities. European capitals are having to come to terms with the idea that Russia is again a strategic rival, rather than a partner.

Addressing conventional weakness

Martial prowess has long been a source of national pride in Russia. The military and its supporting infrastructure for defence research, development and manufacturing formed a keystone of the Soviet Union, but also drew unsustainable levels of economic investment. The collapse of the communist power bloc devastated the military and incapacitated much of the defence industry during the 1990s and the 2000s. In 1991 the army had 32 tank and 100 motor-rifle divisions; by 2015, it had four tank brigades (one of which is now a division again, at least in name) and 40 motor-rifle brigades. But direct comparison is misleading in the sense that less than 20% of the Soviet-era units were at three-quarters strength or more, while the intent now is for units to be at full or near-full strength. The Soviet army was built on a mobilisation structure in which most divisions were held at either half or skeleton strength until an outbreak of hostilities seemed likely, at which point the manning would be brought up to combat levels.

The structural failings of the post-Cold War military were not simply caused by the collapse of the Soviet Union, although the need for fundamental change was underlined by that event as it shed light on a range of pre-existing problems. Marshal Nikolai Ogarkov, who was appointed chief of the general staff in 1977, pushed for reforms and increased military expenditure in the early 1980s, before his demands led in 1984 to his demotion by the political leadership. Ogarkov feared that the structure and equipment of the Soviet military were increasingly ill-suited to meeting the emerging challenge posed by NATO, which was moving to exploit a range of technologies which would enable and support precision engagement. This was particularly apparent in the conventional sphere, where the far-reaching implications of digital technology were becoming clear. That concern still resonates: Moscow watched closely the US-led interventions in Afghanistan and Iraq, particularly the campaigns' use of airpower and precision weaponry that it would have been unable to match.

Announcing his resignation as leader of the Soviet Union in 1991, Mikhail Gorbachev noted that 'all the half-hearted reforms – and there have been a lot of them – fell through, one after the other.' While his comments were made in reference to the Soviet economy, they were equally applicable to the Russian military in the two decades that followed, as it struggled with the dissolution of the state he had inadvertently set in motion. The travails of the military in the 1980s, although evident only in retrospect, prefigured the near-endless array of problems visited upon the armed services and the defence industry by the demise of the Soviet Union. A bewildering set of challenges awaited senior military officers, bureaucrats and the heads of newly privatised defence companies.

Among the most significant difficulties they faced were political fragmentation and the weakening of the Russian economy during the 1990s, as the government strove to make the transition from a centralised to a market-oriented model. Even if the Ministry of Defence had successfully identified the macro-level measures required for military reform and modernisation, the leadership would have been unable to adequately fund the armed forces. The first GPV drafted after the fall of the Soviet Union, covering 1996–2005, reflected the extent of the problems. The armed forces received just one-fifth of the funding that it stipulated, with the result that any planning became fruitless.

Funding problems were often compounded by the retention or setting of unrealistic goals in re-equipment and development projects. One example was the MiG design bureau's project to develop a fifth-generation combat aircraft. Begun in 1983, the programme limped into the mid-1990s with one development aircraft built. It was flown for the first time in February 2000, although by this time the air force had abandoned any plan to buy the aircraft. In fact there had been doubts about the ambition and the affordability of the programme even before the Soviet collapse.

Such was the military's plight in the early 1990s that it could not meet even the basic needs of personnel redeployed from former Warsaw Pact bases to Russia. For example, there was a desperate lack of accommodation, an irritant that was to persist for two decades.

The New Look

It was not until December 1997 that Moscow published its first post-Soviet national-security blueprint, formally laying out its defence policy. With masterful understatement, the document noted that 'the former defence system has been disrupted, and the creation of a new one is proceeding slowly.' The blueprint made clear the Russian government's concerns about what it regarded as an expansionist NATO, a theme that was repeated in subsequent national-security documents and continues to be heard today.

In parallel, a more credible reform and modernisation agenda began to take shape in the Novy Oblik (New Look) plan, announced in the aftermath of the 2008 Georgian campaign. In the Georgian conflict, Russia so overmatched its neighbour that any outcome other than easy victory was unthinkable. Nonetheless, the Russian military displayed shortcomings that could have had far-reaching consequences against a larger, more capable opponent. These included suboptimal command and control, ageing equipment, poor readiness levels and a continued lack of precision-guided munitions.

The process that culminated in the Novy Oblik arguably began with the publication in 2003 of the defence paper 'Priority Tasks', during Sergei Ivanov's tenure as defence minister. The credibility of the new approach centred on an increase in defence expenditure that began in 2005 and would continue over the next ten years, alongside a re-equipment programme that was comparatively modest in its technical aims. Many elements of the programme were based on projects that originated in the Soviet era, such as the Su-35S fighter aircraft, the *Borey*-class ballistic-missile submarine and a range of tactical and strategic missile systems. Yet despite the relatively low technical requirements, annual production rates stipulated in GPV 2011–20 always appeared difficult to achieve.

A core aim of the reform programme was greater professionalisation of the armed forces, moving away from conscription. It also proposed a restructuring of regional commands. But progress in both these areas was limited. The same could be said for the equipment plan for 2006–15, which was intended to complement the reforms. Ivanov said in December 2006 that 'new models of weapons and military equipment, which will determine the Russian army's might in the period until 2020, have not only already been developed, but have largely been accepted into the inventory. Beginning this year, we have begun their massive series-produced purchases.' However, targets in the GPV 2006–15 were missed by a considerable distance. Even when the Ministry of Defence made available the necessary funding, Russian industry – itself operating with outdated equipment and skills – was often unable to fulfil orders in a timely fashion.

Under the Novy Oblik, the ambition of reform was to create armed forces capable of acting across the spectrum of combat, up to and including high-intensity warfare on Russia's periphery. Equipped with modern weaponry and enabling systems, these forces were to be held in a high state of readiness, and to contain significant components capable of rapid mobility. The forces were to be complemented by a nuclear triad of land- and sea-based ballistic missiles, along with air-launched cruise missiles, providing an assured second-strike capability that could defeat any ballistic-missile defence. In the two decades following the collapse of the Soviet Union, Russia's nuclear arsenal had provided the defence-policy crutch for increasingly weak conventional forces. By implication, this reduced the threshold at which Moscow would consider the use of nuclear weapons. Conversely, the present strengthening of Russia's conventional military capability could have the benefit of raising this threshold.

The improvement in conventional capabilities was in tandem with the 2009 National Security Strategy, which indicated that it was to be supported by a properly resourced military-restructuring and re-equipment programme intended to counter the threats identified. The strategy placed emphasis on the capacity to fight wars – including high-intensity conflicts – in Russia's 'near abroad', with strategic deterrence provided by recapitalised nuclear systems.

The Novy Oblik was delivered by Anatoly Serdyukov, who had succeeded Ivanov as defence minister in February 2007. Although he had served as a conscript, he was the first defence minister not to have had a professional career in the military or the intelligence service, and he had no experience of the defence sector. He was a bureaucrat with managerial and financial experience: as head of the tax service during the 2004 nationalisation of oil company Yukos, he had demonstrated both his loyalty to Putin and his effectiveness. His lack of a constituency within the military potentially freed him to act without prejudice in implementing reforms. But as an outsider, it was almost inevitable that Serdyukov would clash with the military and be more willing than his predecessor to confront vested interests in the defence industry. Cuts to personnel in the middle and senior ranks of the military, seeking to slim a top-heavy structure and a swollen officer corps, were greeted with hostility by those whose positions were threatened. Serdyukov later risked domestic criticism by ordering equipment from foreign suppliers, notably *Mistral*-class amphibious assault ships from France, as well as Israeli unmanned aerial vehicles.

In pursuing the reform programme, Serdyukov was supported by General Nikolai Makarov, appointed chief of the general staff in June 2008 to replace General Yury Baluevsky, who had opposed the reform agenda. Clashes between Serdyukov and Baluevsky, who was backed by some senior military leaders, indicated that the main elements of the reform programme were being introduced by late 2007 or early 2008, although they were not made public as part of the Novy Oblik until the following October.

The most contentious issue was personnel cuts, which over a period of three years were intended to reduce the number of officers from 335,000 to 185,000. By 2012 the number of generals had been reduced by nearly 50% to just over 600. The project was not primarily designed to create a smaller military, but rather a more capable force. In an attempt to simplify command and control, Russia's six military districts were to be consolidated into four, with combat forces in each subordinated to the district command – except for the Strategic Rocket Forces, Airborne Troops and planned Aerospace Defence Forces.

Central to the army reform was the shift from a division to a brigade structure, a move that would involve the establishment of heavy, medium and light formations. Air capabilities were to be restructured through the creation of four commands: air force, air defence, long-range aviation and military transport. The main structural element of the air force was to be the *aviabasa* (air base), which would divide into three categories of differing size and capacity, and would adopt the squadron rather than the traditional regimental structure. It was thought that this approach would significantly reduce the number of airfields, bringing auxiliary and support units under the command of the base. The army and air-services restructuring was intended to develop forces that were at permanent combat readiness. Planned organisational changes for the navy were less marked, but had the same aim.

While there was some resistance to the shift to the brigade structure, the army's overall adoption of a smaller unit structure has been implemented, notwithstanding the re-creation of two 'divisions': the 2nd Guards Tamanskaya Motor Rifle Division and the 4th Guards Kantemirovskaya

Tank Division. But in the air force, the language of the *aviabasa* has increasingly been abandoned and regimental and divisional naming conventions reintroduced. Some of the larger air bases may also be being broken down after proving unwieldy. The reforms of the air service do not appear to be finished. In 2014 it became apparent that there was an initiative to merge the air force and the Aerospace Defence Forces, forming what would be known as the Aerospace Forces. The impetus seemed to have come from Moscow's concern over the US Prompt Global Strike programme, particularly the fear that this could provide Washington with a conventional long-range attack that possibly used ballistic missiles for an effective decapitation strike – something previously limited to the realm of the nuclear exchange. It was argued that the combined force would be better able to coordinate a defence against such a threat.

Progress of the armaments programme

Under the GPV 2011–20 re-equipment plan, which complemented Serdyukov's force-restructuring programme, overall capability aims could only be met if both the service reforms and the equipment-modernisation scheme were completed. Discussing the GPV in 2008, Makarov pointed out that 'as of today no more than 10% of equipment is new'. While his exact definition of 'new' has not been established, it is generally viewed as describing equipment that had entered service within the preceding ten years. Moscow aimed to raise the proportion of new equipment to 30% by 2015, and to 70–100% by 2020.

Key programmes for the army were the *Armata* family of heavy armoured vehicles, which included a main battle tank; the family of *Kurganets* tracked infantry fighting vehicles; the *Bumerang* wheeled armoured personnel carrier; the 2S35 *Koalitsiya* self-propelled gun; and the 9K720 *Iskander* theatre ballistic missile. Army aviation was to be re-equipped with the Ka-52 *Hokum* and Mi-28NE *Havoc* attack helicopters, as well as upgraded Mi-17 *Hip* transport helicopters.

The re-equipment programme was meant to provide the air force with 50–60 of the aircraft being tested to meet its requirement for a fifth-generation multi-role combat aircraft, 92 Su-34 *Fullback* strike aircraft and up to 96 of the Su-35S *Flanker G* development of the Su-27 *Flanker* combat aircraft. Some 72 Su-30SM two-seat multi-role variant of the *Flanker* are also on order along with a smaller number of the Su-30M2, the latter replacing the Su-27UB trainer. The programme also includes upgrades to the MiG-31 *Foxhound* interceptor, the Tu-160 *Blackjack*, the Tu-95MS *Bear H* and the Tu-22M3 *Backfire C*. Development work continued on the long-range bomber requirement to provide a successor to the *Bear* and the *Blackjack*. Weapons projects included delivery of the Kh-101/Kh-102 air-launched long-range cruise missile intended to replace the Kh-55 (AS-15 *Kent*). The Kh-102 would function in the nuclear role, while the Kh-101 would provide a very-long-range conventional precision-strike weapon. The scheme also sought to complete the development and purchase of a variety of tactical air-to-surface and air-to-air weapons.

For the navy, the GPV 2011–20 was meant to provide up to 40 surface ships and 36 submarines. These included *Admiral Gorshkov*-class and *Steregushchiy*-class frigates, in addition to the *Borey*-class submarines (eight of which were to be supplied) and four *Mistral*-class ships from France.

Yet the government struggled to deliver on GPV 2011–20. In March 2015, Moscow was forced to announce a review of the delivery schedule of the fifth-generation fighter. By mid-2015, five Sukhoi T-50 flight-test aircraft had been built, but by mid-2015 there were suggestions that only 12 more of the aircraft would be bought before 2020. While the delay of the T-50 was ascribed to the 'new economic conditions' by Deputy Minister of Defence Yury Borisov, reshaping the programme may have helped to manage technical and production issues. Series manufacture of the aircraft is due to be carried out at the Komsomolsk-on-Amur production site, which is also building the Su-35S. The production build-up of the latter aircraft has been comparatively slow, and managing the series production of two types may have proved more demanding than anticipated.

Manufacturing issues also continued to cast doubt on the hull-building and outfitting programme for the navy in meeting the targets of GPV 2011–20. There are ambitious schedules for the *Borey/Borey-A*-class ballistic-missile submarine and *Yasen/Yasen-M*-class nuclear-powered attack submarines, while France has said it will not deliver the *Mistral*-class ships due to the deteriorating relations between NATO and Russia. Ship construction has suffered further in that maritime gas-turbine engines were sourced from Ukraine (as they were during the Soviet era), a process brought to an end by the hostility between Kiev and Moscow. Russian industry is moving to develop replacements for the Ukrainian power plant, but a production engine is unlikely to be available until 2021–22.

The army has encountered difficulties with series production of its armoured-vehicles programme, as well as those for some air-defence systems. Notionally, under GPV 2011–20 the army was to begin to replace its fleet of main battle tanks and to take delivery of new types of armoured fighting vehicles. According to Russian press reports, as many as 2,300 armoured vehicles including a number of the *Armata* main battle tank were to be built during this period, although this figure was very ambitious. While the tank was debuted as part of the Victory Day parade held in Red Square on 9 May 2015, it seems highly unlikely that a large number will be produced annually between 2016 and 2020. The acquisition programme may be recast as part of GPV 2016–25, extending the period over which the *Armata* is bought and possibly reducing planned numbers. The same type of delays and reductions may also affect other elements of the army's re-equipment programme, including the *Bumerang*, a considerable number of which were reportedly to be acquired by 2020.

Alongside the Kh-102 cruise missile and the next-generation long-range bomber, strategic systems to be acquired under GPV 2011–20 included up to 150 *Bulava* ballistic missiles to equip the *Borey*-class submarines. The *Bulava* development proved particularly difficult. The Strategic Rocket Forces were to receive new missiles developed on the basis of the RS-12M2 *Topol*-M intercontinental ballistic missile (ICBM), including the RS-24 *Yars* solid-fuel ICBM and the RS-26 *Rubezh* 'light' ICBM. Funding was also allocated to the development of a heavy liquid-fuel ICBM, dubbed *Sarmat*.

Like the structural reform of the military, GPV 2011–20 has had mixed results. While some significant annual production rates have not been met, and projects have been deferred, the programme has been much more successful than GPV 2006–15. Yet it remains to be seen whether the government and the Ministry of Defence will make further progress under GPV 2016–25, due to be finalised by the end of 2015, as future projects may be undermined by economic weakness and resulting shortfalls in funding. In the interim, it appears that there will be increasing pressure from the Ministry of Finance to reduce spending, as it attempts to offset Western sanctions and other pressures on the Russian economy. Siluanov proposed in April that defence be one of five areas of spending reined in from 2016 onwards. He reportedly suggested that 'a series of tasks' could be put off 'until a later period'. Cuts in annual production rates could be more palatable than overall production delays for both the Ministry of Defence and Putin, who frequently praised the military during the first half of 2015, reiterating that GPV 2011–20 would be fully implemented. Reducing the annual production rates of some systems would help to reduce costs and could also provide respite to those parts of the defence industry that are unable to meet manufacturing targets.

Qualified success

While Moscow's interventions in Crimea and initially in eastern Ukraine were effective, caution should be exercised in drawing broad conclusions. The Crimean operation was executed using elite units mainly from the special forces, while the ground forces deployed in eastern Ukraine were often faced with demoralised and poorly led Ukrainian forces. The Ukrainian military had suffered even more greatly than its Russian counterpart since the collapse of the Soviet Union and had not benefited from any reforms. In addition, Moscow mixed conventional military activity with a range of non-military tactics in what has been called hybrid warfare, which kept the new government in Kiev – as well as Western governments – off balance. Moscow's information campaign appeared more fleet-footed and agile than that of NATO. In truth, there was nothing new about such an approach from Moscow, which had long practised *maskirovka* – tactics including deception, disguise and disinformation in support of military activity – under the Soviet Union.

The main shortcomings of the Georgian campaign have been recognised and addressed within the Novy Oblik, as have the wider challenges of restructuring and re-equipping the Russian military. However, there has been a lack of progress in some areas: for example, the air force still lacks adequate modern tactical air-to-surface weapons. In general, the success of restructuring and re-equipment projects cannot yet be fully measured. But while the 2011–20 equipment programme has not fully met all of its aims, delivery of new and upgraded weaponry has significantly outstripped any previous post-Soviet effort. In shaping the 2016–25 armament programme, the Kremlin and the military will be under pressure on spending. The shift to a higher-readiness – if smaller – force structure also continues, but major challenges remain, not least in terms of the recruitment and retention of personnel.

Overall, the reforms have put the Russian military in its strongest position since the collapse of the Soviet Union. It has the potential to continue on this path, although ambition will be tempered by real-life constraints.

Deadlines for Mitigating Climate Change

Over the last decade and a half, the world's nations and scientists have settled on warming of 2°C since the beginning of the industrial age as the threshold for 'dangerous' climate change and as the target for international emissions-reduction agreements. According to the Intergovernmental Panel on Climate Change (IPCC), almost all scenarios with a better-than-two-thirds chance of keeping warming below this threshold require greenhouse-gas emissions to peak well before 2030, fall to net zero by some time between 2080 and 2100, and thereafter become negative (through a net withdrawal of carbon from the atmosphere). According to the United Nations Environment Programme (UNEP), however, there is a gap between the necessary reductions and the commitments made so far by national governments – including non-binding and conditional pledges – of 7–10 gigatonnes of carbon dioxide by 2025, rising to 14–17Gt by 2030.

This 'gigatonne gap' is the focus of negotiations on a treaty or other instrument that governments hope to conclude at a December 2015 international climate summit in Paris, in line with an agreement made at the United Nations Framework Convention on Climate Change (UNFCCC) conference held in Durban in 2011. As of June 2015, only 43 countries (including the 28 EU member states; the EU operates as a bloc in the UNFCCC process) had submitted their formal emissions-reduction commitments – 'intended nationally determined contributions', or INDCs – for the period after 2020. Together, these countries account for around just under two-thirds of global emissions, but their INDCs, compared to previous pledges, fill no more than 10% of the gigatonne gap. The longer emissions reductions are delayed, the deeper and faster they will have to be to avoid dangerous climate change. If the Paris summit fails to reach an agreement that bridges the gap, the UNFCCC process may be damaged and it will be more difficult to achieve the sharper reductions that would become necessary in the future.

Continued warming, stronger consensus

The calendar year 2014 was the hottest worldwide since instrumental records began. That finding was shared by the four principal independent global temperature sets and analyses, from the United States' National

Oceanic and Atmospheric Administration (NOAA) and National Aeronautics and Space Administration (NASA), the Japan Meteorological Agency and the Hadley Centre of the United Kingdom's Met Office (which noted that, within the limits of error, it was impossible to distinguish between 1998, 2005, 2010 and 2014). NOAA reported that the global temperature was 0.69°C above the twentieth-century average, and 0.04°C warmer than 2005 or 2010. Thirteen of the 15 hottest years on record have occurred since 2000; the exceptions, 1997 and 1998, experienced a strong El Niño event, the warm phase of a multi-year global-temperature oscillation. The records in 2005 and 2010 also came during El Niño years; 2014 was remarkable in that the record high occurred at a neutral point in the cycle. With an El Niño developing at the end of 2014 and extending into the first half of the following year, preliminary data suggested that 2015 might set a new, unequivocal record.

The pattern of extreme weather and volatility linked to global warming continued. (As *Strategic Survey: The Annual Review of World Affairs* noted in 2011, attribution of specific weather events to long-term warming may not be possible, but the trend towards increased extremes is clear.) The Arctic sea ice annual maximum extent fell in February 2015 to its lowest recorded level. Malaysia, Indonesia, Thailand and Singapore suffered exceptionally dry spells; the Balkans experienced near-record flooding, with three months' worth of rain falling in Bosnia and Herzegovina during a three-day period in May. There were unusually strong or early typhoons in both the Western and Eastern Pacific. Australia had abnormally warm weather, and there were huge bushfires in Victoria and South Australia. In 2014, the UK experienced both its wettest-ever January–August, with a record-breaking series of winter storms, and its driest-ever September. In the US, there were record temperatures and drought in the west, as well as record levels of snowfall and unusually cool temperatures throughout the year in the east. According to reinsurance company Aon Benfield, natural disasters caused in 2014 economic losses of US$132 billion, and at least 72% of these events were related to the weather. More than half of the losses came from the ten most severe events: floods in South Asia and the Balkans; tropical cyclones in India and East Asia; droughts in China, Brazil and the US; and severe weather in Japan, Europe and the US. In fact, total global losses in 2014 were 37% lower than the ten-year average and the lowest since 2009.

But there has been a clear upwards trend. After taking into account economic growth – which means there is more wealth at risk overall, but often greater resilience as well – economic losses from weather-related events have increased by an average of 1.1% per year since 1980.

Meanwhile, scientific understanding of the effects of global warming has strengthened. In November 2014, the IPCC published the final synthesis report of its *Fifth Assessment Report* (*AR5*), a comprehensive, multi-volume review of the state of research on the physical science, impacts and mitigation of climate change. The first such review since 2007, the report provided the basis for policymakers to create a global agreement which could keep climate change to a manageable level. It was released one month before the UNFCCC conference in Lima, which laid the final groundwork for the 2015 Paris summit. The report concluded with high confidence that 'without additional mitigation efforts beyond those in place today, and even with adaptation, warming by the end of the twenty-first century will lead to high to very high risk of severe, widespread, and irreversible impacts globally'. In most cases, the evidence, agreement among scientists and confidence in conclusions were stronger than in the 2007 assessment.

Previous editions of *Strategic Survey: The Annual Review of World Affairs* (published in 2007 and 2011) documented the increasing recognition, especially among governments and militaries, that climate change had strategic impacts on human, national and international security. In line with this trend, the Pentagon's *Quadrennial Defense Review 2014* was more definite than previous editions:

> The pressures caused by climate change will influence resource competition while placing additional burdens on economies, societies, and governance institutions around the world. These effects are threat multipliers that will aggravate stressors abroad such as poverty, environmental degradation, political instability, and social tensions – conditions that can enable terrorist activity and other forms of violence.

The 2015 US *National Security Strategy* identified climate change as one of eight strategic risks to US interests. At the launch of the US Department of State's second *Quadrennial Diplomatic and Development Review*, in April 2015, Secretary of State John Kerry noted that 'we are already seeing the negative consequences of climate change, which is a national and global security threat'. Citing the *National Security Strategy*, the review listed mitigating and adapting to climate change as one of the State Department's four strategic priorities, alongside preventing and mitigating conflict and violent extremism; promoting open, resilient and democratic societies; and advancing inclusive economic growth.

Meanwhile, in the second volume of the *AR5*, the IPCC assessed literature on climate change and security (including research published by the IISS) for the first time. The organisation concluded that although it was not yet possible to quantify the influence of climate change and resource scarcity on conflict risk, and the precise mechanisms by which climate influences security had not yet been established, 'climate change can indirectly increase risks of violent conflicts in the form of civil war and inter-group violence by amplifying well-documented drivers of these conflicts such as poverty and economic shocks ... Multiple lines of evidence relate climate variability to these forms of conflict.'

In June 2015, Pope Francis drew on the scientific and academic literature in a groundbreaking encyclical letter that called climate change a global problem with grave environmental, social, economic and political implications. Invoking Pope John XXIII's influential 1963 encyclical, 'Pacem in Terris' (Peace on Earth), on human rights, politics, international relations and nuclear proliferation, Francis explicitly compared global environmental deterioration with a 'world teetering on the edge of nuclear crisis'. He called for an integral environmental, economic, social and cultural ecology based on the principles of the common good, differentiated responsibilities and justice across generations. Called 'Laudato Si'' (Praise Him) after a canticle by Francis of Assisi – the Pope's namesake and the patron saint of the environment – the letter was clearly intended to shape the international debate and cause a paradigm shift in the long term. Its timing suggested that it was also intended to influence the approaching negotiations in Paris.

International negotiations and emissions targets

International climate negotiations are primarily conducted under the aegis of the UNFCCC, although much activity also takes place either bilaterally or in other international forums, such as the G20 and the 17-member Major

Economies Forum. Significant agreements are concluded at the UNFCCC's annual Conference of the Parties (COP) each December. At COP-3 in 1997, for example, the Kyoto Protocol set binding emissions-reduction targets for developed states for the period 2008–12. (The US was the only such state that failed to ratify the protocol.) At COP-13 one decade later, the Bali Road Map called for a long-term goal of global emissions reduction, with measurable, reportable and verifiable commitments for developed countries, and a two-year negotiating process towards a binding global treaty at COP-15, held in Copenhagen. The 2009 conference failed to conclude an agreement, but did 'take note' of the Copenhagen Accord, an informal agreement between the US and the BASIC countries (Brazil, South Africa, India and China) that called for developed countries to submit voluntary emissions-reduction targets for 2020, and for developing states to adopt 'nationally appropriate mitigation actions'. At COP-16 in 2010, the Cancun Agreement formalised many aspects of the Copenhagen Accord.

In 2011, COP-17 produced the Durban Platform, which forms the basis of the current round of negotiations. It established a second commitment period for the Kyoto Protocol, covering 2013–20, and launched a process 'to develop a protocol, another legal instrument or an agreed outcome with legal force under the Convention applicable to all Parties', which would be adopted no later than at COP-21, in December 2015, and would come into effect from 2020. At COP-19 in Warsaw, states were asked to prepare their emissions-reduction commitments – INDCs – in time for COP-21. In Lima, delegates agreed that INDCs would represent advances from the standing commitments of each party, and appended 'elements for a draft negotiating text' for a Paris Accord, which were firmed up into a formal text in February 2015.

This year-by-year process was under the framework of the UNFCCC – opened for signature at the Rio Earth Summit of 1992 – which calls for the 'stabilisation of greenhouse gas concentrations in the atmosphere at a level that would prevent dangerous anthropogenic interference with the climate system'. 'Dangerous' is not defined in the treaty, but in the years following the summit there has emerged a consensus that the term denotes warming of around 2°C above pre-industrial levels. By 2013, around 0.85°C of this warming had already occurred. Although the 2°C level was formalised at the 2009 Copenhagen climate summit, it was essentially arbitrary, based on impressionistic assessments of the risk and severity of impacts across various areas of concern. The intensity of impact that the IPCC considered dangerous in 2001, at 2°C, is projected in the latest report to occur at 1.5°C, 1°C or in some categories even at the level of warming that has already been experienced. Many scientists therefore are now arguing for a threshold of 1.5°C, and some countries pushed for this to be adopted in Copenhagen. The disagreement was reflected in post-Copenhagen negotiations, such as those for the Durban agreement and the draft text for Paris, which have called for a target of '2°C or 1.5°C'.

According to the IPCC's AR5, without additional emissions-reduction efforts beyond those in place, global warming is projected to reach 3.7–4.8°C by the end of the century. There are multiple potential emissions-reduction pathways that would be likely to limit warming to below 2°C; these require cuts of 40–70% by 2050 compared to 2010 and near or below-zero emissions by 2100. A target of 1.5°C requires a 70–95% cut by 2050. According to the UNEP, around 85% of emissions scenarios with a two-thirds chance of keeping warming below 2°C have emissions peaks before 2020, and all require a peak before 2030. But current levels of government pledges mean that emissions will continue to increase beyond that date.

As of June 2015, four of the top five emitters – China, the US, the European Union and Russia – had submitted INDCs; the other 12 submissions came from countries that collectively account for less than 6% of global emissions (Andorra, Canada, Ethiopia, Gabon, Iceland, Liechtenstein, Mexico, Morocco, Norway, Serbia, South Korea and Switzerland). In October 2014, the EU adopted a binding target of at least 40% reduction by 2030 compared to 1990, an advance on its previous commitment of 20% by 2020. Russia's submission suggested an ambition of 25–30% above 1990 levels by 2030, an improvement over its standing 25% commitment for 2020 but one subject to caveats: it is a 'long-term indicator' rather than a 'target', and assumes that carbon-dioxide uptake by forests can be offset against emissions. The US INDC, submitted on 31 March, aimed for a 26–28% reduction by 2025 compared to 2005. It was weaker than ambitions announced before the Copenhagen conference, and in fact had already been announced in November 2014 as part of a bilateral deal with China. In that agreement, Beijing pledged to reach peak emissions no later than 2030, to make its best efforts to do so earlier, and to increase the share of non-fossil-fuel energy sources to 20% by 2030. On 30 June 2015, China submitted an INDC including these pledges, along with new targets for 2030 for reductions in carbon intensity (emissions per unit of GDP) and reforestation.

Beijing's new renewable-energy target actually represents a decline in the rate of uptake of such sources compared to the previous target of 15% by 2020. However, the target of 2030 for peak national emissions is the first such formal commitment by Beijing, and it came earlier than many experts in China had expected. It fit in generally with estimates of peak Chinese emissions by both Chinese and foreign observers that tended to centre on 2030, albeit with considerable leeway in either direction. Previously, Beijing had refrained from formal commitments on emissions reductions, whether unilaterally or under the Kyoto Protocol. Its goals have always been cast in terms of reduction in carbon intensity, and would have resulted in a 2020 emissions level 75% higher than that of 2012. Since China is responsible for around one-quarter of emissions worldwide, global emissions cannot realistically begin to decline before the country reaches its peak.

The US, the EU, China, India and Russia together account for around two-thirds of global emissions and GDP, so efforts to limit global warming are heavily dependent on their collective emissions commitments, as well as on their ability to meet them, and their attitudes towards the shape and strength of a global agreement to reduce emissions after 2020. The next five largest emitters – South Korea, Japan, Brazil, Indonesia and Canada – collectively account for less than 10% of the global total.

Prospects for an agreement in Paris

The 86-page draft text for the Paris summit contains multiple options – up to 11, in some cases – for various sections and paragraphs, all of which are subject to further amendment or substitution in the course of the negotiations. Depending on the language from the draft incorporated in any final agreement, the Paris Accord could be either a robust instrument to limit dangerous climate change in accordance with the UNFCCC, or alternatively it could be vague, weak and incremental – or even useless. Key issues include levels of ambition and the nature of national commitments, the differentiation of responsibility and the legal form of the agreement.

Other outstanding questions relate to adaptation policy, transparency and accountability, financing and compensation.

It seems likely that any agreement will aim to keep warming below 2°C rather than 1.5°C, and that the INDCs submitted before the conference will collectively be insufficient to meet this goal. For it to be effective, countries, especially the biggest emitters, will have to commit to deeper cuts in Paris or agree on a mechanism for frequent reviews and modifications of their national targets. This may include firm target dates for a global peaking of emissions, for specific global percentage cuts and for net-zero emissions.

Article 3 of the UNFCCC mandates that parties pursue the goal of avoiding dangerous climate change 'on the basis of equity and in accordance with their common but differentiated responsibilities': there is a common responsibility to protect the global environment, but appropriate national contributions may depend on degree of economic development, historical responsibility for problems, and other special needs and circumstances. This was the basis for the Kyoto Protocol's differentiation between developed 'Annex I' countries, which had binding emissions targets, and developing countries, which did not. (Washington's failure to ratify Kyoto largely stemmed from the fact that the major emitters among developing countries, such as India and China, were not required to reduce emissions under the protocol.) The 2014 Lima conference affirmed that a Paris Accord should reflect the principle of common but differentiated responsibilities and respective capabilities, but the event marked the first time in which all nations, both developed and developing, agreed to make emissions cuts, and to improve on those ambitions already announced. The Paris negotiating text contains options that could either significantly weaken or strengthen the Kyoto Protocol's formal differentiation between states.

In previous climate negotiations, developing countries have generally worked through the G77 (which, confusingly, has 134 members) to establish common positions. All four BASIC countries, which also work together, are G77 members. There are also many subgroups or other partly overlapping groups with different priorities among issues such as adaptation, finance and compensation; the larger blocs are increasingly fragmented and alliances are becoming more fluid. Positions on legally binding emissions targets, whether universal or differentiated, do not closely correlate with developed- or developing-nation status.

The legal form and force of any agreement is the most critical, and intractable, issue facing the Paris summit. The language of the Durban agreement calling for 'a protocol, another legal instrument or an agreed outcome with legal force' was deliberately vague. It does not necessarily imply that specific national emissions-reduction targets need be legally binding. The UNFCCC itself is a binding international treaty with regard to goals and processes, but specific targets and commitments are either voluntary or subject to separate agreements, such as Kyoto. Several important countries – including the US, China and India – strongly resisted binding targets in a Paris Accord.

Binding targets are a 'red line' for the US in particular, primarily for domestic political reasons. If Washington agrees to a strong treaty in Paris, the document could only be ratified with the consent of two-thirds of the Senate. Such consent is almost unachievable in the current political climate, and US failure to ratify would weaken the agreement, perhaps fatally. Whether particular international treaties are subject to this constitutional requirement depends on factors such as existing authorising legislation or treaty frameworks – but previous Senate debates and resolutions with regard to the UNFCCC treaty and the Kyoto Protocol suggest that any legally binding commitments will face this high barrier. A weaker agreement in Paris taken within the context of the UNFCCC that had legal force in other areas, such as reporting requirements, but only voluntary emissions targets, would be implemented through executive action or legislation that only needed majority approval by both houses of Congress – still a difficult prospect, but less daunting than the alternative. Other nations are aware of this constraint, and it is likely that a Paris treaty will resemble an enhanced version of the Copenhagen Accord rather than the Kyoto Protocol. For instance, it could involve self-defined, voluntary national targets that would be subject to international review and assessment (a process that has proved successful in global trade and tariff negotiations). In the long term, successful implementation could depend as much on bilateral diplomacy as on the formal UNFCCC process, as was the case with the 2014 US–China deal.

Successful implementation also turns on the technical ability and affordability of achieving the necessary emissions reductions, factors which affect countries' willingness to commit to targets, especially unilaterally. The resistance of states such as China and India to emissions reductions rather than improvements in carbon intensity stems from concerns about the effect on economic growth; the same is true of political opposition in the US to emissions-reduction targets, and more widespread opposition to adopting targets that developing nations have avoided. The UNEP reports, moreover, that at least four members of the G20 – Australia, Canada, Mexico and the US – are likely to require further action to meet their 2020 pledges. But Brazil, China, the EU, India and Russia are on track; on a global scale, emissions reductions consistent with avoiding dangerous climate change are technically and financially practical.

Making it work

According to the 2006 review of climate-change economics led by economist Nicholas Stern, the cost of mitigation is estimated to be between –2% and 4% of global GDP per year (the negative number suggesting a possible net gain due to co-benefits), compared to a loss of 5–20% per year for unmitigated climate change. After a decade's delay, the cost will be higher. Yet the Global Commission on the Economy and Climate (co-chaired by Stern and former Mexican president Felipe Calderón) concluded in 2014 that a basket of measures could provide half the emissions reductions needed by 2030 for a two-thirds chance of keeping warming below 2°C. These measures include a strong, predicable carbon price; investment in renewable energy; reduced fossil-fuel investment and subsidies; and changes in urban and land-use planning to promote energy and carbon efficiency. 'Early, broad and ambitious' implementation of these actions could increase the emissions reduction from 50% to 90%. These measures would cost about US$94 trillion over 15 years, but the expected infrastructure investments for a business-as-usual, high-carbon economy would be US$90trn over the same period. The difference amounts to an additional US$270bn a year. Taking into account the co-benefits of a green economy, strong emissions reduction might be cheaper than business as usual, even without factoring in the long-term effects of climate change.

While most such measures require major new policy initiatives, there is evidence that current efforts are bearing fruit. According to the International Energy Agency (IEA), global energy-related emissions of carbon dioxide were the same in 2014 as in the preceding year. This was the fourth time in 40 years that annual emissions failed to rise, but the previous three occurrences (most recently, 2009) coincided with global economic downturns. The global economy grew by 3% in 2014. The IEA attributes the halt in growth to changing patterns of both production and consumption in China and Organisation for Economic Co-operation and Development countries, including an accelerating shift towards renewable energy sources. According to the UNEP, renewables accounted in 2014 for nearly half of new capacity. These energy sources now provide 9.1% of global electricity generation, and save 1.3Gt of carbon dioxide each year over the equivalent production from fossil fuels.

While these figures are based on the energy sector rather than the economy as a whole, overall emissions appear to be decoupling from economic growth. According to the Netherlands Environmental Assessment Agency, this trend began in 2012, when emissions grew by about half the rate of the global economy. According to the IEA, the data 'suggest that efforts to mitigate climate change may be having a more pronounced effect on emissions than had previously been thought'. Furthermore, the decoupling of emissions increases from economic growth suggests that UNEP projections for the gigatonne gap may prove to be too pessimistic. Nonetheless, Maria van der Hoeven, the IEA's executive director, warned that although the trend is encouraging, 'this is no time for complacency – and certainly not the time to use this positive news as an excuse to stall further action'.

Without deep and early cuts in global emissions beyond those already pledged by various countries, the world is likely to experience warming of more than 3°C, and possibly 4°C, above pre-industrial levels by the end of the century. Such cuts are achievable and affordable, but require concerted international action. Many scientists and campaigners have warned that the Paris summit is the world's last chance to avoid dangerous, if not disastrous, climate change. This language has been heard before, especially with regard to the Copenhagen conference in 2009. But whatever the outcome in Paris, if warming is to be kept below 2°C, global emissions must peak within the next 5–15 years. With the effects of climate change likely to contribute increasingly to the twenty-first-century strategic landscape, the next few years will be critical for global climate policy.

Chapter 4

United States

On 3 December 2014, at the lectern of Mount Sinai United Christian Church in Staten Island, flanked by clergy, local politicians and community organisers – most of them African-American – New York Mayor Bill de Blasio spoke in the insistent manner of someone delivering unpalatable truth. He said that he and his wife, who is black, had often warned their biracial son to tread carefully around the police. A few sentences later, he remarked that 'our history, sadly, requires us to say that black lives matter', using a phrase by then better known as a single word – #BlackLivesMatter – appended to thousands of social-media posts about police interactions with black citizens.

De Blasio was speaking at the height of the United States' longest and most intense crisis of race relations in a generation. In his city, protesters had taken to the streets after a grand jury declined to indict the New York Police Department officer who had placed an unarmed African-American man, Eric Garner, in a deadly chokehold. That decision came shortly after another grand jury decided not to indict Darren Wilson, a police officer in Ferguson, Missouri, who had shot and killed an unarmed African-American man named Michael Brown. Since that killing, which took place on 9 August 2014, Ferguson had seen large demonstrations that were met with a forceful response by heavily armed police. On 22 November, three days before the ruling in Ferguson, police in Cleveland shot dead a 12-year-old African-American boy named Tamir Rice. When Wilson escaped indictment, protests in Cleveland grew. And in April 2015, with protests continuing in Ferguson, the city of Baltimore saw large-scale rioting in response to the death of Freddie Gray, a young African-American man who had emerged from a police van in a coma from which he would never wake up.

The substance of de Blasio's remarks was difficult to dispute. Young, dark-skinned men in the US are routinely warned by their parents to avoid attracting police attention, for fear that even innocent behaviour could put them in danger. The worth of black life merited restating. But the timing and symbolism of de Blasio's intervention was seen by the police leadership as a betrayal. The president of the Patrolmen's Benevolent Association said that while police officers had been out protecting New York's sons and daughters, the mayor had been behind a microphone, throwing the police under the bus. A fortnight later, two policemen were shot dead at point-blank range by a mentally unstable African-American man who, shortly beforehand, had written online, 'they take 1 of ours, let's take 2 of theirs'. At each officer's funeral, when de Blasio rose to eulogise, hundreds of police officers, watching outside on big screens, turned their backs.

The divergent judgements made in each of these cases by activists, journalists, politicians, police, prosecutors and judges reflected different relative values being placed on the general and the specific. The argument for calm, for de-escalation of protests and the maintenance of order, often rested on a fastidiously neutral reading of the available evidence. Brown had, the Department of Justice concluded in March 2015, turned back towards Wilson after an initial scuffle and approached him in a way that put him in fear of attack. Garner had resisted arrest. Rice had brandished what looked, to the witness who called emergency services, like a handgun. The police shootings were thus justified – or at least were not to be prosecuted – on the grounds that their specific circumstances did not merit condemnation. In the case of Brown, the legal threshold for pursuing prosecution could not be proven to have been crossed: Wilson's use of force was not, in the language of the relevant test set by the US Supreme Court, 'objectively unreasonable'.

Arguments in the specific were not solely the preserve of the defence. A case in April 2015 showed why witness testimony, and especially that of the officers themselves, was bitterly disputed. A white North Carolina patrolman shot and·killed a black man whom he had stopped at a traffic

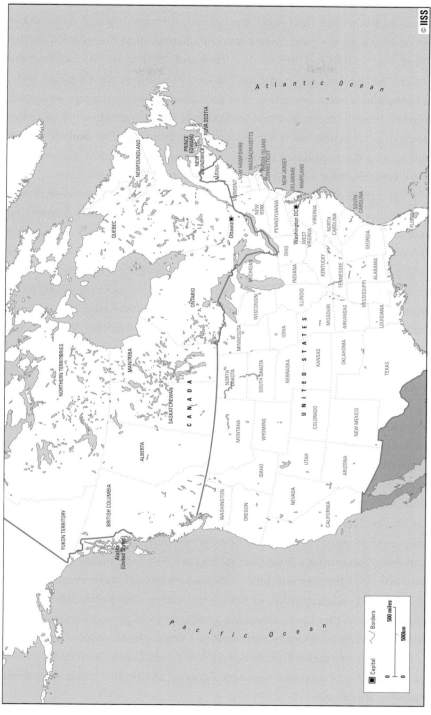

light, and who had then fled from his car on foot. An initial police statement, based on the patrolman's account, claimed that the suspect, Walter
Scott, had fought for the officer's taser and tried to use it, and that the
officer, Michael Slager, had fired his gun in self-defence. One day later,
a bystander's video recording was published. It showed Scott, unarmed,
running away. Slager shot him in the back, firing eight times in all. After
applying handcuffs, he retrieved an object from the site of their earlier
tussle, and then appeared to drop something – which some suspected to
have been his taser – next to Scott's prone form.

Nevertheless, even if triggered by the specific, the broader case for the
prosecution – the case for protesters taking to the streets and demanding
redress – was motivated primarily by the general. The black population
in Ferguson had been wronged, continually, by government institutions,
and particularly by the police. From 2012 to 2014, 93% of those arrested
in this small town were black. Black drivers were twice as likely to be
searched during a traffic stop as whites, but, even after adjusting for non-
racial factors, were 26% less likely to have been carrying illicit goods.
Black people made up almost 90% of those on whom the police used
force; according to records that included racial data, every person bitten
by a police dog was black. Ferguson is only 67% black. The Department of
Justice concluded that this disparity could not have been caused by differing racial rates of criminality. Rather, it occurred, 'at least in part, because
of unlawful bias against and stereotypes about African-Americans'. The
Department of Justice reported a racially targeted pattern of stops without
reasonable suspicion, arrests without probable cause, infringement on free
expression and use of excessive force.

During the 2008 election campaign, then-candidate Barack Obama had
delivered a speech on race relations which *Strategic Survey 2009* judged
capable of becoming a foundational text of US race relations. That speech,
however, was forced upon him – Obama was moved to comment after the
release of damaging video of his former pastor, the Reverend Jeremiah
Wright. Once president, Obama's approach to race was similarly reactive, consisting of sporadic interventions when one flashpoint or another
– the arrest of Harvard professor Henry Louis Gates, Jr in 2009, or the
2013 shooting of unarmed teenager Trayvon Martin in Florida – received
national attention.

'Trayvon Martin could have been me 35 years ago', said the president who had described himself, in the 2004 speech that made his career, as a 'skinny kid with a funny name'. But whatever the symbolic value of Obama's election, and the occasional power of his words, it became evident in the year to mid-2015 that his presidency had done little to bridge America's racial divisions. More than that, long-standing practices to protect and advance African-American civil rights faced serious challenges. Beginning in 2011, states had passed a series of voter-identification laws whose practical impact was to suppress the black vote; and, in two 2013 cases – *Shelby County vs Holder*, and *Fisher vs University of Texas* – the Supreme Court held, firstly, that a section of the 1965 Voting Rights Act was unconstitutional and, secondly, that affirmative action in university admissions had to meet a strict and narrow test. In Ferguson and Baltimore, the most acute racial crises of the civil-rights era were recalled by the sight of protesters fleeing tear gas, police dogs on the advance and officers with batons raised and guns drawn. A *Time* magazine cover featured such an image – a picture of the Baltimore riots – captioned 'America, 1968'. The year was crossed out in red pen, and above it was written a correction: '2015'.

Déjà vu?

Echoes of the 1960s aside, the last time that the American political consciousness had been so focused on police brutality and black protest was 1992 – the year of the Los Angeles riots, which followed the acquittal of four white police officers who had been videotaped beating black motorist Rodney King. That year, a Clinton and a Bush were running for president.

By summer 2015, the dynastic cycle had produced a second President Bush, and had seen a second Clinton – Hillary – beaten to the 2008 Democratic nomination by Obama. Having been rehabilitated by a mostly successful four years as secretary of state, Hillary Clinton was the Democratic frontrunner for the elections of 2016. Her most prominent opposite number in the early weeks of the so-called 'invisible primary' was yet another Bush – John Ellis, known as Jeb.

It was often said that Jeb Bush, George W.'s brother, was the most talented politician in his family. He had made his money in property, chaired the Republican Party of Florida and served briefly as the state's secretary of commerce. After a narrow defeat in 1994, he won the Florida governorship at the second attempt, in 1998. The ragged-edged conservative style that had characterised his first campaign – 'probably nothing' was his response when asked what he would do for the state's African-Americans – was deliberately smoothed in the second. Nevertheless, during Bush's eight years as governor, Florida became the first state to introduce a system of vouchers that parents could spend on private education for children in failing schools, and its state taxes were cut by somewhere between US$13 billion and US$20bn. His efforts to prolong the life of Terri Schiavo – a Floridian woman who was diagnosed as being in a persistent vegetative state, and whose husband wished her to be allowed to die – won him national applause from the right, both as a protector of 'life' (used here in the same sense as in opposition to abortion) and as a defender against an activist judiciary.

As a candidate for the 2016 presidential nomination, however, Bush assumed the profile of a moderate. Partly a matter of presentation, this new reputation was also gained through the adoption of individual policies seriously disagreeable to the party's support base. In Florida his immigration policy had been relatively liberal, and, despite his position on school vouchers, his vocal support for Common Core, an effort to standardise national curriculums, provoked the ire of conservatives who viewed it as an intrusion on states' rights. According to a May 2015 poll by the Pew Research Center, Bush entered the primary race with, at 35%, the highest unfavourable rating among Republican and Republican-leaning voters of any of the likely candidates for the nomination.

Jeb Bush faced another problem: his brother. His family history had brought him national name recognition, formidable fundraising success – by April 2015, his campaign was claiming to have broken the 100-day Republican record – and a roster of high-profile advisers, particularly on foreign policy. It also brought him questions about Iraq. 'Knowing what we know now, would you have authorised the invasion?', asked Fox News' Megyn Kelly in May. 'I would have, and so would have Hillary Clinton', Bush replied. But he claimed afterwards that he had misinterpreted the question – that he was putting himself in the shoes of his brother in 2002–03. After five days of persistent questioning, which had not been defused by the interim line that 'mistakes were made', he told an audience in Arizona that, in fact, 'knowing what we know now, I would not have engaged. I would not have gone into Iraq.'

Superficially, Clinton shared Bush's predicament. Her 2002 Senate vote to authorise the Iraq war, and Obama's public opposition at the time, had been crucial to her 2008 defeat; without it, Obama's insurgency would have lacked its clearest distinguishing policy feature. In May 2015, with the Islamic State of Iraq and al-Sham (ISIS) on the march, and Iraq the subject of daily headlines, Clinton, too, was moved to make clear her position: 'I made a mistake, plain and simple.' As she had in 2008, Clinton, like Bush, appeared vulnerable to a challenge from her party's base, a perception that for several months fuelled calls for a presidential bid by Elizabeth Warren, a populist senator from Massachusetts. Democratic anxieties were not eased by the optics of Clinton's post-State Department speaking engagements, for which she had been charging US$200,000 per appearance – a fee she clumsily justified in a June 2014 interview by claiming that she and her husband had been 'dead broke' upon leaving the White House. Nor were they soothed by the news that, as secretary of state, Clinton had used a personal email account for official business, the contents of which were to be released, in batches, in the run-up to the primaries.

The similarities with Jeb Bush, however, went little further than the superficial. At the beginning of the primary campaign, Clinton was exceptionally popular among Democrats, enjoying a 77% favourability rating (according to the same May 2015 Pew poll). And vulnerability is only relevant if there is an opponent to exploit it. The difference between the Republican and Democratic fields was best expressed by a sporting metaphor: the Republicans had a 'deep bench' – full of viable contenders to take the field – the Democrats a shallow one. Among the Republican contenders were Marco Rubio, senator for Florida, a young, charismatic son of Cuban immigrants; Ted Cruz, also Cuban-American, an arch-conservative, populist senator for Texas; Scott Walker, the governor of Wisconsin, who made his name nationally by confronting the state's labour unions; Rick Perry, the former Texas governor whose promising 2012 campaign had dissolved following a mistake in the TV debates; Carly Fiorina, former chief executive of Hewlett–Packard; Rand Paul, senator for Kentucky, a libertarian in domestic affairs and isolationist in foreign policy, playing the role of an anti-establishment outsider; and irascible businessman Donald Trump, whose political career to date amounted to a quixotic challenge to Obama's American citizenship. As of June 2015, there were at least 12 plausible candidates (announced or presumptive) for the Republican nomination; the most and least popular were, according to national polling averages, separated by no more than ten percentage points.

Clinton, meanwhile, was leading every potential Republican candidate by double digits in head-to-head polls; her strength, and a sense of inevitability even stronger than in 2008, appeared to have warded off several potential challengers. Her defeat to Obama may have resulted from personal vulnerability, but it also stemmed from the emergence of an extraordinary political talent capable of overturning an unprecedented polling lead. It seemed highly improbable that another such talent would surface before 2016.

In sport, having a deep bench makes a team stronger. In US presidential primaries, it may be a liability. The Supreme Court's decision in *Citizens United vs Federal Election Commission*, handed down in 2010, has facilitated the growth of 'super PACs' – large political-action committees legally permitted to accept donations of unlimited size, and to campaign for an individual candidate as long as that candidate does not coordinate the super PAC's activities. This allows candidates to remain in the race for a party nomination longer than they previously would have: early primary and caucus defeats need not necessarily end a candidate's campaign and thereby thin the field. For example, the candidacy of former House speaker Newt Gingrich for the 2012 Republican nomination appeared to be defunct by the end of 2011, but was sustained by Winning Our Future, a super PAC that spent US$17 million on advertising, all but US$1m of which had been contributed by right-wing businessman Sheldon Adelson. In such a scenario, as an unnamed Republican strategist told the *National Review*, 'everyone has nukes – including a whole bunch of non-state actors.' By summer 2015, the accumulation of candidates thus presented the substantial risk of a prolonged race for the Republican nomination – and even, perhaps, the chaos of a brokered convention – taking place alongside a virtual coronation for Clinton.

Jeb Bush was not the only Republican to stumble in passing judgement on the invasion of Iraq. In May, Rubio spent a similarly painful three minutes of television insisting that George W. Bush's decision had been the right one, on the basis of the evidence on Iraqi weapons of mass destruction available at the time (thus avoiding the awkward application of hindsight). It was telling that, for Republican aspirants, this remained a difficult question – although Perry, at least, was willing to concede that the overall outcome of the invasion had been negative. Only Paul, among potential nominees, appeared willing to break decisively with the basic foreign-policy approach of the Bush administration.

In fact, Paul aside, there was little evidence of Republican willingness to appeal to the US electorate by rejecting Bush's political legacy – except when criticising its fiscal indiscipline, as an appeal to the right. Rather, the positions of the Republican Party's candidates for national office reflected a belief that the Obama administration was a historic failure. At the congressional level, the Republican reading of the national mood appeared to be sound. The November 2014 midterm elections were predicted to go badly for the Democrats; they went worse. Republicans outperformed public polling by an average of 4 percentage points to take back control of the Senate after eight years, gaining nine seats for an overall total of 54. In the House of Representatives, they added 13 seats, increasing their lead to 247–188. The gubernatorial races ended in a net gain for Republicans in two states, with victories in traditionally Democratic states including Massachusetts, Illinois and Maryland (where Obama had won in 2012, with 61%, 57% and 62% of the vote respectively).

This marked the second time that decisive victory for Obama in the presidential election had been followed, two years later, by a significant midterm defeat for the Democratic Party. Obama called the 2010 result a 'shellacking'; in 2014, he conceded that the Republicans had had a 'good night'. With an approval rating of 40%, he had played the role of a lame duck; invitations to make campaign visits were conspicuously lacking from Democratic candidates reluctant to defend a presidential record that Republicans were treating, apparently correctly, as an electoral liability. This included a sustained attack on the Affordable Care Act (ACA), also known as 'Obamacare', which the Republican leadership promised to attempt to repeal.

Yet as a referendum on the Obama legacy, or as a test of national political leanings, the midterm elections were hardly conclusive. As *New York Times* writer Nate Cohn observed before polling day in 2014, Republicans have an advantage in midterms: turnout is lower overall, but especially among young and non-white voters, who reliably lean Democratic. In the House of Representatives, gerrymandered districts enabled Republicans to receive 57% of the seats with a 52% share of the vote. Nor, arguably, did the result greatly change the day-to-day functioning of American politics. Obama's legislative agenda had already faced almost immutable opposition from the existing House majority, and the election did not give the Republicans a filibuster-proof 60 seats in the Senate, let alone the two-thirds majority in both houses required to override a presidential veto. That being the case, policies were likely to advance by the same, often non-legislative, often haphazard, means as they had before November 2014.

Government without Congress

Congressional paralysis has made executive action and judicial interpretation the default mechanism of major policy change in the US. In the year to mid-2015, this trend was clearest in two areas in which Congress had been inactive for a decade or more: immigration reform, and measures to combat climate change. On both issues, it took the president little more than a fortnight after the midterms to announce wide-ranging measures dependent on regulatory reform, executive action and, in the case of climate change, international agreement.

Obama had warned, in a major June 2013 speech on climate policy at Georgetown University, that 'if Congress won't act soon to protect future generations, I will'. He promised that, in the absence of congressional action, he would begin to prepare executive orders. This effort was based on a reading of the 1970 Clean Air Act, supported by the Supreme Court, to the effect that the Environmental Protection Agency (EPA) had regulatory authority to manage greenhouse-gas emissions. Proposals for such regulations were unveiled over the course of 2013 and 2014, including measures to reduce carbon emissions from existing power plants by 30% from 2005 levels by 2030. A number of measures began to reach fruition at the end of 2014 and the beginning of 2015, including a limit on smog-causing ozone, although a January 2015 deadline for finalising proposed regulation of emissions by future power plants was extended by five months. The measure with perhaps the most symbolic significance, however, was an accord reached with China on 11 November 2014. The bilateral agreement, signed by Obama and Chinese President Xi Jinping, announced the United States' intention to cut emissions by 26–28% below their 2005 level by 2025, and China's intention for its emissions to peak at 'around 2030', with both countries making their 'best efforts' to exceed those targets, and to 'continue to work to increase ambition over time'. China also declared its intent to increase the share of non-fossil fuels in primary energy consumption to 'around 20%' by 2030. For both sides, these targets were somewhat conservative codifications of existing plans – in the US case, the 26–28% figure was slightly lower than that included in a 2013 climate bill, which passed the House but was never put to a vote in the Senate.

On immigration, Obama proposed to make those undocumented immigrants with children who were US citizens or legal permanent residents eligible for a deferral of deportation, and, after meeting certain criteria, able to receive authorisation to work in the US. He also proposed to broaden an existing scheme, Deferred Action for Childhood Arrivals, which allows those brought illegally into the US as children to defer deportation, and in many cases to be granted the right to work. The non-partisan Migration Policy Institute estimated that the proposals could mean temporary relief from deportation for up to 3.7m undocumented immigrants. When added to the existing numbers already eligible for Deferred Action for Childhood Arrivals or due to become eligible under the new plans, this meant a total of up to 5.2m could benefit from amnesty.

In both areas, Obama's actions were much less ambitious than comprehensive legislation would likely have been; and yet, due to the manner of their execution, they were extremely controversial. As of May 2015, Obama was on average issuing fewer executive orders per year (33) than any president since Grover Cleveland, according to the American Presidency Project at the University of California, Santa Barbara. By comparison, George W. Bush had averaged 36, and Bill Clinton 46. But Obama was taking executive action in major policy areas where his own efforts to encourage legislation had either been explicitly rejected or deliberately stalled. The risk was that accountability and transparency would be sacrificed in the name of good governance – and, citing this risk, opponents sought legal redress.

In a case brought by 26 states and heard by a Texas federal district court, a judge ruled in February 2015 that the Obama administration's instruction to defer action on deportation would inflict 'irreparable harm' on those states forced to accommodate undocumented immigrants, and issued an injunction on the programme's application. The administration appealed, but the fifth circuit court ruled in May that the appeal was unlikely to succeed on the merits, and declined to lift the injunction. The case was likely to reach the Supreme Court; meanwhile, similar challenges were in the pipeline, targeting the EPA's regulations on greenhouse-gas emissions.

The ACA, Obama's single greatest domestic legislative achievement, also faced the possibility of judicial reversal, in a case against the act brought by four Virginia residents, to be heard by the Supreme Court as *King vs Burwell*. For Republicans, however, the case was a poisoned chalice. The campaign to repeal 'Obamacare' had made political sense; over the course of 2014, the ACA's favourability ratings hovered at around 35%. But the issue at stake in *King* was the legality of federal insurance subsidies for residents of states that had not established their own exchanges – subsidies that were much more popular than the ACA as a whole. This left congressional Republicans with a dilemma: letting the subsidies lapse would risk the party appearing responsible for the removal of healthcare coverage from 6.4m Americans. But passing legislation to clarify the intent of Congress and extend the subsidies would risk appearing to have rescued the ACA from judicial defeat, and thus to have undermined a central goal of the party base. The court's decision to maintain the subsidies was therefore a not entirely unwelcome judicial defeat, allowing congressional Republicans to focus on politically safer challenges to Obamacare – including symbolic attempts at repeal alongside smaller-scale tweaks.

Despite political dysfunction, the US economic recovery continued at encouraging speed, with 2014 the best year for American job growth since 1999, both overall and in the private sector; in September 2014, the unemployment rate dipped below 6% for the first time since July 2008. Partisan polarisation was proving a severe obstacle to efficient governance, but not an obstacle to economic growth – although the foundations for recovery had been laid while Obama still enjoyed the support of a Democratic Congress.

In the area of trade policy – a principal tool in shaping future economic growth – executive initiative again met congressional resistance. Ten years of negotiations over the Trans-Pacific Partnership, a 12-country trade pact spanning the Pacific, and on a bilateral agreement with the EU, the Transatlantic Trade and Investment Partnership, were, by summer 2015, reaching fruition. Both agreements focused primarily on hammering out differences between conflicting sets of national and intergovernmental regulations, rather than setting tariffs and market-access conditions. But they both faced resistance, primarily from Democrats, in part because of the political inheritance of the North Atlantic Free Trade Agreement, which was blamed by the populist left for losses of manufacturing jobs, trade imbalances and growing income inequality. Resistance also derived from the opaque nature of the trade negotiations and the leaking in November 2013 of its draft provisions on intellectual-property rights. Faced with the prospect of painstakingly negotiated provisions being opened up individually to congressional redrafting, the Obama administration sought 'Trade Promotion Authority', a fast-track provision to lay the trade agreements before Congress for only 60 days, after which they would be put to an up-or-down vote.

Here, again, the overall lesson was clear: in 2015, the success of presidential policy initiatives, in a condition of divided government, was a function of the extent to which they required congressional approval. The same was increasingly true in foreign policy, the field in which presidential sovereignty had traditionally been strongest.

Beyond the water's edge

'I deeply regret that some perceive my being here as political. That was never my intention.' Israeli Prime Minister Benjamin Netanyahu's regret might (conceivably) have been genuine, but the perception was hardly surprising. He was speaking before a joint session of Congress on 3 March 2015 because he had been invited by House majority leader John Boehner, through Israeli ambassador to the US Ron Dermer, without the White House having been informed. The breach of protocol – as it appeared to most observers – was a statement of opposition, coordinated between the Republican Party and the Israeli prime minister, to an impending nuclear deal with Iran.

While doing his best to reject the charge of partisan interference, Dermer told *Atlantic* magazine reporter Jeffrey Goldberg that Netanyahu had a 'moral obligation ... to speak up about a deal that could endanger the survival of the one and only Jewish state'. He was referring to an agreement between the E3+3 states and Iran that had not yet been struck, but whose basic parameters were becoming public. The clock for the conclusion of a final agreement between the parties had started ticking on 20 January 2014, when the Joint Plan of Action agreed in Geneva in November 2013 came into operation, providing Iran with limited sanctions relief in return for a freeze on the most sensitive of its nuclear activities. An initial six-month deadline for a comprehensive settlement was extended first to November 2014, and then again to 30 June 2015, but with the understanding that the basic principles would need to be settled by the end of March. Delivered at the beginning of March, Netanyahu's speech was therefore his last chance to generate sufficient opposition in the US to make that settlement politically impossible to reach.

Netanyahu's case was not against the deal's details but against its basic logic. It appeared that Iran would, for a period of 10–15 years, be accepting verified limits on its nuclear activities that – if honoured – would make it very difficult to acquire enough fissile material to develop nuclear weapons. In return, the E3+3 would lift the nuclear-related sanctions progressively imposed on the country since 2002 (when its secret enrichment activity was exposed). Iran would still be enriching uranium during this period of limitation, marking the abandonment of the goal of zero enrichment demanded by the negotiating powers since the beginning of the crisis, and enshrined in a series of UN Security Council resolutions. This meant, as Obama put it in a National Public Radio interview in April,

> purchasing for 13, 14, 15 years assurances that the breakout [time] is at least a year ... that if they decided to break the deal, kick out all the inspectors, break the seals and go for a bomb, we'd have over a year to respond. And we have those assurances for at least well over a decade.

This logic, to Netanyahu, meant a double risk: firstly, that Iran would cheat, using the nuclear infrastructure left to it by the deal as the basis for a renewed clandestine programme; and, secondly, that even if it did not cheat, Iran would simply resume its progress towards a nuclear weapon after the deal expired. He insisted that a deal must set back Iran's programme further and that an end to its regional subversion, sponsorship of terrorism and threats towards Israel should be conditions for lifting sanctions.

'We're being told', Netanyahu declared in the most forceful and most quoted line of the speech, 'that the only alternative to this bad deal is war. That's just not true. The alternative to this bad deal is a much better deal.' But little in the preceding years of diplomacy had suggested anything much better was achievable. And when, on 2 April 2015, the State Department announced that parameters for a final agreement had been set, after a last diplomatic push in Lausanne, it became clear that negotiators had secured, in principle, something close to the strongest possible version of the logic Obama described. (See pp. 223–29.)

The agreement was neither final nor perfect. Netanyahu's concern about what would happen after the time limits attached to the deal's provisions were reached was by no means baseless. Indeed, Obama fed those anxieties by sharing with NPR the fear 'that in year 13, 14, 15, they have advanced centrifuges that enrich uranium fairly rapidly, and at that point the breakout times would have shrunk almost down to zero'. Obama's estimate was probably wrong by a measure of some five years: Iran would need some time after the initial ten-year period to develop and test the centrifuge cascades necessary for this breakout path. But the clear implication was that at some point in the 2030s, Iran would be permitted to enrich without restriction, placing it, in theory, dangerously close to acquiring a bomb.

Netanyahu's speech could not stop the Lausanne accord being reached, and it did not persuade Congress to impose additional coercive sanctions, which would have scuppered the Obama administration's negotiating strategy. It did, however, produce a supporting initiative from the junior senator for Arkansas, Tom Cotton, who wrote an open letter to Iran's leaders. Co-signed by 46 other senators, it (condescendingly) aimed to enrich Iranians' 'knowledge of our constitutional system', warning that the nuclear agreement would be regarded as 'nothing more than an executive agreement' between Obama and Supreme Leader Ayatollah Ali Khamenei; that Congress could modify its terms at any time; and that Obama's successor as president could revoke it 'with the stroke of a pen'.

The 1799 Logan Act, passed in response to the efforts of a Pennsylvanian to personally negotiate peace with France, prohibits US citizens from carrying on diplomatic correspondence with foreign powers unauthorised by the executive branch. Since 1800, the accepted doctrine in US constitutional practice has been that, as Representative John Marshall put it, the president is 'the sole organ of the nation in its external relations, and its sole representative with foreign nations'. Boehner's invitation and Cotton's letter appeared to have violated the spirit of this doctrine; Cotton and his co-signatories may even have violated the letter of the Logan Act (although prosecution would have been an absurdity).

After the deal was made public in April, however, congressional disquiet was channelled into a compromise well within the bounds of normal political practice. A bill constructed by senators Bob Corker (the Republican chair of the Senate Foreign Relations Committee) and Ben Cardin (the Democratic ranking member) provided for a 30-day congressional review of a final deal. Passing a joint resolution of disapproval during this period would prevent the administration from lifting congressionally imposed sanctions. This was at some distance from proposals from those, such as Ted Cruz, who had wished for congressional right of approval on the Iran deal in the manner of a treaty. For a joint resolution to be veto-proof, it would have to achieve a two-thirds majority in both houses of Congress. The emerging congressional compromise appeared to demonstrate that the president's achievement of a fundamental realignment of foreign-policy interests could be made to stick at home, albeit narrowly.

Cold wars

On 10 December 2013, in Soweto, Obama rose to speak in memory of Nelson Mandela. On his way to the podium, he had to pass Cuban President Raúl Castro. Obama smiled, lent in, and shook Castro's hand, before doing the same with Brazilian President Dilma Rousseff and Zimbabwean President Robert Mugabe. The ten-second encounter was the first public handshake between American and Cuban presidents since Bill Clinton's hurried interaction with Fidel Castro at a UN summit in 2000, which in turn was the first since Richard Nixon had met Fidel in 1959. It was greeted with some consternation from Cuban-American activists, but not as much as might have been expected; and a number of analysts warned journalists in search of reaction quotes not to read the handshake as a sign of dramatic policy change.

The analysts were wrong. On 17 December 2014, Obama and Castro announced plans to negotiate the restoration of full diplomatic relations between their countries. By the time they shook hands in South Africa, a two-man American team had been talking to Cuban officials for six months. The channel remained open throughout 2014, with nine secret meetings in Canada, helped by the mediating efforts of Pope Francis. The decision to go public in December brought the release of Alan Gross – a US Agency for International Development employee detained since 2009 for work the Cuban government deemed espionage – and a spy exchange. Obama announced a review of Cuba's inclusion on the list of state sponsors of terrorism – from which it was duly removed in May – and his intention to discuss with Congress the lifting of the trade embargo. (See map, *Strategic Geography* p. XX.)

Washington's shift marked the end of a five-decade strategy of isolating Cuba, which appeared to have achieved little. At the turn of the millennium, a Gallup poll showed 71% of Americans in support of normalising relations. It took US policy 15 years to catch up. The support of Cuban-American constituencies and activists notwithstanding, Obama had little to lose in adjusting US policy, and perhaps something to gain: the beginnings of economic opening in Cuba that could eventually lead to political change; and a reduction in Cuba's political and economic reliance on an increasingly unstable and anti-US Venezuela. Again, however, the core of the reopening to Cuba – the lifting of the trade embargo – would still be subject to congressional approval, and vulnerable to obstruction, as was made clear by the two Cuban-American senators and presidential candidates, Cruz and Rubio.

Nevertheless, Obama was able to tell a press conference at the April 2015 Summit of the Americas in Panama, shortly after a meeting with Raúl Castro, that 'the Cold War is over'. Mending relations with Cuba was the clearest tangible result of Obama's effort to shape a post-Cold War presidency, by removing the one glaring leftover from the Cold War order in Latin America. In Asia, despite increasingly assertive Chinese actions in the South China Sea, Obama had scrupulously avoided allowing the US 'pivot' to the Asia-Pacific to be governed by the rhetoric of power competition, and appeared to be at least forestalling a decisive increase in offensive balancing, let alone Cold War-style containment. Chinese land-reclamation efforts in the South China Sea were making the drift to confrontation harder to avoid, but a November 2014 agreement on military notifications and possible 'rules of the road' gave some hope for preventing direct hostilities (although the risk of inadvertent escalation remained troubling). (See pp. 345–50.)

Instead, Obama's second term was increasingly being shaped by the need to avert a new Cold War with Russia. Moscow's destabilisation of eastern Ukraine brought US–Russian relations to their lowest ebb since the end of the Cold War. The annexation of Crimea in March 2014 had already led to the suspension of most bilateral cooperation projects, and the hope that some areas could be insulated from the effects of the Ukrainian crisis began gradually to erode: in November, for example, Russia effectively put an end to the long-standing Nunn–Lugar programme of cooperative nuclear-threat reduction, and announced that it would not attend the 2016 Nuclear Security Summit in Washington. As a ceasefire agreement hammered out in September 2014, 'Minsk I', unravelled, the US announced sanctions on Russian banks, oil companies and other major firms, to bolster the individual sanctions applied at the start of the crisis. A further round of sanctions followed in March, expanding the list of targeted individuals to include members of the deposed, Russian-aligned Ukrainian government, and the administration expanded its programme of non-lethal defensive assistance to Ukrainian forces, which included communications equipment and armoured (but unarmed) Humvees.

The Obama administration had been under considerable pressure, however, to go further. As Ukrainian President Petro Poroshenko put it in an address to a joint session of Congress in September 2014, 'blankets and night-vision goggles are important', referring to the delivery of non-lethal defensive aid, 'but one cannot win a war with blankets.' Congress agreed, and passed a resolution authorising the president to intensify sanctions and provide lethal defensive aid. On the latter point, as Vice President Joe Biden told Poroshenko in a November visit to Kiev, the administration's position was that it had 'made no decisions'; such a move was clearly not Obama's preferred option, but was not ruled out.

This dynamic formed the backdrop to the second round of ceasefire talks, held in Minsk in February. As Russia negotiated with Germany,

France and Ukraine, the possibility of a more bellicose US response provided a convenient foil for the Europeans – deal with us, or risk US escalation. Yet, as the resulting agreement, 'Minsk II', became increasingly fragile during the first half of 2015, the balance of the administration's position became harder to sustain, not least because of the need to reassure NATO allies that, should Russia's hybrid-warfare tactics be used on their soil, the US would respond. The middle way of imposing sanctions while avoiding military escalation continued vis-à-vis Ukraine, but as the crisis continued, the foundations of the broader post-Cold War order in Europe were coming under strain. The US was readying plans to pre-position heavy weaponry for up to 5,000 troops in Eastern Europe – the first time it had done so since the end of the Cold War.

Middle Eastern realignment

Obama's presidency was born in the shadow of the Iraq War. His 2002 speech in opposition to the invasion made possible his primary challenge to Hillary Clinton from the left. His effort to withdraw all US troops from Iraq subsequently became a central, self-consciously legacy-defining feature of his presidency. His extreme reluctance to intervene in Syria, even as President Bashar al-Assad crossed the White House's infamous chemical-weapons 'red line', was almost certainly a product of the Iraq experience. So as ISIS transformed from 'al-Qaeda's JV team' (in the British vernacular, their second eleven), as Obama had put it, into a fearsome army and quasi-state stretching from deep inside Syria almost to Baghdad, his desire to avoid direct military re-engagement in Iraq was understandable.

The administration's hand was forced, however, by the spectacle of an American-trained Iraqi army in all-out retreat, followed by the looming possibility of humanitarian catastrophe. As ISIS forces trapped around 40,000 members of the primarily Kurdish-speaking Yazidi minority community on Mount Sinjar, in northern Iraq, and the Kurdish capital Erbil appeared under threat, Obama announced on 7 August 2014 the start of limited US airstrikes against ISIS forces, while insisting that he would 'not allow the United States to be dragged into another war in Iraq'. Yet the precise meaning of that disavowal quickly became a matter for debate. In testimony to the Senate Armed Services Committee on 16 September, Chairman of the Joint Chiefs of Staff Martin Dempsey suggested that he would, if he deemed it necessary, recommend that US military 'advisers' already on the ground be deployed to fight directly alongside Iraqi troops, and that the president was prepared to approve such operations on a 'case-by-case basis'. The White House insisted that Dempsey's remarks were purely hypothetical, but they had raised a reasonable question. If the fight against ISIS was to develop into an offensive to retake major Iraqi cities, would Iraqi forces be sufficient for the task?

As the campaign against ISIS developed, it became clear that it could neither be limited to the borders of Iraq, nor rely solely on the fighting power of the Iraqi army. But the way in which the campaign expanded was politically fraught. A quickly assembled coalition, said by Washington to number 62 states (although only a small fraction of these were contributing to offensive operations), was unwieldy, and uneven in its relative application of force; Obama announced the beginning of coalition airstrikes in Syria on 10 September, but in practice more than 90% were carried out by the US. The US-led campaign, on the side of the Iraqi government and Shia militias, was in tacit alignment with Tehran's interests and reliant on Iranian power: for some critics in the Arab world, this went as far as alliance. However, the reality was more complicated. Aside from the substantial supply of weaponry to Gulf states, the US was simultaneously supporting a Saudi-led struggle against Iranian-backed Houthis in Yemen, notably forcing an Aden-bound Iranian supply convoy to turn back to Iran in April 2015, after several days of being tracked by the aircraft carrier USS *Theodore Roosevelt*.

Nevertheless, in combination with the negotiations over a nuclear deal, there was plenty to fuel long-standing anxieties that a 'grand bargain' between the US and Iran would be made above the heads of the Gulf states. These fears were perhaps reflected in the fact that Saudi King Salman bin Abdulaziz declined to attend a May 2015 summit of Gulf states at Camp David. This feeling of uncertainty about Washington's priorities in the Middle East was further amplified by the continuing turmoil of the US–Israeli alliance. Boehner's congressional power play had only made sense, after all, because of the near-total dysfunction of the Obama–Netanyahu relationship. Since 2011, the political revolutions of the Arab Spring and their consequences had been remaking the Middle East piece by piece, with the collapse of autocracies followed in some cases by chaos, in others by autocratic revival, and in one or two instances by something approaching democracy. In the year to mid-2015, the United States' strategic choices in the Middle East had begun to promise a systemic transformation of relations with the region. However, the steady increase in US military advisers in Iraq suggested that the old and familiar dilemmas would not be easy to escape.

©IISS

Atlantic Ocean

MEXICO

Havana

THE BAHAMAS

Mexico City

BELIZE

CUBA

DOMINICAN
REPUBLIC

JAMAICA   HAITI

Santo Domingo

GUATEMALA

Belmopan

Tegucigalpa

Kingston

Port-au-
Prince

Guatemala City

HONDURAS

EL SALVADOR

NICARAGUA

San Salvador

COSTA RICA

TRINIDAD & TOBAGO

Managua

Panama
City

Caracas

Georgetown

San Jose

Paramaribo

PANAMA

VENEZUELA

Cayenne

Bogotá

GUYANA

SURINAME

FRENCH GUYANA

COLOMBIA

Quito

ECUADOR

PERU

B R A Z I L

Lima

La Paz

Brasília

B O L I V I A

PARAGUAY

Asunción

CHILE

URUGUAY

Santiago

Buenos Aires

Montevideo

A R G E N T I N A

Pacific Ocean

Falkland Islands (UK)

South Georgia (UK)

■ Capital   〜 Borders

0   1,000 miles

0   1,000km

Chapter 5

Latin America

Much of Latin America and the Caribbean began 2015 lacking the confidence that had defined the region in the preceding decade. Economic growth had become sluggish and public finances imbalanced, and both were projected to remain disappointing until the end of 2016. Corruption scandals rocked governments in several countries, undermining public trust in politics and institutions. Attempts at regional integration and cooperation had mostly come up short, and Latin America found itself fragmented and polarised, with many states going in their own direction and pursuing a national agenda. A tide of violent crime continued to sweep across parts of Mexico and Central America. Meanwhile, anti-US and anti-imperialist rhetoric – staples of Latin American nationalism – seemed to be growing stale, in part due to the sudden opening between the United States and Cuba, the year's most dramatic diplomatic development. The region was left without a clear sense of the path forward, and had few unifying elements.

The biggest factor behind these trends was the end of what was called the 'commodities super-cycle', a decade-long period of high prices for raw materials caused by rapidly rising demand from East Asia. Exports of commodities and other low-value-added goods were the driving force behind the boom from 2003 to 2013, and many Latin American countries have been deeply reliant on them. As demand faded, economic growth slowed in 2014 and 2015, and studies indicated that the prospects for a rebound in the short term were not bright. The slowdown harmed markets and profits across the region, and exposed Latin America's failure to diversify economies and become more competitive during the boom years. Without a strong export market for raw materials and other commodities, the region is relatively inefficient and uncompetitive, particularly in manufacturing and high-skill industries.

The direct and indirect effects of the economic slowdown cascaded across Latin American societies. In the energy sector, the decline was striking. As the price of crude fell below US$50 per barrel (before recovering somewhat), there were significant repercussions for oil-producing countries, especially Venezuela – where falling oil revenues contributed to a fiscal and macroeconomic meltdown – as well as Ecuador and Colombia. And while low energy prices had some benefits, particularly for countries in the Caribbean and Central America that were heavily reliant on imports, they were also an obstacle to much-needed energy-industry reform. In Mexico, lower prices posed some challenges for President Enrique Peña Nieto's ambitious attempt to liberalise the state oil company Pemex, and to reinvest in energy infrastructure. Similarly, in Brazil, lower revenues combined with a massive corruption scandal to make the state oil company, Petrobras, a tremendous drag on the economy and the political system. Not only did the development of offshore 'pre-salt' reserves seem improbable, but the future of the firm was far from clear. At the same time, Latin America faced a series of energy and environmental disasters, including floods in Chile and droughts in Brazil, the latter causing significant problems for the hydroelectricity industry.

In broader terms, growing fiscal imbalances called into question many of the expensive social policies financed by the boom years and, by extension, the progress the region had made in combating poverty and inequality, and expanding the middle class. Moreover, while some countries responded to the slowdown by pursuing economic liberalisation, others stepped up protectionism and state involvement in the economy – a difference that tended to widen the divide between the region's Atlantic and Pacific countries. However, with the 'open regionalist' Pacific Alliance grouping losing some momentum, and Brazil and other Mercosur countries showing signs of moving back towards orthodox policies, this split seemed less pronounced than it had been a few years earlier.

At the same time, partly because of slowing economic growth and uncertainty over public spending, public discontent with politics and political figures rose steadily across the region. While most elections in the year to mid-2015 resulted in victories for the status quo, few were resounding endorsements of those in power. Indeed, Brazilian President Dilma Rousseff narrowly won a national vote (as had Colombian President Juan Manuel Santos in the first half of 2014). More importantly, from September 2014 to April 2015, a surge of corruption scandals broke across the region, implicating figures close to the presidency in countries from Chile to Mexico. Unprecedented in scale and breadth, these scandals were more than just a series of unrelated events. They were, in large part, a product of falling public tolerance for corruption as prospects for economic growth and prosperity began to seem more tenuous. They also represented growing confidence on the part of journalists, prosecutors and other actors supporting democratic accountability. The scandals contributed to weariness, frustration and dissatisfaction with government and the political process in general.

These cases formed part of a broader trend in which institutions in Latin America were decaying or simply failing to keep pace with rapidly changing societies. In Mexico, the disappearance of 43 students from a teachers' college in Ayotzinapa – as well as the less publicised Tlatlaya massacre – called into question the ability of the state to protect its citizens, even from itself. It became clear that the problem in Mexico was not just a fight against drug cartels, but also weak and corrupt institutions involved with criminal activity.

The most serious crisis in the region occurred in Venezuela. In the two years following the death of President Hugo Chávez, the economy entered a steep recession and inflation spiked to 68%, according to official figures. Capital controls and fixed exchange rates led to shortages of basic consumer goods. Although falling oil revenues contributed to the down-turn, much of the hardship was the result of policy failings and economic mismanagement. President Nicolás Maduro cracked down on demon-strators and opposition leaders, imprisoning protest leaders Leopoldo López and Daniel Ceballos in 2014 and Caracas mayor Antonio Ledezma in early 2015. After the US government imposed sanctions on seven mid-level Venezuelan officials for human-rights violations in March 2015, the Venezuelan Congress responded by granting Maduro emergency powers, giving him de facto rule by decree until the end of 2015. Crime and violence spiralled out of control, and Venezuela teetered on the brink of chaos.

Commodities bust and economic discontent

After seven years averaging 4.3% across the region, economic growth fell to 1.3% in 2014 and was expected to drop below 1% in 2015. From the peak in 2011 to the end of 2014, the three major World Bank commodity-price indexes – energy, metals and minerals, and agricultural raw materials – all declined by more than 35%. The decline was steepest between October 2014 and January 2015, when prices dropped by more than 25% in four months. As commodities weakened while the prices of manufactured goods stayed relatively constant, most Latin American economies saw their terms of trade fall sharply, placing significant strain on both economies and governments.

To many, the downturn was a sign of a gift wasted. Critics claimed that various Latin American governments had squandered a decade of prosperity on consumption rather than investment. However, the real picture was more complicated. Latin America had changed since the 1980s in several important respects: savings rates were higher; the middle class was more robust; debt loads were lower; macroeconomic management was more effective; and governments were better prepared to deal with economic slowdown.

Yet at the same time, the region still found itself lacking in terms of productivity and global competitiveness. Latin America largely failed to take advantage of the commodities boom to address persistent underlying weaknesses. For example, the gap between demand for, and supply of, skilled labour continued to be one of the largest in the world, according to a report by Deloitte and the World Economic Forum. Education remained poor and infrastructure was neglected. Progress on economic reforms and on diversification was inadequate. But by 2014 and 2015, when the effects of these inadequacies were being felt, the region had entered into a new period of tighter budgets, giving policymakers much less room to manoeuvre.

The burden of the slowdown was not distributed evenly. For example, Venezuela, Argentina and Brazil fared far worse than Chile, Mexico and Peru. Those economies that were more closely integrated with that of the US generally performed well, in contrast to those that were not. There was also a divide between east and west. Even as the policy divide between the two groups grew smaller, the older, more protectionist Mercosur bloc continued to struggle economically and the countries of the younger, trade-friendly Pacific Alliance (Chile, Colombia, Mexico and Peru) weathered the storm relatively well. Yet even within those two blocs, countries pursued somewhat divergent strategies towards prosperity.

By 2015, there were some indications that several Mercosur countries were reversing course towards economic liberalisation. Rousseff unexpectedly appointed Joaquim Levy, an orthodox economist and fiscal hawk, as Brazil's finance minister – an indication that she was ready to make difficult financial adjustments. Almost immediately, his aggressive approach to fiscal stabilisation won favour with international investors. Even in Argentina, there were signs that the hard line of unorthodoxy was softening: all three main candidates for the October 2015 election were arguing for some degree of economic liberalisation.

The relative fragmentation of economic and trade strategies highlighted the persistent issue of China's role in Latin America. Even with the relative slowdown in commodities demand, China was a progressively more important trade partner for almost every country in Latin America. Chinese leaders regularly visited the region, and demonstrated an increasingly extrovert approach to trade and investment there. Beijing expressed a particularly strong interest in large-scale projects boosting trans-Pacific trade, including new port infrastructure in the region and a Nicaraguan canal, as well as a transcontinental railway that would extend across Brazil and Peru. At the same time, it was unclear whether China was simply an export market for raw materials or a more comprehensive, long-term partner. China's influence renewed questions about the role of the US in the region, and how the two would interact and balance in the future. In particular, the pending Trans-Pacific Partnership trade agreement – which included Chile, Peru and Mexico – heralded escalating competition between Washington and Beijing.

Crime, instability and the rule of law

On 26 September 2014, students from a teachers' college in Ayotzinapa commandeered several buses and travelled to the nearby town of Iguala, intending to protest against a conference led by the wife of the mayor. En route, local and state police stopped the buses, a shootout occurred and 43 students subsequently disappeared. While many of the details of the case remained unknown, the official investigation concluded that the students had been kidnapped, handed over to a gang and murdered, before their bodies were burned beyond recognition and thrown into a river. As of May 2015, only one of the student's remains had been identified. The brutality of the case led to public outcry across Mexico.

Beyond shock value, the Ayotzinapa massacre changed perceptions about crime and violence in the country. Previously, drug cartels and other criminal groups had been seen as discrete entities that were in conflict with law-enforcement agencies. However, government involvement in the Ayotzinapa incident – the kidnapping supposedly having been ordered by the mayor of Iguala and carried out by the police – seemed to reveal a disturbing truth: that Mexico's gangs and cartels were deeply intertwined with various levels of government and law enforcement. To make matters worse, many accused the federal government of indifference to the case. Peña Nieto hesitated to address the incident until public pressure made it difficult to ignore. In subsequent months, nearly 100 people, including the then-mayor of Iguala and his wife, were detained in connection with the incident.

The scandal in Iguala built upon the July 2014 massacre in the town of Tlatlaya, southwest of Mexico City, in which Mexican troops killed 22 civilians. Although accounts of this incident were also murky, and the military claimed the victims had been killed in a shoot-out, forensic evidence indicated that they had been shot at extremely close range with their own weapons. A working-group report by the Mexican House of Representatives described the massacre as an 'extrajudicial execution', and criticised an alleged cover-up by various officials, including the head of the military in the region.

The two incidents – as well as a broader trend of violence, crime and corruption across Mexico – underlined how deep the problem of institutional weakness had become. The burden of crime is staggeringly high.

In the past eight years, between 60,000 and 100,000 people have been killed in drug-related violence in Mexico. Without substantial reforms to judicial, security and political institutions, the death toll is likely to grow quickly.

The problem went far beyond Mexico. Violence in the 'northern triangle' of Central America – comprising El Salvador, Guatemala and Honduras – sent a wave of migrants into the US, most of them children unaccompanied by a parent or guardian. The exodus was facilitated by a 2008 US law designed to prevent human trafficking, which gave substantial protection to children who entered the country alone. This, along with false rumours about a US policy deferring deportation for undocumented children, led to more than 68,000 unaccompanied minors crossing the US–Mexico border between October 2013 and September 2014. Most of the children crossed the border and simply handed themselves in to law-enforcement agencies, hoping that they would be allowed to stay. This placed enormous strain on immigration authorities, with thousands of unaccompanied children detained in inadequate temporary facilities, often set up on military bases. To deal with the crisis, the Obama administration requested US$3.7 billion in emergency funding for immigration and customs operations.

While generally discussed in the US as a question of immigration policy, the surge was a symptom of violent crime in Central America. El Salvador, Guatemala and Honduras reported some of the highest homicide rates in the world in 2014. The vast majority of crimes went unpunished. In Guatemala, for example, 95% of homicides that occurred during the year remained unsolved. And while homicide rates in Honduras and Guatemala fell slightly, El Salvador's rose by 57%, to 3,942. This was almost certainly due to the breakdown of a 2012 truce between the country's two largest street gangs, Mara Salvatrucha and Barrio 18. In Guatemala and Honduras alone, more than half a million people were driven from their homes by crime and violence in 2014.

In response to the child-migrant crisis and instability in Central America, the Obama administration proposed a US$1bn aid package to support the region's 'Alliance for Prosperity', a joint road map developed by El Salvador, Guatemala and Honduras with the Inter-American Development Bank. The plan sought to stimulate economic activities, improve public safety, enhance access to the legal system and strengthen state institutions. It also set out benchmarks for energy integration (including a natural-gas pipeline from Mexico), law-enforcement reform and anti-corruption measures. Additionally, a Central America Regional Security Initiative aimed to coordinate counter-narcotic measures, and to make security institutions more self-sustaining.

Unfortunately for Central America, the plan risked losing momentum in Congress in the US by mid-2015, as the number of children crossing the border dropped sharply, almost returning to normal levels. This was largely a result of the Mexican government cracking down at its southern border, and an information campaign in Central America discouraging parents from sending their children to the US. Although the conditions that had spurred the rise in child migration remained largely unchanged, the fate of the aid package was unclear. As of June, only US$300 million was due to be allocated in aid to the three countries, the vast majority for security initiatives.

Overall, the incidents in Mexico and violent crime in Central America were revealing indicators of the regional problem of institutional weakness. Police, judiciary, regulatory and other state institutions remain inadequate, and even well-designed laws are often enforced poorly, if at all. From democratic breakdown in Venezuela and corruption in Brazil to political dysfunction in Argentina, many of Latin America's problems stemmed from this failing.

Brazil: Troubled Regional Power

The 2014 presidential, legislative and state elections in Brazil were seen as a referendum on President Rousseff's Workers' Party (PT) and its 12 years in power. Although Rousseff remained the favourite to win throughout the campaign, the PT faced a considerably more difficult fight than in its last three presidential elections, which were easily won by Rousseff and her predecessor, Luiz Inácio Lula da Silva. Initially, the race appeared to be a three-way competition between Rousseff, Aécio Neves of the centrist Brazilian Social Democracy Party (PSDB) and Eduardo Campos of the Brazilian Socialist Party (PSB). However, Campos was killed in a plane crash on 13 August. In his place, the PSB nominated his running mate, Marina Silva, a prominent former Green Party activist, an environment minister under Lula and a seasoned presidential candidate. Silva's candidacy surged in the first weeks after her nomination, with one poll showing her tied with Rousseff, seemingly sure to make the run-off and a contender to win. Yet after a torrent of negative campaigning by Rousseff and without a strong national party structure to compete with the PT and PSDB, Silva and the PSB later dropped sharply in the polls.

In the first round of voting, on 5 October, Rousseff took 41%, Neves 33% and Silva 21%, resulting in a run-off on 26 October. After a late surge by Neves, Rousseff narrowly won re-election by a margin of 51.6% to 48.4%, making the presidential election the closest since the 1980s. In her victory speech, Rousseff struck a distinctly conciliatory tone, seeking to rebuild bridges with those who had voted for her opponent. Instead of 'increasing differences and creating gaps', she said, 'I strongly hope that we create the conditions to unite.' At the time, this goal still seemed possible. While no longer thriving, Brazil had still managed to avoid a serious political or economic crisis. The staging of the World Cup in June and July 2014 had been a success (despite the host team being routed 7–1 by the eventual champion, Germany, in the semi-finals). Rousseff retained significant support among her party's base, particularly in the poorer northeast of the country. While the economy was slowing, extensive state-run social programmes had reduced the effects for many of the most vulnerable Brazilians. During the campaign, Rousseff had made much of the claim that if the PT was not re-elected, the social progress it represented could be reversed – a resonant message for much of Brazil's poor and lower-middle class.

Nevertheless, there were plenty of signs of the economic and political distress to come. The public was increasingly vocal in its disapproval of the government, particularly of the high costs of both the World Cup and the 2016 Summer Olympics, to be held in Rio de Janeiro. The World Cup's estimated US$11.3bn price tag motivated thousands of protesters to take to the streets both before and during the tournament, insisting that the money would have been better spent on public services. Simmering discontent, while not enough to oust Rousseff in October, had grown further by mid-2015.

Most immediately troubling was the economy, as it felt the effect of the weakening commodities-export market. Growth predictions for 2015 were lowered from 1.6% to 0.7%. Inflation was rising fast, precluding an expansionary monetary policy to jump-start the economy. By April 2015, it reached 8%. The budget deficit rose to 6.7% of GDP and public-sector debt exceeded 60% of GDP. Exports were falling and foreign investment was flagging. In the months preceding the election, Rousseff had put off fiscal and monetary adjustment. This was now overdue, and would be difficult for a president and party that had built success on state-centric growth and welfare programmes.

It was in this fragile situation that the Petrobras corruption scandal broke in December 2014. A federal investigation, code-named *Operation Carwash*, revealed that for more than ten years, the state oil company had been inflating contracts with suppliers. Some of the extra cash was kicked back to prominent government figures, politicians and political parties, including the PT. As details emerged, it became clear that the Petrobras scandal was one of the largest graft and money-laundering schemes in the history of Latin America. Many of those indicted held high positions in Rousseff's government and the PT, including Renan Calheiros, president of the Senate; Eduardo Cunha, president of the Chamber of Deputies; former energy minister Edison Lobão; and former president Fernando Collor de Mello, who had been impeached for corruption in 1992 and had been a senator since 2007. Maria das Graças Foster, Petrobras's chief executive, resigned along with five other executives at the firm, and the treasurer of the PT, João Vaccari Neto, was arrested. All told, by mid-2015 over 100 people had been charged in connection with the scheme, and more than 50 others were under investigation.

While as of June 2015 no evidence directly linked the president to the scandal, opinion polls indicated that more than two-thirds of the country saw her as responsible. From 2003 to 2005, Rousseff as minister of mines and energy had chaired the company, and she retained a seat on the board until she was elected president in 2010. Most Brazilians viewed the scheme as something the president should have prevented. If nothing else, many saw her as guilty of negligence and incompetence.

By March and April 2015, large numbers of protesters across the country were taking to the streets calling for Rousseff's resignation. Estimates of the size of the marches ranged from hundreds of thousands to as many as a million, spread across São Paulo, Rio, Brasilia and other cities. Brazilians even borrowed the *cacerolazo* – an angry protest that involved banging pots and pans, common in neighbouring countries – for their own interpretation, the *panelaço*. For a period, impeachment even seemed to be a possibility: a March 2015 poll showed that 60% of Brazilians supported her being forcibly removed from office.

However, by mid-2015 Rousseff appeared to have survived the worst of the crisis. Most calls for her resignation had died down, and public attention had turned towards prosecution of those involved and recovery from the scandal. At Petrobras, political appointees had been removed from the board and the company was able to release long-delayed results for 2014 showing losses of US$7.2bn, of which US$2.1bn was directly attributable to past kickbacks. The figure also reflected a US$14.8bn write-down of the value of its assets because of the fall in the oil price and delays to projects.

Rousseff also showed signs of willingness to move forward with economic reforms. Newly appointed finance minister Levy implemented austerity measures, including cuts to unemployment benefits. 'We need these measures, which are indispensable for the economy to recover', he said. 'The biggest risk for Brazil is a fiscal imbalance.' But their immediate effect was to stifle economic growth, and Levy's approach was controversial among voters and in the highly polarised Congress. Rousseff's approval ratings, which reached 13% by March 2015, were almost certain to remain low. The road to economic recovery was likely to be difficult and long.

Beyond Petrobras: A regional wave of corruption

The Petrobras scandal was far from the only case of its kind in Latin America. Between mid-2014 and mid-2015, the region suffered what seemed almost an epidemic of corruption scandals and allegations. The intensity and political impact was unprecedented even for a region familiar with the phenomenon. In some countries the revelations seriously undermined trust in leaders.

In Guatemala, a political fight over the continued mandate of a UN prosecutorial assistance group, the International Commission against Impunity in Guatemala (CICIG), was overshadowed when the commission uncovered corruption extending to the highest reaches of the government. President Otto Pérez Molina had been resisting CICIG's renewal, arguing that it could violate his country's sovereignty. However, he was forced to acquiesce in April 2015, when the commission uncovered a customs graft scheme allegedly led by his vice-president's former personal secretary, Juan Carlos Monzón. There were large protests in Guatemala City, and Vice-President Roxana Baldetti faced calls to resign, including from prominent business associations. On 6 May, the Supreme Court ruled that Baldetti's immunity from prosecution could be revoked and, the next day, Congress formed a commission to examine her role in the misconduct. It was widely suspected that she had tipped off Monzón about the investigation, giving him time to flee the country. On 8 May, Baldetti resigned, albeit while protesting her innocence. By June, the authorities had arrested 24 people, including the country's top tax official. It was unclear what the long-term impact would be for the government, but public outcry over the scandal persisted. Pérez is due to leave office in 2016.

In Mexico, there were allegations that Peña Nieto's wife had engaged in improper housing deals with a prominent businessman. The first lady, Angélica Rivera, a singer, model and *telenovela* star, was in the process of acquiring a luxury home owned by the businessman Juan Armando Hinojosa when the details surfaced. At the same time, his consortium was awarded a US$3.75bn railroad contract. While the contract was cancelled once the allegations came to light, it was later revealed that Peña Nieto had used a house owned by the same group as campaign headquarters, without being charged rent. The finance minister, Luis Videgaray, had also bought a house from Hinojosa shortly before he was appointed. In June 2015, Peña Nieto was accused of hiding the provenance of a lakefront vacation property by falsely claiming he had inherited it from his parents. While the president claimed there was no conflict of interest in any of the four cases, questions and accusations remained. These were only the most high-profile accusations of financial misconduct levelled at the administration. In a further twist, Carmen Aristegui, a prominent journalist, was fired from a privately owned radio network along with two of her staffers after they helped break the scandal. The network stated that she had been sacked because of internal disagreements and her combative working style. Aristegui claimed it was an attempt to silence her criticism of the government.

Most surprising of all, though, was Chile – which, while not a stranger to such problems, had in recent years been relatively free of them. Two corruption and influence-peddling scandals surfaced on opposite sides of the political spectrum. Firstly, in February 2015, details emerged that the son of President Michelle Bachelet, Sebastián Dávalos, had received a US$10m loan for his wife's Caval holding company (a firm valued at only US$6,000) from the Bank of Chile on 16 December 2013, one day after Bachelet was elected for a second term. The loan was used to buy land that was sold shortly afterwards at a considerable profit. Dávalos, who was alleged to have used his connections to secure the loan, resigned as the head of a state charity. Secondly, at approximately the same time, executives of Chilean financial group Penta were accused of tax evasion and arrested. The indictments claimed that the executives had for years illegally financed the campaigns of political candidates, mostly from the right-wing Independent Democratic Union party. Subsequent investigations eventually revealed a long-running money-laundering scheme.

The Penta and Caval scandals seemed to many Chileans an indictment of the political system as a whole, highlighting the extent of corruption and shadowy money in politics. Bachelet, who had been president from 2006 to 2010, had a reputation for honesty. Although she was not accused of any wrongdoing and stated that she found out about the Caval loan through the media, her popularity fell considerably, with only 24% of respondents expressing approval of her government in a June 2015 poll. In response, Bachelet announced plans for a sweeping anti-corruption overhaul covering campaign financing and including bans on corporate and anonymous donations. New oversight measures were to be written into the constitution. On 6 May 2015, she asked for the resignation of her entire cabinet, hoping that a political shake-up could help her move beyond the scandals and refocus attention on ambitious political and economic reforms. The main outstanding question concerned how much political credibility Bachelet could regain.

Scandals also occurred in other countries of the region. In Argentina, President Cristina Fernández de Kirchner had faced allegations of graft and abuse of power for years, but these were overshadowed by political turmoil as elections approached. In Colombia, several cabinet ministers and the chief of staff of former president Alvaro Uribe were arrested on charges that they had electronically eavesdropped on Santos's re-election campaign, as well as peace talks with rebel group FARC. In May 2015, Uribe testified before the Supreme Court in defence of his officials. Meanwhile, the Colombian customs agency was alleged to have engaged in a scheme that allowed large quantities of goods to enter the country without being declared.

In Bolivia, the ruling Movement Towards Socialism party lost several regional and municipal elections in March 2015, after details of corruption emerged, including videos of party leaders accepting bribes. In Peru, voters saw corruption as almost commonplace. Luis Castañeda, a candidate for mayor of Lima, won the race in October 2014 despite a poll in which almost half of respondents said they expected him to steal state funds if he took office. Most of the potential candidates for the 2016 presidential election have been accused of corruption: two former presidents who are expected to run again, Alan García and Alejandro Toledo, have both come under scrutiny for involvement with improper enrichment schemes. Keiko Fujimori, expected to be the frontrunner, is the daughter of a former autocratic president, Alberto Fujimori, who in January 2015 was given an eight-year prison sentence for corruption, on top of the 25 years he is serving for human-rights abuses. At the same time, Nadine Heredia, wife of President Ollanta Humala and herself a potential contender, was under investigation by the government's budget auditor, who accused her of using public funds to promote herself. And in Panama, President Juan Carlos Varela announced in May 2015 that corruption under his predecessor Ricardo Martinelli may have cost the country as much as US$100m through inflated government contracts.

These were only the major scandals to break in this period. Dozens, if not hundreds, of smaller-scale and more local scandals struck nearly every country in the region. This trend contributed to cynicism and low support for elected officials. Even if, as some observers argued, overall corruption levels had not actually worsened compared with past years, the situation was troubling. Anti-corruption and transparency efforts had generally not come to anything. Alejandro Salas, regional director for the Americas at Transparency International, argued, 'each year that passes without things improving is a lost year for the process of strengthening state institutions'. Moreover, the scandals were coinciding with an economic slowdown in most countries that made political leaders more vulnerable. Corruption, although familiar, was seriously undermining institutions and public trust.

However, the degree of public outcry seemed to indicate that Latin Americans were no longer willing to tolerate the phenomenon. Moreover, prosecutions of politicians and business figures in Brazil, Chile, Colombia, Guatemala and other countries showed that judicial institutions were functioning. Independent public prosecutors in particular had played a key role in bringing down powerful political interests, and the media too was responsible for uncovering many critical details. Anti-corruption reforms began to be pursued in Chile, Mexico and Brazil. While similar efforts may not have been successful in the past, they could mean that flagrant public misconduct is less likely in the future.

Energy crises and reform

Of all the drops in commodity prices, the most dramatic was in oil. In June 2014, crude traded at around US$115 per barrel. By the following March, prices had dropped below US$50, although they later partially recovered. As for other commodities, the pace of demand in East Asia had slowed, while increases in efficiency and shifts to other fuel sources pushed demand down worldwide. More importantly, though, the massive boom in unconventional oil and gas in North America altered the balance between supply and demand.

In Latin America, the worst consequences were for Venezuela, which, as the world's seventh-largest oil exporter, received 90–96% of its export revenues from energy. Oil revenues account for 45% of the budget and around 12% of GDP. The oil-price fall therefore destabilised the country's economy and political system. The economy slid into a recession and inflation rose sharply. Price restrictions led to widespread shortages in basic goods, including flour, milk and eggs.

Elsewhere in the region, lower oil prices complicated attempts by governments to reinvigorate domestic energy sectors and to stimulate growth and investment. In particular, they hindered Mexico's ambitious effort to liberalise its energy sector and loosen the control of the state oil company, Pemex. After nearly 80 years of government monopoly, Peña Nieto sought to open up oil exploration to other companies in a bid to expand production by up to 500,000 barrels per day and boost investment in energy infrastructure. The government hoped to attract more than US$12bn per year in foreign investment but, as oil prices fell, foreign companies began scaling back their commitments. The government also cut the budget of the loss-making Pemex by US$4bn in 2015, making it much more difficult for the company to invest in relatively untapped deep-water reserves in the Gulf of Mexico. While the reforms were continuing, they proceeded more slowly than the government had intended.

Energy was also a growing political issue in Brazil. The corruption scandal at Petrobras – which produces more than 90% of the country's oil and natural gas, as well as owning most pipelines, all of the refining capacity and the largest chain of service stations – had a huge impact on industry and the economy as a whole. The company suspended all new contracting and wrote down the value of many of its assets. Although a benchmark Brazilian borrower, it was unable to raise funds on international bond markets. These effects, combined with the fall in oil prices, contributed to large losses for Petrobras and related contractors, as well as to Brazil's economic slowdown. The full consequences of the scandal were yet to be seen at mid-2015. But it was expected that Petrobras would give larger opportunities for exploration to foreign oil companies in future. China announced a US$3.5bn investment in Petrobras to support exploration and production activities.

At the same time, parts of Brazil confronted an electricity shortage caused by the worst drought in 80 years. In 2014, hydroelectric power supplied almost three-quarters of Brazil's electricity – only China produces more electricity in this way. But by early 2015, the Cantareira reservoir system around São Paulo, Brazil's largest and wealthiest city, had dropped to just 5% of capacity, and the situation was just as serious around Rio. Strict water rationing was introduced, and the fall in electricity generation caused rolling blackouts in several cities. While the use of natural gas was stepped up to make up for the loss of hydroelectric power, the costs were substantial.

Energy also took centre stage in Central America and the Caribbean, in countries of the region with the fewest resources and the highest energy costs. For the Caribbean, the economic collapse in Venezuela was troubling news. Since 2005, Caribbean states (plus Nicaragua, El Salvador and, until 2013, Guatemala) had been able to buy oil under a generous deferred-payment scheme initiated by Chávez, called Petrocaribe, worth a total of US$2.3bn annually. But with Venezuela on the brink of collapse, the arrangement began to show cracks. The terms became stricter, and in January 2015 Venezuela sold all the debt owed to it by the Dominican Republic in order to raise cash. Moreover, because Petrocaribe required a higher proportion of the price to be paid upfront when the cost of crude was lower, the global price fall was only of limited benefit to Central America and the Caribbean. According to a study published by Barclays in March 2015, overall shipments under Petrocaribe had fallen by half since 2012.

However, as Venezuelan energy support faded, the US became more interested in stepping up its assistance, sensing an opportunity for re-engagement. On 9 April 2015, President Barack Obama met Caribbean leaders in the Jamaican capital, Kingston, to discuss deepening energy cooperation. Through the Caribbean Energy Security Initiative, the US announced plans to finance and support energy projects in the region, especially those from clean and sustainable sources. The projects included new wind- and solar-generation capacity, improved efficiency initiatives, regional collaboration networks and green-tourism efforts. In Central America, the US also continued to support greater energy integration, including a pipeline connecting Mexico with the region.

Cuba: Dawn of a New Age?

The most seismic shift in regional relations came on 17 December 2014, when Obama and Cuban President Raúl Castro jointly declared a mutual effort to restore diplomatic relations between the US and Cuba, and to work towards reconciliation. The surprise announcement was one of the most audacious foreign-policy moves of Obama's presidency. Not since the Torrijos–Carter treaties transferred control of the Panama Canal to Panama in 1977 had a diplomatic effort between the US and a Latin American country had as much impact.

In 1961 the US and Cuba broke off diplomatic relations, and in 1962 Washington imposed a full trade embargo – the Cuban missile crisis was to follow later that year. The regime of Fidel Castro, who had assumed power in 1959, persisted until 2008, when he handed over the presidency to his brother Raúl. In 2013, after quiet pressure for change had built up in both countries, Obama decided to explore a new course – he later said 'I do not believe we can keep on doing the same thing for over five decades and expect a different result.' Over the following year and a half, senior National Security Council staffers conducted nine rounds of secret talks in Canada and at the Vatican – discussions in part brokered by Pope Francis. The most immediate result of the agreement was the simultaneous release of US Agency for International Development contractor Alan Gross, who had been held prisoner in Cuba since 2009, and the last three of the so-called 'Cuban Five', a group of Cuban intelligence officers imprisoned in the US. While both governments claimed Gross's release was not part of a prisoner swap, the Cuban government also released an unnamed US spy.

At the same time, Obama eased restrictions on travel by US citizens to Cuba, and quadrupled the limit on remittances by Cuban-Americans to the island. Special export and import allowances were expanded and direct telecommunications links were opened across the Straits of Florida. Commercial interests across the US, especially agricultural and tourism businesses, began positioning themselves for access to the Cuban market.

Perhaps unsurprisingly, the pace of subsequent negotiations on the reopening of relations was slower than was hoped. The opening of embassies was delayed by disputes over the level of access that American diplomats would have to ordinary Cubans. Removal of the US trade embargo would be more difficult: while Obama was able significantly to adjust the terms of the sanctions, the Helms–Burton Act of 1996 governed the embargo itself. It stipulated that the embargo could only be lifted if a democratically elected or transitional government was in power in Cuba. As a result, lifting the embargo while the Castro regime was still in power would have required the act to be repealed – an unlikely prospect in light of the legislative environment in the US Congress.

Optimism that the opening with Havana could re-energise strained relationships between the US and Latin America was dampened by a confrontation with Venezuela. In March, the White House's announcement of congressionally mandated sanctions against individual members of the Maduro government drew widespread condemnation from the region, especially the statement that Venezuela represented an 'unusual and extraordinary threat to the national security and foreign policy of the United States'. Maduro used the declaration to launch a tirade against the Obama administration, even holding air-raid drills in preparation for a potential US attack on Caracas. The tension placed Cuba – reliant on Venezuelan aid – and the rest of Latin America in a difficult position: supportive of the opening, but unwilling to cease criticism of perceived American aggression.

Nevertheless, the rapprochement with Cuba spurred several key developments. Cuba attended the 7th Summit of the Americas, held in Panama City on 10–11 April, for the first time in the forum's 21-year history. Obama and Castro sat down for an hour-long face-to-face discussion, the first formal meeting between the US and Cuban heads of state since that between Dwight Eisenhower and Fulgencio Batista in 1958, the year before Fidel Castro took power. For Obama, the encounter was 'candid and fruitful', while Castro referred to it as a 'historic meeting'. While he still talked extensively about the history of US intervention in Latin America, Castro had almost nothing but praise for Obama. Moreover, the issue of Venezuela, predicted by many to be a major distraction at the summit, became a sideshow: the rhetoric of *yanqui* imperialism lacked its usual bite.

Further progress was made after the summit. Obama announced that he would remove Cuba from the US list of state sponsors of terrorism, a decision that the Republican-controlled Congress tellingly decided not to contest. This eliminated an important obstacle to reconciliation.

Public opinion in both countries firmly supported the opening. One poll showed that 64% of US voters supported ending the embargo, including 74% of Democrats, 64% of independents and 51% of

Republicans. Cuban-Americans in Florida, especially those under 30, had become much less opposed to engagement with the Castro regime – in fact, many expressed direct support. Public opinion in Cuba was even more overwhelmingly favourable. A rare survey, carried out entirely through 1,200 in-person interviews by Univision Noticias and Fusion in April, showed that 97% of Cubans thought that the embargo should end. A similar percentage said a better relationship with the US would benefit Cuba. However, most Cubans had realistic expectations of the reconciliation process and few believed that material conditions for Cubans would change overnight. A full 80% of respondents had a positive opinion of Obama, compared to 47% for Raúl Castro and 44% for his brother, Fidel. Given the momentum on both sides, the question was when, rather than whether, diplomatic relations would be restored and the embargo lifted.

The process seemed certain to bring tangible benefits for both sides. Cuba stood to gain several hundred million dollars a year in exports while, according to the US Chamber of Commerce, the embargo currently costs the US at least US$1.2bn in lost exports. Yet the transition was likely to prove challenging for Cuba: the emergence of small private enterprises (especially *paladares,* or privately owned restaurants) and loosening of state control of the economy gave an indication of what was to come. Havana also faced political transition as its ageing governing class – Raúl Castro is 84, Fidel 88 – was set to give way to a new generation. For its part, the White House was confident that the process would bring substantial dividends for the US in Cuba and across the region. At the very least, it removed a persistent irritant in hemispheric relations: regional opposition to the Cuban embargo had stalled many efforts at cooperation and empowered vocal critics of the US. While the thaw did not necessarily create a diplomatic restart in the Americas, it did eliminate this barrier. Perhaps most importantly, by moderating its stance on Cuba the Obama administration hoped it could combat the perception that democracy and human-rights advocacy was often just a veil for US geopolitical manoeuvring. According to the *New York Times,* Obama stated at the Summit of the Americas, 'when we insert ourselves in ways that go beyond persuasion, it's counterproductive … [and] why countries keep on trying to use us as an excuse for their own governance failures'. To him, reconciling with Cuba was partially a way to take away that excuse.

Argentina: End of the Kirchner Era

Political chaos is nothing new for Argentina. Since becoming a democracy, in 1983, Argentina has seen, by turns, hyperinflation; market-oriented reforms; economic collapse; a constitutional crisis in which there were five different presidents in 12 days; and a large international-debt default. Yet even by these standards, 2014 and 2015 have been chaotic years.

The government again entered into default with international creditors on 30 July 2014, although this was only on some of its obligations, and was the result of a long-standing dispute stemming from its much larger default in 2002. The leftist governments of Néstor Kirchner, and then his wife Cristina Fernández de Kirchner, struggled to negotiate with international bond funds, known in Argentina as 'vulture funds', which had refused earlier restructuring deals and demanded full payment. Since the funds successfully sued Argentina in a US federal court in 2012, the two sides have been locked in a legal struggle. The core question is the legality of Argentina continuing to make payments on the rest of its reduced debt without also paying the holdouts. The US court ruling stated that doing so was in violation of the terms of the original bonds, which stipulated that all debt must be treated equally. This trapped financial institutions, most importantly Citibank Argentina, in the middle. When processing the government's debt, Citibank was required by Argentine law to make payments on the reduced debts alone, but was also banned from doing so by US law. As a result, by April 2015, the conflict escalated to include a simultaneous legal fight between Argentina and Citibank, with the government suspending the bank from capital-market operations and sending regulators into its headquarters to monitor its activity. Argentina, meanwhile, remained unable to borrow on international capital markets, from which it has been excluded since 2002.

Meanwhile, with Fernández in her last year in office after two four-year terms, the economy was stagnating, inflation rising and foreign-exchange reserves falling. Argentina suffered from the collapse of the commodities market, especially in agricultural products. In three months in 2014, the price of soy beans, Argentina's principal export, fell by almost 35%. With the central bank and other financial institutions highly politicised – especially after central-bank governor Juan Carlos Fábrega resigned over conflicts with the administration, and was replaced by a ruling-party loyalist – monetary and fiscal policy seemed dysfunctional. The government resorted to capital and exchange controls that fed a thriving underground market known as the 'blue dollar'. As the difference between the official and blue-dollar rates grew, the street corners of Buenos Aires and other Argentine cities filled with trench-coat-wearing currency vendors. In late 2014, the blue dollar peaked at 16 pesos to the US dollar, almost twice the official exchange rate. Inflation rose steeply to over 30%, according to independent estimates. While this was far from the hyperinflation of the 1980s – which topped 12,000% at one point – the memory of that period made inflation politically toxic in Argentina.

The most bizarre twist in Argentina's political chaos, however, came on 18 January 2015, when federal prosecutor Alberto Nisman was found dead in his high-rise apartment in Puerto Madero, a prosperous Buenos Aires neighbourhood. Discovered locked in his bathroom with a gun nearby and no signs of forced entry, Nisman's death appeared to be a suicide. But the circumstances of his death immediately drew scrutiny. Days before, Nisman had published a 300-page report accusing President Fernández and foreign minister Héctor Timerman of collusion with Iran to cover up details of a 1994 bombing of a Jewish cultural centre in Buenos Aires, in which 85 people were killed. Nisman claimed that they had tried to reach a secret agreement whereby Argentina would help lift international arrest warrants on Iranian citizens in connection with the bombing in exchange for oil. Nisman had been scheduled to testify before Congress about the allegations within hours of when his body was found. In the garbage in the apartment was a draft of arrest warrants for both Fernández and Timerman.

Nisman's death triggered a public outcry. Hundreds of thousands braved torrential rain to march silently through the streets of the capital, gathering in front of the presidential palace. Similar silent demonstrations took place across the country. The manner of Nisman's death remained a mystery.

At first, Fernández dismissed it as suicide, but within days she reversed course, claiming that Nisman had been killed by a rogue network of current and former spies. At the centre of the web, she claimed, was the main intelligence organisation, the Intelligence Secretariat (SI). In particular, Fernández blamed former spymaster Antonio Stiusso, an enigmatic figure who had served with the SI for 12 years before being ousted one month before Nisman's death. She alleged that the killing was part of a plot to destabilise her government. The episode lowered her approval ratings by approximately five points, to less than 30%. Stiusso and the journalist who broke the story of Nisman's death both fled the country, claiming that they feared for their lives. Nisman's accusations and death fed cynicism about the government and state institutions. In February, a poll found that over 70% of Argentines had no expectation that the case would be solved.

In the lead-up to the October 2015 presidential elections, all of these factors – Nisman, the economy and the debt dispute – were contributing to an inauspicious end for the Kirchner dynasty, which had held power in Argentina for the preceding 12 years. (Néstor Kirchner died in 2010.) Fernández lacked the political capital to anoint a chosen successor or change the constitution so as to run again, and all three major candidates were to some degree running against her legacy. Mauricio Macri, the centre-right mayor of Buenos Aires, espoused a rapid shift back to market-friendly and export-oriented policies, and seemed poised to be the first serious non-Peronist challenger since 2003. Sergio Massa, a former Fernández cabinet member turned dissident Peronist, ran somewhere in the middle, hoping to move the ideology of Peronism back towards the political centre. However, the candidate most likely to win the election was Daniel Scioli, governor of Buenos Aires Province, who captured the nomination of the president's Front for Victory (a sub-party of the Peronist movement). He also advocated a moderation of Kirchnerist policies, albeit on a slower timescale. Yet his choice to nominate Kirchner loyalist Carlos Zannini as his running mate cast doubt on his commitment to economic reforms. To many, the selection was a clear gesture towards Fernández, if not an outright demonstration of her power over Scioli. According to one poll, 61% of Argentines believed the choice to have been made by the president alone.

Yet Scioli still seemed most likely to win simply because of the challenges faced by the other two candidates. Although Macri was popular, well known and represented a widely desired break from the status quo, his party lacked officeholders and infrastructure outside Buenos Aires. In Argentina's machine-dominated politics, without a party structure to compete nationwide and in the sprawling *conurbano* industrial suburbs around the capital, Macri fought an uphill battle against the better-organised Peronists. As a result, he was forced to try to build a heterogeneous coalition of former Radicals and defected Peronists. Massa, meanwhile, faced the even larger difficulty of defining a political space in the middle of the spectrum, drawing voters away from both candidates and inspiring a passionate following – a difficult task for a centrist candidate. By June, he seemed to be falling firmly into third place, and so was unlikely to make the run-off. Scioli, on the other hand, seemed to overcome his most significant challenge: dealing with Fernández. Even though the two were hardly allies, Fernández's endorsement of Scioli (ensured by his choice of Zannini as running mate) seemed almost certain to prevent a split in the party vote. This gave him a significant, if not unassailable, position of strength. But Scioli still needed to maintain the impression of opposition to the Fernández government's policies and to pledge economic reforms without alienating the party base, an increasingly difficult line to walk.

In perhaps a final ironic twist, by mid-2015 the political weight seemed to be lifting from Fernández's shoulders. She was cleared by a federal court of any wrongdoing in the Nisman affair. Her approval ratings bounced back to the low to mid-40% range, and the economy showed surprising signs of life. The stock market rallied and consumer confidence rose. Most unexpectedly of all, despite the ongoing struggle with debtors, investors were buying Argentine debt. In a local debt sale in May worth US$590m, the economy ministry received bids for almost three times as many bonds as it was selling. While much of this came from expectations that the elections would bring a change in policy, these developments gave Fernández an unexpected boost. It was likely that she would remain an important force in the country's politics even after she stepped down in December.

Causes for optimism

For most of its history, Latin America has had an unusual balance of commonality and discord. Its nations have faced situations strikingly similar to those of others in the region, but with divergent outcomes. To view them all as one misses considerable nuance. In politics, economics and culture, the Latin American story must be painted in both broad strokes and precise details.

This dual reality was on full display in the year to mid-2015. The region as a whole faced the same commodities-market bust and with it an end to easy prosperity, but individual countries weathered the storm very differently. Corruption scandals of similar tenor broke across the region, and most states share a common history of impunity and weak judicial institutions. But each scandal also reflected a different reality, and required a separate path forward. Democratic governance suffered a blow in several parts of Latin America in 2014 and 2015, but other areas of the region showed surprising resilience. Regional groupings the Pacific Alliance and Mercosur may be integration efforts with similar goals, but the long-term strategies they represent are very different. Violence and crime may be serious issues throughout the Americas, but to say that homicide rates in Venezuela and Mexico reflect a common reality would surely be a serious misreading of the situation.

Despite the fact that Latin America and the Caribbean experienced a series of setbacks in the year to mid-2015, the region's challenges were hardly monolithic. While there was a relative economic decline, most countries – in their own way – avoided outright crisis. And while public discontent increased, it did not translate into widespread political upheaval. Yet even as elections mostly maintained the status quo, political realities and the general mood in many countries evolved in different and important ways. For some countries, this was the fallout of scandal and resulting pushes for better governance. For others, political turmoil drove the government towards more authoritarian practices.

Above all, while the broad trends in the region were not always positive, some political and economic progress often lay beneath them. Economic hardships were damaging, but they shed light on long-standing structural issues that had never been resolved. Corruption scandals were disheartening, but they were for many countries a step on the path to transparency and justice. And even increasing economic and political polarisation showed that – in separate ways – Latin American countries were determining their own futures to a greater extent. The region has never been a homogeneous entity. The Latin America of 2015 was no exception.

Chapter 6

Europe

By 30 June 2015, the last day of the year covered by *Strategic Survey 2015: The Annual Review of World Affairs*, Europe had reached an important moment. On that day, Greece missed a €1.6 billion payment to the IMF, becoming the first developed country to go into arrears with the fund; and the country's bailout arrangements with European institutions expired, leaving it without access to external finance. In the absence of an agreement with creditors, developments could not be predicted. But if the outcome of the crisis was to be Greece's exit from the euro, the common currency of 19 European nations, this would mark the largest step backwards in more than 60 years of moves towards European integration.

Another potential breaking point was looming due to the United Kingdom's decision to hold a referendum on whether to remain a member of the European Union. While the vote, to be held by the end of 2017, was expected to affirm the UK's membership, major risks were involved in an awkward negotiation with other governments that Prime Minister David Cameron hoped would produce a deal he could recommend to British voters. No country has previously left the EU, and the departure of its second-largest economy would substantially undermine the 28-member grouping's future.

These fissures in European solidarity were unfortunate in light of the renewed focus on the continent's security. There was no alleviation of concern about Russia as, after annexing Crimea in 2014, the country continued to directly assist and enable separatist forces in the conflict in eastern Ukraine. In July 2014, the shoot-down of a Malaysia Airlines aircraft over rebel-held Ukrainian territory, with the loss of 298 lives, strengthened European resolve to impose sanctions on Russia (which denied responsibility). NATO allies then took significant steps to improve unity and military readiness, as well as to boost defence spending, seeking to deter Russia from attempting similar destabilising activities in other Eastern European countries.

Security worries also persisted because of the growth of Islamic State of Iraq and al-Sham (ISIS) and the ability of jihadist groups to attract recruits in Europe. European countries were the targets of multiple terrorist attacks.

Meanwhile, conflicts in the Middle East and North Africa contributed to a large flow of migrants to Europe, thousands of whom died while being trafficked across the Mediterranean Sea. The EU launched a small operation in November 2014, mainly in Italian waters, but military activities against traffickers and to rescue migrants were broadened in 2015 as the scale of the problem grew.

Threats to integration ...

Greece had triggered the European sovereign-debt crisis by announcing in 2009 that it had been under-reporting its budget deficit. As investors lost confidence, the debts not only of Greece but also of several other countries became unsaleable on capital markets. Financial rescues were arranged for Greece, Ireland, Portugal and Cyprus, as well as for Spain's banks. With this support, the economies began to recover, albeit with substantial burdens being placed on their citizens by austerity programmes. The sacrifices demanded of the Greeks – the price of many years of political mismanagement – were the largest. Their frustrations were expressed in the January 2015 election victory of the radical leftist Syriza party, led by Alexis Tsipras.

Tsipras wanted an end to austerity, and to dealing with the hated 'troika', composed of the European Commission, the European Central Bank and the IMF. But as the months passed, there was no getting round the need to negotiate terms of continuing financial support with creditors, which were mainly EU institutions and governments. After a four-month extension to the existing €240bn of rescue loans, matters came to a head in

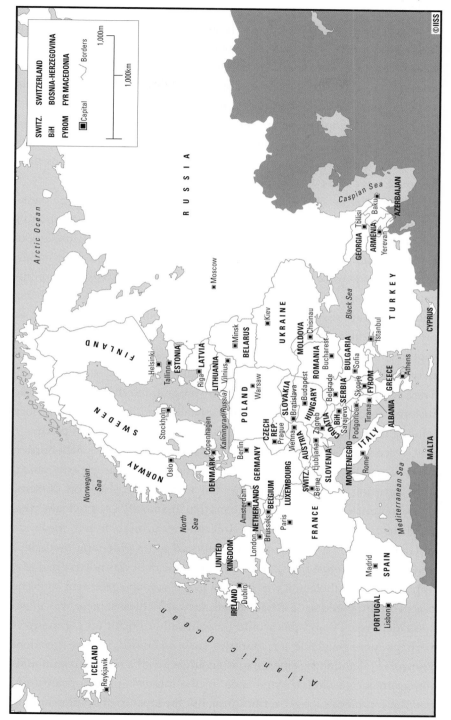

©IISS

SWITZ. **SWITZERLAND**
BiH **BOSNIA-HERZEGOVINA**
FYROM **FYR MACEDONIA**

■ Capital
〜 Borders

1,000km
1,000m

a series of ill-tempered meetings in June. With a draft deal almost agreed, Tsipras announced that the terms would be put to a referendum within a week, on 5 July – five days after the expiry of the bailout. However, even as Greek banks suffered large withdrawals of deposits and capital controls were imposed, he advocated rejection of the terms – a choice that would have serious, if unpredictable, consequences. The Greeks duly voted 'no' by a margin of 61% to 39%, increasing expectations in financial markets that the country would have to depart from the euro. Negotiations then resumed, but events were unpredictable.

At the extreme of possible outcomes were debt defaults, large bankruptcies and Greece's exit from the euro, necessitating the recreation of the previous currency, the drachma. This scenario would condemn Greeks to deeper and more prolonged suffering, and to partial isolation within Europe. Efforts were likely to continue to be made to avoid these contingencies. Although Tsipras alienated his European counterparts with his antagonistic approach, they wished to accommodate Greece's wishes as far as they could, and to keep the country within the euro. But creditors, especially Germany, the country with the largest exposure, were limited in what they could offer by their own beliefs and democratic constraints. They wished to see a structural-reform programme that could credibly restore Greece's financial and economic health, and they could not justify lending the country more money without having such a plan in place.

Greece's fate was, therefore, in the balance. The country's debt burden was near to 180% of GDP. Tsipras was trying to break the cycle in which, after agreeing to difficult reforms that impose hardships on citizens, debtor countries are given rescue loans that are mostly used to make payments to creditors rather than to spur economic growth. In fact, the terms of Greece's debts had already been adjusted to provide long maturities and very low interest rates, so the burden of the debt was not as great as it appeared. Nevertheless, it was difficult to see how an agreement could be reached that would set a credible path forward unless Greece was given some debt relief – and this would be politically difficult for Germany, if perhaps more palatable for countries such as France. French President François Hollande was emerging as an advocate of a more accommodating approach to Greece's demands, in the interests of European unity and the continent's longer-term future. But the balance of opinion among eurozone governments still appeared to favour taking a tough line with Athens.

In contrast to the market turmoil that surrounded previous rescue packages for Greece and other countries in difficulties, investors took Greece's 2015 negotiations in their stride. It was a small economy. Default on its debts would have seriously affected private banks five years ago, but by now its creditors were mainly governments. The financial system had had time to absorb the risks. Nevertheless, Greece's continuing membership of the euro remained very important to its eurozone partners. The departure of any country would expose the fact that the adoption of the common currency from 1999 onwards was not, in fact, permanent – and could be reversed if a member ran into problems. The next time another country encountered similar difficulties, market speculation about its departure from the common currency would be intense. Thus, the very foundations of the currency union – and accordingly of European integration – were under threat.

An even greater danger to the European project – although one less likely to come to pass – was posed by the UK. In May 2015, the Conservative Party unexpectedly won an outright majority in Parliament, ending five years of unusual (for Britain) coalition government. The party has for years had a potent eurosceptic wing, which was strengthened by the emergence of an even more strident and right-wing force in the form of the UK Independence Party. The eurosceptics cast the EU as an unelected Brussels bureaucracy that had encroached upon the sovereignty of the Westminster parliament. Cameron made numerous concessions to try to appease this element; the most significant of these was his promise in 2013 to hold a referendum on EU membership, after first trying to negotiate a new deal for the UK. Having won a majority in the 2015 election, Cameron therefore had to keep his pledge. Perhaps sensibly, he had remained vague on the precise demands that he would make, and these remained unclear even as he held private discussions with other European leaders in June 2015. But one demand was likely to be an opt-out from the 1957 Treaty of Rome's commitment to an 'ever closer union'. There was widespread expectation that Cameron would reach an accommodation he could recommend to British voters, who would then endorse continuing membership. But such an outcome could by no means be taken for granted.

Meanwhile, the UK's own make-up remained in question: despite a vote against Scottish independence in a September 2014 referendum, the pro-independence Scottish National Party became the third-largest bloc at Westminster, thus ensuring that the issue of Scotland's separation would continue to simmer.

Although it is not an EU member, Turkey's erratic foreign policy and domination by President Recep Tayyip Erdogan have been increasingly troubling for European governments. The Turkish elections of June 2015 provided the first sign that this era may be ending, with Erdogan's Justice and Development Party failing to win a parliamentary majority. Having founded the party before serving as prime minister between 2003 and 2014, Erdogan had hoped for a large majority in order to push through constitutional changes that would allow him to concentrate power in the presidency. Although this goal appeared to have been blocked, the difficulties in forming a coalition government indicated considerable political uncertainty and more elections ahead.

... but stronger cooperation on defence

In contrast to the developments within the EU described above, European governments showed signs of willingness to bolster their defence capabilities and to work together more closely in response to the perceived threat from Russia. After displaying unexpected unity in imposing sanctions on Moscow despite the economic costs of doing so, they took steps to signal that the NATO commitment to collective defence remained intact. This was intended to deter Russian President Vladimir Putin from employing in a NATO country the 'hybrid' tactics – a mix of military and non-military measures – that were used in Crimea and eastern Ukraine.

At a NATO summit held in the UK in September 2014, Alliance leaders agreed on a Readiness Action Plan under which troops, equipment and command facilities would be constantly deployed to Eastern European member countries. (See map, *Strategic Geography* pp. VI–VII.) The purpose was both to reassure allies who felt under threat, and to deter Moscow. A 'spearhead' high-readiness force was set up for quick reaction. In addition, exercises were stepped up: for example, 2,100 troops from nine countries took part in the *Noble Jump* NATO exercise in Poland in June 2015. Overall, the events in Ukraine were reinforcing NATO's original role in collective defence, following the end of its combat operations in Afghanistan at the end of 2014 (although it maintained a presence in the latter country). New NATO secretary-general Jens Stoltenberg, former prime minister of Norway, said: 'as we see another major shift in the security landscape, NATO is once again making fundamental changes. Today, we do not have the luxury to choose between collective defence and crisis management. For the first time in NATO's history we have to do both at the same time.'

This would be challenging given the long decline in European defence spending, which had eroded capabilities across the continent. However, there were significant indications that this trend was beginning to reverse. Plans for defence-budget increases were announced by the Czech Republic, France, Germany, Hungary, Latvia, Lithuania, the Netherlands, Norway, Poland, Romania and Sweden. While it remained unclear how much of the additional funding would be spent on the enhancement of actual military capabilities and technologies, and to what degree cooperation would be stepped up in order to receive the maximum benefit from higher budgets, there was no doubt that Russia's actions had decisively altered European threat perceptions. Important defence-policy reviews were under way in the UK, Europe's largest defence spender, and Germany, the third largest, which broke with a 70-year tradition by publicly sending arms to a live conflict, in support of Kurdish Peshmerga fighters opposing ISIS. Meanwhile, Islamist attacks such as the *Charlie Hebdo* murders in France and the killing of 38 tourists, of whom 30 were British, in Tunisia strengthened the case for more robust defence and security measures.

France: Growing Foreign Engagement

France experienced a highly eventful year on the international stage, involving major diplomatic and military engagement in several crucial theatres. Terrorist attacks in Paris and new partnerships in the Middle East redefined the country's complex relationship with the Muslim world. But the government's agenda was also dominated by economic challenges and party political upheavals.

The government of French Prime Minister Manuel Valls was shaken by several crises in summer 2014, just months after being installed to inject rigour and consistency into public policy. Strikes in the transport sector (affecting railways, air-traffic controllers and Air France) and elsewhere reflected growing discontent with the leadership's austerity and restructuring policies. Matters came to a head in September when, emboldened by public opposition to belt-tightening, economy minister Arnaud Montebourg openly defied both Valls and President François Hollande, opining that France should not be 'pushed around by Germany'. Montebourg was summarily dismissed, along with fellow dissidents Benoît Hamon and Aurélie Filippetti, ministers of education and culture respectively.

Embattled leadership

The economics portfolio passed to 36-year-old technocrat Emmanuel Macron, who had previously served as Hollande's principal economic adviser. The *loi Macron* – legislation geared towards liberalising specific sectors of the economy – became the most contentious political issue of the following six months. Macron's appointment was designed to signal the government's firmness and consistency in economic policy, even at the price of a thinning of the Socialists' parliamentary majority. From September 2014 onwards, he faced equally vocal hostility from both left and right. Yet there was scant evidence that his austerity measures were succeeding. France's fiscal deficit of around €60 billion, which the measures were designed to cut significantly, remained almost unchanged between June 2013 and spring 2015, hovering at 4–4.5% of GDP. The country was not expected to meet the 3% limit imposed by the European Union before 2017.

Like Italian Prime Minister Matteo Renzi, Hollande engaged in shadow-boxing with European institutions, proclaiming noisily to his Socialist Party (PS) base that he was resisting pressure from Brussels, while in reality toeing the EU line (albeit inadequately). The government's consistency, however, did not help to maintain its credibility with the French electorate. Valls took office with approval ratings of almost 50%, and it was hoped that he would pull Hollande up to this level. In fact, Hollande's continuing decline – his approval rating had fallen to just 12% by the end of 2014 – dragged Valls down with it, the prime minister losing 20 percentage points in just eight months.

Finance Minister Michel Sapin's 2015 budget was announced in October 2014, and featured a further €70bn in spending cuts – mainly to welfare and local-authority entitlements – during 2014–17. His predictions of 1% growth in 2015 and 2% by 2018 were widely regarded as optimistic. Public debt rose for the first time to €2 trillion (95% of GDP). Critics insisted that, as Keynes had argued, sustained retrenchment at a time of economic recession only made matters worse. But Hollande was determined to be consistent. Even so, France's public spending, at 57% of GDP, still remained way above the EU average of around 50%, and a full 12 percentage points above that of Germany and the United Kingdom. In October, the last-minute announcement of further savings aimed at cutting the structural budget deficit by 0.5% probably staved off a formal reprimand from the European Commission (and possibly a fine). Paris heaved a sigh of relief, and all eyes turned to Macron.

The 'Bill on Growth, Economic Activity and Equality of Opportunity', as the Macron measures were formally entitled, was approved by the cabinet in December 2014 and submitted to parliament the following month. It featured a range of sectoral reforms designed to promote growth and competition: more Sunday opening of businesses (with a strictly volunteer workforce who would receive appropriate overtime pay); liberalisation of inter-city coach services to spur competition with railways (only 110,000 French people travel by coach each year, as opposed to eight million in Germany and 30m in the UK); and deregulation of notoriously closed professions such as notaries (85% of legal administrators in France are over 50 years of age). The package was presented as an indispensable dynamic to increase individual choice, particularly for small firms, young people and start-ups; to stimulate growth and investment; and to create jobs.

But the legislation was considerably watered down by parliamentary committees in an attempt to depoliticise it, while lobbyists from the pharmaceutical industry and other sectors succeeded in defanging some of its deregulatory objectives, and it failed to end the controversial 35-hour working week that Macron had aggressively targeted in public. Nonetheless, enough Socialist lawmakers were prepared to vote down the bill that Valls was obliged on 17 February 2015 to force it through the

National Assembly by decree, thereby triggering a vote of no confidence from the Union for Popular Movement (UMP), the centre-right opposition. With the government narrowly winning the vote, the legislation passed on a constitutional technicality. Although the bill was approved by the Senate the following May, there were doubts about whether the new measures – which the government needed Brussels and Berlin to believe were liberal, and the PS to believe were not – would suffice to fix France's sclerotic economy. In light of this, Macron presented in summer 2015 a new round of initiatives to stimulate investment, promote digitisation and support small- and medium-sized firms. These were widely greeted as being too timid to make any real difference.

Rise of the far right

The diminishing popularity of the Hollande administration was highlighted by Senate elections held in September 2014, in which the centre-right once again took control of the Upper House, just three years after having lost it to the Socialists. Departmental elections held in March 2015 produced a minor political earthquake. The PS gained only 21% of the vote in the first round, and was totally eliminated from 580 cantons, suffering particularly heavy losses in rural areas (in the southeastern Var department, not one Socialist regional councillor was elected). The party even lost between one-third and half of its supporters in working-class bastions such as the Nord, Bouches-du-Rhône, Seine-Maritime and Côtes d'Armor. It ceased to be a nationwide party. Despite the fact that the Socialists' final tally after the second round of voting was not as catastrophic as had been predicted, the results suggested that there had been, in the words of Valls, 'a lasting transformation of France's political landscape'.

This was not only because the left fared so badly. While the PS lost 28 of the 57 departments it controlled before the vote, the UMP won all of those seats conceded by its centre-left rival. The opposition's victory in 60 out of 101 departments in the second round confirmed it as the leading political force in France. Yet the shift in the country's politics was perhaps most clearly demonstrated by the performance of the National Front (FN), which in the first round beat the Socialists into third place and took 25% of the vote (marginally improving on its gains in the 2014 European elections). The FN thus established a greater presence across France than the

PS. While the structure of the electoral system prevented the FN from controlling any departments, the message was clear: France had undergone a silent revolution.

Conservative voters were little reassured by the UMP's reinstatement of Nicolas Sarkozy as party leader in November 2014, as the former president had been deeply unpopular on leaving office two years earlier. Yet he had secured only 64% of the vote in the leadership poll, far below the 85% he won in 2004. Sarkozy has remained vague about his political programme, equivocated about relations with the FN and sought – with a large measure of chutzpah – to position himself as a symbol of renewal. He also worked to rename the party, which was relaunched as 'Les Républicains' at the beginning of June 2015.

Sarkozy faces several internal challenges in his bid to secure the party's nomination for presidential candidate in the 2017 elections, as well as a string of pending lawsuits relating to allegations of corruption and abuse of power. The challenges come from François Fillon and Alain Juppé, former prime ministers under Sarkozy and Jacques Chirac respectively. Juppé is regarded as a serious alternative candidate, despite having had legal problems of his own and the fact that he will be 72 by the time the election is held. He has staked out a clear claim to the centre-right, while Sarkozy has flirted with the extreme right. But Juppé is poor at campaigning, an area in which Sarkozy excels. A poll conducted in April 2015 placed Juppé four points ahead of Sarkozy in first-round voting intentions for 2017, and identified him as a much more decisive winner in the second round, against both Hollande (70% to 30%, as opposed to Sarkozy's 60% to 40%) and FN leader Marine Le Pen (70% to 30%, as opposed to Sarkozy's 63% to 37%). The same poll found that Hollande would only just prevail over Le Pen (52% to 48%).

Marine Le Pen was probably strengthened by her May 2015 decision to suspend her father, FN founder Jean-Marie Le Pen who, by pursuing racist provocation, continued to defy her efforts to 'normalise' the party. In a series of televised outbursts, Le Pen *père* praised Vichy leader Marshal Philippe Pétain, questioned the patriotism of Prime Minister Valls (who was born in Barcelona) and quipped that France was 'run by immigrants'. Marine Le Pen accused her father of 'wobbling between a scorched-earth policy and political suicide', and blocked his designation as a candidate in regional elections scheduled for December 2015. Having been appointed honorary president of the FN in 2011, he was formally stripped of his position and expelled from the leadership following a meeting of the party congress. Disowned by her father, Marine Le Pen risked splitting the party – although such a rift had the potential to benefit those in the FN who were intent on breaking with its origins on the extreme right. The expulsion of her father helped Marine Le Pen create a formal group of right-wing lawmakers in the European Parliament in late June, over which she now presides.

Much of the FN's political success has derived from its hardline stance on immigration. Relations between France's Muslim community and wider society became much more complex in the year to mid-2015, owing to three factors. The first was the flood of French citizens (estimated at more than 1,000) who left the country to fight for the Islamic State of Iraq and al-Sham (ISIS). The second was the Israeli offensive in Gaza in summer 2014, which was followed by an increase in anti-Semitic attacks: two Paris synagogues were assaulted in July 2014, along with a Jewish restaurant and kosher grocery, leading the government to ban all anti-Israel demonstrations. The third was the increase in attacks on French citizens carried out by Islamist extremists. This followed a declaration made by ISIS on 22 September: 'if you can kill an American or European infidel – especially the spiteful and cursed French – or an Australian or a Canadian ... then rely upon God and kill them in any way possible'. Two days later, French kidnapping victim Hervé Gourdel was beheaded by Islamists in Algeria, who posted a video of the murder online. The following December, an Islamist 'lone wolf' attacked a suburban Paris police station and, in separate incidents in Dijon and Nantes, extremists drove their vehicles into crowds of shoppers, killing one person and injuring more than 20 others. Valls ordered 300 additional troops to join the 800 that had earlier been assigned to protect public spaces. He declared that France faced an unprecedented threat from terrorism.

Charlie Hebdo

The most high-profile jihadist attacks of the year began on 7 January 2015, when brothers Said and Chérif Kouachi stormed the offices of satirical magazine *Charlie Hebdo*, shooting dead 12 people. The magazine had been under police protection for several years because of its publication of cartoons depicting the Prophet Mohammad. The following day, Amedy Coulibaly, an associate of the Kouachi brothers who claimed to be acting in the name of ISIS, murdered a French policewoman before taking 15 shoppers hostage in a kosher supermarket, executing three of them on the spot. He shot a fourth hostage shortly before being killed by riot police as they retook the supermarket. Meanwhile, the Kouachi brothers had been cornered in an industrial estate close to Charles de Gaulle airport. They claimed to be acting in the name of al-Qaeda in the Arabian Peninsula. Both were shot dead by marksmen from the riot police.

These incidents, which led to 17 French civilians and three Islamists dying over a 48-hour period, constituted for France a shock akin to that of 9/11 for the United States. On 11 January, an estimated four million people demonstrated across France, more than two million of them in Paris alone, joined by 40 heads of government from across the world. As the largest street demonstration in French history, the event brought together people from every age group, class, faith and political affiliation. The movement popularised the slogan 'nous sommes tous Charlie' in honour of those killed, reaffirming republican values and a commitment to freedom of speech. The government subsequently enacted several measures to prevent a recurrence of the Charlie attacks, although it was unclear whether they would prove to be effective. In an attempt to deal with the social and cultural disaffection felt by many young people from minority groups, the authorities decided to intensify the teaching of republican values in French schools. And to keep track of would-be jihadists, the government passed in May 2015 a bill giving the intelligence services almost unlimited rights to track phone calls, text messages, emails and internet usage, with virtually no judicial oversight. Just as the US was doubting the merits of the Patriot Act and the extensive powers afforded to the National Security Agency in the wake of revelations by former government security contractor Edward Snowden, France was moving decisively in the opposite direction.

Extrovert foreign policy

In foreign and security policy, Paris was proactive on several fronts. Hollande and German Chancellor Angela Merkel worked closely in

February 2015 to resolve the Ukraine crisis. They held talks with Ukraine's leaders in Kiev on 5 February, followed the next day by further discussions with Russian President Vladimir Putin in Moscow. These meetings paved the way for the relaunch of the stillborn 'Minsk agreements' of September 2014, signed under the aegis of the Organisation for Security and Cooperation in Europe. On 8 February, Merkel and Hollande held long teleconferences with Putin and Ukrainian President Petro Poroshenko, before travelling to Minsk together on 11 February to sign a new agreement. This plan centred on a ceasefire and the withdrawal of heavy weaponry from contested territory; the acknowledgement of borders for the disputed areas of eastern Ukraine; and provisions for the exchange of prisoners. Ukraine was called upon to reform its constitution to respect the rights of pro-Russian citizens in the east, but – contrary to much speculation – there was no mention of a federal constitution. The US House of Representatives' proposal to deliver 'lethal aid' to Ukrainian forces was firmly opposed by both Hollande and Merkel. Privately, neither Hollande nor Merkel had any illusions that Minsk II would solve the crisis, and indeed this scepticism proved well founded in the days after the agreement was signed, as intense fighting broke out around Debaltsevo.

Like Merkel, Hollande was adamant that there was 'no military solution' to the crisis. He stressed in several press conferences that a war between Russia and Ukraine would result in a decisive victory for the former. Post-Minsk II diplomacy was largely managed by the French and German foreign ministers, Laurent Fabius and Frank-Walter Steinmeier, who met a few times each week for several months and hosted further discussions with the foreign ministers of Russia and Ukraine, in the so-called 'Normandy format'. This diplomatic effort proceeded even as events on the ground suggested that Minsk II was moribund. Despite the work of France and Germany, it appeared that Europe had limited options when faced with an assertive Russia.

Nonetheless, in spring 2015, Paris sought to establish more cordial relations with Moscow. France had already explicitly ruled out extending NATO membership to Ukraine. At a summit in Latvia during 21–22 May, the future of relations between Brussels and the six countries of the ill-fated 'Eastern Partnership' (Armenia, Azerbaijan, Belarus, Georgia,

Moldova and Ukraine) was shown to be a divisive subject for EU members, with the Scandinavian countries joining the Baltic states and Poland in pressing for a harder line against Moscow. France's position was that confrontation with Russia should be avoided, and that relations with the six Eastern countries should properly take account of Moscow's concerns. Having vacillated on France's sale to Russia of *Mistral* amphibious-assault warships for much of 2014, a decision was taken in September to place the deal on hold, given Russian military incursions into Ukraine. By November, it had become clear that the sale would not go ahead. As a result, Russia demanded reimbursement of the €1.2bn it had paid for the vessels, while threatening to claim additional penalties for delays in delivery, as stipulated in the contract. France reportedly repaid around €800m and asked Russia's permission to sell the vessels to other countries. Moscow refused the request on the grounds that the two *Mistral* ships had been specifically designed for Russian military equipment, the details of which could not be revealed to a third party. As the issue went before the courts, both Paris and Moscow sought to downplay its significance.

The revitalisation of the Franco-German relationship in security and defence overshadowed the 2010 defence-cooperation agreements signed by Paris and London at Lancaster House. The UK was absent from the Minsk II process, and generally had a much lower profile in collective-security issues. This was in stark contrast to Germany, which under Merkel strengthened its position as a leader in European security, taking initial command of NATO's Very High Readiness Joint Task Force and entering into multiple defence–industrial agreements with France – mainly in space and unmanned aerial vehicles. The 17th Franco-German Council of Ministers, held on 31 March 2015, generated the sense that Paris and Berlin had achieved the meeting of minds in security and defence policy that had long eluded them.

French military forces were deployed in multiple theatres in the year to mid-2015. *Operation Chammal* was France's contribution to anti-ISIS air missions in Iraq, conducted by a US-led coalition. From 14 September 2014 onwards, France deployed 700 troops to Iraq supporting surveillance and strike missions carried out by six *Rafale* and six *Mirage* 2000D combat aircraft, an E3F airborne warning and control system (AWACS), and an

Atlantique 2 maritime-patrol aircraft. As part of the missions, French air-craft typically carried out around 20 sorties against ISIS positions per week, at the request of the Iraqi government.

Operation Sangaris, meanwhile, has involved the deployment of 2,000 troops to Central African Republic, in an effort to prepare the way for a larger force led by the African Union. *Operation Barkhane* in the Sahel, which succeeded the Mali-focused *Operation Serval* in August 2014, has involved the deployment of 3,000 troops on anti-Islamist operations, in coordination with the governments of Mauritania, Mali, Niger, Chad and Burkina Faso. Designed as a long-term mission to be carried out across a large expanse of North Africa, *Operation Barkhane* has involved the deployment of 200 armoured vehicles, 20 helicop-ters, 200 logistics vehicles, seven transport aircraft, six fighter-bombers and four unmanned aerial vehicles. The operation was credited with the killing in May 2015 of two jihadist leaders in the Sahel. At the same time, France has been operating a frigate and a Djibouti-based maritime-patrol aircraft in *Operation Atalanta*, the EU's anti-piracy mission in the Gulf of Aden. The French base in Djibouti has also been used to provide medical facilities to the mission. In addition, almost 1,000 French troops are assigned to the United Nations Interim Force in Lebanon. France has contributed AWACS and fighter planes to NATO patrol missions in the Baltic and Black Sea regions, and has deployed a *Leclerc* tank division to Poland.

On the home front, over 7,000 troops have been mobilised in the domes-tic counter-terrorism effort, *Operation Sentinelle*, which followed the *Charlie Hebdo* attacks. In support of this initiative, Hollande argued in April 2015 in favour of the defence ministry and against the finance ministry. The latter, with an eye on the EU requirement to reduce the deficit to 3% of GDP, had pressured the government to stick rigorously to the planned cuts in the defence budget that had been agreed in 2013. Yet Hollande decided in January 2015 that, of the 34,000 defence jobs originally sched-uled to disappear by 2019, 18,500 would be retained. In addition, he increased the defence budget for 2016–19 by €3.8bn, stating that there could be no haggling over the security of the country. A new law on the military programme incorporating these changes was put before parlia-ment the following June.

New ties with the Middle East

Some of the additional resources needed to fund the shift in policy were to derive, in a roundabout way, from the long-delayed sale of *Rafale* combat aircraft to India, Egypt and Qatar (which were to buy 36, 24 and 24 jets respectively). There were also ongoing negotiations with the United Arab Emirates for the proposed purchase of 60 *Rafale* jets. The defence contracts French suppliers won in the Middle East appeared to be part of France's exploitation of an opening unintentionally created by US President Barack Obama, whose foreign policy was interpreted by the Gulf states as showing indifference to their concerns. Disputes between Washington and Riyadh over the Iranian nuclear deal, as well as the wars in Syria and Yemen, have facilitated a strong French rapprochement with the Gulf states, particularly Saudi Arabia. While the US dependency on Gulf oil is rapidly decreasing, France continues to import almost 40% of its oil from the region.

Sarkozy's unexpected emphasis on relations with Doha, Riyadh's regional Sunni rival, has been replaced with a strategy of close links to the authoritarian regimes in Algeria, Egypt and Saudi Arabia. In parallel, Hollande and Fabius have taken a tough line on the Iranian nuclear deal, arguing that there should be no sanctions relief before Tehran provides clear evidence of compliance. Fabius believes strongly that, as a Shia and Persian state, Iran cannot solve the increasingly complex problems of an Arab world that is overwhelmingly Sunni. This position has endeared France to Saudi Arabia, which invited Hollande to become the first Western leader to attend a summit of the Gulf Cooperation Council – an invitation he accepted, joining Gulf leaders in Riyadh on 5 May 2015. King Salman bin Abdulaziz has apparently decided that France offers the strongest and most consistent support to Saudi policy of any Western state, which in part explains his decision to boycott Obama's Camp David summit of Gulf allies on 14 May. Nobody imagines that Saudi Arabia is tempted to abandon its seven-decade alliance with the US. But Riyadh is sending a clear message to Washington that the kingdom has a strong and seemingly reliable new partner in France. There were considerable benefits for Hollande: he left Riyadh with 20 large contracts in the defence, transport, energy and health-care sectors, estimated to be worth around €30bn. Such deals can significantly ease his budgetary problems with the European Commission.

United Kingdom: Risks Remain after Election Surprise

'It Couldn't Be Closer' ran the headline of the *Guardian* newspaper on 7 May 2015, as Britons cast their votes in the general election. Reflecting widespread expectations that there would be no clear outcome, the *Times* went with 'Queen [Elizabeth] to Take Control of Election Aftermath.' But in fact there was no need for the monarch to intervene in the nation's politics – even if she had the constitutional power to do so. Confounding all predictions, the Conservative Party won an outright majority in the House of Commons, enabling it to end a five-year experiment with coalition government.

This result confounded much of the analysis that, shaped by wayward opinion polls, had dominated politics in preceding months. With the prospect of an uncertain result, the coming end of the two-party system was widely discussed, and coalitions were predicted to become the norm. But in the event, both the Conservatives and the opposition Labour Party strengthened their positions in England, while the Liberal Democrats, long Britain's third party, were cruelly punished for the policy compromises that followed their decision in 2010 to enter into coalition with the Tories. After the Liberals' humiliation, reduced to eight seats from 57, no smaller party will want to follow its example if future elections fail to deliver a winner with a decisive majority.

The pollsters were not completely wrong. They did predict the election's most extraordinary phenomenon: the sweep of Scottish seats by the Scottish National Party (SNP), making it a political force not just in Scotland but in the United Kingdom as a whole – a country it wants to break up. In September 2014, the SNP – which has had a majority in Scotland's devolved parliament since 2011 – lost a referendum among Scottish voters on separation from the UK by a margin of 55% to 45% (on a voter turnout of 85%). But its surge in the general election gave it 56 out of 59 Scottish seats, 50 more than it held previously. This meant that the independence issue had not, after all, been 'settled for a generation', as Prime Minister David Cameron had hoped.

This was not the only fundamental risk faced by the UK. The Conservative victory meant that Cameron would hold to his promise of an in-or-out referendum on Britain's continued membership of the European Union by 2017. He began to engage in a negotiation with other European leaders in which his agenda was obscure and their participation reluctant. It was unlikely that he could achieve the sort of assurances about British sovereignty and immigration control that were craved by the anti-EU right wing of his party, as well as by the more strident UK Independence Party (UKIP), which won 14% of English votes in the election (but only one seat). This meant that, while the eventual referendum result was widely predicted to be in favour of staying in the EU, the possibility of British departure could not be ruled out. People who were uncertain about how to vote could well be influenced by the financial problems of the eurozone (though the UK is not part of the common currency), as well as migration flows from within and outside Europe.

Meanwhile, Cameron faced broader questions about the UK's role in the world. The government was criticised for its low profile on major strategic issues affecting Europe, such as the conflicts in Ukraine, Syria and Iraq. Questions about its vision and foreign policy would be thrust into focus by a pending Strategic Defence and Security Review. Decisions taken in the previous review, in 2010, formed part of an effort to reduce the budget deficit, resulting in a significant diminution of military capabilities, although the government said at the time that there would be no 'strategic shrinkage'. The 2015 review was being viewed as a litmus test of the UK's future posture.

Political conundrum

The May 2015 election was a puzzle that was solved only by its eventual outcome. The overriding aim of the Conservative/Liberal Democrat coalition had been to restore Britain's fiscal and economic health following the global financial crisis of 2008, which not only triggered a steep recession but also forced up the budget deficit to an unsustainable level. The previous government, led by Labour Prime Minister Gordon Brown, won credit for dealing with the crisis effectively, but was perceived as having indulged in excessive spending. Government borrowing in the last year of Brown's government rose steeply to 11% of GDP. This gave George Osborne, the Conservative finance minister, a fair wind as he acted to cut public spending. He played a canny game, introducing an 'austerity' programme of which one purpose was to ensure the confidence of financial markets and prevent any possibility that British government debt could be viewed with the same distaste as that of Greece, Italy or Spain, all of which were suffering from the eurozone debt crisis. Over five years, he cut spending in real (inflation-adjusted) terms and as a proportion of GDP. With health and education ring-fenced from cuts, the burden fell heavily on other state-provided services, including welfare benefits. However, Osborne's fiscal tightening was not in fact so draconian as to choke off economic recovery, and there was also substantial monetary stimulus provided in a 'quantitative easing' programme by the Bank of England. By 2014, the UK was showing the highest economic growth among large European countries and had record employment levels.

In most elections, an economic recovery such as this would be enough to keep the governing party in office. The puzzle was that this was not reflected in opinion polls, which for months showed the Conservatives and Labour locked together with 33–34% of the national vote. The most common explanation was that wages were not rising sufficiently and many of the new jobs created by the recovery were low-paid, and therefore that the growth of the economy had not yet sufficiently relieved the recession-induced hardships of many people. Labour put considerable emphasis on societal inequalities. But as it transpired, the message of economic competence projected by the Conservatives, contrasted with the perception of Brown-era fiscal profligacy, was enough – even though it was combined with a lot of tactical playing on voters' fears about Labour, the SNP and UKIP. Cameron's almost deliberately unexciting campaign easily defeated that of Ed Miliband, the Labour leader, who was perceived as anti-business and held to a more traditional socialist agenda than had Tony Blair, who won three elections as Labour leader under the modernising banner of 'New Labour'.

The election produced a 36.9% vote share for the Conservatives, and 30.4% for Labour. This meant that, instead of being close together in Parliament as many polls predicted, the Conservatives with 331 seats (out of 650) had 99 more than Labour's 232, a decisive victory. This was despite the new prominence of the right-wing UKIP, which campaigned on an anti-EU, anti-immigration agenda and won 12.6% of the national vote (but because of the first-past-the-post electoral system secured only one seat). Undoubtedly, UKIP cut into the Conservative vote, but perhaps more surprisingly, it also appealed to disgruntled Labour voters. The contrasts can be seen more starkly in England alone, which makes up 533 of the 650 seats in the Westminster parliament. The Conservatives won 41% of the vote in England, an increase of 1.4 percentage points, and UKIP took 14.1%, a rise of 10.7 percentage points. Labour also increased its vote share by 3.6 percentage points to reach 31.6%, but this was not nearly enough to capture sufficient seats.

The Liberal Democrats were the casualty; their UK vote share of 7.9% was only one-third of their share in 2010. Participation in the coalition had been a disaster for the party, whose supporters deserted it for backing Tory fiscal austerity and especially for acquiescing in a sharp rise in university tuition fees, going against their explicit promise. The party had also failed to secure any progress on electoral reform, another key part of its policies. It was especially rough justice that the Liberal Democrats' coalition partner captured most of the English seats they lost.

Miliband resigned immediately after the election and was heavily criticised for his negative campaign. The departure of the 'Brownite' Miliband, who had defeated his 'Blairite' brother David in the previous party-leadership contest, triggered a new war between Labour's socialist and centrist factions – one that was scheduled to be resolved with the election of a new leader in September 2015.

Although the coalition had been replaced by the Conservatives' slim parliamentary majority of 12 seats, it would certainly not be plain sailing for the government over the subsequent five years. The party had not shed the divisions on Europe that had plagued it in the past. Its rightist anti-Europe wing was essentially composed of the same members of parliament who were particularly sensitive about England's rights vis-à-vis Scotland. To have 56 SNP members facing them in the House of Commons, arguing insistently for greater devolution of powers to the Scottish Parliament (a separate elected body, sitting in Edinburgh, with an SNP government in power), was likely to provoke them to stand up even more for English rights. Cameron had in fact already acknowledged this pressure when he said on the morning after the Scottish referendum: 'we have heard the voice of Scotland – and now the millions of voices of England must also be heard. The question of English votes for English laws ... requires a decisive answer.'

The issue to be addressed was whether Westminster members of parliament representing Scottish constituencies could vote on matters that were primarily of concern to England, as powers to manage Scotland's affairs had increasingly been devolved to the Scottish Parliament since its establishment in 1999. Events in the lead-up to the referendum served to exacerbate the problem: shortly before the September 2014 vote, an opinion poll suggested that the 'yes' campaign advocating independence would win. This caused panic among political leaders at Westminster, who flocked north to try to influence the outcome by professing their devotion to Scotland as part of the union. Cameron, Miliband and Nick Clegg, then Liberal Democrat leader and deputy prime minister, signed 'The Vow' on the front page of a Glasgow tabloid newspaper, promising 'extensive new powers' for the Scottish Parliament. This was almost certainly an overreaction, given the 'no' campaign's subsequent victory by a decisive margin. Afterwards, the SNP was able to exploit the move, arguing that the promise – which was vaguely worded – was already being broken.

This set of circumstances, along with the SNP's extraordinary showing in the May election, has created several challenges at Westminster – on top of the continuing threat to the 308-year-old union between England and Scotland. Firstly, it brought to the fore of British politics a dynamic new personality, Nicola Sturgeon, who became the SNP leader following the referendum defeat. She spoke passionately against the Conservatives' austerity policies and positioned the party firmly to the left of Labour. With a slim majority, Cameron would need to deal with her on many issues – not least because she unambiguously carried the weight of Scotland behind her, with the latent threat to call a new referendum on Scottish independence, a vote that she might well win. The SNP's sweep of Scotland showed the country's profound disillusionment with a Westminster system that, the party argued, consistently failed to take Scottish interests into account.

Secondly, there was the immediate question of which additional powers would be devolved to Edinburgh. Some politicians called on Cameron to give Scotland full fiscal autonomy, since this would place clear responsibility for managing Scotland's finances on the SNP, without support from the UK budget. Given the fall in the price of oil, revenues from which would account for much of an independent Scotland's tax income, this could be challenging for Sturgeon in her capacity as leader of the Scottish government. A parallel move to give more control of English affairs to English members of parliament could undermine the new SNP contingent at Westminster.

Thirdly, the SNP success was a disaster for the Labour Party, which was reduced from 41 Scottish seats to just one. Scotland was once a heartland of Britain's coal, steel and shipbuilding industries, and Labour had long dominated its politics. Many of its leading ministers in the Blair and Brown governments, including Brown himself, came from Scotland. Unless it could regain ground against the SNP in future elections, Labour would find it very difficult to command a majority at Westminster. Overall, the rise of the SNP created many new uncertainties for the future of the UK as a whole.

In or out of Europe?

In a programme set out in May 2015, the government pledged to 'renegotiate the United Kingdom's relationship with the European Union and pursue reform of the European Union for the benefit of all member states'. A referendum on the UK's continued membership of the EU would be held before the end of 2017. Cameron had first announced this plan in January 2013, in an attempt to appease the right wing of his party and to quell the rise of UKIP. But he steadfastly avoided mention of the specific demands he would make in negotiations with other European leaders – and by mid-2015, even after an initial tour of European capitals, his precise ambitions were only just beginning to emerge.

While opinion polls indicate that British people favour participation in Europe, and do not count the issue as one of their top concerns, there have always been anti-European elements in the two main parties, especially the Conservatives. In the 1990s, John Major's government – which, like Cameron's, had a small majority – was riven by internal dissent on Europe. Subsequent Labour governments were quietly pro-European but did not take the UK into the euro, which as of June 2015 was the common currency of 19 EU members. Tory euroscepticism gained new expression with the Conservatives' return to office in 2010, after which UKIP steadily gained popularity until it won (on a low turnout) the 2014 elections to the European Parliament. Fear of large-scale defections to

UKIP – as well as his shaky position as leader, after his failure to win the 2010 elections outright – forced Cameron into a series of concessions to the eurosceptics.

According to the anti-EU narrative championed by UKIP leader Nigel Farage, Westminster had ceded sovereignty to an 'out-of-sight, unaccountable, pan-European bureaucratic elite which has the final say'. Britain's economic performance and freedom are held back by EU regulation, so this argument goes, and 'we have nothing to lose and everything to gain by leaving the EU.' Farage's party asserts that after leaving the EU, Britain could strike new free-trade agreements with the Union and with countries further afield. As UKIP gained momentum, its arguments focused increasingly on immigration, with migrants from eastern EU countries said to be swamping the UK and taking British jobs and welfare benefits. Here at least UKIP was touching a nerve, as immigration was viewed as a key issue by many voters. In response, Cameron vowed to restrict annual net immigration to below 100,000, from figures of more than 200,000 – a promise that, given the laws on freedom of movement within the EU, he lacked the tools to enforce. Labour was also forced to say that it 'got it wrong' on immigration in the past.

It seemed a valid contention that the UK's growing population – in 2014 it increased by 0.76% to 64.6m, with more than half of the increase due to net migration – was putting pressure on public services and especially on housing, with the construction of affordable homes falling far short of demand. But it was equally clear that public services, especially state-provided health care, depended on an influx of professionals from abroad – and that economic growth was spurring the creation of jobs that could not be filled without a flow of migrant labour. Statistics showed that immigrants were net contributors to Britain's finances, paying significantly more in taxes than they extracted in benefits. But politicians did not deem it useful to make much of such points. Nor did they pick up on more scientific arguments, such as those made by the late Philip Whyte, of the think tank Centre for European Reform. In a 2013 essay 'Do the UK's European Ties Damage its Prosperity?', revised and re-released after his death in 2015, Whyte cited evidence that Britain's product and labour markets were among the least regulated in the developed world, and that EU membership did not impose a straightjacket. He wrote: 'Britain's economic failings have nothing to do with the regulatory burdens of EU membership. The supply-side deficiencies that do most damage to Britain's long-term prosperity originate at home, not in Brussels.'

As of mid-2015, it was unclear what arguments the major parties would develop as the EU referendum approached. There seemed little willingness on any side to take up strategic and security-based rationales for membership of the Union – for example, that it provided a guarantee against future intra-European conflicts, or that Britain was a stronger, more secure and more influential nation within the EU than it would be outside. Thus, Washington's pro-European cheerleading along these lines gained little traction. Rather, the focus seemed likely to be on the transactional aspects: what did Britain get out of its EU membership, and what were the disadvantages? Therefore, quite a lot seemed to hang on Cameron's gains in negotiations with other European leaders, and how these would be presented to voters. Cameron has been a decidedly pragmatic prime minister. He professed to favour continued EU membership, on the right terms; and it seemed unlikely that, come the referendum, he would want to support a British exit. But the prime minister would face considerable pressure from within his own party, not least Boris Johnson, the volubly anti-European mayor of London, who was seen as a future contender for the Conservative leadership.

Despite his reluctance to discuss specifics, the prime minister appeared likely to have several aims in the negotiations with his European counterparts. At the transactional level, he would seek to restrict the benefits that EU governments were required to grant to migrants, including child benefits for children living outside the UK. Poland – the birthplace of around 600,000 migrants living in the UK – is one of several EU states to have argued against any discrimination. More symbolically, Cameron could seek a derogation from the commitment in the preamble of the 1957 Treaty of Rome to 'lay the foundations of an ever closer union'. In between would come broad but practical reforms, such as loosening some EU regulations and safeguarding the single market for all 28 EU nations to avoid penalising those that have not adopted the euro. Some potential UK proposals could find favour in other European capitals, while others could meet with strong resistance. Overall, European leaders would not want the EU to be weakened by the exit of such a significant member country. While

Cameron's path ahead seemed very challenging, both at home and in dealing with European governments, German Chancellor Angela Merkel adopted a conciliatory tone, stating that 'you cannot completely rule out treaty change if it's necessary to do that.'

Britain's role in the world

One way in which London could gain favour in its EU negotiations would be to show willingness to take on more responsibility in dealing with the principal security issues facing Europe. The UK has been largely uninvolved in the Union's response to conflict in Ukraine, leaving Merkel and French President François Hollande to take the lead in negotiating a second ceasefire agreement with Moscow and Kiev. Although the UK sent a military detachment to Sierra Leone to help deal with the Ebola outbreak, it was France that had taken the lead in dealing with a series of African conflicts in recent years. Frustration was growing in the UK and elsewhere at what was seen as a widening vacuum in foreign policy, with the country's neuralgia about Europe and preoccupation with domestic issues a perennial handicap. As the *Financial Times* noted in an editorial published in February 2015, 'far from leading the West's response to bestial jihadism in the Middle East or Russian aggression in Ukraine, Britain is everywhere absent.'

London could counter that the UK was Europe's largest spender on defence in 2015, retained capable armed forces and was committed to leading NATO's new high-readiness spearhead force in 2017. But reductions in spending since 2010 had considerably diminished UK combat capability. The Ministry of Defence was expected to come under pressure to reduce its budget further as part of a new round of spending cuts. This meant that defence spending would soon fall below the NATO target of 2% of GDP, despite pledges to the contrary made at the September 2014 NATO summit in Wales. Among the 28 NATO members, the UK is one of five exceeding the 2% benchmark, but the Conservatives have refused to commit to staying above it.

The heightened threat to the Alliance resulting from Russia's actions in Ukraine exposed UK capability gaps, such as those in maritime-patrol aircraft following the cancellation of the *Nimrod* programme in 2010, as well as in air defence and in sheer numbers of available combat aircraft and ships. The pending defence review would thus be crucial both for the tone of its language in discussing threats and strategy, and in setting out plans for future capabilities. It would be a key indicator of whether the UK still wished to continue being one of the world's larger and more influential powers.

Germany: Wider Security Role

Throughout Europe, security-policy establishments spent the year to mid-2015 coming to terms with a security environment in which, to the east, there was military conflict in Ukraine, driven and enabled by Russia, while to the south there was chaos and fragility, with Iraq and Syria consumed by insurgency and sectarian violence. In Berlin, an important shift was taking place as officials and experts increasingly debated the value of military might to supplement political and economic clout. The nation's defence policies were under review, with a new set of strategy documents due in 2016.

European crisis diplomacy, both in the travails of the eurozone and following Russia's annexation of Crimea and aggression in eastern Ukraine, has been led in recent years by Germany and in particular by Chancellor Angela Merkel, who heads a 'grand coalition' between her centre-right Christian Democratic Union and the centre-left Social Democratic Party (SPD). Merkel played a vital role alongside President François Hollande of France in brokering the Minsk II ceasefire agreement in Ukraine. German willingness to play a more proactive security role abroad was seen in an August 2014 decision to equip and train what amounts to a light infantry brigade of Peshmerga fighters combating the Islamic State of Iraq and al-Sham (ISIS) in the Kurdish region of northern Iraq. This decision broke a taboo in Germany, which does not usually supply weapons to an active conflict zone. The rationale for the move had three elements: that ISIS was causing a humanitarian catastrophe; that it posed an existential threat to people in the areas it controlled; and that it was attracting foreign fighters, many of whom were coming from Europe and could become a direct terrorist threat on their return.

Crisis leadership

While Berlin was in the practice of playing a leading role in shaping international responses to crises, its decisions often seemed to follow a reactive pattern. Germany appeared to lack a coherent framework for crisis response, beyond a general desire to do more in the realm of global security. However, during the year to mid-2015 Defence Minister Ursula von der Leyen was prominent in crafting new security policies and structures. At the 2015 Munich Security Conference, she outlined a vision for Germany's role that she described as 'leadership from the centre'. While its substance was not immediately obvious, the concept brought together some mainstays of German security policy, such as multinational cooperation to generate European capabilities, and support for capacity-building, in the form of train-and-equip programmes and security-sector reform, to enable other actors to deal with regional security problems outside Europe. Germany had pushed for such ideas within the European Union and NATO, for which it had generated the Framework Nations Concept on defence cooperation. Von der Leyen said leadership from the centre would use the legitimacy generated by working through alliances. Writing in *Berlin Policy Journal*, German analyst and commentator Constanze Stelzenmüller paraphrased the concept as meaning that 'Germany should assume responsibilities commensurate with its power, but that it is also dependent on and vulnerable to its neighbours and partners. Therefore, it must work together with them, offering its own resources to bolster the capacities of others.' Germany would neither seek to dominate, nor attempt to sit back.

Meanwhile, Foreign Minister Frank-Walter Steinmeier led a review of German foreign policy that found in February 2015 that Germany sometimes faced unrealistic expectations from its partners. According to essays by external analysts that Steinmeier commissioned for the review, Germany should 'revitalise Europe', 'europeanise Russia' and 'multinationalise America'. At the same time, Steinmeier argued, these partners appreciated Germany's willingness to 'work for mediation and peaceful conflict resolution worldwide, for justice and the rule of law, for human rights and for sustainable economic models'. Steinmeier's review, which involved wide consultation, promoted a narrative in which Germany was a good international citizen. However, its concrete proposals focused almost exclusively on adjusting structures within the foreign ministry to better enable it to deal with challenges in three key areas, as Steinmeier perceived them: crisis management, international order and Europe. The inward-looking character of the exercise was inadvertently underlined by a quotation from one ministry official in the document that 'German foreign policy is 99.9% not on the military side'. This sentence seemed to indicate a failure to consider holistically the relationship between different foreign-policy tools.

Yet the moves undertaken by von der Leyen suggested a broader and more integrated approach. She initiated a government-wide effort to draft a new White Paper on security policy and the future of the German armed forces. A new strategic document was required, she argued, because of the changing international security environment, of which important features included Russia's challenge to the European order, the adoption of 'hybrid' tactics in conflicts, transnational terrorism and the security implications of epidemics such as that caused by the Ebola virus. In addition, there was a need to examine the progress of reforms to the armed forces following the suspension of conscription and problems in the procurement of equipment. The review, the first since 2006, is due to be completed in 2016. Von der Leyen said the process would provide an opportunity to reflect on Germany's international role and should set its level of ambition, as well as providing a supporting narrative, outlining why and where Germany would choose to engage, amid a changing strategic culture. Germany had to accept greater responsibility, she argued, because of its historical responsibility for peace and stability, its humanitarian obligations and its security-policy interests.

End of defence cuts

At the September 2014 NATO summit held in the United Kingdom, government leaders pledged to increase defence spending towards 2% of GDP over the next ten years, in light of the deteriorating security environment. Germany, which spent only 1.14% of GDP on defence in 2014, had long argued that metrics focused on output would be more meaningful than input measures such as the 2% target. Berlin, along with several other allies, initially opposed the spending pledge and succeeded in diluting its language. On 30 June 2015, the 60th anniversary of Germany's membership of NATO, von der Leyen argued that 'we stand by the 2% goal. But in the future we have to ask a second additional question: what does the result of the financial effort look like?'

Nevertheless, after the summit von der Leyen began to argue in favour of an increase in the defence budget. She carefully avoided any talk of quickly reaching 2%, a target that has almost no domestic political support, but stressed that the spending level should be driven by Germany's ability to play the role of a reliable and capable ally in NATO. The subtext was that spending 2% of GDP on defence might be unrealistic, but that defence cuts had gone too far. By March 2015, she had built enough support within Merkel's government to announce plans for a 6.2% defence-spending increase over the period 2016–19. Spread out over four years, the German armed forces would thus benefit from an additional €8bn in funding.

A closer look at the plan revealed, however, that the impact would be rather limited. First of all, on the basis of current projections for economic growth in Germany, the percentage of GDP spent on defence would probably be lower in 2019 than in 2014, despite the budget increase. Secondly, around €5.5bn of the additional spending would be directed towards personnel, covering wage increases, pension payments, and redundancy or retraining measures. These payments might be necessary, but would not generate new capability. Approximately €1.85bn was earmarked for fresh investment, but most of this would go towards procurement programmes that had been delayed, as well as to upgrading accommodation for military personnel. Around €250m would support increased involvement in exercises within the context of NATO reassurance measures in Eastern Europe – the one line item that could truly be linked to the changes in the security environment. Thus, the increase itself would not alter the overall picture, but sent an important political signal that the era of defence-spending cuts was over. In addition, the Ministry of Defence published in June 2015 a joint report with the Federation of German Security and Defence Industries, outlining the results of a six-month dialogue between the two. The report made the case that the proportion of the defence budget allocated to investment should be increased from 15% to 20%, and that 10% of that investment should be directed towards research and new technology.

The scale of the modernisation challenge facing Germany's armed forces, the Bundeswehr, was illustrated in May 2015 by Lieutenant

General Bruno Kasdorf, the outgoing chief of the army. Arguing that the army's equipment budget had been systematically underfunded since the 1990s, he pointed to equipment shortfalls, sluggish reform efforts and low stocks of ammunition. He indicated that it was necessary to pull together equipment from units across the country to adequately equip Germany's contribution to NATO's new Very High Readiness Joint Task Force (VJTF). (See map, *Strategic Geography* pp. VI–VII.) Germany, together with Norway and the Netherlands, took responsibility for providing the first rotation of the VJTF, which would serve as a test bed for its procedures and capabilities. Projecting to 2025, Kasdorf said that even with the higher budget, the army would be underfunded by roughly €20bn. It was not just the army that faced such challenges: a report sent to the parliamentary defence committee by the defence ministry suggested that all services had problems marrying platforms with advanced weapons systems. The effects of previous years' defence cuts had become more obvious: force structures had been hollowed out, and readiness reduced, putting a question mark over the ability of the armed forces to fulfil NATO obligations.

In addition to boosting spending, von der Leyen was also questioning the principles that lay behind the reform efforts of her predecessors, Karl-Theodor zu Guttenberg and Thomas de Maizière. The so-called 'breadth before depth' concept meant that cuts should be implemented in a way that ensured the armed forces would still be able to cover a broad spectrum of contingencies, but with reduced sustainability. In other words, it was accepted that the price of a broad-spectrum capability would be limits on the concurrency of the missions the Bundeswehr would be able to conduct, as well as on the length of time that such missions could be sustained. To von der Leyen, this concept was too rigid: in practice, Germany already had capability gaps yet was determined to protect the depth of certain areas of excellence, such as battlefield medicine. She stated in March 2015 that 'to me it is important to be able to breathe and have an appropriate breadth, together with multinational partners, and then also a differentiated depth, where we need this in specialised areas.'

A similar line of thinking seemed to inform her approach to defence technology, leading her to question which technologies needed to be acquired from national suppliers in order to protect German sovereignty. In an attempt to define defence–industrial strategy, the Ministry of Defence indicated that German companies should supply systems for networked command and control, and cryptology, and sensors for intelligence, surveillance and reconnaissance (ISR), as well as some aspects of force protection – and that the government would need to make sufficient investments to sustain these capacities. However, Germany would be prepared to rely on European or global providers of command-and-control hardware; ISR platforms; some missile and air-defence capabilities; surface vessels; rotary and fixed-wing aircraft; unprotected land platforms; and medical capacity. Submarines, armoured vehicles and small arms – all areas in which Germany boasts prominent manufacturers that rely on exports in order to balance a shrinking domestic market – were initially identified as being in need of further inter-ministerial discussion. If these defence–industrial capacities were deemed critical, the government would be forced to support the defence-export industry. But Sigmar Gabriel, SPD leader and minister for economic affairs and energy, has led a drive to tighten Germany's arms-export policy. These tensions between Gabriel and von der Leyen delayed the decision until summer 2015, when armoured vehicles and submarines were deemed to be key technologies that Germany would maintain on a national basis, and the development of which would be supported with government funding.

A further strand of von der Leyen's reformist approach was a shake-up in the procurement of defence equipment. Following a review of large-scale procurement programmes commissioned from a consortium led by consultants KPMG, von der Leyen appointed Katrin Suder, of the consultancy McKinsey, as the ministry's acquisition chief. The KPMG report found that delivery of equipment began after a six-year delay, on average, and that the period from first to final delivery averaged almost 11 years. This meant that defence-procurement projects often spanned 30 years from beginning to end. Suder launched an 'Armaments Agenda' initiative that focused on three core elements: more transparent risk assessment, improved project management and a focus on filling the Bundeswehr's capability gaps. The first test cases for the new approach will come with two important decisions announced in June 2015: the selection of the US–European MEADS anti-missile system; and the commencement of an international tender for multi-role combat ships. Each has a contract value of around €4bn.

In the realm of foreign affairs and defence, shifts in German policy thus appeared to be under way, reflecting the greater security risks within Europe and in its neighbourhood, and Berlin's enhanced role as a pillar of Europe following the 2008 financial crisis and the eurozone's subsequent woes.

Turkey: End of the Erdogan Era?

The Turkish general election of 7 June 2015 put an end to almost 13 years of single-party rule by the conservative Justice and Development Party (AKP), which failed to secure a parliamentary majority for the first time since November 2002. But the result arguably dealt an even greater blow to Recep Tayyip Erdogan, who co-founded the AKP in 2001 and served three successive terms as prime minister, before being elected to the largely ceremonial post of president in August 2014. In the run-up to the general election, Erdogan made it clear that, if the AKP secured another majority, he would use his still-considerable influence within the party to ensure that it formulated a new constitution concentrating virtually all power in the presidency. In the immediate aftermath of the vote, these dreams appeared to be in ruins. Although Erdogan seemed likely to continue trying to shape the manner in which Turkey was governed, there was a sense that an era was drawing to a close and that his influence was now in permanent, if slow and perhaps turbulent, decline.

Despite losing its majority, the AKP remained the largest party in parliament and had begun negotiations with the opposition in the hope of remaining in power as the head of a coalition. Even if these efforts succeeded, there seemed little prospect that a coalition would provide political stability or even survive a four-year term. It appeared inevitable that there would be an early general election, either in 2016–17 or, if the coalition negotiations collapsed, even as early as November 2015.

There was also uncertainty about the impact that the AKP's loss of its parliamentary majority would have on government policy, both domestically and in foreign relations. Few doubted that the election result was partly caused by a reaction against Erdogan's growing authoritarianism.

With the president palpably weakened, the fear that he had engendered also began to fade, and opposition journalists started to relax what had become almost instinctive self-censorship. Similarly, there looked set to be a loss of momentum in the centralised attempts to reshape Turkish society in line with Erdogan's conservative interpretation of Sunni Islam. Yet there was little sign that a new government would emerge to energetically drive policy in a different direction. Indeed, there were indications that the post-election period would be characterised by introspection and the lack of a clear path forward.

Strengthened political opposition

In summer 2014, Erdogan appeared confident that not only would his decade-long domination of Turkish politics continue indefinitely, but that he would soon establish what he termed the 'New Turkey' as the dominant power in both the Middle East and the broader Muslim world.

On 10 August 2014, Erdogan secured victory in the first round of Turkey's first direct presidential election, winning 51.8% of the popular vote, ahead of the 38.4% garnered by Ekmeleddin Ihsanoglu, the joint candidate of the social democratic Republican People's Party (CHP) and the ultranationalist National Action Party (MHP), and the 9.8% won by Selahattin Demirtas, chair of the pro-Kurdish Peoples' Democratic Party (HDP). In his victory speech, Erdogan proclaimed that the result was a triumph for all of the world's Muslims and vowed that, as their representative, he would continue to defend their rights against predatory outsiders.

On 27 August 2014, one day before Erdogan was sworn in as president, the AKP held an extraordinary party congress to approve the appointment of Foreign Minister Ahmet Davutoglu, who had been handpicked by Erdogan, as party leader and prime minister. The following month, Erdogan's aides informed journalists that he had decided to use a newly built 1,150-room complex in Bestepe, on the outskirts of Ankara, as his presidential palace. Originally intended as the prime minister's new residence and paid for out of the budget for that office, the palace cost more than US$615 million and was built on environmentally protected land, in violation of two court orders. The site was part of a forest that had once belonged to Mustafa Kemal Atatürk, the fierce secularist who had founded the modern Turkish Republic in 1923.

The AKP announced in October 2014 a 97% increase in the presidency's budget for 2015, in comparison to that of the previous year. Under Erdogan's predecessors, the president's advisers had been divided into four directorates. In December 2014, Erdogan increased the number of directorates to 13, equipping each with a staff of experts in what became almost a shadow cabinet. Starting in January 2015, Erdogan chaired monthly meetings of the actual cabinet in the new presidential palace. He also began bypassing Davutoglu, the ostensible head of the executive, by regularly issuing instructions to, and receiving briefings from, individual ministers.

Erdogan made clear that his conception of the New Turkey was rooted in, and sought to revive, past imperial glories. References to the Ottoman Empire had already become regular features of his public speeches. In December 2014, Erdogan abruptly announced that he had decided that the Ottoman language, which was written in the Arabic script, would become a compulsory subject in all Turkish schools. Starting from January 2015, foreign dignitaries visiting the presidential palace were greeted by an honour guard of actors dressed as soldiers from past Turkish empires.

However, a detailed analysis of the presidential election suggested that Erdogan's power had already peaked, particularly in terms of his ability to galvanise his supporters. The turnout in Turkish elections is usually relatively high, at around 84–5%. But in the presidential election, it was only 74%. At 51.8%, Erdogan's share of the vote was higher than the 49.8% won by the AKP in the preceding general election, held in June 2011. Yet although the electorate had grown from 50.2m in 2011 to 55.7m in 2014, Erdogan's tally of 21m votes in the presidential election was slightly less than the 21.3m won by the AKP in 2011. Equally significant was the fact that the 9.8% share gained by Demirtas in the presidential election was well above the 6–7% usually won by Kurdish nationalists. This suggested that the Gezi Park protests of summer 2013 had created a sense of solidarity among the government's opponents, eroding the traditional reluctance of many Turks to back a Kurdish politician and prompting some to vote tactically to confound Erdogan's ambitions.

Under Turkish law, the support of 367 parliamentarians is required to promulgate a new constitution, although 330 are sufficient to put such a document to a referendum. In the run-up to the 2015 election, opinion polls suggested that the AKP would again win the largest share of the vote, and that both the CHP and the MHP would comfortably cross the 10% threshold required for representation in parliament. The only question appeared to be whether they would be joined by the HDP, thereby splitting the seats between four rather than three parties and reducing, if not ending, the AKP's majority.

In the event, the AKP took 40.9% of the vote and 258 seats in parliament, ahead of the CHP with 25% and 132 seats, and the MHP with 16.3% and 80 seats. Boosted by the support of conservative Kurds alienated by Erdogan's relentlessly abrasive rhetoric and tactical votes from Turks hoping to thwart his dreams of formally introducing a presidential system, the HDP won 13.1% and took 80 seats in parliament. As a result, far from initiating a transition from a de facto to a *de jure* presidential system, the election halted Erdogan's ambitions in their tracks. Indeed, opinion polls conducted shortly after the vote indicated that many supporters of the AKP had deserted the party for fear that Erdogan was trying to create a dictatorship.

Ascendant Kurdish minority

For Turkey's Kurdish nationalists, the HDP's entry into parliament in the general election crowned a tumultuous year, in which hopes for their decades-old campaign for greater cultural and political rights inside the country fluctuated amid a rising sense of identification with Kurdish minorities abroad, particularly those in Syria.

In September 2014, the mood among Kurdish nationalists in Turkey was one of frustration and fear. No progress was being made in the two-year dialogue between the government and Abdullah Ocalan, the imprisoned founder of the militant Kurdistan Workers' Party (PKK), and the latter organisation was heavily involved in helping the Kurds of Syria and Iraq in their efforts to halt the advance of the Islamic State of Iraq and al-Sham (ISIS). At that time, although the situation in Iraq appeared to have stabilised, in Syria ISIS had made deep inroads into the de facto Kurdish autonomous enclave of Rojava – which was administered by the Democratic Union Party (PYD), the PKK's Syrian affiliate – and appeared to be poised to take the town of Kobane, on the Turkish border. The government refused to allow either volunteers or supplies to cross from

Turkey into Kobane and, on 7 October, Erdogan dismissively described the town as having already fallen to ISIS. The result was the worst civil unrest in Turkey for more than 20 years, as tens of thousands of Kurdish nationalists took to the streets in the southeast, conducting violent demonstrations in which over 50 people were killed. Backed by airstrikes carried out by a US-led coalition (which had begun such operations in August), the defenders of Kobane first halted ISIS and eventually, on 27 January, drove the last of the jihadists out of the city. The victory prompted more demonstrations across southeastern Turkey, this time in celebration.

The PKK successfully deployed its forces in support of Kurdish fighters in Syria and Iraq, thereby boosting its prestige both in the region and further afield. In practice, the PKK also allied with the United States and its EU partners in the coalition – even though Washington and Brussels still officially classified the group as a proscribed terrorist organisation. This further strained Ankara's already tense relations with Washington, not least because some of the weapons and equipment supplied to the PYD's military wing in Rojava, the People's Protection Units (YPG), ended up in the hands of the PKK, as did some of the materiel supplied by EU countries to Iraqi Kurdish Peshmerga fighting ISIS in Iraq. Most Kurdish nationalists in Turkey dismissed the protestations of neutrality made by Erdogan and the AKP, and regarded them as sympathetic to ISIS. Critically, thousands of Turkish Kurds found ways to cross into Syria to join the YPG, and remained with the group even after the siege of Kobane had been lifted. By June 2015, more than 500 Turkish Kurds were estimated to have died fighting for the YPG against ISIS. Pro-YPG symbols and graffiti proliferated across southeastern Turkey, and Turkish municipalities in which the HDP had strong support started to closely cooperate with the PYD's local structures in Syria.

The defence of Kobane combined with territorial gains made by the more well-established Kurdish enclave in northern Iraq to enhance the sense of ethnic solidarity among Kurds across the Middle East, and to promote the belief among Turkey's Kurds that history was finally moving in their direction. This in turn fuelled hopes of creating a Kurdish autonomous region in southeastern Turkey. The relative success of the HDP in the Turkish general election raised expectations even higher. Managing these expectations is likely to present a major challenge to both the new

Turkish government and, once the euphoria of entering parliament has dissipated, to the leadership of the HDP itself. The party will need to extract significant concessions from the government to convince its supporters that politics is more effective than violence as a means of achieving their aims.

Entanglement with Syria

The turmoil in Syria continued to pose not only the greatest challenge to Turkey's foreign policy but also a major risk to the country's internal stability. According to the government, there were 1.8m Syrian refugees in Turkey as of mid-2015, although officials privately put the figure at more than 2m and rising, of whom only 15% resided in organised refugee camps. In some towns close to the Turkey–Syria border, refugees outnumbered locals. Many who had escaped Syria found work in Turkey's unregistered economy, driving down wages and increasing unemployment, while compounding social tensions that occasionally erupted into violent clashes. With no end in sight to the fighting in Syria, it was unclear when, if ever, the majority of refugees would return home. Yet the government had still not formulated a long-term strategy to absorb or accommodate them. Although the conditions in organised camps were generally good, refugees who lived outside these facilities had only limited access to health and education services, a problem exacerbated by the fact that around half of them were younger than 18.

Nor did the Turkish government have a coherent strategy for dealing with other potential repercussions of the Syrian civil war. It stuck stubbornly to the policy that it had adopted in mid-2011, which prioritised the overthrow of Syrian President Bashar al-Assad and held that the threat posed by Islamic extremist groups such as ISIS was secondary and would effectively resolve itself once Assad had been ousted.

Turkey's focus on removing Assad led it to allow anyone wishing to fight against him – including foreign fighters joining jihadist organisations – to travel through Turkey on their way to Syria. Even if it had always had strained relations with ISIS, the AKP remained confident that this approach would act as a safeguard against any terrorist threat to Turkey. Indeed, Turkish court documents leaked in 2014 and early 2015 appeared to show that the country's National Intelligence Organization had facilitated covert arms shipments to extremist groups active in Syria, and that Turkish artillery units deployed inside Turkey had provided covering fire for alliances of Syrian opposition groups, which included extremist elements, during attacks against Assad's forces. It thus came as a shock to the AKP that on 11 June 2014, five days after ISIS began its attack on the Iraqi city of Mosul, the group stormed the Turkish consulate there and took 49 personnel hostage.

Turkey refused to provide substantive support to the US-led coalition conducting airstrikes against ISIS, or to sign an agreement to combat the group put forward by the US and ten Arab states on 11 September 2014. On each occasion, Turkish officials cited concerns about the safety of the 49 hostages held by ISIS. But Ankara declined to join the coalition even after negotiating the release of the hostages on 21 September, and subsequently insisted that any military action in Syria should be directed at the ouster of Assad.

Nevertheless, starting in late 2014, increasing fears of an ISIS attack inside Turkey resulted in a partial tightening of restrictions on foreign fighters travelling through the country on their way to Syria. These efforts were stepped up after a lone suicide bomber killed a policeman in central Istanbul on 6 January 2015, in what Turkish officials erroneously interpreted as an ISIS attack and a prelude to a possible campaign against foreign diplomats in Turkey. (No information emerged about the motive of the attacker.) On the night of 21 February, fear of an ISIS attack even prompted the Turkish government to evacuate the tomb of Suleiman Shah – grandfather of the Ottoman Empire's founder – from a site around 27 kilometres inside Syria. Both the tomb's contents and its honour guard of 40 Turkish soldiers were moved to a location on the Turkey–Syria border.

Despite the new measures focused on ISIS, as of mid-2015 Ankara had made few attempts to clamp down on the activities of other extremist organisations, such as Jabhat al-Nusra and Ahrar al-Sham. Operating in Turkish towns close to the Syrian border, these groups often openly used cafes and apartments as liaison offices and staging posts for foreign fighters arriving from other countries. Nor had the Turkish authorities attempted to suppress propaganda and recruitment activities by extremist Islamist groups targeting young Turks. Perhaps most strikingly, the Turkish authorities had blocked access to more than 80,000 websites, including many that were critical of Erdogan and the AKP, but had not restricted those used by jihadist groups to recruit fighters for the conflict in Syria. Overall, the AKP appeared unconcerned that the growing number of radicalised Turkish citizens could eventually pose a threat to Turkey's own security, and imposed no controls on fighters returning home from Syria.

Strategic drift?

When Ankara's policy on Syria was first formulated, Erdogan was confident that Turkey would soon emerge as the pre-eminent power in the Middle East. He argued that rather than seeking to exercise influence through its membership of an alliance led by others, the country would become a power centre in its own right and a magnet for states seeking leadership, particularly other predominantly Sunni countries. Yet by 2015, Turkey had become more isolated than at any other time since the AKP came to power. The government's refusal to join the anti-ISIS coalition and Erdogan's harsh rhetoric against the military regime in Egypt even distanced Turkey from Saudi Arabia and Qatar – states with which it had previously cooperated in providing aid to the Syrian rebels.

Nevertheless, Turkey's foreign policy was still based on the assumption that it was strong enough to go it alone, pursuing tactical partnerships in different areas with countries that regarded one another as strategic rivals. Although Turkey remained officially committed to its membership of NATO and its candidacy for EU membership, Ankara irked its Western allies by refusing to join them in imposing sanctions on Russia in response to Moscow's annexation of Crimea and support for separatists in Ukraine. On 1 December 2014, just as the West was trying to isolate Moscow, Erdogan and Russian President Vladimir Putin announced an agreement to build a new pipeline carrying Russian natural gas through Turkey to international markets – the so-called 'Turkish Stream' – after objections from the European Union forced Russia to shelve the South Stream project, which would have carried the product through Bulgaria.

Turkey announced on 19 February 2015 that it was pushing ahead with a US$3.4-billion deal to buy a missile-defence system from the China Precision Machinery Import–Export Corporation. The contract, which had first been awarded in 2013, had been intensely criticised by Turkey's NATO allies, who warned that it would be impossible to integrate the Chinese system with Turkey's existing air-defence architecture – much of which is comprised of elements of NATO's Air Defence Ground Environment – without compromising the security of sensitive data. As a result, Ankara will only be able to install the system as a stand-alone, without any integration with NATO assets, a move that would effectively strip Turkey of around half of its radar capabilities.

Uncertain future

Erdogan's hopes of introducing a presidential system were a step towards his goal of establishing Turkey as a global player, the head of an informal alliance of Sunni states. The international dimension of this plan never appeared to have a realistic chance of success. Indeed, Erdogan's insistence on Turkey's leadership role appears to have alienated other Muslim countries. By mid-2015, the result of the general election also appeared to have dealt a fatal blow to Erdogan's hopes of dominating domestic politics. Although there was no expectation that he would fade quickly from the political arena, there was a sense that his power was now in irreversible decline. The only questions were when and how the Erdogan era would come to an end.

Yet, if one era was drawing to a close, there was no sign that a new one was about to begin. Instead, the mood was rather one of uncertainty, and of an interregnum before the dynamics of the post-Erdogan era could assert themselves. Although he was loved and loathed in equal measure by his domestic supporters and opponents – and in recent years had attracted increasing international opprobrium – there was a general acknowledgement that Erdogan had brought momentum to Turkish politics, albeit of a kind that many found disturbing. Consequently, for Erdogan's opponents, the 2015 election brought not only feelings of relief but a sense of a loss of direction as the pressures against which they had railed and rallied were suddenly lifted. There was no immediate prospect that another politician or party would emerge to shape Turkish policy as decisively as Erdogan had done at the height of his power.

Some hoped that a new government would try to repair Turkey's frayed foreign relations, as well as heal some of the damage to the country's social fabric caused by the deliberately divisive policies adopted by

Erdogan following the Gezi Park protests. But such hopes were tempered by the knowledge that any new government would be a weak and probably short-lived coalition. The new government might be able to soften some of the harsher aspects of Erdogan's policies, but would struggle to implement effective solutions to the challenges the country faced. These included a slowdown of economic growth, rising Kurdish aspirations and, perhaps most critically, the continuing risk of spillover from the conflict in Syria.

Strategic Geography 2015

II
The shifting economics of oil

IV
China's growing foreign investments

VI
NATO's Readiness Action Plan

VIII
Europe's home-grown Islamic extremism

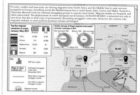

X
Flows of migrants across the Mediterranean

XII
Long road to recovery after West Africa's Ebola outbreak

XIV
Challenges facing Nigeria's new president

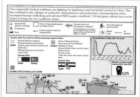

XV
Libya divided

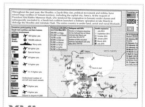

XVI
Yemen in the grip of Houthi insurgency

XVII
Expansion of Iraq's Kurdish Regional Government

XVIII
Syria and Iraq: increasing complexity of crises

XX
Improved US relations hold promise for Havana

The shifting economics of oil

In the second half of 2014, the global oil price suffered its biggest tumble for nearly 20 years. Even after a small upturn in mid-2015, Brent crude was about US$60 per barrel, half the level of the past three years. This 'correctio[n]' came about because US shale oil had increased supply just as poor economic growth weakened demand. The 12 members of the Organization of the Petroleum Exporting Countries (OPEC) unusually did not curb production [to] stabilise prices, because the cartel's most influential member, Saudi Arabia, considered that reduced OPEC outp[ut] would benefit rivals Iran and Russia, and decided to put its market share first. Despite continued conflict in man[y] oil-producing countries, the market now seems more robust against such geopolitical risks, and some analysts now wonder whether the underlying economics of oil have fundamentally changed. The many variables at play make any definitive forecast impossible, but a period of lower oil prices seems likely.

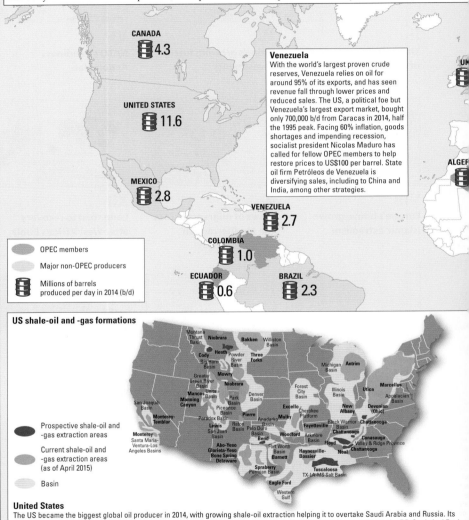

CANADA
4.3

Venezuela
With the world's largest proven crude reserves, Venezuela relies on oil for around 95% of its exports, and has seen revenue fall through lower prices and reduced sales. The US, a political foe but Venezuela's largest export market, bought only 700,000 b/d from Caracas in 2014, half the 1995 peak. Facing 60% inflation, goods shortages and impending recession, socialist president Nicolas Maduro has called for fellow OPEC members to help restore prices to US$100 per barrel. State oil firm Petróleos de Venezuela is diversifying sales, including to China and India, among other strategies.

UNITED STATES
11.6

MEXICO
2.8

VENEZUELA
2.7

COLOMBIA
1.0

ECUADOR
0.6

BRAZIL
2.3

OPEC members

Major non-OPEC producers

Millions of barrels produced per day in 2014 (b/d)

US shale-oil and -gas formations

Prospective shale-oil and -gas extraction areas

Current shale-oil and -gas extraction areas (as of April 2015)

Basin

United States
The US became the biggest global oil producer in 2014, with growing shale-oil extraction helping it to overtake Saudi Arabia and Russia. Its average daily output of crude oil, shale oil and liquids separated from natural gas hit 11.6 million barrels, according to the BP *Statistical Review of World Energy 2015*. However, fracking is costly and continued low oil prices, especially as OPEC carried on pumping at high capacity, saw half of the 1,600 US rigs idled between October 2014 and April 2015. The US Department of Energy estimates the world has 345bn barrels of recoverable shale-oil reserves (58bn of them are in the US) and 7,299 trillion cubic feet of shale-gas reserves. Meanwhile, as the world's large[st] oil consumer, the US still imported 7.3m b/d of crude oil in 2014.

Sources: BBC; Bloomberg; BP Statistical Review of World Energy 2015; CNN; The Economist; Financial Times; Forbes; International Energy Agency; Reuters; Wall Street Journal; US Department of Energy; US Energy Information Administration

Russia

The World Bank forecast in mid-2015 that Russia's economy would contract by around 3% this year because of the combined impact of lower oil prices and Western sanctions over Russia's support for separatists and other actions in war-torn eastern Ukraine. The bank predicted a 3.5% contraction with an average US$53 per barrel, or a 2.9% fall with an average US$65 price. Russia relies on oil and gas for 70% of its income and loses up to US$2bn for every dollar fall in the oil price. After oil prices plummeted and sanctions were imposed, the Kremlin moved swiftly to try to avert recession. In late 2014, there was a dramatic interest-rate rise, from 10.5% to 17%, to prop up the rouble currency. Nevertheless, sanctions have seen Western partners withdraw from oil joint ventures and the overall economic outlook remains sluggish.

Global oil supply 2014, millions of barrels per day

88.7 Global production

36.6 of which produced by OPEC-member countries

2,718 OECD commercial inventory, millions of barrels – end of 2014

WAY 1.9

RUSSIA 10.8

KAZAKHSTAN 1.7

KUWAIT 3.1

IRAQ 3.3

IRAN 3.6

CHINA 4.2

IBYA 0.5

SAUDI ARABIA 11.5

UAE 3.7

INDIA 0.9

QATAR 2.0

A 2.4

ANGOLA 1.7

Daily crude oil prices per barrel, June 2014–June 2015

Brent crude
US$115.7, Jun 2014
WTI crude
US$102.4 Jun 2014

Brent crude
US$59.0, Jun 2015
WTI crude
US$58.3 Jun 2015

Brent crude
US$46.6, Jan 2015
WTI crude
US$56.2 Jan 2015

Brent crude – Global benchmark
WTI crude – US benchmark

bya

litants have targeted refineries and her Libyan infrastructure in an attempt undermine the fragile post-Gadhafi ate. But while Tripoli relies heavily on e revenue, the return of Libyan oil to e global market in mid-2014 – as ports ere unblocked and production rose – nted prices by adding to world er-supply. Libya once had a 1.6m b/d tput; this fell to 150,000 b/d in the aos immediately following the 2011 ab spring uprising that toppled uammar Gadhafi.

Saudi Arabia

OPEC's purpose has been to keep oil prices stable by unifying its members' policies. But at a cartel meeting in November 2014, leading member Saudi Arabia, the world's largest oil exporter, broke with this practice by declining to cut production to prop up prices. This squeezed the growing US shale-oil and -gas industry, and some high-cost shale extraction was abandoned due to continuing low prices. While Saudi Arabia has a US$700bn reserve fund to survive leaner times, it needs US$85 per barrel to break even, and will not be able to hold off the rival shale industry forever.

Iran

Tehran had already been hit by Western sanctions over its disputed nuclear programme, when low oil prices worsened its liquidity, investor confidence and ability to balance its budget. The US$20bn–25bn it is expected to earn from its crude in 2015 is only around one-quarter of its 2011 oil earnings. On the other hand, a global deal over its nuclear programme and the lifting of sanctions could see a glut of Iranian oil hit the international market, further weakening prices.

© IISS

China's growing foreign investments

Chinese investment in other countries has surged, increasing Beijing's global influence. Among the world's top five investors, its annual outward flow of non-financial foreign direct investment (FDI) officially surpassed US$100 billion in 2013. In 2014, its outbound investment, at more than US$116bn, possibly exceeded money coming into the country. Chinese capital has traditionally been concentrated in Asia. However, investment in Africa, Latin America, the United States and other Western countries has grown rapidly in the past five years.

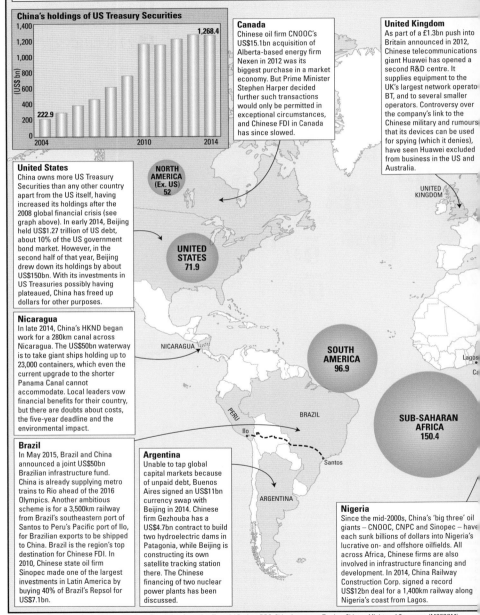

China's holdings of US Treasury Securities

(US$ bn), 2004 to 2014: rising from 222.9 to 1,268.4

Canada
Chinese oil firm CNOOC's US$15.1bn acquisition of Alberta-based energy firm Nexen in 2012 was its biggest purchase in a market economy. But Prime Minister Stephen Harper decided further such transactions would only be permitted in exceptional circumstances, and Chinese FDI in Canada has since slowed.

United Kingdom
As part of a £1.3bn push into Britain announced in 2012, Chinese telecommunications giant Huawei has opened a second R&D centre. It supplies equipment to the UK's largest network operator BT, and to several smaller operators. Controversy over the company's link to the Chinese military and rumours that its devices can be used for spying (which it denies), have seen Huawei excluded from business in the US and Australia.

United States
China owns more US Treasury Securities than any other country apart from the US itself, having increased its holdings after the 2008 global financial crisis (see graph above). In early 2014, Beijing held US$1.27 trillion of US debt, about 10% of the US government bond market. However, in the second half of that year, Beijing drew down its holdings by about US$150bn. With its investments in US Treasuries possibly having plateaued, China has freed up dollars for other purposes.

Nicaragua
In late 2014, China's HKND began work for a 280km canal across Nicaragua. The US$50bn waterway is to take giant ships holding up to 23,000 containers, which even the current upgrade to the shorter Panama Canal cannot accommodate. Local leaders vow financial benefits for their country, but there are doubts about costs, the five-year deadline and the environmental impact.

Brazil
In May 2015, Brazil and China announced a joint US$50bn Brazilian infrastructure fund. China is already supplying metro trains to Rio ahead of the 2016 Olympics. Another ambitious scheme is for a 3,500km railway from Brazil's southeastern port of Santos to Peru's Pacific port of Ilo, for Brazilian exports to be shipped to China. Brazil is the region's top destination for Chinese FDI. In 2010, Chinese state oil firm Sinopec made one of the largest investments in Latin America by buying 40% of Brazil's Repsol for US$7.1bn.

Argentina
Unable to tap global capital markets because of unpaid debt, Buenos Aires signed an US$11bn currency swap with Beijing in 2014. Chinese firm Gezhouba has a US$4.7bn contract to build two hydroelectric dams in Patagonia, while Beijing is constructing its own satellite tracking station there. The Chinese financing of two nuclear power plants has been discussed.

Nigeria
Since the mid-2000s, China's 'big three' oil giants – CNOOC, CNPC and Sinopec – have each sunk billions of dollars into Nigeria's lucrative on- and offshore oilfields. All across Africa, Chinese firms are also involved in infrastructure financing and development. In 2014, China Railway Construction Corp. signed a record US$12bn deal for a 1,400km railway along Nigeria's coast from Lagos.

NORTH AMERICA (Ex. US) 52

UNITED STATES 71.9

SOUTH AMERICA 96.9

SUB-SAHARAN AFRICA 150.4

Sources: American Enterprise Institute and Heritage Foundation; Australian Financial Review; BBC; China Investment Tracker; Chinese Ministry of Commerce (MOFCOM); EY (formerly Ernst & Young); Financial Times; Foreign Policy; Railway Gazette; Reuters; The Star (Toronto); UNCTAD; Wall Street Journal

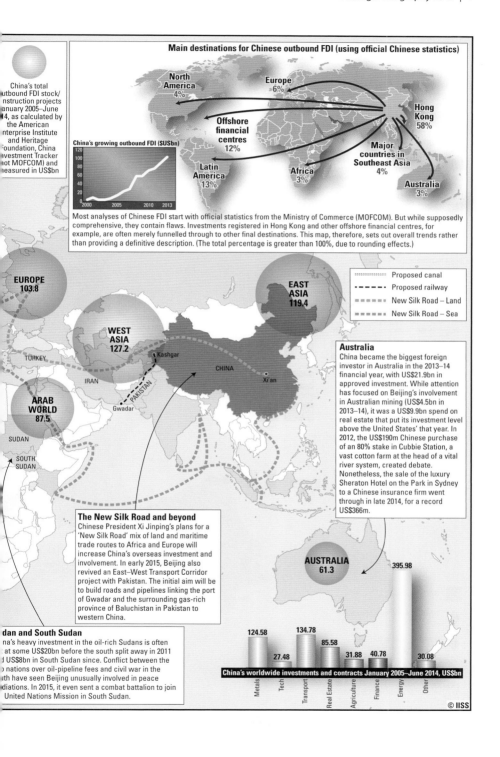

Main destinations for Chinese outbound FDI (using official Chinese statistics)

China's total utbound FDI stock/ nstruction projects anuary 2005–June 4, as calculated by the American nterprise Institute and Heritage oundation, China vestment Tracker ot MOFCOM) and easured in US$bn

North America 4%

Europe 6%

Hong Kong 58%

Offshore financial centres 12%

China's growing outbound FDI ($USbn)

Latin America 13%

Africa 3%

Major countries in Southeast Asia 4%

Australia 3%

Most analyses of Chinese FDI start with official statistics from the Ministry of Commerce (MOFCOM). But while supposedly comprehensive, they contain flaws. Investments registered in Hong Kong and other offshore financial centres, for example, are often merely funnelled through to other final destinations. This map, therefore, sets out overall trends rather than providing a definitive description. (The total percentage is greater than 100%, due to rounding effects.)

EUROPE 103.8

EAST ASIA 119.4

WEST ASIA 127.2

Kashgar

CHINA

Xi'an

TURKEY

IRAN

PAKISTAN

ARAB WORLD 87.5

Gwadar

SUDAN

SOUTH SUDAN

Proposed canal

Proposed railway

New Silk Road – Land

New Silk Road – Sea

Australia
China became the biggest foreign investor in Australia in the 2013–14 financial year, with US$21.9bn in approved investment. While attention has focused on Beijing's involvement in Australian mining (US$4.5bn in 2013–14), it was a US$9.9bn spend on real estate that put its investment level above the United States' that year. In 2012, the US$190m Chinese purchase of an 80% stake in Cubbie Station, a vast cotton farm at the head of a vital river system, created debate. Nonetheless, the sale of the luxury Sheraton Hotel on the Park in Sydney to a Chinese insurance firm went through in late 2014, for a record US$366m.

The New Silk Road and beyond
Chinese President Xi Jinping's plans for a 'New Silk Road' mix of land and maritime trade routes to Africa and Europe will increase China's overseas investment and involvement. In early 2015, Beijing also revived an East–West Transport Corridor project with Pakistan. The initial aim will be to build roads and pipelines linking the port of Gwadar and the surrounding gas-rich province of Baluchistan in Pakistan to western China.

AUSTRALIA 61.3

395.98

dan and South Sudan
na's heavy investment in the oil-rich Sudans is often at some US$20bn before the south split away in 2011 d US$8bn in South Sudan since. Conflict between the o nations over oil-pipeline fees and civil war in the uth have seen Beijing unusually involved in peace diations. In 2015, it even sent a combat battalion to join United Nations Mission in South Sudan.

124.58

134.78

27.48

85.58

31.88 40.78

30.08

China's worldwide investments and contracts January 2005–June 2014, US$bn

Metals

Tech

Transport

Real Estate

Agriculture

Finance

Energy

Other

© IISS

NATO's Readiness Action Plan

At its 2014 Wales summit, NATO announced a series of measures intended to reinforce Alliance solidarity, capability and credibility following Russia's actions in Crimea and eastern Ukraine. Collectively known as the 'Readiness Action Plan' (RAP), these proposals include both short-term 'assurance' measures and longer-term 'adaption' changes to NATO's military capability.

NATO Response Force and Very High Readiness Joint Task Force
The NATO Response Force currently comprises 13,000 personnel, including a 5,000-strong combat brigade, and is intended to be able to deploy with five to 30 days' notice. These forces are drawn from multiple NATO members on an annual basis. The RAP envisages using the current combat brigade to form an equivalent strength Very High Readiness Joint Task Force (VJTF), capable of deploying in two to five days, and expanding the total force to around 30,000 personnel by adding two more brigades intended to act as follow-up forces to the VJTF at lower readiness. These changes are scheduled to be implemented between 2016 and 2018.

Interim VJTF 2015
The land component of NATO's Response Force 2015 is currently acting as an interim version of the intended VJTF. Under the command of the 1st German/Netherlands Corps, it comprises a Dutch brigade headquarters, with Dutch, German and Norwegian infantry battalions and a multinational artillery battalion.

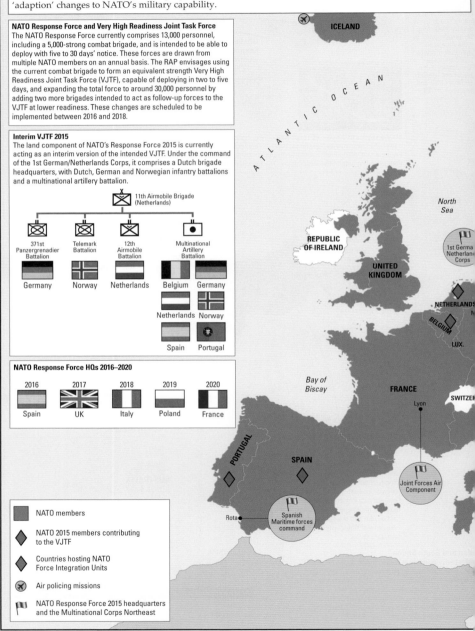

Sources: IISS; Bundesministerium der Verteidigung, Germany; Forsvarsdepartementet, Norway; NATO; Ministerie van Defensie, The Netherlands; United States Air Force

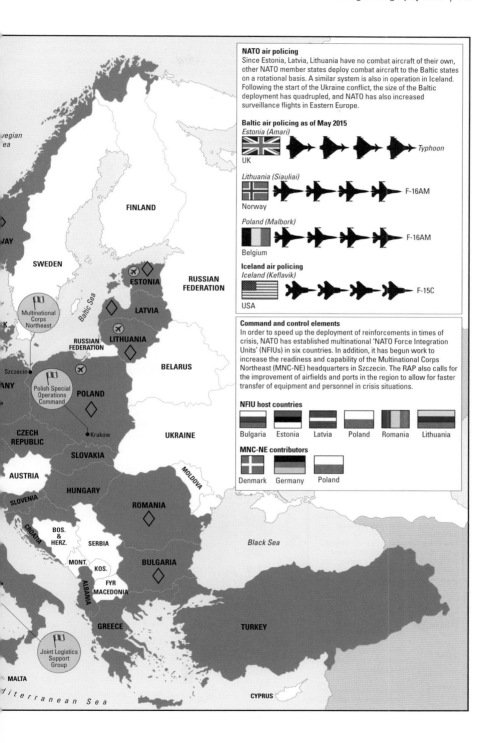

NATO air policing
Since Estonia, Latvia, Lithuania have no combat aircraft of their own, other NATO member states deploy combat aircraft to the Baltic states on a rotational basis. A similar system is also in operation in Iceland. Following the start of the Ukraine conflict, the size of the Baltic deployment has quadrupled, and NATO has also increased surveillance flights in Eastern Europe.

Baltic air policing as of May 2015
Estonia (Amari)
UK — Typhoon

Lithuania (Siauliai)
Norway — F-16AM

Poland (Malbork)
Belgium — F-16AM

Iceland air policing
Iceland (Keflavik)
USA — F-15C

Command and control elements
In order to speed up the deployment of reinforcements in times of crisis, NATO has established multinational 'NATO Force Integration Units' (NFIUs) in six countries. In addition, it has begun work to increase the readiness and capability of the Multinational Corps Northeast (MNC-NE) headquarters in Szczecin. The RAP also calls for the improvement of airfields and ports in the region to allow for faster transfer of equipment and personnel in crisis situations.

NFIU host countries
Bulgaria Estonia Latvia Poland Romania Lithuania

MNC-NE contributors
Denmark Germany Poland

Europe's home-grown Islamic extremism

Nearly 4,000 Western Europeans are thought to have travelled to Syria and Iraq to join the Islamic State of Iraq and al-Sham (ISIS), out of a total of more than 20,000 from 81 countries. As a result, the subject of home-grown Islamic extremism and how to tackle it has been pushed to the top of European domestic and foreign-policy agendas.

How foreign fighters are radicalised and recruited

Citizens travelling to Iraq/Syria as foreign fighters

- Online
- In person

Middle East, North Africa, South Asia: 70% / 30%
Europe incl. Caucasus and Balkans: 50% / 50%
North America: 10% / 90%

Region of origin

France
Criminal measures: Authorities have extensive powers to prosecute terrorists. Common criminal provisions with enhanced penalties have been employed for anti-terror cases, and special investigative judges can prosecute individuals for attending terror training camps abroad.
Response to returnees: Authorities assess threats and monitor with a view to prosecution.

Belgium
Criminal measures: There is legislation against taking part in the activities of a terrorist group, incitement or recruitment, and providing or receiving instruction or training in Belgium or abroad.
Non-criminal measures: The Coordination Unit for Threat Assessment distributes lists of 'at risk' or 'dangerous' individuals. There are also measures to prevent minors from leaving the country, and an agreement with Turkey to stop particular Belgian nationals from entering Syria via its territory.
Response to returnees: Threat assessment and monitoring, efforts at reintegration for those not prosecuted.

Denmark
Criminal measures: Any individual who engages in activities covered by Danish terrorism legislation during a stay in a foreign country can be prosecuted.
Non-criminal measures: Emphasis is placed on deterrence before departure, including confiscating the passports of minors. There are wide-ranging local initiatives to prevent radicalisation.
Response to returnees: Threat assessment and monitoring; efforts to reintegrate and de-radicalise at a local level, including psychological support and mentoring schemes.

SWEDEN
FINL
NORWAY — 60
70
180
DENMARK — 150
UNITED KINGDOM
700
NETHERLANDS — 250
600 GERMANY
30
IRELAND
BELGIUM — 440
FRANCE
SWITZERLAND — 150
40
AUSTRIA
1,200
ITALY
80
SPAIN
100
3,000 TUNISIA
1,500 MOROCCO
200 ALGERIA
900 LIBYA

Legend:
- 100 → Estimated flows of foreign fighters from Western Europe
- 360 Estimated flows of foreign fighters from countries beyond Western Europe
- EGYPT
- Measures taken to counter radicalisation and foreign fighters

Number of fighters per million people
- >20
- 15–20
- 10–15
- 5–10
- 0–5

- Attack on military
- Attack on civilians
- Attack on police
- 17 Number of dead
- 22 Number of wounded

Sources: IISS; Brookings Institute; Centre for Security Studies; Economist; European Parliamentary Research Service; Foreign Policy Research Institute; Guardian; Institute for St Dialogue; International Centre for Counter-Terrorism; Organisation for Economic Co-operation and Development; Quilliam Foundation; Radio Free Europe; Spiegel Online; The Sou Washington Post

United Kingdom
Criminal measures: Those who commit any crimes related to plans to fight overseas can be prosecuted. The UK has ramped up efforts to make preventative arrests.

Non-criminal measures: The Prevent strategy aims to make individuals less susceptible to extremist propaganda. Mentoring schemes at a local level are used to counter the spread of extremist narratives within communities.

Response to returnees: If an individual has contravened the Terrorism Act while abroad, they can be prosecuted. Arrests of individuals 'preparing' to travel for terrorism purposes have been made since 2014. Home Secretary can confiscate the passports of dual-nationality citizens while they are abroad, without recourse to a judge.

The Netherlands
Criminal measures: Prosecution is used to stop individuals leaving for Syria, often on the basis that participation in jihad or jihadi training abroad is a criminal offence. It is illegal to recruit, train or instruct, and efforts to gather resources or intelligence to aid terrorism can result in prosecution.

Non-criminal measures: Surveillance and disruption by intelligence agencies; protection of minors including custody; rescinded residency permits for non-Dutch citizens; cancelled passports; frozen bank accounts; pressure to accept education or employment placements.

Response to returnees: Aim is to prosecute if possible, or to achieve both de-radicalisation and reintegration.

Selected Islamist attacks in Europe

 March 2011 Muslim gunman targets a US Air Force bus parked outside Frankfurt Airport

 March 2012 Three separate shootings target French soldiers and Jewish civilians in Toulouse and Montauban

 May 2013 British soldier is killed outside Royal Artillery barracks in Woolwich, London

 May 2013 French soldiers are attacked by a man in the La Defense suburb of Paris, apparently inspired by the London attack several days earlier

 May 2014 Gunman opens fire at the Jewish Museum of Belgium in Brussels. The perpetrator, a French national called Mehdi Nemmouche, is believed to have spent over a year in Syria. It is the first attack in Europe by a returning foreign fighter

 December 2014 Knife attack at a police station near the city of Tours, central France

 December 2014 A driver runs down pedestrians in Dijon, France. The perpetrator targets citizens at random in five different parts of the city over the space of half an hour

 January 2015 Over three days, three Muslim men carry out the deadliest terrorist attacks in France for over 50 years. Targets include the Paris offices of *Charlie Hebdo*, a satirical magazine, and a kosher supermarket in the city's suburbs

Germany
Criminal measures: Section 129a of the German Penal Code punishes acts deemed as support for, participation in, or the formation of a terrorist organisation. Those with involvement in terrorist training or instruction can also be prosecuted.

Non-criminal measures: A 'travel disruption plan' includes approaching suspected individuals and notifying local authorities, such as the police, about specific cases. German citizens can have passports seized if they pose a threat; non-Germans can be ordered to remain in Germany. Counter-radicalisation schemes and early warning systems have been established.

Response to returnees: Prosecution is a possibility. There is also the Schengen Information System for tracking foreign fighters when they are known to have returned, increased detection capabilities at border posts, and revocation of visas for non-Germans.

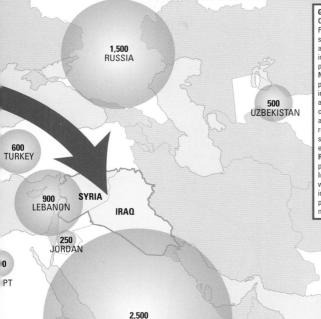

Flows of migrants across the Mediterranean

Poverty, conflict and insecurity are driving migrants from North Africa and the Middle East to seek out new prospects in Europe, travelling across the Mediterranean Sea to reach Spain, Italy, Greece and Malta. Turmoil in Libya has allowed room for criminal smuggling groups to operate more freely. Migrant deaths are frequent, and often unrecorded. The deployment of a new European naval mission, EUNAVFOR MED, is intended not only to save lives, but also to find ways of permanently disrupting smugglers' networks. However, the reasons why migrants embark on such perilous journeys remain unchanged.

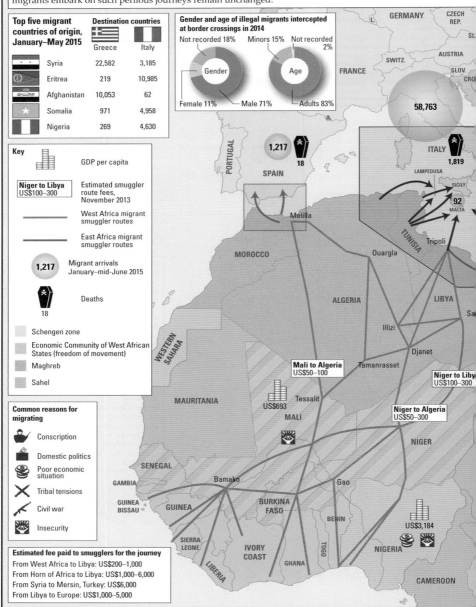

Top five migrant countries of origin, January–May 2015

		Greece	Italy
	Syria	22,582	3,185
	Eritrea	219	10,985
	Afghanistan	10,053	62
	Somalia	971	4,958
	Nigeria	269	4,630

Gender and age of illegal migrants intercepted at border crossings in 2014

Gender: Not recorded 18% — Female 11% — Male 71%

Age: Minors 15%, Not recorded 2% — Adults 83%

Key

GDP per capita

Niger to Libya US$100–300 — Estimated smuggler route fees, November 2013

West Africa migrant smuggler routes

East Africa migrant smuggler routes

1,217 — Migrant arrivals January–mid-June 2015

18 — Deaths

Schengen zone

Economic Community of West African States (freedom of movement)

Maghreb

Sahel

Common reasons for migrating

Conscription

Domestic politics

Poor economic situation

Tribal tensions

Civil war

Insecurity

Estimated fee paid to smugglers for the journey

From West Africa to Libya: US$200–1,000
From Horn of Africa to Libya: US$1,000–6,000
From Syria to Mersin, Turkey: US$6,000
From Libya to Europe: US$1,000–5,000

GERMANY   CZECH REP.
SL
AUSTRIA
SWITZ.   SLOV.
FRANCE   CRO

58,763

PORTUGAL
1,217   18
SPAIN

ITALY   1,819
LAMPEDUSA
SICILY
92   MALTA
TUNISIA   Tripoli
Melilla
MOROCCO   Ouargla

ALGERIA   LIBYA
Illizi
Djanet
Mali to Algeria US$50–100   Tamanrasset   Niger to Liby US$100–300
US$693   Tessalit   Niger to Algeria US$50–300
MALI   NIGER

WESTERN SAHARA
MAURITANIA

SENEGAL
GAMBIA   Bamako   Gao
GUINEA BISSAU   GUINEA   BURKINA FASO
BENIN
SIERRA LEONE   IVORY COAST   TOGO   NIGERIA   US$3,184
LIBERIA   GHANA
CAMEROON

Sources: IISS; Altai Consulting; Atlantic; BBC; Council of the European Union; Economist; European Commission; EUROPOL; FRIDE; Frontex; Global Initiative Against Transnational Organized Crime; Guardian; International Organization for Migration; International Maritime Organization; Independent; International Business Times; New York Times; UNHCR; UN

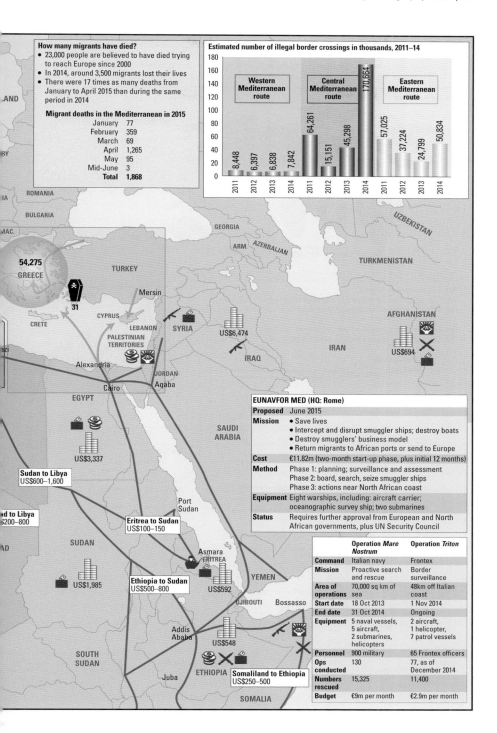

How many migrants have died?
- 23,000 people are believed to have died trying to reach Europe since 2000
- In 2014, around 3,500 migrants lost their lives
- There were 17 times as many deaths from January to April 2015 than during the same period in 2014

Migrant deaths in the Mediterranean in 2015

January	77
February	359
March	69
April	1,265
May	95
Mid-June	3
Total	**1,868**

Estimated number of illegal border crossings in thousands, 2011–14

Western Mediterranean route: 2011: 8,448; 2012: 6,397; 2013: 6,838; 2014: 7,842

Central Mediterranean route: 2011: 64,261; 2012: 15,151; 2013: 45,298; 2014: 170,664

Eastern Mediterranean route: 2011: 57,025; 2012: 37,224; 2013: 24,799; 2014: 50,834

54,275
GREECE
31

Mersin
CYPRUS
CRETE
LEBANON
SYRIA   US$6,474
PALESTINIAN
TERRITORIES
IRAQ
Alexandria
JORDAN
Cairo   Aqaba
EGYPT

AFGHANISTAN
IRAN   US$694

SAUDI ARABIA

US$3,337

Sudan to Libya
US$600–1,600

...d to Libya
...200–800

Port Sudan

Eritrea to Sudan
US$100–150

SUDAN
Asmara
ERITREA
US$1,985
Ethiopia to Sudan
US$500–800   US$592   YEMEN

DJIBOUTI   Bossaso

Addis Ababa   US$548

SOUTH SUDAN

Juba   ETHIOPIA   Somaliland to Ethiopia
US$250–500

SOMALIA

EUNAVFOR MED (HQ: Rome)

Proposed	June 2015
Mission	• Save lives • Intercept and disrupt smuggler ships; destroy boats • Destroy smugglers' business model • Return migrants to African ports or send to Europe
Cost	€11.82m (two-month start-up phase, plus initial 12 months)
Method	Phase 1: planning; surveillance and assessment Phase 2: board, search, seize smuggler ships Phase 3: actions near North African coast
Equipment	Eight warships, including: aircraft carrier; oceanographic survey ship; two submarines
Status	Requires further approval from European and North African governments, plus UN Security Council

	Operation *Mare Nostrum*	Operation *Triton*
Command	Italian navy	Frontex
Mission	Proactive search and rescue	Border surveillance
Area of operations	70,000 sq km of sea	48km off Italian coast
Start date	18 Oct 2013	1 Nov 2014
End date	31 Oct 2014	Ongoing
Equipment	5 naval vessels, 5 aircraft, 2 submarines, helicopters	2 aircraft, 1 helicopter, 7 patrol vessels
Personnel	900 military	65 Frontex officers
Ops conducted	130	77, as of December 2014
Numbers rescued	15,325	11,400
Budget	€9m per month	€2.9m per month

ROMANIA
BULGARIA
MAC.
GEORGIA
ARM. AZERBAIJAN
UZBEKISTAN
TURKMENISTAN
TURKEY

Long road to recovery after West Africa's Ebola outbreak

As of early July 2015, the West African outbreak of Ebola virus disease had claimed the lives of 11,229 in Guinea, Sierra Leone and Liberia. Although the number of new infections has diminished significantly since its peak in 2014, all three governments must overcome severe public-health and economic challenges on the road to recovery.

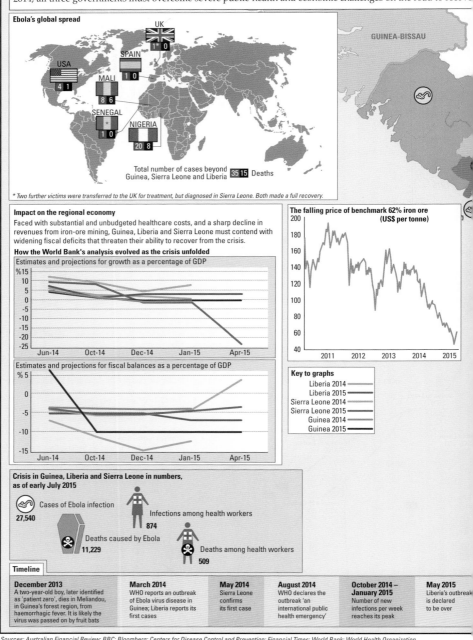

Ebola's global spread

UK
1* 0

SPAIN
1 0

USA
4 1

MALI
8 6

SENEGAL
1 0

NIGERIA
20 8

GUINEA-BISSAU

Total number of cases beyond
Guinea, Sierra Leone and Liberia 35 15 Deaths

* Two further victims were transferred to the UK for treatment, but diagnosed in Sierra Leone. Both made a full recovery.

Impact on the regional economy

Faced with substantial and unbudgeted healthcare costs, and a sharp decline in revenues from iron-ore mining, Guinea, Liberia and Sierra Leone must contend with widening fiscal deficits that threaten their ability to recover from the crisis.

How the World Bank's analysis evolved as the crisis unfolded

Estimates and projections for growth as a percentage of GDP

%15, 10, 5, 0, -5, -10, -15, -20, -25 — Jun-14, Oct-14, Dec-14, Jan-15, Apr-15

Estimates and projections for fiscal balances as a percentage of GDP

%5, 0, -5, -10, -15 — Jun-14, Oct-14, Dec-14, Jan-15, Apr-15

The falling price of benchmark 62% iron ore
(US$ per tonne)

200, 180, 160, 140, 120, 100, 80, 60, 40 — 2011, 2012, 2013, 2014, 2015

Key to graphs
Liberia 2014
Liberia 2015
Sierra Leone 2014
Sierra Leone 2015
Guinea 2014
Guinea 2015

Crisis in Guinea, Liberia and Sierra Leone in numbers,
as of early July 2015

Cases of Ebola infection
27,540

Infections among health workers
874

Deaths caused by Ebola
11,229

Deaths among health workers
509

Timeline

December 2013	March 2014	May 2014	August 2014	October 2014 – January 2015	May 2015
A two-year-old boy, later identified as 'patient zero', dies in Meliandou, in Guinea's forest region, from haemorrhagic fever. It is likely the virus was passed on by fruit bats	WHO reports an outbreak of Ebola virus disease in Guinea; Liberia reports its first cases	Sierra Leone confirms its first case	WHO declares the outbreak 'an international public health emergency'	Number of new infections per week reaches its peak	Liberia's outbreak is declared to be over

Sources: Australian Financial Review; BBC; Bloomberg; Centers for Disease Control and Prevention; Financial Times; World Bank; World Health Organization

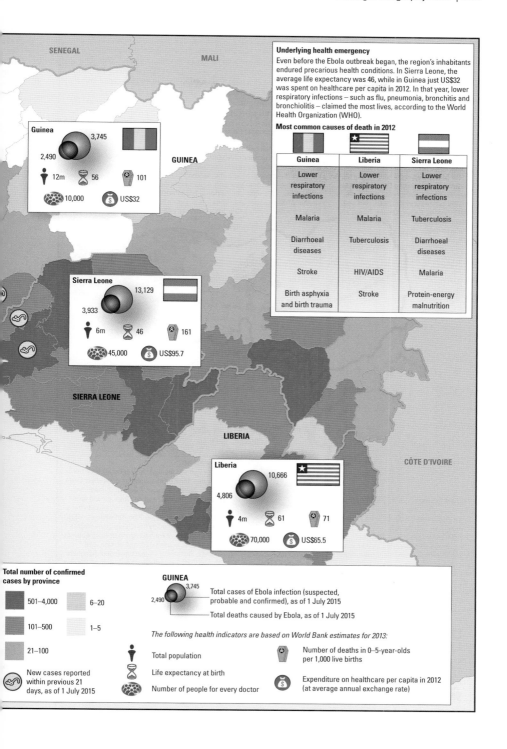

SENEGAL

MALI

GUINEA

Guinea

3,745

2,490

👤 12m   ⌛ 56   ⚰ 101

🦠 10,000   💰 US$32

Underlying health emergency

Even before the Ebola outbreak began, the region's inhabitants endured precarious health conditions. In Sierra Leone, the average life expectancy was 46, while in Guinea just US$32 was spent on healthcare per capita in 2012. In that year, lower respiratory infections – such as flu, pneumonia, bronchitis and bronchiolitis – claimed the most lives, according to the World Health Organization (WHO).

Most common causes of death in 2012

	Guinea	Liberia	Sierra Leone
	Lower respiratory infections	Lower respiratory infections	Lower respiratory infections
	Malaria	Malaria	Tuberculosis
	Diarrhoeal diseases	Tuberculosis	Diarrhoeal diseases
	Stroke	HIV/AIDS	Malaria
	Birth asphyxia and birth trauma	Stroke	Protein-energy malnutrition

Sierra Leone

13,129

3,933

👤 6m   ⌛ 46   ⚰ 161

🦠 45,000   💰 US$95.7

SIERRA LEONE

LIBERIA

CÔTE D'IVOIRE

Liberia

10,666

4,806

👤 4m   ⌛ 61   ⚰ 71

🦠 70,000   💰 US$65.5

Total number of confirmed cases by province

- 501–4,000
- 101–500
- 21–100
- 6–20
- 1–5

〰 New cases reported within previous 21 days, as of 1 July 2015

GUINEA

3,745 — Total cases of Ebola infection (suspected, probable and confirmed), as of 1 July 2015

2,490 — Total deaths caused by Ebola, as of 1 July 2015

The following health indicators are based on World Bank estimates for 2013:

👤 Total population

⌛ Life expectancy at birth

🦠 Number of people for every doctor

⚰ Number of deaths in 0–5-year-olds per 1,000 live births

💰 Expenditure on healthcare per capita in 2012 (at average annual exchange rate)

Challenges facing Nigeria's new president

Nigerian President Muhammadu Buhari faces Boko Haram rebels and many other difficulties, having taken the reins of Africa's most populous nation and largest economy in May 2015. The Islamist insurgency waged by Boko Haram in the country's poor northeast flared under Buhari's predecessor, Goodluck Jonathan, a Christian from the south. Buhari, a Muslim northerner and ex-military ruler, has vowed to step up efforts against the group. He must also tackle corruption, recurring petrol shortages at the pumps, and communal violence across the 'Middle Belt' – all while diversifying the economy, avoiding renewed unrest in the southern oil-producing Niger Delta and convincing a young population impatient for change that he can lead democratically.

Communal violence
Hundreds have been killed in the latest round of inter-communal violence between Fulani cattle herders and Christian villagers in the Middle Belt of the country. The Muslim Fulani have long battled Christian farmers over land and grazing rights, with earlier violent outbreaks in 2001, 2004, 2008 and 2010. Plateau, Benue, Kaduna, Taraba and Nasarawa states suffered deadly attacks in 2014–15.

Boko Haram
Despite a last-ditch military onslaught by the Jonathan government, Boko Haram remains one of Nigeria's most serious challenges. Not only did it declare allegiance to ISIS this year, but the group also advanced into more Nigerian towns and villages, and increasingly targeted neighbouring Chad and Cameroon. According to the most reliable calculations, 5,000–7,000 people died in Boko Haram violence in 2014; another 2,000 may have been killed in and around Baga in early 2015. Some 1.5 million civilians have been displaced by the insurgency.

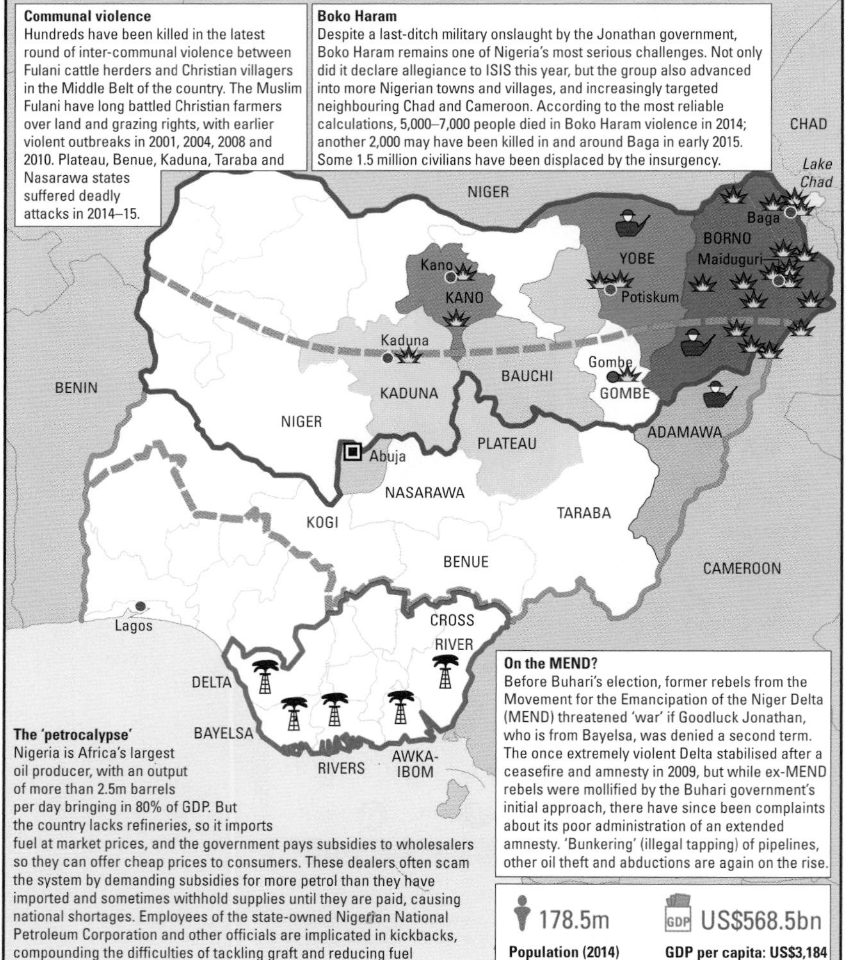

The 'petrocalypse'
Nigeria is Africa's largest oil producer, with an output of more than 2.5m barrels per day bringing in 80% of GDP. But the country lacks refineries, so it imports fuel at market prices, and the government pays subsidies to wholesalers so they can offer cheap prices to consumers. These dealers often scam the system by demanding subsidies for more petrol than they have imported and sometimes withhold supplies until they are paid, causing national shortages. Employees of the state-owned Nigerian National Petroleum Corporation and other officials are implicated in kickbacks, compounding the difficulties of tackling graft and reducing fuel subsidies.

On the MEND?
Before Buhari's election, former rebels from the Movement for the Emancipation of the Niger Delta (MEND) threatened 'war' if Goodluck Jonathan, who is from Bayelsa, was denied a second term. The once extremely violent Delta stabilised after a ceasefire and amnesty in 2009, but while ex-MEND rebels were mollified by the Buhari government's initial approach, there have since been complaints about its poor administration of an extended amnesty. 'Bunkering' (illegal tapping) of pipelines, other oil theft and abductions are again on the rise.

178.5m Population (2014)		**GDP US$568.5bn** GDP per capita: US$3,184
18.2 years Median age		**46%** Living in poverty
	38% Youth under- and unemployment	**136/175** Global corruption ranking (2014)

Legend:
- Under Sharia law
- MEND stronghold
- The Middle Belt
- Top oil-producing states
- State of emergency (in force since 2013)
- Major Boko Haram attacks (mid-2014 to mid-2015)

Number of deaths in the course of the Boko Haram insurgency (2009–14): >4,000 | 501–1,000 | 401–500 | 201–300 | 101–200

Map labels: CHAD, Lake Chad, NIGER, Baga, BORNO, YOBE, Maiduguri, Kano, KANO, Potiskum, Kaduna, KADUNA, BAUCHI, Gombe, GOMBE, BENIN, NIGER, PLATEAU, ADAMAWA, Abuja, NASARAWA, TARABA, KOGI, BENUE, CAMEROON, Lagos, CROSS RIVER, DELTA, BAYELSA, RIVERS, AWKA-IBOM

Sources: IISS; Armed Conflict Location & Event Data Project; BBC; CIA World Factbook; Guardian; IHS Jane's; Transparency International; United Nations; US State Department; World Bank

Libya divided

Two regionally backed coalitions are fighting for legitimacy and territorial control in Libya. This has resulted in the collapse of authority, disruptions to oil production, a humanitarian crisis, increased human trafficking and allowed ISIS to gain a foothold. UN-led peace efforts have so far failed to bring the two coalitions closer.

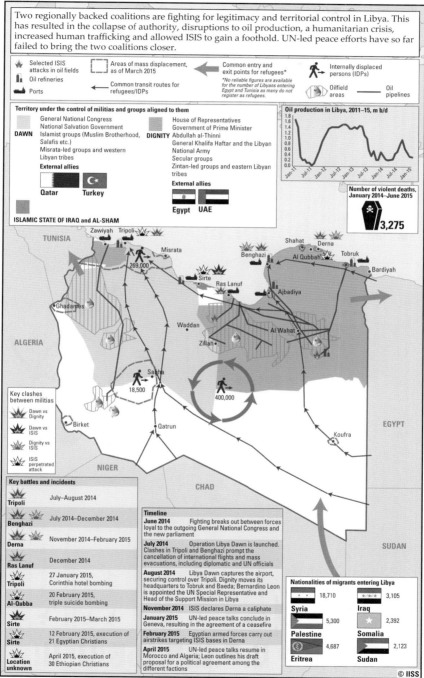

Sources: IISS; Internal Displacement Monitoring Centre; libyabodycount.org; UNHCR

Yemen in the grip of Houthi insurgency

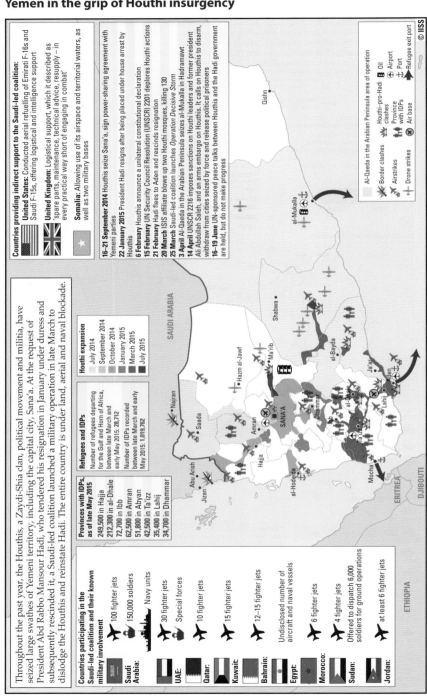

Throughout the past year, the Houthis, a Zaydi-Shia clan, political movement and militia, have seized large swathes of Yemeni territory, including the capital city, Sana'a. At the request of President Abd Rabbo Mansour Hadi, who tendered his resignation in January under duress and subsequently rescinded it, a Saudi-led coalition launched a military operation in late March to dislodge the Houthis and reinstate Hadi. The entire country is under land, aerial and naval blockade.

Countries participating in the Saudi-led coalition and their known military involvement

Saudi Arabia: 100 fighter jets; 150,000 soldiers; Navy units

UAE: 30 fighter jets; Special forces

Qatar: 10 fighter jets

Kuwait: 15 fighter jets

Bahrain: 12–15 fighter jets

Egypt: Undisclosed number of aircraft and naval vessels

Morocco: 6 fighter jets

Sudan: 4 fighter jets; Offered to dispatch 6,000 soldiers for ground operations

Jordan: at least 6 fighter jets

Provinces with IDPs, as of late May 2015
249,500 in Hajja
212,300 in al-Dhale
72,700 in Ibb
62,500 in Amran
51,800 in Abyan
42,500 in Ta'izz
35,400 in Lahij
34,700 in Dhammar

Refugees and IDPs
Number of refugees departing for the Gulf and Horn of Africa, between late March and early May 2015: 28,712
Number of IDPs recorded between late March and early May 2015: 1,019,762

Houthi expansion
July 2014
September 2014
October 2014
January 2015
March 2015
July 2015

Countries providing indirect support to the Saudi-led coalition:

United States: Conducted aerial refuelling of Emirati F-16s and Saudi F-15s, offering logistical and intelligence support

United Kingdom: Logistical support, which it described as 'spare parts, maintenance, technical advice, resupply – in every practical way short of engaging in combat'

Somalia: Allowing use of its airspace and territorial waters, as well as two military bases

16–21 September 2014 Houthis seize Sana'a, sign power-sharing agreement with Yemeni parties

22 January 2015 President Hadi resigns after being placed under house arrest by Houthis

6 February Houthis announce a unilateral constitutional declaration

15 February UN Security Council Resolution (UNSCR) 2201 deplores Houthi actions

21 February Hadi flees to Aden and rescinds resignation

20 March ISIS affiliate blows up two Houthi mosques, killing 130

25 March Saudi-led coalition launches *Operation Decisive Storm*

3 April Al-Qaeda in the Arabian Peninsula seizes al-Mukalla in Hadramawt

14 April UNSCR 2216 imposes sanctions on Houthi leaders and former president Ali Abdullah Saleh, and an arms embargo on Houthis. It calls on Houthis to disarm, withdraw from cities seized by force and release political prisoners

16–19 June UN-sponsored peace talks between Houthis and the Hadi government are held, but do not make progress

Al-Qaeda in the Arabian Peninsula area of operation
Houthi-pro-Hadi clashes
Border clashes
Airstrikes
Drone strikes
Province with IDPs
Air base
Oil
Airport
Port
Refugee exit port

© IISS

Sources: IISS; Bureau of Investigative Journalism; UNOCHA; WHO

Expansion of Iraq's Kurdish Regional Government

Although the Iraqi Kurdistan Regional Government's (KRG) military, known as the Peshmerga, has played a pivotal role in the fight against ISIS, Erbil has also taken advantage of the crisis to expand the size of the territory it controls by as much as 40%. The KRG has presided over a period of substantial economic growth thanks to the region's oil reserves, but it remains to be seen what impact its unilateral expansion into more ethnically diverse territory will have on future regional stability.

An estimated 50,000 members of the minority Yazidi sect fled to Mount Sinjar in August 2014 as ISIS forces seized control of the city of Sinjar. In response, the United States launched airstrikes against ISIS positions, while the Peshmerga played an instrumental role in breaking the siege on the ground.

Kurdistan Regional Government

5.2   US$23.6bn

Deployment of the Peshmerga to Kobane
In late October 2014, the Turkish government agreed to allow 200 Kurdish Peshmerga fighters to enter the besieged town of Kobane via its border. The Peshmerga deployed by air, landing in the Turkish town of Sanifula, and on the ground, travelling from Erbil and passing through Suruc, Turkey, from where they could access Kobane via the Mursitpinar border crossing.

Make-up of the Peshmerga
A predominantly light-infantry force, comprising at least 80,000 fighters, but it could in fact be three times as large. It has limited access to heavy weapons, but its inventory does include a number of main battle tanks, armoured personnel carriers and artillery systems acquired primarily from within Iraq. Recent international military assistance has provided training to counter ISIS forces; it has also acquired new equipment, including modern anti-armour weapons.

TURKEY 18%

Mursitpinar border crossing

Kobane

SYRIA 7–10%

Sinjar

Dohuk
Nineva
Mosul
Makhmour

Erbil

Sulaimaniya

Kirkuk

IRAN 10%

IRAQ 15–20%

Kermanshah

With an estimated 45 billion barrels of oil reserves, and production targets for 2015 projected at 750,000 barrels per day, Kurdistan is emerging as an important international energy supplier. This oil boom has enabled the KRG to become one of the fastest-growing economies in the world.

Baghdad

28%	Population surge in Iraqi Kurdistan as a result of conflict in wider Iraq and Syria
US$1.4bn	World Bank estimate of how much it will cost to stabilise Iraqi Kurdistan following the influx
5%	Percentage points by which economic growth in Iraq has contracted

Internally displaced persons

Kirkuk 370,986

Dohuk 445,164

Erbil 253,158

Nineva 192,312

Sulaimaniya 174,066

Pre-2014 KRG territory	Oil field
De facto KRG territory	Supergiant oil field
Predominantly Kurdish areas	Oil refinery
15-20% Percentage of national population represented by Kurds	Planned oil refinery
Population, in millions	Oil pipeline
	Planned oil pipeline
Gross domestic product in 2011	Gas pipeline
	Planned gas pipeline
	Internally displaced persons

© IISS

Sources: IISS; BBC; CIA World Factbook; Daily Telegraph; Economist; IHS Global Insight; International Organization for Migration; Invest in Group; Kurdistan Regional Government; NPR; pietervanostaeyen.wordpress.com; World Bank

Syria and Iraq: increasing complexity of crises

The Syrian civil war and Iraqi crisis grew in complexity from June 2014 onwards, with the expansion of ISIS forcing a United States-led military intervention against the militant group. The Iraqi government struggled to rebuild its forces to counter ISIS, and Syrian rebel coalitions formed to better challenge the Assad regime. The anti-ISIS coalition included Arab nations and focused on airstrikes and training, while Iran provided support to Kurdish, Iraqi and militia forces. ISIS suffered setbacks in Iraq and Syria, but seized Ramadi in Iraq and Palmyra in Syria in May 2015.

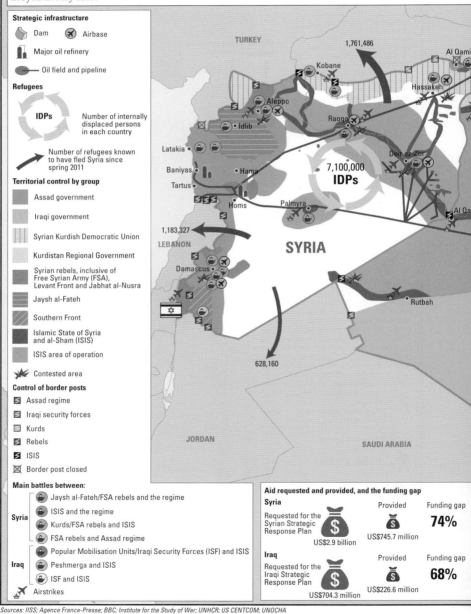

Strategic infrastructure

- Dam
- Airbase
- Major oil refinery
- Oil field and pipeline

Refugees

IDPs — Number of internally displaced persons in each country

Number of refugees known to have fled Syria since spring 2011

Territorial control by group

- Assad government
- Iraqi government
- Syrian Kurdish Democratic Union
- Kurdistan Regional Government
- Syrian rebels, inclusive of Free Syrian Army (FSA), Levant Front and Jabhat al-Nusra
- Jaysh al-Fateh
- Southern Front
- Islamic State of Syria and al-Sham (ISIS)
- ISIS area of operation
- Contested area

Control of border posts

- Assad regime
- Iraqi security forces
- Kurds
- Rebels
- ISIS
- Border post closed

Main battles between:

Syria
- Jaysh al-Fateh/FSA rebels and the regime
- ISIS and the regime
- Kurds/FSA rebels and ISIS
- FSA rebels and Assad regime

Iraq
- Popular Mobilisation Units/Iraqi Security Forces (ISF) and ISIS
- Peshmerga and ISIS
- ISF and ISIS

- Airstrikes

Aid requested and provided, and the funding gap

Syria
Requested for the Syrian Strategic Response Plan
US$2.9 billion
Provided: US$745.7 million
Funding gap: **74%**

Iraq
Requested for the Iraqi Strategic Response Plan
US$704.3 million
Provided: US$226.6 million
Funding gap: **68%**

TURKEY — 1,761,486

Al Qami
Kobane
Hassakeh
Aleppo
Raqqa
Idlib
Latakia
Deir ez-Zor
Baniyas
7,100,000 IDPs
Tartus
Hama
Homs
Palmyra
Al Qa
1,183,327
LEBANON
SYRIA
Damascus
Rutbah
628,160
JORDAN
SAUDI ARABIA

Sources: IISS; Agence France-Presse; BBC; Institute for the Study of War; UNHCR; US CENTCOM; UNOCHA

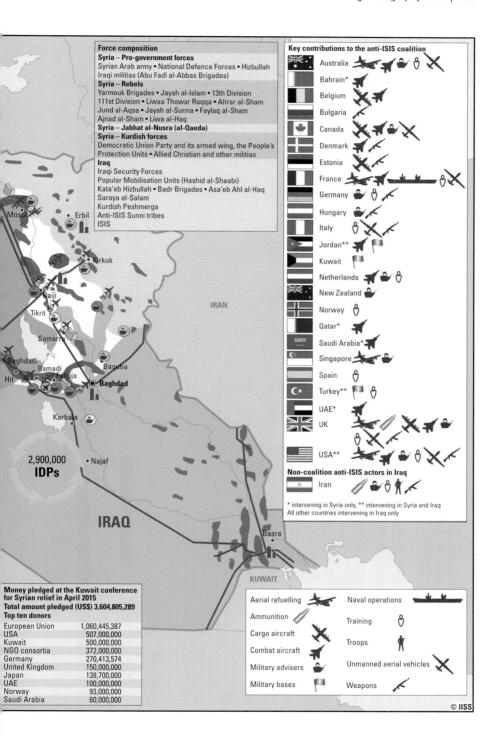

Force composition

Syria – Pro-government forces
Syrian Arab army • National Defence Forces • Hizbullah
Iraqi militias (Abu Fadl al-Abbas Brigades)

Syria – Rebels
Yarmouk Brigades • Jaysh al-Islam • 13th Division
111st Division • Liwaa Thowar Raqqa • Ahrar al-Sham
Jund al-Aqsa • Jaysh al-Sunna • Faylaq al-Sham
Ajnad al-Sham • Liwa al-Haq

Syria – Jabhat al-Nusra (al-Qaeda)

Syria – Kurdish forces
Democratic Union Party and its armed wing, the People's
Protection Units • Allied Christian and other militias

Iraq
Iraqi Security Forces
Popular Mobilisation Units (Hashid al-Shaabi)
Kata'eb Hizbullah • Badr Brigades • Asa'eb Ahl al-Haq
Saraya al-Salam
Kurdish Peshmerga
Anti-ISIS Sunni tribes
ISIS

Mosul
Erbil
Kirkuk
Baiji
Tikrit
Samarra
IRAN
Al-Baghdadi
Ramadi Baquba
Hit Falluja
Baghdad
Karbala

2,900,000
IDPs

Najaf

IRAQ

Basra

KUWAIT

Key contributions to the anti-ISIS coalition

Australia
Bahrain*
Belgium
Bulgaria
Canada
Denmark
Estonia
France
Germany
Hungary
Italy
Jordan**
Kuwait
Netherlands
New Zealand
Norway
Qatar*
Saudi Arabia*
Singapore
Spain
Turkey**
UAE*
UK

USA**

Non-coalition anti-ISIS actors in Iraq
Iran

* intervening in Syria only, ** intervening in Syria and Iraq
All other countries intervening in Iraq only

Money pledged at the Kuwait conference
for Syrian relief in April 2015
Total amount pledged (US$) 3,604,805,289
Top ten donors

European Union	1,060,445,387
USA	507,000,000
Kuwait	500,000,000
NGO consortia	372,000,000
Germany	270,413,574
United Kingdom	150,000,000
Japan	138,700,000
UAE	100,000,000
Norway	93,000,000
Saudi Arabia	60,000,000

Aerial refuelling		Naval operations	
Ammunition		Training	
Cargo aircraft			
Combat aircraft		Troops	
Military advisers		Unmanned aerial vehicles	
Military bases		Weapons	

© IISS

Improved US relations hold promise for Havana

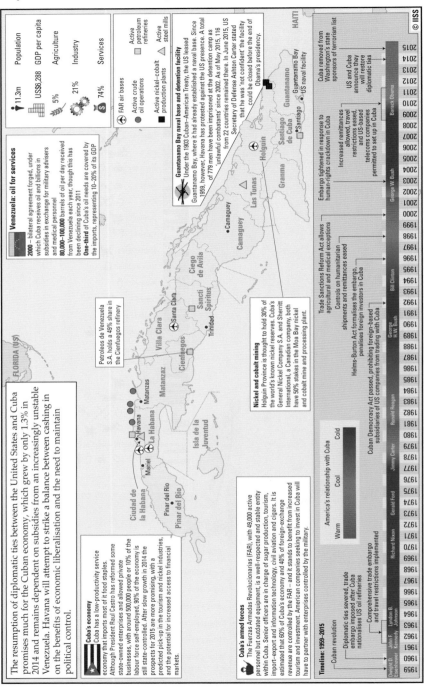

The resumption of diplomatic ties between the United States and Cuba promises much for the Cuban economy, which grew by only 1.3% in 2014 and remains dependent on subsidies from an increasingly unstable Venezuela. Havana will attempt to strike a balance between cashing in on the benefits of economic liberalisation and the need to maintain political control.

Cuba's economy

Cuba has a low-productivity service economy that imports most of it food staples. Although President Raul Castro has reformed some state-owned enterprises and allowed private businesses, with around 500,000 people or 10% of the labour force self-employed, 90% of the economy is still state-controlled. After slow growth in 2014 the prospects for 2015 are more promising, with a predicted pick-up in the tourism and nickel industries, and the potential for increased access to financial markets.

Cuba's armed forces

The Fuerzas Armadas Revolucionarias (FAR), with 49,000 active personnel but outdated equipment, is a well-respected and stable entity within Cuba. Senior officers are in charge of sugar production, tourism, import–export and information technology, civil aviation and cigars. It is estimated that 60% of Cuba's economy and 40% of foreign-exchange revenue are controlled by the FAR – and it stands to benefit from increased tourism and investment. American companies seeking to invest in Cuba will have to partner with enterprises controlled by the military.

Venezuela: oil for services

2000 – bilateral agreement forged, under which Cuba receives oil and billions in subsidies in exchange for military advisers and medical personnel.

80,000–100,000 barrels of oil per day received from Venezuela each year, though this has been declining since 2011

One-third of Cuba's oil needs are covered by the imports, representing 10–20% of its GDP

Population 11.3m

GDP per capita US$6,288

Agriculture 5%

Industry 21%

Services 74%

FAR air bases

Active crude oil operations

Active nickel–cobalt production plants

Active petroleum refineries

Active steel mills

Guantanamo Bay naval base and detention facility

Under the 1903 Cuban–American Treaty, the US leased Guantanamo Bay, where it had already established a naval base. Since 1959, however, Havana has protested against the US presence. A total of 779 men have been imprisoned at the detention camp as 'unlawful combatants' since 2002. As of May 2015, 116 from 22 countries remained there. In June 2015, US Secretary of Defense Ashton Carter stated that he was 'not confident' the facility could be closed before the end of Obama's presidency.

Petroleos de Venezuela S.A. holds a 49% share in the Cienfuegos refinery

Nickel and cobalt mining

Holguin Province is thought to hold 30% of the world's known nickel reserves. Cuba's General Nickel Company S.A. and Sherritt International, a Canadian company, both have 50% stakes in the Moa Bay nickel and cobalt mine and processing plant.

Timeline: 1959–2015

America's relationship with Cuba

Warm | Cool | Cold

Cuban revolution

Diplomatic ties severed, trade embargo imposed after Cuba nationalises US oil refineries

Comprehensive trade embargo and travel restrictions implemented

Cuban Democracy Act passed, prohibiting foreign-based subsidiaries of US companies from trading with Cuba

Helms–Burton Act formalises the embargo, penalises foreign investors in Cuba

Trade Sanctions Reform Act allows agricultural and medical exceptions

Controls on humanitarian shipments and remittances eased

Embargo tightened in response to human-rights crackdown in Cuba

Increased remittances allowed, travel restrictions eased, and US-based telecoms companies permitted to set up in Cuba

US and Cuba announce they will restore diplomatic ties

Cuba removed from Washington's state sponsors of terrorism list

Dwight D. Eisenhower | John F. Kennedy | Lyndon B. Johnson | Richard Nixon | Gerald Ford | Jimmy Carter | Ronald Reagan | George H.W. Bush | Bill Clinton | George W. Bush | Barack Obama

1959 1960 1961 1962 1963 1964 1965 1966 1967 1968 1969 1970 1971 1972 1973 1974 1975 1976 1977 1978 1979 1980 1981 1982 1983 1984 1985 1986 1987 1988 1989 1990 1991 1992 1993 1994 1995 1996 1997 1998 1999 2000 2001 2002 2003 2004 2005 2006 2007 2008 2009 2010 2011 2012 2013 2014 2015

FLORIDA (US)

Ciudad de la Habana

Mariel · Havana · La Habana · Matanzas

Pinar del Rio

Isla de la Juventud

Cienfuegos

Villa Clara · Santa Clara

Sancti Spiritus · Trinidad

Ciego de Avila

Camaguey

Las Tunas

Granma

Holguin

Santiago de Cuba · Santiago

Guantanamo · Guantanamo Bay · US naval facility

HAITI

© IISS

Sources: IISS; American Civil Liberties Union; Brookings Institution; Economist Intelligence Unit; Petersen Institute of International Economics; Politico; US Geological Survey; USITC; Wall Street Journal; World Affairs Journal

Chapter 7

Russia and Eurasia

The Ukraine crisis continued to transform Russia and Eurasia in the year to mid-2015. The conflict in Ukraine's east went through several peaks of escalation, creating devastation on the ground in the Donetsk Basin area (called Donbas) and raising tensions in the international system. The situation remained highly unstable, with frequent ceasefire violations and a largely moribund political process. Although the outcome of the conflict is unpredictable, it is certain that the effects of the crisis will shape the region for many years to come.

The conflict in Ukraine has shaken the relationship between Russia and the West to its core. As the West heightened pressure on Moscow through economic sanctions, ties deteriorated to levels of antagonism not seen since the early 1980s. Indeed, the effects of this rivalry now extend far beyond Ukraine, justifying talk of a new Cold War. A continuing series of close calls between Russian military planes and Western civilian and military aircraft paralleled emerging diplomatic clashes, such as Moscow's decision not to participate in the US-led Nuclear Security Summit process. US President Barack Obama and other NATO leaders have sought to strike a balance between the imperative of responding to Russian actions and the equally important need to avoid an all-out confrontation with Moscow. 'It's not a new Cold War', Obama said in July 2014, 'it is a very specific issue related to Russia's unwillingness to recognise that Ukraine can chart its own path.'

Yet such statements did little to stop the escalatory spiral. In part, a classic security dilemma was unfolding, whereby defensive steps taken by one side (for example, NATO reassurance measures in Eastern Europe) are perceived by the other as a security threat. But rhetoric emanating from Moscow suggested that the Kremlin had abandoned the strategic goal of integrating with the West, since integration was impossible on terms the Russian leadership could accept. Instead, Moscow focused on strengthening its integration efforts in post-Soviet Eurasia, deepening strategic ties with China and minimising Western influence within Russia.

At home, that meant increasing controls on media and non-governmental organisations, and selective repression of prominent opposition figures. It also meant virulent rhetoric on the three state-controlled television channels, which portrayed opponents of the Kremlin as traitors, the Ukrainian government as a 'fascist junta' and the West as innately hostile to Russia. In this toxic environment, Boris Nemtsov, an opposition leader and former deputy prime minister, was gunned down just outside the walls of the Kremlin. His assassins appeared to be linked to the administration of Ramzan Kadyrov, leader of the Chechen Republic. If so, it would seem that Kadyrov acted without first receiving approval from the Russian leadership, reflecting both weak federal control and the increasingly wilful and defiant behaviour of the Chechen strongman.

Early gains by the Ukrainian army

Although a succession of ceasefires allowed for periods of respite in the Ukraine conflict, both government and Russian-backed separatist forces entrenched their positions, setting the stage for a protracted war. As of mid-2015, the conflict-resolution process teetered on the verge of collapse.

Following his inauguration as president of Ukraine, Petro Poroshenko declared a seven-day ceasefire on 20 June 2014, halting the government's so-called 'anti-terrorist operation' against separatists in the east. During the ceasefire, government forces and separatists from the self-styled Donetsk and Lugansk 'People's Republics' (DNR and LNR respectively) often accused one another of violating the agreement, with both sides reporting casualties. After the end of the ceasefire, which was extended to 30 June, violence rapidly escalated. Buoyed by volunteer battalions, government

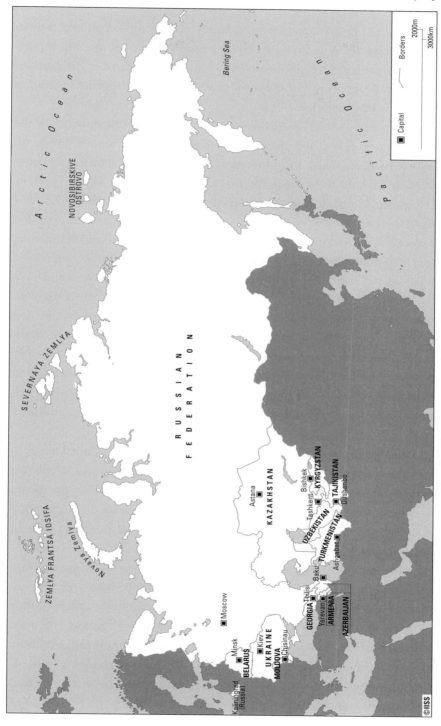

©IISS

forces began to achieve tactical victories against the separatists, whom they outnumbered and outgunned by a wide margin. Meanwhile, reports began to surface of overt Russian involvement in the conflict. Russian servicemen allegedly crossed the border into Ukraine, training the separatists and delivering materiel.

On 17 July, Malaysia Airlines flight MH17 was shot down over the Donetsk region as it flew from Amsterdam to Kuala Lumpur, killing all 298 civilians on board, including 193 Dutch citizens. The incident further internationalised the conflict. Ukraine and the West blamed Russia and the separatists, claiming that the plane was downed by a Russian 9K37 *Buk* (NATO designator: SA-11 *Gadfly*) surface-to-air missile system operated in rebel-held territory. Moscow and the separatists blamed Kiev, alleging that a Ukrainian military jet was responsible. Western outrage intensified when Russia seemed to be obstructing access to the crash site. The Dutch Safety Board, the organisation coordinating the international investigation of the crash, released its initial report on the event on 9 September, stating that the plane broke apart in the air after being hit by a burst of 'high-energy objects from outside the aircraft'. The investigators subsequently issued a call for evidence that suggested they believed the tragedy had been caused by a 9K37 *Buk* that had been brought into separatist-held territory from Russia. The final report was due to be published in autumn 2015.

Ukrainian government forces recaptured separatist-controlled territory throughout July – beginning with Slovyansk, a city around 90 kilometres north of Donetsk city – and slowly moved south and east. But the tactics they used seemed unsuited to winning the hearts and minds of a population that had been deeply alienated by the change of power in Kiev in February. Government forces employed Soviet counter-insurgency tactics, pummelling cities with long-range unguided munitions before sending in shock brigades for clean-up operations. During the course of the conflict, the Ukrainian side targeted heavily populated areas with long-range artillery, mortars, BM-21 *Grad* multiple-launch rocket systems and even 9M79-1 *Tochka-U* (NATO designator: SS-21 *Scarab-B*) short-range ballistic missiles. Human Rights Watch documented the use of cluster munitions, while Amnesty International chronicled human-rights abuses perpetrated by pro-Kiev volunteer battalions in 'liberated' areas.

Separatist counter-offensive

In late August, just as the separatist forces seemed on the verge of defeat, Russia intervened far more directly. With heavy backing from Moscow, the separatists launched a counter-offensive, moving south and capturing towns and cities towards the Sea of Azov. The Ukrainian military suffered a crushing defeat in the town of Ilovaisk, when its servicemen were encircled by forces armed with advanced weaponry, widely assumed to be Russian regulars. It was reported that more than 360 Ukrainian servicemen were killed, while around 180 went missing.

The counter-offensive was intended to demonstrate to Kiev that an outright military victory over the separatists would be impossible. Indeed, these defeats drove the Ukrainian government to the negotiating table. Russian President Vladimir Putin unveiled a draft plan to end the conflict at a press conference in Mongolia on 3 September. The seven-point plan foreshadowed the negotiations that were to come a few days later. Putin and Poroshenko spoke during a series of phone calls, reaching a mutual understanding on key requirements for peace before allowing the details to be formalised by the Trilateral Contact Group (TCG), comprised of representatives from Russia, Ukraine and the Organisation for Security and Co-operation in Europe (OSCE).

On 5 September, the TCG met in Minsk, where its members signed a 12-point protocol for de-escalating the conflict. The agreement called for, inter alia, an immediate bilateral ceasefire; monitoring by the OSCE; the decentralisation of power within Ukraine, including a law on 'special status' for rebel-held areas of the Donetsk and Lugansk regions; a permanent OSCE presence along the Ukraine–Russia border, with an established security zone; the release of all hostages; an amnesty law for combatants; early local elections for the rebel-held areas of Donetsk and Lugansk; and the withdrawal of illegal armed groups and equipment.

Despite declarations from the Ukrainian government and separatist leaders that they would abide by the ceasefire, fighting continued, albeit at lower levels, throughout the conflict zone. In this context, the TCG met again in Minsk on 19–20 September. During this new round of negotiations, the group hammered out a more detailed plan intended to facilitate implementation of the ceasefire. The resulting memorandum included the following stipulations: a renewed commitment to the ceasefire by both sides; the creation of a Line of Contact (LoC), determined by the sides' positions on 19 September; an end to the use of all types of weapons and offensive operations; and the withdrawal, within 24 hours, of all weapons with a calibre of more than 100 millimetres to at least 15km away from the Line of Contact, in order to create a 30km buffer zone.

Although the provisions of the Minsk Protocol and Memorandum were only partially implemented, they prompted a sharp decline in violence: the United Nations reported 331 deaths in the month following the 5 September ceasefire, compared to around 756 fatalities, or 42 people per day, in the 18 days before the agreement was signed. In addition, hundreds of prisoners were exchanged. Nonetheless, heavy fighting continued in key areas, such as Donetsk airport (located 10km northwest of Donetsk city). Additionally, both sides used the respite to reinforce their positions on the front lines.

On 16 September, Ukraine's parliament passed a law designed to introduce a special form of self-rule in the separatist-held areas of Donetsk and Lugansk, as stipulated in the Minsk Protocol. It also passed a limited amnesty, offering immunity to separatists who released hostages, turned over their weapons and vacated occupied buildings within one month of the legislation's enactment – conditions that made the law practically meaningless. The special-status law called for local elections to be held on 7 December 2014. However, in open defiance of the measure, the DNR and LNR held a vote on 2 November. A top Putin aide stated that Moscow 'respected but did not recognise' the ballot, while Kiev and the West denounced the vote, noting the Minsk Protocol provision that it should take place in accordance with Ukrainian law. At a meeting with visiting foreign experts in October, Putin claimed that there had been an understanding that the vote would be held by 3 November and that the Ukrainian authorities had decided on 7 December 'without consulting anyone'. Yet even if there had been such an understanding, the violation of the protocol was clear. Regardless of their legality, the elections demonstrated to residents of separatist-held areas the degree to which the Ukrainian central government had lost control of governance there. In response to the early vote, Poroshenko threatened to abolish the special-status law. As a result, tensions increased significantly within Ukraine and internationally.

Minsk II

Following a meeting between the leaders of Ukraine, Germany, France and Russia on 12–13 February 2015, the parties to the Ukraine conflict agreed to:

- A ceasefire that would begin at midnight on 15 February.
- The creation of a buffer zone through both sides' removal of all heavy weaponry. Initiated no later than the second day after the ceasefire began and completed within 14 days, the zone was to be at least 50km wide for artillery with a calibre of 100mm or more; 70km for most multiple-launch rocket systems; and 140km for the tactical-missile systems 9A52-4 *Tornado-S*, 9K57 *Uragan*, 9A52-2 *Smerch* and *Tochka-U*.
- Negotiations after the withdrawal on conducting local elections in separatist-controlled areas, which would be carried out on mutually agreed terms, reflected in Ukrainian law and monitored by the OSCE.
- Amnesty for all combatants.
- Release of all hostages.
- Unlimited access to conflict areas for humanitarian aid.
- Full restoration of Ukraine's social safety net in the east, including pension payments and the banking system.
- Reform of the Ukrainian constitution by the end of 2015, the key element of which was the decentralisation agreed to in consultation with the separatists.
- Return of control of the Russia–Ukraine border to Kiev after reform of the constitution.
- Withdrawal of all foreign armed groups, military equipment and mercenaries from conflict areas.

A footnote detailed the authorities that would be charged with the administration of separatist-held areas. These authorities would have the power to, inter alia, appoint prosecutors and judges, and form 'people's militias' to maintain public order.

On 9 December, Kiev and the separatists agreed to suspend combat operations indefinitely, under what was termed a 'silence regime'. According to reports by the OSCE Special Monitoring Mission (SMM), in the following days no major ceasefire violations were recorded by the Joint Centre for Control and Coordination (JCCC), a monitoring body that had been quietly launched in October and was staffed by officers of the Russian and Ukrainian militaries. This began a period of diminished violence that lasted until early January 2015. Nonetheless, despite the work of the JCCC, the demarcation of the LoC was not finalised, and hence the sides did not implement the 30km buffer zone stipulated in the Minsk Memorandum. Reports also continued to surface of Russian military personnel and equipment in Ukraine.

While the silence regime tamped down the violence for a short time, fighting escalated in the new year. Backed by what seemed to be a second direct Russian intervention, as reports surfaced of additional Russian troops and materiel entering the region, the separatists began pushing government troops into retreat. The forces of the DNR advanced in the vicinity of Donetsk city, pushing northwest towards the airport and southwest towards the village of Bugas, while LNR forces seized additional territory along the northern flank of the LoC. Donetsk airport fell to separatist forces on 22 January. By February, the rebels had gained control over 300 square kilometres of additional territory. They also shelled Mariupol and Kramatorsk, cities well within government-controlled territory.

Flawed peace deal

In a bid to end this renewed violence and prevent a broader war, German Chancellor Angela Merkel and French President François Hollande travelled to Kiev and then Moscow on 5–6 February, meeting with the Ukrainian and Russian presidents to pave the way for new talks. The four leaders agreed to meet in Minsk on 11 February, in parallel with a meeting between the TCG and separatist representatives. And on 12 February, after 16 hours of negotiations, they finalised a set of 'implementing measures' intended to revive the principles of the original Minsk Protocol.

The new document, commonly referred to as Minsk II (see box for details), definitively placed Ukrainian domestic political compromise at the centre of the negotiation process. Furthermore, the agreement was much more specific than the September protocol and memorandum about how to sequence the provisions; in particular, Russia did not have to cede control of the border until Ukraine reformed its constitution. In these respects, Minsk II included significant gains for Russia and major concessions from Ukraine.

Regardless of which side it benefited most, Minsk II had serious shortcomings. Firstly, the parties did not agree on an official armistice line, only demarcations from which heavy weaponry was to be withdrawn. Secondly, there was no effective means to enforce the ceasefire and withdrawal provisions. The SMM was, by design, not a formal peacekeeping or humanitarian mission, in contrast to analogous initiatives in other conflict zones. The group's mandate was limited to monitoring and reporting on security and human rights, as well as facilitating dialogue. Staffed by unarmed civilians rather than uniformed military personnel, it was unable to intervene to ensure compliance by either side.

Another flaw in Minsk II related to the feasibility of its political compromise. In the short term, Poroshenko needed to surmount domestic opposition to a deal that, if fully implemented, would require Kiev to make significant political concessions to the separatists. In the medium-to-long term, the political settlement needed to function. If enacted as written, Minsk II would essentially transform Ukraine into an asymmetric confederation, requiring Kiev to participate in a continuous bargaining process whereby Russophile regions – which comprise a small fraction of the country – had significant powers of self-rule, while the rest of the country continued to be ruled by Kiev.

These shortcomings began to manifest themselves almost immediately. The lack of an armistice line exacerbated conflict over strategically significant points along the LoC, as was demonstrated most clearly by the battle for Debaltsevo. A transportation hub between Donetsk and Lugansk cities, Debaltsevo was originally captured by the separatists in April 2014, before being recaptured by Ukrainian forces the following July. At the end of 2014, the town and its surrounding territory remained in Kiev's control, flanked by the separatists on three sides. Separatist forces, allegedly with Russian backing, began a campaign to retake the city once and for all in late January 2015. They reportedly paused the offensive as leaders met in Minsk to negotiate. The subject of Debaltsevo consumed many hours of the talks. Apparently, Poroshenko and Putin could not agree on how to proceed, so it was decided to exclude any mention of the town from Minsk II. In a press conference after the agreement was announced, Putin referenced the situation in Debaltsevo, warning that separatist forces had surrounded 6,000–8,000 Ukrainian servicemen. Subsequent reports suggested that Putin offered Poroshenko a negotiated retreat, but he refused.

The fighting intensified once the negotiations in Minsk had concluded. The main highway into the town from government-controlled territory became virtually impassable, damaged by artillery fire and heavily mined. By 17 February, separatist forces had fought their way into the town proper. Government troops began withdrawing the following day, suffering significant losses in a haphazard retreat. Estimates of casualties varied, ranging from one dozen to hundreds, and at least 100 Ukrainian soldiers were captured. The UN reported that 500 civilians were found dead in their homes.

With the capture of Debaltsevo and surrounding territory, the LoC had metastasised into a jagged semicircle bounded by the Russian border to the east and tracing far north of Lugansk city, northwest of Gorlovka and Donetsk city, and west of Novoazovsk, on the Sea of Azov. In subsequent months, the violence intensified in several areas, especially Donetsk airport and Shirokino (a village 20km east of Mariupol). Indeed, the SMM issued reports of heavy fighting and shelling near both of these locations, while noting large troop movements across the region and an increase in the construction of defensive fortifications along the LoC. The SMM stated on 26 April that the area around Shirokino was experiencing its most intense period of fighting since February. On 3 June, the Russian-backed separatists launched an assault on Marinka, a town approximately 25km southwest of Donetsk city centre. The town sits on a strategic highway near checkpoints along the LoC. After witnessing the movement of tanks and heavy weaponry in the area, the SMM reported the use of artillery and *Grad* multiple-launch rocket systems by both sides. After both sustained significant casualties, they retreated to previous positions.

By mid-2015, the political process called for in Minsk II had not progressed as envisioned. A Ukrainian law passed on 17 March defined the special-status area along lines that did not reflect separatist gains in January and February, particularly those around Debaltsevo. While such a definition was permissible under Minsk II, it suggested that the Ukrainian government was not serious about implementing the legislation. The law also required that all illegal armed groups be removed before elections were held, and that the designation of special status would not apply until after the elections were held – sequencing that was absent from Minsk II. Moreover, the government did not consult the separatists on holding local elections, as stipulated in the document. Finally, Kiev instituted an economic blockade against rebel-held areas, despite Minsk II's stipulation that economic ties be restored.

A potentially positive development occurred in May, when the TCG launched four working groups to assist in the implementation of the Minsk agreements. These groups focused on security; political affairs, including elections and constitutional reforms; internally displaced persons, refugees and humanitarian assistance; and economic affairs and rehabilitation. They brought Ukrainian officials and separatists into direct contact with each other on such matters for the first time.

Growing humanitarian crisis

The conflict has resulted in a humanitarian catastrophe for Ukraine. According to the most recent estimates by the UN, the war has killed at least 6,400 people and injured nearly 16,000 (unofficial figures are much higher), as well as causing destruction across large parts of Donetsk and Lugansk regions, both key industrial and urban areas. Violence also threatens parts of the country outside the conflict zone, as evidenced by a string of bombings in Kharkov and Odessa since autumn 2014.

In May, the UN Office for the Coordination of Humanitarian Affairs (OCHA) estimated that at least 1,315,000 people had been internally displaced, while more than 870,000 had fled the country as refugees, the majority of them to Russia. (The latter figure does not include Ukrainians who fled to Russia but did not seek refugee status – of whom there are more than one million, according to Russian officials.) For those who remained in the conflict zone, the situation was dire. The OCHA reported in January 2015 that at least 1.4m people in rebel-held areas of Donbas were highly vulnerable and required assistance, facing serious danger from the harsh winter. Many residents could barely afford basic necessities such as food and medication.

The problem was complicated by the Ukrainian government's policy towards contested areas. In November 2014, Kiev responded to the separatists' elections by closing state offices and ending benefit payments in areas not controlled by the government. The UN High Commissioner for Refugees expressed concern that the move would 'have unintended negative effects such as increasing internal displacement ... while causing serious hardship to those unable or unwilling to leave their homes'. An order enacted on 21 January by the Ukrainian security service required those who wished to travel to separatist-held territory to obtain a permit, and to pass through one of seven government-controlled checkpoints. There were onerous restrictions on obtaining permits, and the process was subject to long delays. Furthermore, the SMM reported that the locations where permit applications could be submitted were 'situated within areas of active hostilities that can only be reached through roads prone to shelling and crossfire'. While the self-proclaimed governments of the DNR and LNR have attempted to set up governance institutions, their ability to provide basic services is limited. Moreover, there were widespread reports of looting and arbitrary detention by LNR and DNR 'officials'. While Russia regularly sends humanitarian-aid convoys to the conflict area, Moscow has not taken financial responsibility for the population's health and security.

Fractious Ukrainian politics

In July 2014, two months after he was elected, Poroshenko dissolved parliament and called for snap elections to be held on 26 October (moving the vote forward from 2017). There was a clear political logic to the decision, as parliament contained a large number of officials loyal to former president Victor Yanukovich. Yet conducting the vote amid war in the east did little to heal the wounds in the Ukrainian polity.

The election result was somewhat surprising, with Prime Minister Arseniy Yatsenyuk's People's Front taking 22.2% of the party-list vote while Poroshenko's bloc won 21.8%, despite the fact that pre-election polls gave the latter a double-digit lead. Two other parties also had unexpected success: the newly formed Samopomich (Self-reliance), led by Lvov mayor Andriy Sadovyi, won 11% of the party-list vote; and the Opposition Bloc, successor of Yanukovich's Party of Regions, took 9.4%, and had a strong showing in several single-member districts in the south and east. The conflict prevented voting in nine of 21 constituencies in Donetsk and six of 11 in Lugansk, and there was no participation by residents of the 12 districts of Russian-controlled Crimea. Half of parliamentary representatives were elected through proportional representation, and the other half through single-member districts.

Together with Oleg Lyashko's Radical Party and Yulia Tymoshenko's Fatherland party, Samopomich, the Poroshenko bloc and the People's Front formed a pro-Western constitutional majority of 288 deputies out of 421. While many commentators rushed to conclude that Ukraine had finally made a definitive turn towards the West, closer analysis revealed that the key difference between this and previous elections was a drastic decrease in the overall number of ballots cast – a function of low turnout in the south and east, the annexation of Crimea and the war in Donbas. In the previous two parliamentary elections (held in 2007 and 2012), there were 10.6m and 10.7m pro-Western voters respectively; this time, there were 11.9m. There were 23.2m and 20.8m ballots cast in 2007 and 2012 respectively; in the 2014 election, there were only 16m.

It appeared that many voters in the south and east had refused to participate, amid a climate of growing fear and intimidation. In the run-up to the elections, pro-Maidan activists assaulted several Party of Regions members of parliament, in some cases throwing them into rubbish bins in what they called acts of 'people's lustration'. In September 2014, a group of young men toppled the Lenin statue in central Kharkov, a city home to many Russophile Ukrainians. The police protected the mob of activists, with Interior Minister Arsen Avakov commenting, 'I ordered the police to protect the people and not the idol.' In 2015, this nationalist fervour took on a far more sinister character when several public figures linked to the Yanukovich government were found dead. On 15 April 2015, for example, Oleg Kalashnikov, a former Party of Regions member of parliament, was found shot to death in his home in Kiev. The next day, a journalist known for his pro-Russian views was shot dead outside his home.

Despite the large pro-Western majority in parliament, the popular mandate from the Maidan revolution of February 2014 and the existential threat from Moscow, Ukraine's political establishment was wracked by infighting and seemed incapable of fundamentally reforming the country. These battles permeated the highest echelons of Ukrainian politics, as demonstrated by the highly combative relationship between Poroshenko and Yatsenyuk. The two leaders were only able to finalise the terms of the coalition agreement at the last minute (allegedly reaching a deal after the intervention of US Vice President Joe Biden), and the situation grew worse thereafter. Although there was some disagreement about the policy agenda, Poroshenko and Yatsenyuk mostly seemed to be fighting over control of decision-making in the executive branch.

Ukraine's economy had been in a tailspin since the change of government. The country's GDP contracted by 7.5% in 2014, and in the first quarter of 2015 this contraction accelerated to 17.6% year-on-year, with the World Bank predicting that GDP would contract by at least 7.5% in

2015. Ukraine's currency, the hryvnia, lost nearly half its value and there was inflation of 24.9% in 2014; inflation continued to soar in 2015, hitting 61% year-on-year by May. Moreover, the conflict gutted Donbas, which accounted for 16% of GDP, 25% of industrial output and 27% of exports before the crisis. Poroshenko stated that the conflict cost the government somewhere between US$5.5m and US$8m per day; if that number is accurate, Kiev had by the end of May 2015 spent between US$2.3bn and US$3.4bn, or roughly 1.5–2% of 2013 GDP, on the war.

The economic situation appeared particularly dire in early 2015, as Ukraine's central-bank reserves were barely able to provide two months of import cover. The IMF approved in March a four-year programme for Ukraine worth US$17.5bn – which included an immediate disbursement of US$5bn – to replace the two-year agreement reached in April the previous year. The loan was provided on the condition that Kiev implement an austerity programme. Measures mandated by the IMF included fiscal consolidation, modification of the exchange-rate regime to allow the hryvnia to float and the elimination of subsidies in the natural-gas sector. Those important steps allowed the first tranche to be disbursed, but subsequently reforms largely stalled.

The new $17.5bn programme was part of what the IMF and the Ukrainian government described as a US$40bn 'package' needed to cover Kiev's fiscal gap. The other elements were US$7.5bn in bilateral and multilateral financing – most of which was yet to be delivered – and US$15bn in debt relief from renegotiated terms with Ukraine's private creditors, talks on which were continuing as of mid-2015.

Deteriorating Russia–West relations

In response to the conflict in Ukraine, the United States and the European Union expanded in July 2014 the sanctions they had imposed on Russia the preceding March and April, which consisted of travel bans and asset freezes for Russian and Ukrainian officials and targeted, firm-specific transaction bans for several companies allegedly linked to Putin's inner circle. On 16 July, the US Treasury Department implemented sanctions that prohibited financing debt with a maturity of more than 90 days for several large Russian banks – a far more extensive measure than the previous steps. The department also imposed sanctions on more individuals including senior Russian officials and Donbas separatist leaders, as well as several Russian weapons manufacturers and a Crimean shipping company.

It was initially unclear whether Brussels would follow suit, as Europe's extensive economic ties with Russia meant that the potential blowback from sanctions would be significantly greater for EU member states than for the US. Yet the downing of MH17 altered the political dynamic in Europe, facilitating agreement on harsher measures among EU member states. On 25 July, the EU expanded its list of sanctioned individuals from the Russian government and Russian companies. Critically, Brussels followed Washington by limiting Russian financial institutions' access to capital markets, banning the export of dual-use technology to Russia (a step which the US had taken in March) and preventing the country from acquiring 'sensitive technologies' in the oil sector. Four days later, the US added three new financial institutions to the debt-maturity-limits list.

In response to the separatist offensive in early September, the debt-financing restrictions were applied to further Russian entities, and the maturity period allowed on debt was reduced to 30 days. In addition, the US issued a directive that forbade 'the provision, exportation, or re-exportation, directly or indirectly, of goods, services (except for financial services), or technology in support of exploration or production for deep-water, Arctic offshore, or shale projects' in Russia. As a result, ExxonMobil announced on 19 September that it was 'complying with all US sanctions' and would wind down its operations in the Kara Sea, where the company had been participating in a joint venture with Russian state-owned energy company Rosneft. The EU coordinated its sanctions with those of the US later that month, expanding the regime to include more Russian banks, arms companies and energy companies, as well as 24 more individuals.

In December, the US and the EU jointly coordinated and implemented a round of sanctions related specifically to economic activity in Crimea. Obama issued an executive order that barred US citizens and businesses from investment and other economic activity on the peninsula. The EU quickly followed suit. The severity of these measures was similar to that of EU and US sanctions on Iran, albeit limited to a much smaller territory.

Canada, Japan, Australia and Norway also introduced restrictive measures against Russian companies and government officials. Canada and

Australia largely followed the US lead, while Norway primarily imple-mented Brussels' rulings. Japan was initially reluctant to participate, but came under significant pressure from the US to join the sanctions regime. Tokyo froze the assets of 40 individuals and two Crimean companies on 5 August, and the following month instituted measures targeting Russia's defence industry and the five banks that had been sanctioned by the US. However, unlike its Western counterparts, the Japanese government did not target Russia's energy companies and no financing restrictions were imposed.

The international sanctions were remarkable in three respects. Firstly, they were unprecedented in scope (for example, 151 individuals and 37 entities had been sanctioned by the EU by mid-2015) and severity for such a large economy. A US official remarked that Russia's GDP was more than twice that of all countries previously subject to sanctions combined. Secondly, the July and September restrictions on debt issuance were far more targeted and narrow than any previous measures. Western policy-makers had found an innovative middle ground between designations of individual entities and blanket sectoral sanctions, the latter of which were untenable for an economy as deeply interwoven with the West as is Russia's. (In the event, 'overcompliance' by Western financial institutions – that is, refusal to conduct non-sanctioned, legal activity with Russian entities to avoid the appearance of sanctions evasion – led to a far wider impact than policymakers had intended.) Just as the West innovated, so did Russia, devising clever mechanisms to evade sanctions, such as forcing Mastercard and Visa to clear transactions through a national-pay-ments system, thereby allowing their cards to be used in Crimea. Thirdly, although the measures were highly damaging to the Russian economy, they had no impact on Russian strategic objectives in Ukraine. Western officials stated that the sanctions served as a deterrent against further aggression in Ukraine, but such claims were impossible to prove. Yet they came to symbolise transatlantic solidarity in the face of Russian aggres-sion, and as such acquired significant political weight.

On 7 August 2014, the Russian government retaliated against Western sanctions with a one-year import ban on agricultural goods and foodstuffs from the US, the EU, Australia, Canada and Norway. These measures were enacted under the banner of 'import substitution', an idea that became a key rallying cry for Russian officials with their domestic audience. While the ban provided new opportunities for some Russian producers, its main effect in the short term was to increase inflation.

Tension between Russia and the West went far beyond sanctions and counter-sanctions. Moscow pushed brinkmanship in the skies to dangerous new levels, resulting in several close encounters between Russian air patrols and Western jets (both civilian and military). The most serious incident occurred on 7 April 2015, when a Russian Su-27 *Flanker* flew dangerously close to a US RC-135 reconnaissance aircraft in international airspace over the Baltic Sea; Washington protested Russia's 'unsafe' actions in diplomatic channels, while Russian officials claimed that the US plane had been flying with its transponder turned off. On 30 May, US officials reported that another Russian Su-27 had flown within ten feet of a US reconnaissance aircraft in international airspace over the Baltic Sea.

Overall, the West attempted to chart a middle ground between an all-out confrontation with Russia and engaging in the kind of diplomatic give and take that could bring sustainable peace to Eastern Europe. This strategy was driven by the need to maintain cooperation with Moscow on key global issues while keeping up the pressure on Russia over its actions in Ukraine.

The difficulty was that avoiding escalation in Ukraine while maintaining such cooperation was becoming politically untenable. In the US, this dual-track approach – condemning Moscow as an aggressor one day, while seeking to work with it the next – provided Obama's critics with frequent opportunities to decry him as weak and feckless. Indeed, accusations of appeasement could be heard on Capitol Hill each time senior US and Russian officials conferred on global issues or the administration avoided steps to escalate US involvement in Ukraine (such as providing lethal military assistance).

Meanwhile, officials on both sides gave in to the urge to link the conflict to other aspects of cooperation. The US began to do so almost immediately after the annexation of Crimea, in March 2014. Washington suspended all joint work considered non-essential, including by ending meetings of the US–Russia Bilateral Presidential Commission and cutting off talks on economic ties. What remained of the relationship therefore reflected what mattered most to the US, from the Iran nuclear talks to the purchase of the

Russian rockets needed to launch US military satellites. Moscow has for the most part continued to cooperate on these issues, insulating them from the Ukraine dispute. But what mutual compartmentalisation there was has already started to fray. In November 2014, Moscow announced its decision to boycott the US-led Nuclear Security Summit in 2016. The following May, Putin lifted the ban on the sale of the S-300 air-defence system to Iran. It seemed only a matter of time before tensions over Ukraine undermined remaining areas of cooperation in the relationship.

These tensions, both intergovernmental and domestic, were exacerbated by the US debate over providing lethal military assistance to Ukraine. Congress passed the Ukraine Freedom Support Act of 2014 in December, authorising – but not requiring – the president to supply Ukraine with such assistance. However, the Obama administration chose not to do so, citing concerns about uncontrolled escalation and requests from EU leaders, particularly Merkel. In February, Deputy National Security Advisor Ben Rhodes said 'we don't think the answer to the crisis in Ukraine is simply to inject more weapons and get into that type of tit-for-tat with Russia.' Within the Washington Beltway, Obama came under increasing pressure to change course from retired senior military officers and other prominent experts. The debate typified the challenge facing Western strategy on the crisis, whereby options for increased involvement offered few opportunities to gain the upper hand; in this instance, there was no coherent case that lethal assistance would actually affect the military balance on the ground.

As the conflict in Ukraine intensified, Putin's rhetoric became more aggressive and anti-Western. During the annual Valdai International Discussion Club meeting held in Sochi in October 2014, he accused the US government of undermining the existing international order and spreading chaos around the globe. Discussing Western sanctions in an 18 December press conference, Putin stated that 'the policy of containment ... has been carried out against our country for many years, always, for decades, if not centuries. In short, whenever someone thinks that Russia has become too strong or independent, these tools are quickly put into use.'

In the context of this near-complete breakdown of ties, Moscow sought to deepen its partnership with Beijing. After signing a US$400-billion gas deal in May 2014, Russia and China inked another pipeline agreement on the sidelines of the Asia-Pacific Economic Cooperation summit, held in November. Once operational, this pipeline would provide northwest China with 30bn cubic metres of gas from western Siberian fields (which also supply Europe). The Chinese and Russian militaries also conducted several joint exercises in the East China Sea, the Mediterranean and elsewhere, both bilaterally and under the aegis of the Shanghai Cooperation Organisation. Moscow agreed in autumn 2014 to a US$3bn contract to provide Beijing with S-400 air-defence systems. The sides are reportedly conducting talks on a sale of the advanced Su-35 fighter to the Chinese military. While there are limits to Russia–China ties, the two states are growing closer, with barriers to bilateral cooperation falling particularly fast on the Russian side due to the Ukraine crisis.

Russia's climate of intolerance

The Ukraine crisis galvanised domestic support for Putin, while at the same time turning the majority of Russians against the West. According to polls conducted by the Levada Center, the president's approval rating remained at around 85% in the year to mid-2015. Although Western sanctions may have been intended to turn the Russian population against the Kremlin, the measures had the opposite effect. Levada polls found that a majority of Russians viewed the sanctions as specifically targeting the Russian population: while in May 2014 around 42% of respondents thought the sanctions were directed against a small group of individuals responsible for Moscow's Ukraine policy, that number fell to 15% by December. A May 2015 study by the Institute of Sociology found that 69% of Russians blamed the negative economic trends in their country on Western sanctions. Yet despite the deteriorating economic situation, 86% of Russians expressed a willingness to tolerate the sanctions, while only 14% thought the government should take measures to have them lifted.

A poll taken in January 2015 found that 65% of Russians considered relations with the EU to be either tense or hostile; according to another study, conducted three months later, a majority of Russians regarded the US as a threat. In short, the Western response to the Ukraine crisis elicited a defensive reaction from the Russian population, creating the perception of an external threat that the government leveraged to boost its support.

At the same time, Moscow tightened its control over the media and the internet, introducing legislation designed to further marginalise the political opposition. In June 2014, Putin signed amendments to a 2012 law regulating the behaviour of non-governmental organisations, giving the Ministry of Justice the authority to independently register these groups operating in Russia as 'foreign agents', without a court order. In July, the government enacted a law criminalising the instigation and support of extremism on the internet. New legislation was introduced to increase the penalties for separatists and protesters. Putin also signed into law a bill requiring all internet companies to store data on Russian citizens on servers located inside the country.

Further restrictions on the internet came with the so-called 'blogger law', which defined any blog with more than 3,000 daily readers as a media outlet. The legislation required popular blog writers to submit to registration and licensing procedures. A law enacted in August 2014 required all Russians with dual citizenship to disclose their non-Russian citizenship to the government. In May 2015, Putin signed into law a bill allowing the prosecutor's office to brand as 'undesirable' foreign non-governmental organisations that 'threaten constitutional order, defence capabilities or national security'. An organisation designated as such is forbidden from opening offices in Russia and disseminating its work in the country, and is not permitted to work with banks and state agencies.

Media personalities and pro-government politicians regularly used the terms 'fifth column' and 'national traitors' to describe the Kremlin's opponents, terminology that Putin popularised in his March 2014 speech announcing the annexation of Crimea. Politicians and journalists who spoke out against government policies online were hounded by what investigations revealed to be a paid army of pro-government internet trolls. However, many online attacks – including some that contained violent threats – came from nationalist elements of Russian society, which did not need to be paid to condemn Putin's opponents.

This outpouring of vitriol reached a tragic peak with the killing of Nemtsov, who was shot four times in the back while crossing the Bolshoi Zamoskvoretsky bridge in Moscow at midnight on 27 February 2015. In the last decade of his life, he led various opposition movements and parties, regularly publishing reports alleging malfeasance by senior government figures, as well as energetically criticising Putin himself. But Nemtsov also served in government in the 1990s – including as deputy prime minister under President Boris Yeltsin – and as a member of the Russian parliament until 2003, during which time he supported Putin's presidency. Before the assassination, it was thought that Nemtsov's status as a former senior official protected him from the fate that has befallen other outspoken opposition figures.

On 1 March, tens of thousands of Muscovites took to the streets to commemorate the opposition leader. Putin condemned Nemtsov's assassination as 'vile' and ordered a criminal investigation, which initially proceeded quickly. Within days, the authorities had arrested five Chechen men suspected of involvement in the killing, including the alleged assassins. The evidence trail suggested a link with senior Chechen Republic officials in the Kadyrov administration. One of the suspects, Zaur Dadayev, was a lieutenant in Chechnya's Ministry of Interior forces until being fired on 28 February 2015, the day after Nemtsov's murder. The federal authorities also questioned Ruslan Geremeev, a member of Chechnya's special forces, in late March. They were unable to interrogate him again, however, as he allegedly escaped to the United Arab Emirates in early April.

The investigation revealed a conflict between federal law-enforcement agencies and Kadyrov, one that the latter appeared to be winning. That conflict was also on public display on 19 April, when police officers from the Stavropol region, which neighbours the Chechen Republic, shot and killed a suspect during a raid in Grozny. Kadyrov warned that failure to forewarn him of such actions would give Chechen security forces the right to 'shoot to kill' law-enforcement officers from other regions. The federal Ministry of the Interior denounced Kadyrov's position as 'unacceptable'.

Broad economic downturn

Along with an increasingly severe sanctions regime, the Russian economy had to contend with a large drop in the price of oil and the cumulative effects of long-term underinvestment. Russia's GDP grew by 0.6% in 2014, nearly half the amount forecast by the World Bank in January of that year. At the same time, the country faced a collapsing rouble and inflation of 11.4% in 2014. The IMF estimated that the economy would contract by 3.4% in 2015, but would return to growth the following year.

Between June 2014 and January 2015, the price of Brent crude oil fell by around 60%. The drop was damaging to the Russian government's budget, which relies in large part on revenues from oil and gas. The Ministry of Finance originally based its 2015 budget on an assumed oil price of US$100 per barrel, and in January that year Finance Minister Anton Siluanov warned that if oil prices remained at around US$50 per barrel, the budget would be underfunded in 2015 by approximately three trillion roubles, a deficit of around 4% of GDP. (By comparison, the deficit was 0.5% and 0.7% of GDP in 2013 and 2014 respectively.) As a result of the squeeze, the ministry imposed spending cuts of 10% across all sectors, except for defence.

Pressure on the rouble intensified in 2014, leading the Central Bank of Russia to take steps to increase foreign-exchange liquidity in late October and, a few weeks later, to allow the currency to float freely, eliminating a previously existing target band. Interest rates were raised incrementally throughout the year, from 5.5% in February to 7% in March, to 7.5% in April, to 8% in July and to 9.5% in October. After OPEC decided in late November not to cut oil production – as it had traditionally done to buoy the oil price – the rouble fell sharply as capital outflows spiked. In response, the central bank hiked interest rates to 10.5% on 11 December and then to 17% five days later. In total, the rouble fell by 46% against the US dollar in 2014. Interest rates were slowly cut back from 17% in the first half of 2015, reaching 11.5% by 15 June.

The Duma attempted to bolster the banking sector – which faced high servicing costs for non-rouble debts due to sanctions, and a large increase in funding costs as a result of the tightened monetary policy ensuing from the rouble's depreciation – by establishing in December 2014 an emergency, one-trillion-rouble recapitalisation fund. More than 80% of the fund had been disbursed by the end of the following month, during which period another 500bn roubles were earmarked to provide additional support to the sector. Western sanctions also affected a much wider range of Russian companies than those that were directly targeted, and many firms lost access to capital markets.

Counter-sanctions implemented by the Russian government and the fall in the value of the rouble contributed to a rise in inflation from 7.5% to 11.2% year-on-year between June and December 2014. Throughout the first quarter of 2015, this trend continued: inflation hit 16.9% year-on-year in March, accelerating at the fastest annual rate since 2002, before falling back to around 15.8% in May. Food inflation was particularly severe, reaching 20.7% in January 2015 and placing significant strain on most Russian consumers.

While the quick response of the government mitigated some of the damage, the outlook for the economy was nonetheless grim. In January 2105, Standard & Poor's downgraded Russia's sovereign credit rating to junk status, and Moody's Investors Service soon followed suit. Net capital outflows reached US$130.5bn, or 7% of GDP, in 2014. However, by mid-2015, there were some indications that the economy was adapting. The rouble had rebounded by 21% by May 2015 as the price of oil stabilised, and the stock market also rose.

Although the central bank refrained from large-scale intervention in currency markets, the crisis and the resulting budget deficit forced the government to draw on its reserve funds. As a result, Russia's foreign-currency reserves fell from US$469.9bn in June 2014 to US$350.5bn in April 2015. Whether or not the Kremlin can avoid further depleting the reserve will largely depend on the oil price, since Russia remains unable to access international capital markets.

The country's economic woes reverberated throughout the region. The economies of the former Soviet states (with the exception of the Baltic countries) are still deeply dependent on Moscow. Across the board, Armenia, Azerbaijan, Belarus, Georgia, Kazakhstan, Kyrgyzstan, Moldova, Tajikistan and Uzbekistan reported falling exports to Russia – and in some cases, increases in imports from Russia – as well as currency pressure from a devalued rouble, increases in import prices and disruptions to labour migration, among other knock-on effects.

The devaluation of the rouble dragged down all currencies in Central Asia: Kazakhstan's tenge fell by 40% in 2014; Kyrgyzstan spent US$109.82m (1.5% of 2013 GDP) in the first two months of 2015 alone, in order to prop up the som; and Tajikistan's somoni and Uzbekistan's som also plunged in value. The latter two countries closed their currency-exchange markets in mid-2015 in an effort to restore stability. Moreover, a large decrease in remittances from Russia had serious ramifications for Tajikistan and Kyrgyzstan, both of which rely heavily on income from labour migrants. In Tajikistan, remittances from migrants working in Russia, which constitute roughly half of GDP, fell by 40%.

Competing integration initiatives

The Eurasian Economic Union (EEU) was officially launched on 1 January 2015, beginning what Putin called a 'new epoch' in regional relations. According to the Eurasian Economic Commission, the union's governing body, the EEU will provide for the free movement of goods, services, capital and labour, and will pursue harmonised policies in sectors including energy, transport and agriculture. The organisation's founding treaty also created single services and labour markets, while calling for the coordinated regulation of financial markets based on step-by-step harmonisation. The EEU's predecessor, the Eurasian Customs Union (which comprised Belarus, Kazakhstan and Russia), was folded into the EEU.

The EEU expanded Eurasian integration efforts beyond the Customs Union's three founding countries to include Armenia and Kyrgyzstan. Following Armenian President Serzh Sargsyan's abrupt turn from deeper integration with the EU in autumn 2013, Yerevan spent much of 2014 negotiating the specifics of its accession to the EEU. The talks produced a variety of concessions from Moscow, including lower import duties and subsidised natural gas. Armenia signed the treaty on accession to the EEU on 10 October 2014, joining the organisation at its launch.

Kyrgyzstan also sought accession to the EEU, although there were multiple delays in the attempt. While President Almazbek Atambayev signed Kyrgyzstan's accession treaty on 21 May 2015, the finalisation of the country's membership was contingent on its ability to upgrade border checkpoints to the EEU's standards and the broader approval of the organisation's four existing members. Heavily dependent on remittances from Russia, Kyrgyzstan was drawn to the union by the promise of an open labour market, which would ensure that many Kyrgyz workers no longer needed to obtain work permits. While the EEU was theoretically open to all states in the region, Tajikistan was the only other country considering accession.

Despite the moves towards economic integration, Russia's trade ties with the other two founding members of the Eurasian grouping, Belarus and Kazakhstan, came under strain. After being unable to convince the two countries to join counter-sanctions against the West within the Customs Union, Moscow implemented the measures unilaterally, thereby undermining the core principle of any such union: a unified external tariff.

Belarus actively facilitated evasion of the Russian sanctions, allowing banned European products, such as Norwegian salmon, to be re-exported into Russia. In response, Russia's food-safety regulator set up inspection points at the Belarus–Russia border on 24 November 2014, and refused entry to such goods. Minsk retaliated by ordering customs officers to inspect imports from Russia at the border for the first time since July 2011, when the border posts were removed as part of Customs Union integration efforts. Both sides backed down before the end of the year, however, as Moscow attempted to smooth the way for the impending launch of the EEU.

Russia and Kazakhstan had a trade spat of their own in early 2015. Due to the devaluation of the rouble, Russian goods suddenly became far cheaper than those produced in Kazakhstan, prompting Astana to take measures to protect domestic producers. In February, Russian newspaper *Kommersant* published rumours that Kazakhstan was planning to impose restrictions on Russian natural-resources and consumer goods, citing sources in the Kazakhstani Ministry of Agriculture. On 5 March, Astana enacted a 45-day embargo on Russian oil products. A few weeks later, officials removed many Russian food products from the shelves of Kazakhstani shops, purportedly because they violated health codes. In late March, the Russian consumer-safety regulator announced that some Kazakhstani food products did not comply with health codes in several regions of Russia. While the media was quick to label this a 'trade war', the Kazakhstani government stressed it was only targeting suppliers who violated regulations and that the policy was not designed to block Russian imports. Russian officials, meanwhile, described the label as a 'big exaggeration'. The situation remained unresolved in mid-2015.

While Moscow strengthened and enlarged the EEU, Ukraine, Moldova and Georgia continued to pursue integration with the EU. All three countries signed Association Agreements (AAs) with the EU on 27 June 2014. The far-reaching deals included political association, visa liberalisation and the establishment of a Deep and Comprehensive Free Trade Area (DCFTA). However, all three states are embroiled in protracted conflicts that prevent them from meeting technical requirements of the AA such as visa liberalisation, while also creating political obstacles to potential EU membership in the future.

Moldova's December 2014 parliamentary elections resulted in the formation of a minority government comprising the Liberal Democratic Party and the Democratic Party (which together held 40 out of 101 seats). The pro-Russian Socialist Party made up the largest faction in parliament, with 25 seats. Moldovans were deeply dissatisfied with their pro-EU government: a March 2015 poll conducted by the US National Democratic Institute found that 48% thought their country was headed in the wrong direction (up from 37% in October 2014). Moldova also experienced a corruption scandal in early 2015, after the central bank discovered that more than US$1bn – roughly one-eighth of the country's GDP – had vanished shortly before the November parliamentary elections. Three banks made a series of loans to unidentified recipients, and the money may have ended up in offshore accounts. The government was subsequently forced to intervene to keep the banks afloat. It dismissed top officials and promised to appoint special investigators. Thousands took part in street protests in May. Meanwhile, Georgia's fractious political scene suffered from weak institutions and the departure of several prominent figures from the government in 2015.

After Ukraine signed the AA, Moscow's threat to implement retaliatory trade measures against Kiev drove Brussels to the negotiation table. The EU foreign-policy chief met the presidents of Russia, Ukraine, Kazakhstan and Belarus for talks in Minsk on 26 August 2014. Putin made his position clear:

> Russia has stated on numerous occasions that full acceptance by our Ukrainian friends of all the tariff liberalisation requirements and the adoption of the European Union technical, sanitary and veterinary norms will have a negative impact on the scope and dynamics of trade and investment cooperation in Eurasia.

While Poroshenko held his ground, little came of the meeting. But the EU later announced that while it would proceed with ratification of Ukraine's DCFTA, it would postpone implementation until 1 January 2016 in order to allow the trilateral talks time to produce results. In subsequent months, Russian officials put forth both concrete technical concerns and a politically charged demand to postpone DCFTA implementation for another year. However, at a ministerial meeting in May 2015 there was a striking departure from the intransigence and vitriol that had characterised prior discussions. The parties said they had agreed to address Russia's concerns using 'flexibilities' within the DCFTA and by adjusting other agreements governing Ukraine–Russia trade. They also agreed that they would 'intensify their efforts and task their experts to achieve practical solutions to the concerns raised by Russia'. Customs cooperation, technical barriers to trade, and sanitary and phytosanitary issues would be addressed in future consultations. This seemed to suggest that if the technical changes were made, Russia would not implement retaliatory trade measures when the DCFTA entered into force. The EU representative at the meeting, Trade Commissioner Cecilia Malmström, pointed out that 'the reference [in the joint statement] that the [DCFTA] enter into force on January 1, 2016, was not contested by the Russian delegation.' By mid-2015, however, the Russian government had not repealed trade sanctions that would enter into force ten days after Ukraine started implementing the DCFTA.

The tentative progress on the trilateral talks on Ukraine's DCFTA demonstrated the potential for mutually beneficial solutions on regional integration. This followed a similarly positive signal in the aftermath of the negotiations over Minsk II, in which the leaders of Russia, Ukraine, Germany and France jointly declared they were 'committed to the vision of a joint humanitarian and economic space from the Atlantic to the Pacific'. But in reality, the leaderships and institutions of the West and Russia continued to compete for influence in the so-called 'countries in-between'. This competition had been the original trigger of the Ukraine crisis, and promised to further deepen geopolitical tensions in the future.

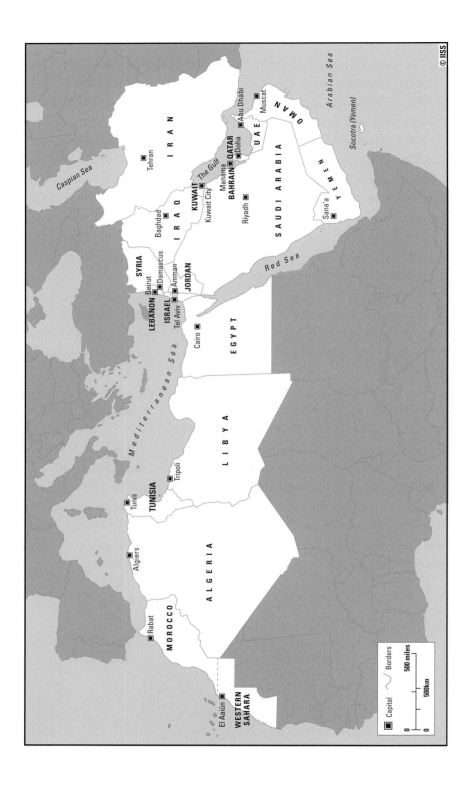

© IISS

Chapter 8

Middle East and North Africa

The year to mid-2015 saw significant flux in the Middle East. Nuclear diplomacy between Iran and major powers appeared to have defused a very important source of international tension, but its effect on regional security remained uncertain, with no sign of detente emerging between Iran and other major Middle Eastern countries.

As the Iranian nuclear deal approached, and was eventually sealed in July 2015, regional governments viewed it with scepticism. Israeli Prime Minister Benjamin Netanyahu remained a vociferous critic of Washington's dialogue with Tehran, while Saudi Arabia, the United Arab Emirates and other Gulf states sought to extract reassurances about US policy and diversify their security relationships rather than express vocal opposition. For them, the counter-proliferation benefits of the agreement seemed to be outweighed by the political and symbolic returns that would accrue to Iran.

Their concern about Tehran's potential behaviour after reaching an agreement was discussed at a summit convened with Gulf allies by US President Barack Obama at Camp David in May 2015. This took place against the backdrop of rhetorical and military escalation between Iranian-allied and Saudi-supported factions in troubled countries across the region. Arab states were worried that radical factions in Iran would demand even more aggressive regional policies in exchange for assenting to the deal – and that Washington's response to such an increase in Iranian activities would be inadequate.

The long-standing rivalry between Iran and Saudi Arabia was being played out primarily in Arab states that had fragmented – notably in Syria and Iraq, but also, since March 2015, in Yemen. In Syria, the four-year-old civil war showed no sign of ending, while in Iraq there was a resurgence of conflict as jihadist group the Islamic State of Iraq and al-Sham (ISIS) captured territory. In Yemen, civil war broke out between the internationally recognised government and Houthi rebels. This provoked foreign intervention, direct and sizeable in the case of Saudi Arabia's backing of the government, and indirect and limited in the case of Iran's support of the rebels. The conflict threatened Yemen's long-term viability and cohesiveness.

So too in Libya, civil war broke out that reflected regional fault lines, between an Islamist government in Tripoli with the support of Turkey and Qatar, and the internationally recognised government in Tobruk that was backed by the United Arab Emirates and Egypt. Disorder in a divided Libya facilitated flows of migrants from the Middle East and Africa across the Mediterranean, seeking refuge in Europe – though many, in the hands of traffickers, died at sea. Meanwhile in Egypt, the consolidation of power by Abdel Fattah el-Sisi following his election as president was paralleled by the emergence of a mid-level Islamist insurgency.

The campaign against ISIS, intended to push the group back first in Iraq and then in Syria, had a mixed record. While ISIS suffered significant setbacks against Kurdish and Iraqi security forces, backed by mostly American airpower, it demonstrated endurance and sustained appeal, seizing the Iraqi city of Ramadi, expanding within Syria and conducting operations in other countries across the Middle East. ISIS also gained important footholds across North Africa.

In Iraq, the ISIS threat to Baghdad and to non-Sunni areas appeared to have receded by mid-2015. But Sunnis were not reassured by the performance of anti-ISIS forces, the Iraqi government's disjointed response or the tentative strategy of the US-led coalition. Meanwhile, the prominence of Shia militias in the battle against ISIS, as well as Kurdish territorial boldness and disarray amongst Sunnis, further weakened the central government.

In Syria, the regime of Bashar al-Assad showed signs of growing structural weakness in the first half of 2015. Exhausted and lacking manpower and resources, the Syrian government increasingly struggled militarily and territorially. While it continued to control the large cities and the coastal regions, it lost significant areas to rebel forces, which were better organised and more coherent than in previous years. In the north, these forces were dominated by an array of Islamist groups, including the al-Qaeda affiliate Jabhat al-Nusra, while in the south, nationalist rebels appeared to be in the ascendant. The regime owed its survival to airpower and Iranian support, as well as apprehension among Western and local states that a rapid regime collapse would primarily benefit Islamist groups.

The regional picture gained complexity with the mounting role and assertiveness of Kurdish militias in Iraq and Syria. Well-organised Kurdish groups were able to attract Western support in their fight against ISIS, sharpening concerns in Turkey about Kurdish ambitions for statehood. For their part, Kurdish factions blamed Turkey for being complicit in the spread of jihadist movements.

In Iran, the credibility of President Hassan Rouhani appeared to hinge on the nuclear agreement. Rouhani and his negotiating team came under sustained attacks by hardline elements, which believed the diplomacy would lead to undue concessions. But Rouhani, in pursuing a deal that could end the country's isolation and jump-start the economy, enjoyed the qualified support of Supreme Leader Ayatollah Ali Khamenei.

The accession to the Saudi throne of King Salman bin Abdulaziz, accompanied by personnel changes at the top and a more assertive tone at home and abroad, energised the kingdom. The Saudi military operation in Yemen had broad Arab and Sunni backing and reluctant Western support, but the feasibility of Riyadh's political and military objectives remained questionable given the Houthis' military prowess and significant political influence.

Anxieties in the Gulf states were heightened by adversarial Iranian statements, ISIS attacks in Saudi Arabia and Kuwait (primarily against Shia targets) and a sense of US strategic disinterest, combined with low oil prices. These challenges compelled the Gulf states to put aside, if only for a time, a serious dispute between Qatar on the one hand, and Saudi Arabia and the UAE on the other, over Doha's support of the Muslim Brotherhood. This tentative reconciliation allowed the members of the Gulf Cooperation Council to announce ambitious, if speculative, plans for defence and security collaboration. Meanwhile, governments on the Arabian Peninsula were increasingly cracking down on dissent.

Syria: New Rebel Alliances

By the end of 2014, Bashar al-Assad had looked more secure as president of Syria than at any time since 2011, when the revolution against his regime began. As ISIS expanded dramatically within Syria and into Iraq, Western states prioritised the fight against the jihadist movement over the weakening of his regime, with governments calling for a dialogue between Syria's leadership and the main political opposition and rebel groups, and some former officials advocating cooperation with Assad against the jihadists. However, by mid-2015 there had been no reconciliation between the parties and the overall situation looked very different, with the regime seemingly in its weakest state since 2012, albeit in control of central Syria and still benefiting from superior firepower.

The Syrian government struggled to raise the funds and manpower it needed, was shaken internally by diminishing domestic support and was increasingly dependent upon foreign Shia forces, particularly the Lebanese militant group Hizbullah, to stave off rebel advances. The infighting that had plagued rebel forces since 2012 largely subsided. Moderate rebels established themselves as the most powerful faction in the south, while Islamist rebels dominated the northwest and Kurdish forces, supported by members of the Free Syrian Army (FSA), led in the northeast. By June 2015, the rebels had succeeded in capturing major towns and cities from both ISIS and the regime. Nonetheless, ISIS continued to gradually seize territory controlled by the regime. The de facto partition of Syria seemed irreversible.

Rising profile of ISIS

The lightning advance of ISIS in Iraq in June 2014 was a turning point for the conflict in Syria. After capturing Iraq's second-largest city, Mosul, the group seized large quantities of weapons, which it used to recapture lost territory and then expand in Syria.

It first attacked rival groups and regime forces in the eastern provinces of Ar-Raqqah and Deir ez-Zor, ousting al-Qaeda affiliate Jabhat al-Nusra and other rebels from the latter region. After the fall of Al-Tabqa air base, where ISIS executed hundreds of government soldiers, the regime retreated from much of the northeast, clinging on to the south of Al-Hasakah city, as well as western parts of Deir ez-Zor city and the air base just outside it. Only the Kurdish-held areas of Al-Hasakah province remained outside the group's control. It also made gains beyond its strongholds in the east, seizing towns and villages in the provinces of Hama, Homs and Rif Dimashq.

The group employed extraordinary brutality in both Syria and Iraq: it paraded captured fighters on camera before executing them en masse; kidnapped foreign journalists and aid workers, either collecting ransoms for their return or else beheading them; and sought to purge captured territory of minorities, the Yazidis in Iraq and the Assyrians in Syria. This strategy succeeded in generating local and international publicity, terrorising foes and potential victims, and inspiring would-be jihadists to join ISIS. Despite awareness of the problem in many countries, thousands of recruits joined jihadist groups in the year to mid-2015 – most of them from elsewhere in the Middle East and North Africa, but also hundreds from Western states.

Yet ISIS is different from other Islamist and jihadist groups in terms of both ideology and strategy. Whereas its rivals wanted to impose Islamist governance on Syria gradually once Assad had been defeated, ISIS sought the immediate, wholesale 'purification' of Syria (and Iraq) by ridding the territory it controlled of non-Sunni residents and imposing puritanical law. The group prioritised Islamist governance and territorial expansion even against other anti-Assad factions, creating dissent within Islamist ranks. Its bureaucracy oversaw and at times subsidised schooling, food distribution and basic public services, allowed business and trade, and imposed strict social mores. To finance its operations, ISIS resorted to taxation and extortion, exploiting oilfields and other sources of income.

The group's expansion and rule were met with opposition, both violent and non-violent. To deter such resistance, ISIS crushed the al-Sheitaat tribe, executing hundreds of its members before burying them in mass graves. However, guerrilla attacks and acts of civil disobedience against the group persisted.

In September 2014, the group advanced from its stronghold in the east towards Kobane, a Kurdish-majority town on the Turkish border. It rapidly captured approximately 70% of the town and threatened to overrun the border crossing. Coming on the heels of the Yazidi exodus in Iraq, this prompted the first US airstrikes in Syria. Supported by US airpower and Peshmerga heavy artillery, the Kurdish People's Protection Units (YPG) and fighters from the FSA were able to reverse the ISIS advance, at considerable cost to all sides.

This marked another turning point. From January 2015 onwards, Kurdish and FSA forces moved beyond Kobane to seize towns and villages in Aleppo province that had long been occupied by ISIS, pushing the jihadists south towards the Euphrates River. At the same time, Kurdish fighters in Al-Hasakah province seized two strategically important towns from ISIS, Tel Hamis and Tel Birek. In June, while ISIS made forays into Aleppo province, YPG and FSA forces were able to press their offensive and for the first time captured territory in Ar-Raqqah province – including the strategically important towns of Ayn Issa and Tal Abyad, on the border with Turkey – thereby cutting the jihadists' supply lines.

By this time, there were signs of growing dissent within the ranks of ISIS. Reports emerged of infighting over power and resources, and discontented foreign fighters attempted to desert the group. Although ISIS was able to capture the ancient city of Palmyra in May after government forces retreated, its territory looked vulnerable to Kurdish and FSA advances. The group began another major offensive against government-held areas in Al-Hasakah in June, but was unable to advance as easily as it had in the past.

Nevertheless, its brutality, effective use of social media, success as a fighting force, attacks in the West and establishment of a so-called 'caliphate' across national borders combined to place ISIS at the top of the Western political and media agenda, diminishing the attention given to the Assad regime. This was despite the fact that ISIS was both less of a danger to Syrian civilians and less of an impediment to the overthrow of the regime than were Assad's forces and allied militias. As a result, tensions increased between the Syrian opposition, which was committed to ending the rule of Assad, and Western countries that prioritised the fight against ISIS, especially the United States.

Weakened regime

The rise of ISIS relieved political pressure on the Syrian regime. Assad had long described the civil war as a fight against terrorists, and he looked to use advances made by ISIS as evidence of this, despite the regime's ambiguous relations with the group. However, the ISIS offensive in Iraq spurred a change in the Syrian government's policy. Regime forces subsequently began operations targeting the group, carrying out airstrikes against it in Ar-Raqqah, Deir ez-Zor and Al-Hasakah. Nevertheless, the regime was not able to recapture territory from the group or avert further losses. Nor were Assad's forces able to make any major territorial gains against the rebels, in contrast to the previous year.

The main regime offensive centred on Aleppo in the belief that, were the large northern city to fall to pro-government forces, the rebels would suffer a debilitating blow. Assad's forces worked for months to surround the city and cut off rebel supply lines, but made only stuttering progress. Although sudden gains were made when foreign forces spearheaded a surprise offensive north of the city in mid-February, the rebels subsequently recaptured many of the villages they had lost. By mid-2015, the encirclement and conquest of Aleppo no longer seemed feasible for the regime.

The regime continued the offensive against its opponents in Eastern Ghouta, to the north and east of Damascus. The siege and perpetual bombardment of the area caused widespread suffering among civilians, exacerbated by the government's repeated refusal to allow international aid organisations to distribute medical supplies and food there. Despite the humanitarian cost, the rebels held fast, ceding only the district of Adra to the regime. The southern Damascus suburb of Yarmouk faced a similar fate to Eastern Ghouta.

The regime continued to use barrel bombs, missiles and mortars across the country, causing enormous human and environmental damage in rebel-held territory. Accordingly, tens of thousands of civilians were killed and millions fled their homes to seek refuge abroad. The Syrian government also deployed chlorine as a weapon in breach of an international ban, leading to protests that the chemical-weapons agreement it signed in 2013 had been broken.

The regime seemed increasingly brittle, as dwindling resources were directed towards the war effort rather than the provision of services. Subsidies and salaries were cut, while taxes were raised and fees imposed on administrative procedures. In turn, the regime had a diminished ability to govern the areas under its control, making financial assistance from Iran crucial to its survival. The Syrian government also became more dependent on local loyalist militias to control territory and provide services.

Thus, domestic support for Assad eroded. The Syrian Arab Army's dramatic defeats at the hands of ISIS, and the resulting loss of hundreds of men, damaged morale among regime supporters. Frustration simmered over the high casualty rate, the fate of hundreds of missing soldiers and the failure of the regime to win outright victories despite official announcements. The government nevertheless tried to recruit more fighters, imposing mandatory enlistment for males of fighting age. This also met with resistance in all pro-Assad communities. Deprived of pay for several weeks, the National Defence Forces became increasingly dissatisfied with the regime, resulting in clashes between local pro-regime militias and the professional Syrian Arab Army in late April. The regime was also plagued by internal infighting. A struggle between two senior intelligence commanders, Rafiq Shehadeh of the Military Intelligence Directorate and Rustom Ghazaleh of the Political Security Directorate, ended with the dismissal of the former and the death of the latter in unclear circumstances.

Such tension further increased the regime's reliance on the support of Iran and Hizbullah. Iranian and Hizbullah officers played key command and operational roles in the fight against the moderate Southern Front alliance in the provinces of Quneitra and Daraa, as well as – to Israel's discomfort – areas close to the Golan Heights. With many Iraqi Shia militiamen recalled to the battle against ISIS in their home country, Iran also facilitated the recruitment and deployment of Afghan and Pakistani Shia fighters. Hizbullah focused on battling ISIS and Jabhat al-Nusra in the Qalamoun area, along the Lebanese border.

Partnerships among rebels

By mid-2015, Islamist brigades had unequivocally established themselves as the dominant rebel force in northwestern Syria. In doing so, they had defeated moderate, US-backed groups such as Harakat Hazm and the Syrian Revolutionaries Front. The remaining moderate groups in the north joined Kurds fighting around Kobane or worked alongside the Islamist-dominated alliances in Aleppo and Idlib. In Aleppo city, rebels worked together under the Levant Front and its successor, the Conquest of Aleppo operations room. In June, the Conquest of Aleppo alliance included at least 31 groups.

Rebel infighting in the north had largely ended by spring 2015. Ahrar al-Sham recovered from a bombing in September that had killed almost all of its leadership and joined with other Islamist factions, including Jabhat al-Nusra and Jund al-Aqsa, to form Jaysh al-Fateh (Army of Conquest). The alliance quickly proved to be the most effective force opposing the regime. In March, using heavy weapons and supported by an array of small FSA units, Jaysh al-Fateh began a major offensive in Idlib province, quickly seizing Idlib city from the regime. This was the first time that a provincial capital had fallen to the rebels. Jaysh al-Fateh pressed the advance, seizing the strategically important town of Jisr al-Shughour, then Al-Mastumah military base and the town of Ariha. By the end of May, the alliance controlled almost all of the province. Other victories in the north put Latakia and Hama provinces within the rebels' reach. These advances were made possible by rapprochement between Turkey, Qatar and Saudi Arabia, the opposition fighters' main patrons. Frustrated by US policy and the shift of focus away from the fight against Assad, all three states sought to reconcile their Islamist clients.

Nevertheless, international supporters continued to shun Jabhat al-Nusra due to its affiliation with al-Qaeda. In the second half of 2014, Jabhat al-Nusra expelled the Syrian Revolutionaries Front and Harakat Hazm, the major US-backed rebel factions, from northern Syria. However, in 2015, Jabhat al-Nusra allied with other Islamist factions and focused on fighting the regime as part of Jaysh al-Fateh. This raised hopes that the group might cut its ties with al-Qaeda in an attempt to gain the external support enjoyed by its allies, but its leader, Abu Muhammad al-Jolani, dispelled any such notion in a June interview with Al-Jazeera.

The YPG and other moderate rebel groups coordinated their fight against ISIS in northern Aleppo province through the Euphrates Volcano operations room, an undertaking that also bore fruit, as ISIS was successfully pushed south. Cooperation between the YPG, the FSA and the Peshmerga in Kobane, supported by US airstrikes, spurred a marked improvement in international perceptions of Syria's Kurds.

In the south, the Islamist Jaysh al-Islam remained the strongest rebel group in the area around Damascus, and Islamist factions retained a strong presence along the border with Lebanon and Iraq. However, the moderate Southern Front alliance emerged as the most powerful force in Daraa province. Although progress in the province was slow compared to the Islamist advance in the north, the Southern Front, supported by Jabhat al-Nusra, captured a series of towns and military bases from the regime, including the strategically important town of Al-Shaykh Maskin. By mid-2015, it was poised to launch an offensive to oust the regime from the provincial capital, and looked to expand further into As-Suwayda province.

But the rebels remained at a military disadvantage, struggling to match or overcome the regime's greater firepower. The supply of weapons, especially anti-aircraft missiles, to moderate rebels continued to be constrained by the reservations of Western countries, which feared that the arms could fall into the hands of jihadists – a concern sharpened by Jabhat al-Nusra's seizure of weapons the US had provided to Harakat Hazm – and that such action might deepen the rivalries between anti-government factions.

Syria's political opposition and moderate rebel groups therefore criticised Western states for failing to offer more support. When the White House announced a Pentagon-run train-and-equip programme for vetted rebels in June 2014, anti-Assad factions greeted the plan with scepticism: the US designed the programme to combat ISIS rather than the Assad regime, and to train only 5,000 men per year. After first stalling in Congress and then being delayed by wrangling over which countries would host the training, the programme finally began in May 2015. But the rebels' fears were realised. Stringent vetting meant that few fighters were able to participate in the programme and, among those who were, many were unwilling to commit to fighting only ISIS. As a result, by mid-2015 fewer than 100 fighters were to be trained under the programme.

The opposition-in-exile, the National Coalition for Syrian Revolutionary and Opposition Forces (NC) and its interim government, was repeatedly criticised for its disconnection from the situation on the ground, its dependency on foreign patrons and its internal bickering. The opposition struggled to define a strategy, build its profile and mobilise resources. Led by Ahmad Tohme, the interim government made a series of controversial decisions; for example, it dismissed the entire military council in June 2014, then reinstated it days later. The following month, Hadi al-Bahra was elected as the new president of the NC. Bahra quickly dismissed Tohme and his cabinet, only for the NC to re-elect Tohme in October. Such drama paused in January 2015 with the NC's election of Khaled Khoja, a relatively neutral figure, as the new president. Khoja sought to establish closer relations with fighters on the ground, including Islamist factions, and encouraged coordination between the Islamists in the north and moderates in the south.

The opposition worked, with limited success, to support the development of Local Administrative Councils (LACs) in Syria and draw them together in an overarching coordination structure. The LACs offered the best chance of effective local governance in rebel-held territory. Across the country there were around 1,385 LACs, in one form or another, almost 500 of them in rebel-held territory and around 150 in areas controlled by ISIS. But former civil servants with expertise in water management, electricity transmission and engineering were reluctant to work with the LACs due to poor pay and fear of being associated with the opposition. Funding shortages and a lack of strategy further hampered the LACs' work.

International intervention

In August 2014, concern that ISIS would slaughter Yazidis trapped on Mount Sinjar prompted the US to begin airstrikes against the group in Iraq. Similar fears of genocide, this time affecting Syria's Kurds, were generated by the ISIS advance on Kobane. In response, Washington cobbled together an alliance with Bahrain, Jordan, Saudi Arabia and the United Arab Emirates to conduct airstrikes against ISIS in Syria, under *Operation Inherent Resolve*. (Canada joined the coalition in March 2015.) Coalition airstrikes targeted the group's fighters around Kobane, command centres, military hardware, oil facilities and fighting positions elsewhere in Syria, with the aim of degrading its combat capabilities.

The airstrikes did little to stem the advance, until the coalition began to coordinate its operations with the YPG, using the Iraqi Kurdish Peshmerga as intermediaries. This dismayed Ankara because the YPG had strong relations with the Kurdistan Workers' Party, a banned Turkish–Kurdish organisation classified as a terrorist group by the US and the European Union.

The decision to conduct airstrikes against ISIS but not the Syrian regime infuriated Ankara further, and sparked criticism from the NC and rebels inside Syria. With coalition aircraft sharing airspace with Assad's air force, Syrians increasingly questioned the motives of the US. Airstrikes against select members of al-Qaeda, whom the US labelled the 'Khorasan Group', were vocally condemned by rebel groups that fought alongside Jabhat al-Nusra.

Regime airstrikes and attacks using barrel bombs remained a primary cause of civilian casualties, hampering the rebels' ability to govern areas they controlled, demoralising communities and undermining efforts at reconstruction and stabilisation. Several prominent figures subsequently pushed for the imposition of a no-fly zone in northern Syria. Turkish President Recep Tayyip Erdogan championed the idea, gaining support from France and a coalition of Syrian civil-society organisations. Yet the US remained unreceptive, as a no-fly zone would have required military operations against the regime and faced legal challenges. Washington also dismissed the proposal to establish safe zones inside Syria to accommodate displaced persons and repatriate refugees, for similar reasons. Turkey and Jordan were left to contemplate setting up buffer zones inside Syria independently of the US, in part to prevent ISIS from establishing a presence on their borders.

Failed peacemaking

Following the failure of the Geneva II conference in early 2014, Lakhdar Brahimi stood down as joint UN–Arab League envoy to Syria. His successor, Italian–Swedish diplomat Staffan de Mistura, designed a process based on the hope that local truces and reconciliations could lead to a national compromise between the warring parties. In November, he set out his vision for a series of such local truces, seeking to persuade the Assad regime to establish the first such 'freeze zone' in Aleppo.

By February, de Mistura's undertaking had fallen apart. He lost the confidence of opposition politicians and rebel fighters, who dismissed his Aleppo plan as benefiting Assad politically and militarily. In response, UN Secretary-General Ban Ki-moon directed his envoy to focus on relaunching the political process. In May, de Mistura began a series of consultations with all parties to the conflict, purposefully keeping expectations low. Rebels again refused to participate, accusing de Mistura of favouritism towards the regime and criticising the process as primarily helpful to Assad.

Russia independently set out to host talks between the regime and parts of the opposition. This resulted in the Russian Ministry of Foreign Affairs hosting two 'Moscow Forums' in January and April 2015; while some opposition members attended, the NC boycotted the events, seeing little prospect for success in Russian-mediated talks.

The rare diplomatic success that had facilitated the destruction of Syria's chemical weapons – in the first half of 2014 – was undermined by the regime's continued use of chlorine gas. The damage caused by the indiscriminate nature of the weapon was compounded by the fact that it disproportionately affected women, children and the elderly. On 8 May 2015, almost one year after all of Syria's chemical weapons had supposedly been handed over to the Organisation for the Prohibition of Chemical Weapons, it was reported that traces of sarin and VX nerve agent had since been found in an undisclosed military research facility in Syria.

Shortfalls in international aid

With the violence in Syria continuing unabated, there was a further deterioration of the humanitarian situation in the country. In June, the Syrian Observatory for Human Rights stated that the conflict had killed more than 230,000 people, approximately 70,000 of whom were civilians. However, the real death toll was thought to be in excess of 300,000. The organisation estimated that around 1.5m Syrians had been seriously wounded. By the end of May 2015, more than 4m Syrian refugees resided in Lebanon, Jordan, Turkey, Iraq and Egypt. The United Nations calculated that a further 7.5m people were in need of humanitarian aid in the country, including 4.8m in hard-to-reach areas.

In July 2014, the UN Security Council passed Resolution 2165, providing UN agencies with a six-month authorisation to deliver aid in Syria without the approval of the government. In December, the Security Council passed another resolution extending the authorisation for a further year.

Although these measures allowed for some improvements in the delivery of aid, practical obstacles still prevented the process from being carried out efficiently. Much of Syria remained inaccessible to international aid workers. Indiscriminate government bombing posed a significant threat to anyone working in rebel-held Syria, while the regime also impaired aid efforts through its use of siege tactics, which involved restricting the entrance of food, water and medical supplies into affected areas. Likewise, attempts by ISIS to assert absolute control in its territory and the group's execution of aid workers prevented international organisations from operating in much of northern and eastern Syria. By April 2015, vital medical supplies had reached just 58,000 of the people in hard-to-reach areas in need of humanitarian aid.

In order to distribute supplies in rebel-held areas, aid agencies increasingly partnered with local Syrian and diaspora non-governmental organisations. These groups enjoyed better access across front-lines and in besieged communities. However, aid agencies were slow to build effective remote-management programmes, and struggled to resolve the tension between logistical difficulties and their aversion to the risk of supplies falling into the hands of armed groups, especially proscribed ones.

Winter struck particularly hard among communities of displaced persons and Syrian refugees, with severe weather in Syria, Lebanon and Jordan exacerbating the dire humanitarian situation. The World Food Programme ran out of funds for its food-voucher system in December, after scaling back the programme repeatedly in the preceding months, leaving millions of refugees in Lebanon and Egypt without support. Although a major campaign raised enough money to resume the programme, funding remained in such short supply that in summer 2015 the World Food Programme had to reduce its support to refugees once again.

When states gathered in Kuwait at the end of March for the third international donors' conference, the UN asked for US$8.4 billion to meet the humanitarian needs of civilians in Syria and refugee communities in neighbouring countries for the coming year. Aid agencies voiced their frustration when states pledged less than half the sum required, just US$3.8bn.

Iraq: Battling ISIS

Iraq's current crisis engulfed the country on 10 June 2014, when Mosul, the country's second-largest city, was seized by ISIS. The expanding conflict resulted in the deaths of around 18,000 people in Iraq during 2014, a five-year high. With a further two million people displaced by the violence, the country returned to a level of internecine strife last seen during the civil war triggered by the 2003 US-led invasion.

After capturing Mosul, the highly motivated and mobile ISIS forces exploited popular discontent among Iraq's Sunni minority to sweep southward towards Baghdad. With the advance halted in August at Samarra, barely 100 kilometres short of the capital, ISIS redeployed its troops and pushed into Mount Sinjar – a region of northwestern Iraq along the Syrian border dominated by the country's Yazidi minority – forcing 130,000 people to flee into Kurdish territory. The jihadists then advanced towards Erbil, capital of the Kurdish Regional Government, overrunning Kurdish Peshmerga fighters who were defending the city's outskirts. These moves prompted an intervention by the United States: on 8 August, President Barack Obama authorised airstrikes against ISIS. However, the group retained the military initiative, taking Ramadi, capital of the western province of Anbar, in May 2015.

The resilience of ISIS, in the face of an extensive air campaign by a US-led coalition, indicates that the group is a violent symptom of a much larger set of problems, which have undermined the Iraqi state since it was reconstructed following the deposal of President Saddam Hussein. These problems, largely political, were responsible for the ensuing civil war. For Iraq to be stabilised and a sustainable peace established, not only will ISIS have to be vanquished on the battlefield, but the Iraqi state and its political institutions will need to be rebuilt in a way that gives a large majority of Iraqis a stake in the political system – and hence a commitment to maintaining stability.

Rise of ISIS

The predecessor of ISIS emerged long before the seizure of Mosul, and was intimately linked with Iraq's post-2003 political situation: the Islamic State of Iraq was created in 2006, at the height of the civil war. As a radical Sunni jihadist organisation, it was designed to capitalise on an increasingly sectarian conflict, and bore the hallmarks of that war's brutality. Its ideology evolved to become even more hardline and ruthless than that of its forerunner, al-Qaeda in Iraq. In contrast to al-Qaeda, ISIS is uncompromising on doctrinal issues, demanding complete adherence to its interpretation of Islam. Members of the group are seen to be the only 'true' Muslims, and as such are expected to dissociate themselves from all other Muslims. Failure to live in accordance with its interpretation of Islam constitutes unbelief, and opposing ISIS is tantamount to apostasy – both are punishable by death. Shi'ites, who make up the majority of Iraq's population, are therefore seen as apostates who must be killed. Accordingly, ISIS promotes an 'offensive jihad', the main targets of which are the Shia populations of Iraq and Syria.

In 2007 al-Qaeda in Iraq, along with radical Shia militias, became the main target of the US-led surge of foreign troops into the country. By 2010, when current ISIS leader Abu Bakr al-Baghdadi took charge of the group, the US military had succeeded in reducing its number of active members to the low hundreds. The group's subsequent renewal was driven by three separate but interlinked dynamics. Firstly, all US military forces were withdrawn from Iraq at the end of 2011 after the failure of negotiations on a new Status of Forces Agreement, which would have governed the legal status of American troops deployed there. This left the US government with comparatively little influence in Iraq.

Secondly, Iraq's prime minister from 2006 to 2014, Nuri al-Maliki, repeatedly tried to bolster his own legitimacy and solidify his vote among the Shia majority through the demonisation of Sunnis, associating them with the former Ba'athist regime and with continued terrorist violence. This approach reached its peak in 2013, when the popular and effective minister of finance, Rafi al-Issawi, a Sunni member of the Iraqiyya political bloc, was driven from the cabinet on trumped-up charges.

Thirdly, Baghdadi skilfully led the rejuvenation of ISIS by launching a series of campaigns to seize territory vacated by departing American troops, while also capitalising on an increasing sense of alienation and persecution among Sunnis. In 2012 Baghdadi launched what amounted to a hostile takeover of the Syrian jihadist campaign against President Bashar al-Assad, using his battle-hardened forces to take territory and gain control over new fighters and resources flowing into Syria. Baghdadi's commitment to both the civil war in Syria and the campaign in Iraq was symbolised by his April 2013 decision to rename the group the 'Islamic State of Iraq and al-Sham' (an Arabic word denoting Syria or the Levant).

The subsequent rebranding of ISIS as simply the 'Islamic State', following the capture of Mosul, indicated another expansion of the organisation's ambition. The declaration of a universal caliphate ruled by Baghdadi was indicative of the group's offensive jihad and of its recognition, as a central trait of both its strategy and ideology, that to survive it needed to continually increase the territory and numbers of people under its control.

Due to the success of its campaign, ISIS was able to attract new recruits into its ranks. By mid-2015, it was estimated that the group could mobilise around 25,000 fighters across both Iraq and Syria. Although ISIS has attracted many foreigners, a large majority of its fighters are Iraqi and Syrian, and its leadership primarily comprises Iraqis who were once middle-ranking personnel in Saddam Hussein's military and intelligence services. The rank and file is mostly made up of local fighters who joined either because they are angry with the governments in Baghdad or Damascus, or because they defected from other, less successful jihadist groups.

The organisation's finances were damaged by coalition airstrikes targeting oil wells it controlled near its stronghold of Ar-Raqqah, in Syria. It is estimated that the group's daily oil revenues may have been reduced from a high of US$1–2m in 2014 to as little as US$300,000 in 2015. However, according to a February 2015 report by the Financial Action Task Force, an international body combating money laundering and terrorist financing, the majority of revenues received by ISIS are extracted from the territories it controls through the extortion of businesses, fees for government services and 'taxation'. This money funds the estimated monthly wage bill of US$10m needed to keep its fighters in the field.

The US-led air campaign broke the group's momentum and played a role in ending its siege of the Syrian Kurdish town of Kobane. The operation engendered optimism at the Pentagon and in the Iraqi military that ISIS could be first geographically contained and then militarily defeated. In January 2015, the Pentagon announced that ISIS had lost 700 square kilometres of territory in the first four months of the campaign, and by April it was claiming that ISIS had lost control of between 12,950 and 15,540 sq km.

This optimistic view gained credence from a ground campaign by the Iraqi army and Shia militias to retake the northwestern Iraqi town of Tikrit. The assault, which began in March 2015, was seen as a dress rehearsal for the much larger task of retaking Mosul. But the fluidity of the 27,000 troops that made up what were styled 'government forces' was indicated by the fact that 70% of the operations to retake Tikrit were undertaken by Shia militias. In addition, a central role in the planning and execution of the military campaign was reported to have been played by General Qassem Suleimani, leader of the Iranian Revolutionary Guard Corps' elite Quds Force, and Hadi al-Ameri, senior commander in Iraqi militia the Badr Brigade, a violent sectarian actor in Iraq's civil war. (The Quds Force runs covert foreign operations for the Iranian government.) The US military lent its support with tactical intelligence and airstrikes. After a 29-day campaign, the combined forces drove ISIS from Tikrit.

Yet the renewed confidence created by victory in Tikrit was short-lived. Demonstrating its ability to regroup quickly, ISIS redeployed its forces two weeks later, overrunning the villages of Sjariyah, Albu-Ghanim and Soufiya, near Ramadi. It soon became apparent that this was a precursor to the group's main objective, the capture of Ramadi itself. In the event, ISIS seized control of eastern Ramadi before moving across the Euphrates to rout a much larger government force and take control of the whole city. The operation was well planned, with earth-moving equipment, heavy explosives and suicide bombers used to break Ramadi's defences, and with flanking forces deployed to stop government reinforcements from reaching the city.

The speedy and unexpected capitulation of Iraq's regular armed forces triggered a debate about their fighting ability. According to US Secretary of Defense Ashton Carter, the city had been lost because 'Iraqi forces showed no will to fight'. This conclusion was especially damning when it emerged that the counter-terrorism troops of Iraq's elite 'Golden Division' were among those who had fled. Iraqi analysts stressed that troops stationed in the city had not been rotated for 12 months, had only been reinforced by a police brigade and locally raised irregulars, and had not been sufficiently supported by US airstrikes. Ultimately, as with the fall of Mosul one year earlier, the defenders were made highly vulnerable by low morale, poor coordination and incoherent command and control.

Carter's derogatory remarks cast doubt on the credibility of US plans in which Iraq's security forces were relied on to defeat ISIS. From 2004 to 2011, the US had spent US$24.5 billion on rebuilding these forces; by 2012, they employed 933,000 people, spread between the Ministry of Defence, the Ministry of Interior and the prime minister's counter-terrorism force. But significant parts of the forces collapsed in the face of the ISIS campaign. The army's First Division lost two brigades fighting ISIS in Anbar before the capture of Mosul. The Second Division fell apart as it fled after Mosul was overrun, and the First Division lost two more brigades. The Third, Sixth and Ninth divisions fled ahead of the ISIS march on Sinjar and Erbil, while the Fourth was routed during the jihadists' seizure of Tikrit, reportedly leading to the massacre of large numbers of soldiers. Then came the flight from Ramadi.

Army reforms and growing militias

Prime Minister Haider al-Abadi adopted a three-pronged strategy to reform and rebuild the army. Firstly, he purged its senior ranks of corrupt, incompetent or politically tainted officers. Having become prime minister in September 2014, he quickly disbanded the Office of the Commander in Chief, the institutional vehicle that Maliki had used to concentrate military power in his own hands, thus breaking the chain of command and *esprit de corps*. Over the next two months, he sacked 320 senior officers, many of whom had responsibility for the areas of northwestern Iraq where ISIS had triumphed. Those sacked or forced to retire included the secretary-general of the defence ministry, the heads of the Baghdad, Samarra, Babil and Anbar operations centres, and the head of military intelligence. In June 2015, Abadi accepted the retirement of the army's chief of staff, General Babakir Zebari.

Secondly, Abadi sought to tackle the corruption that had become endemic in the security forces. He did this through an audit of the army's payroll to identify 'ghost soldiers', who were paid by the ministry of defence but did not show up for work, instead splitting their wages with senior military officers complicit in the deception. The audit uncovered 50,000 cases of such fraud.

Thirdly, as part of a plan to devolve power to the provinces, Abadi embarked on the creation of a locally raised National Guard. This, he hoped, would create a more religiously balanced security force, diminishing the sense among Sunnis that the army was used as a tool to persecute them – one primarily aligned with Shia religious parties. Political organisations whose allies dominated the higher ranks of the military, primarily Shia and Kurdish parties, vehemently opposed the initiative. In February 2015, after prolonged negotiations, parliament passed the National Guard bill. But it contained significant amendments: the National Guard would be managed by the prime minister rather than provincial governors; split between full- and part-time members; and raised only in provinces other than those controlled by the Kurdistan Regional Government. Despite these compromises, the majority of lawmakers from Shia religious parties voted against the bill.

Even as Abadi sought to reform the regular forces, the number of irregulars combating ISIS grew sharply. Since June 2014, when the army collapsed in the face of the group's abortive march on Baghdad, the capital and the whole of the Iraqi state had remained in an extremely vulnerable position. Recognising the perilous nature of the situation, Iraq's most senior Shia religious authority, Grand Ayatollah Ali al-Sistani, issued a fatwa calling on all able-bodied men to defend 'their country and their people and their holy places'. Two days later, the Iraqi government announced the formation of Hashd al-Shaabi (Popular Mobilisation Forces) to manage the tens of thousands of young men who, following the fatwa, had volunteered to fight.

However, although Sistani had explicitly asked volunteers to join Iraqi government forces and Baghdad had quickly moved to set up Hashd al-Shaabi, the main beneficiaries of this popular mobilisation were the militias run by Shia religious parties. The government could not organise, let alone deploy, so many volunteers. Instead, violent and radically sectarian Shia militias who had been active in the civil war – groups such as Asa'ib Ahl al-Haq, Kata'ib Hizbullah and the Badr Brigade – took centre stage, arming and deploying the recruits and rapidly growing in size, power and influence. Ameri, the senior Badr commander, became their public face. Together, the militia and Hashd al-Shaabi were estimated to have at least 100,000 men under arms.

The problems of raising a primarily Shia force mobilised through sectarian appeals and controlled by Shia militias soon became apparent. As the militias and Hashd al-Shaabi began to retake Sunni-dominated areas theretofore controlled by ISIS, there were reports, from Human Rights Watch and others, of summary executions, human-rights abuses and deliberate attempts at religious cleansing. This raised profound doubts about the sustainability of the victories against ISIS, based as they were on population transfers that exacerbated resentment among the Sunni population, making it even more difficult to find Sunni allies for the fight against the jihadists. Beyond this, the prospect of another civil war was raised by the dominant position of Shia militias – which, for example, controlled roadblocks across Baghdad – and their participation in a renewed campaign of sectarian violence and intimidation.

Political shift

The turmoil and fear engendered by the fall of Mosul prompted the removal of Maliki, who had become increasingly authoritarian in his eight years as prime minister. The ouster came despite his success in the April 2014 elections, in which his State of Law coalition won 95 seats in the 328-seat parliament and Maliki himself gained the highest individual backing of any Iraqi politician, with 721,000 votes. In theory, this put him in a position to control the formation of a new government. But the success of the ISIS campaign solidified opposition to a third Maliki term among the ruling elite. He was blamed for the army's weakness, and for the high level of resentment among Sunnis.

Moves to block Maliki's reappointment started in earnest in July 2014, after a Sunni politician, Salim al-Jibouri, was appointed speaker of parliament. This appointment triggered a constitutional countdown that gave parties 30 days to elect a president, who would then have 15 days to name a prime minister. On 24 July, veteran Kurdish politician Fuad Masum was elected to the presidency, a largely ceremonial position. A two-week deadlock on the selection of the prime minister was broken when Shia parties chose Abadi over Maliki, reportedly by a margin of 130 votes to 40, and Masum named Abadi as his chosen candidate. On 10 August, Maliki reacted by deploying soldiers around Baghdad and saying that he would challenge the decision in court. Amid intense diplomatic negotiations to avoid a crisis, a senior army general was reported to have visited Masum to reassure him that the military would stay out of politics. A delegation of senior officials pleaded with Maliki to stand down. At this point, the Iranian government, which previously supported Maliki, changed its stance. The secretary of Iran's Supreme National Security Council, Ali Shamkhani, offered his congratulations to Abadi, as did the Iranian foreign ministry. On 13 August, Sistani issued a handwritten letter to senior leaders of Maliki's party, Dawa, saying 'I see the need to speed up the selection of a new prime minister'. Negotiations with Maliki then focused on a guarantee that he would not be prosecuted for his actions while in office, along with the offer of a lesser government post. On 14 August, Maliki appeared on television with Abadi to announce that he was withdrawing his candidacy 'in order to preserve the high interests of the country'.

Abadi moved quickly to appoint a cabinet, although there was disagreement on who would become the defence minister and interior minister. Ameri was put forward for the latter post, but this recalled the 2005–06 period, when a Badr member held the position, with the ministry and its special-police commandos becoming important and very violent actors in the civil war. In October, parliament agreed to appoint Mohammed Salim al-Ghabban, a younger Badr member who did not have Ameri's controversial history, as interior minister and Khaled al-Obeidi as defence minister.

Abadi's cabinet looked remarkably similar to those that had followed each election since 2005. It divided up cabinet posts according to a sectarian quota and the electoral success of each political party. This approach has tended to encourage incoherence and corruption, as political parties, rather than the prime minister, control the ministries that they have been allocated. However, Abadi's appointment was seen in Iraq and across the region as a positive step. He appeared to be sincerely committed to national reconciliation, and quickly put in place bold policies to strengthen the armed forces and reduce their reputation for sectarianism. Still, his powers were limited and his popular support open to question. Moreover, the real military power lay with the Shia militias and Hashd al-Shaabi, neither of which he controlled. With sectarian violence increasing and no sign that ISIS would be defeated in the medium term, it was unclear whether Abadi could maintain enough popular support among his Shia constituency to push through the political reforms he desired, and to thereby mobilise Iraq's Sunnis against the jihadists.

ISIS: Widening Impact

The surprise takeover of Mosul and establishment of a self-styled 'caliphate' by ISIS in mid-2014 widened pre-existing sectarian, ethnic and political fault lines in the Middle East. The emergence of a jihadist pseudo-state at the heart of the region unnerved all Middle East powers, forcing a reluctant Washington to once more conduct a military intervention in Iraq, out of fear that the country would otherwise collapse. By mid-2015, ISIS looked set to become a lasting feature of the Middle East landscape.

An heir to the Islamist movements that grew out of the US occupation of Iraq, ISIS attracted a considerable number of fighters who had served in the Iraqi military and security services under Saddam Hussein, as well as foreign jihadists. Surviving in a weakened form in the last years of the US occupation, the group was reinvigorated by the Syrian civil war and the divisive, sectarian-based rule of Iraqi Prime Minister Nuri al-Maliki. By mid-2014, it had seized large swathes of northwest Iraq and northeast Syria, including the cities Fallujah and Ar-Raqqah. Primarily directed by Iraqi commanders, ISIS attracted recruits from the Arab world, Western countries and Central Asia, and by mid-2015 was estimated to have 25,000 fighters. The prominence in the media of the group's atrocities served the dual purpose of terrorising its enemies and appealing to would-be recruits.

Abu Bakr al-Baghdadi, leader of ISIS, proclaimed on 11 July 2014 the establishment and imminent expansion of his caliphate from the recently captured city of Mosul. His group distinguished itself from al-Qaeda in both ideology and strategy. It sought to conquer and govern territory; aimed to dominate all other groups, including other jihadist movements; prioritised expansion over the defeat of the Syrian regime; and engaged in large-scale, systematic acts of brutality against minorities and Shi'ites.

As part of its attempts to carry out widespread ethnic and sectarian cleansing, ISIS targeted Iraq's Yazidis, trapping and besieging them on Mount Sinjar in summer 2014. Along with the concurrent collapse of the Iraqi security forces, the plight of the Yazidis prompted Washington to build a broad international coalition, which included several Arab countries, to conduct airstrikes against ISIS. The US also provided military assistance to the Iraqi security forces. However, Washington refused to deploy ground troops in combat roles due to fears of mission creep, and out of mistrust of the Iraqi government.

The most organised, determined and effective local forces to fight ISIS were the Kurdish fighters in Iraq and Syria, at times aided by Turkish Kurds. In northern Iraq, the Peshmerga received support from several countries and was able to seize Kirkuk, rolling back ISIS advances in many areas and establishing defensive lines across disputed areas.

Further south, ISIS met with resistance from Sunni tribes in Anbar Province, as well as Shia militias that had mobilised at the request of Grand Ayatollah Ali Sistani and fell ostensibly under the command of the Iraqi prime minister. But in reality, while some militias supported government forces, the most powerful among them were aligned with Iran. Tehran's involvement created tension among fighters opposing ISIS – particularly as many Sunnis feared the Shia groups they joined in the effort – and created the perception that Baghdad would be unable to control, and would eventually succumb to, Shia militias.

The battle against ISIS led to complex entanglements between states, with the US and Iran operating uncomfortably alongside each other on the battlefield. Washington's policy was predicated on working with the Iraqi government on the training and equipping of reconstituted military units, and prioritised Iraq over Syria (except in Kobane, where coalition aircraft assisted the Kurdish resistance and counter-offensive against ISIS).

Iran directed significant resources towards the fight against ISIS, partly due to the group's frequent use of anti-Shia rhetoric and threats to Shia shrines, and provided political and material support to the Iraqi government and the Peshmerga, as well as Iraqi Shia militias. General Qassem Suleimani, head of the Iran Revolutionary Guard Corps' elite Quds Force, made appearances on battlefields across Iraq so as to convey Tehran's commitment to the fight, while Iranian officers embedded in Shia militias helped coordinate the efforts of these groups.

The US-led coalition against ISIS faced several strategic and operational challenges. The Gulf states had joined the coalition partly because of the danger posed by the jihadist group and partly to steer US strategy. However, there was increasing friction between Washington and the Gulf states due to the growing influence of Iran in Iraq, as well as the perception that the coalition's air campaign in Syria was benefiting Assad. Yet in February 2015 the immolation of captured Jordanian pilot Moaz al-Kasasbeh by ISIS reinvigorated Arab support for the mission, with the United Arab Emirates and Jordan playing the leading roles among Arab states.

In the first half of 2015, the jihadist group reconquered territory it had lost to the Syrian rebels in early 2014, and established a presence in Damascus and surrounding areas while conducting operations in Homs and Hama provinces, increasing its presence in Deir ez-Zor and capturing Palmyra. Ar-Raqqah continued to be governed as the de facto ISIS capital, as it had been since 2013.

In addition to Iran and the US-led coalition, ISIS faced an array of opposing forces – from al-Qaeda affiliate Jabhat al-Nusra and other hardline Islamist factions to Kurdish and nationalist rebel forces. Baghdadi's group presented itself as the champion of the Sunni community. Operating by what seemed to be an unspoken understanding, ISIS and pro-Assad forces focused their firepower on mainstream Syrian rebels, which both regarded as their more immediate enemy. But in August 2014, sensing weakness in the Syrian regime, ISIS attacked Al-Tabqa airport and massacred hundreds of government soldiers there. The group later captured Palmyra, putting it within reach of Damascus and other important cities.

The campaign against ISIS succeeded in blocking important sources of revenue for the group, especially through airstrikes on oilfields. It also led to the deaths of around 10,000 ISIS fighters, according to US estimates, and the destruction of some of the group's military and training facilities.

But the coalition failed to achieve decisive successes against ISIS, and by mid-2015 seemed unable to quickly meet the objective to 'degrade and ultimately destroy' the group that was articulated by US President Barack Obama. Indeed, ISIS proved to be adaptable and resilient. In March and April 2015, it mounted a strong defence of Tikrit against Iraqi forces, Shia militias and US airpower. Less than two months later, it captured Ramadi, delaying a long-awaited campaign to retake Mosul. This forced Washington to incrementally increase its military assistance to Iraq, despite remaining reluctant to change strategy out of fear that the burden of fighting ISIS would fall on US troops rather than local forces. The jihadist group also demonstrated its operational prowess and discipline, fighting ferociously in urban environments while acting with opportunism and stealth. It combined the agility of a light-infantry force with the terror tactics of a jihadist group, deploying sleeper cells and building powerful improvised explosive devices.

While ISIS displayed some internal weaknesses, as of mid-2015 these factors had not had a major effect on its fortunes. Many foreign recruits have attempted to desert the group in the face of harsh conditions, however, and civilians in Syria and Iraq have become discontented with its puritanical rule and excesses. There has also been a lack of support for ISIS among prominent jihadist thinkers, with figures such as the Jordanian Abu Muhammad al-Maqdisi expressing their disapproval of its methods.

Jordan: Struggle to Preserve Stability

Jordan faced a wide variety of challenges in the year to mid-2015, as it struggled to deal with the effects of the conflicts in Syria and Iraq, mounting domestic insecurity and sluggish political and economic reform. Nevertheless, King Abdullah II maintained tenuous stability in the country by balancing global, regional and domestic interests.

While Jordan maintained ambivalent neutrality in the early stages of the Syrian conflict, this policy changed with the rise of ISIS and at the insistence of the country's Gulf allies, which wanted the country to take on a more assertive role. It was reported in July 2014 that Jordan was covertly training moderate Syrian rebels on its soil. In September, with ISIS operating increasingly close to its borders, Jordan joined the US-led coalition and conducted airstrikes against the group. Amman suspended these operations in December 2014 after ISIS shot down a Jordanian aircraft over Syria and captured its pilot, Moaz al-Kasasbeh. But the release in February 2015 of footage showing Kasasbeh being burned alive by ISIS caused public outcry across Jordan, and galvanised support for more intensive operations in Syria and Iraq.

King Abdullah preserved stability in the country by securing international military and other aid, while walking a fine line between US, Saudi and Iranian interests in the Middle East. In May 2014, Jordan expelled the Syrian ambassador in Amman on the grounds that he had insulted the monarchy; in December, the country submitted a draft UN resolution in support of Palestinian statehood, a move that was backed by the Gulf states but strongly opposed by the US, which vetoed the proposal. In March 2015, the Jordanian foreign minister made a rare visit to Tehran, to discuss terrorism in the region and to convey Amman's alarm at Iranian activity in the Golan Heights. Amman subsequently joined the Saudi-led coalition conducting airstrikes against Houthi rebels in Yemen. Jordan's shift to a more active defence policy was particularly significant given that its military had remained largely uninvolved in regional wars for nearly 40 years.

Jordanians' primary domestic concern was the lack of substantive political and economic reform. They saw only superficial benefits in 2013 changes to electoral law purportedly designed to address the marginalisation of Palestinian–Jordanians and to allow parliament to appoint the prime minister. The Islamic Action Front, a political arm of the Muslim Brotherhood and Jordan's largest political faction, continued to criticise the monarchy's reforms, all the while suggesting that corruption at the heart of the government remained a perennial problem. The Muslim Brotherhood split in March 2015 into two competing branches, one of which remained loyal to the monarchy while the other that had a more militant outlook.

As host to more than one million Syrian refugees, Jordan was forced to set up another camp to shelter them at Azraq even as pressure on its fragile economy grew. The burgeoning number of refugees also stretched the country's scarce water and energy resources, while increasing internal tensions.

Against a background of high youth unemployment and the arrest of hundreds of citizens in connection with jihadist activities, senior government officials estimated that 1,500 Jordanians had joined extremist groups in Syria since 2011. Dozens of political activists were also arrested under expanded anti-terrorism legislation passed in April 2014. In September 2014, radical cleric Abu Qatada was cleared of terrorism charges, owing to a lack of sufficient evidence to connect him to a bomb plot targeting the millennium celebrations in Amman. In May 2015, the arrest and heavy-handed treatment of suspects, particularly those from the poor southern city of Ma'an, led to the resignation of the interior minister and several police chiefs.

Lebanon: Burden of Syrian War

Lebanon remained paralysed and under mounting pressure in the year to mid-2015, with parliament unable to resolve a political stalemate that had begun in May 2014 after it failed to elect a new president. Despite expectations that the rapid changes occurring across the Middle East would galvanise the Lebanese political scene, the lack of a president delayed important decisions and appointments to be made by state institutions, thereby reducing their power. Intent on seeing Michel Aoun elected president – although it did not have the votes to achieve this – the pro-Iran March 8 alliance boycotted presidential sessions, denying the constitutional quorum to the larger, pro-Saudi March 14 alliance. With regional and international attention focused on other Middle East crises, Lebanon was largely left to its own devices.

The legitimacy of the government was increasingly called into question: the lack of a president meant that all executive powers rested within the cabinet of Prime Minister Tammam Salam, and parliament voted in November 2014 to extend its own term until 2017. Although the government comprised ministers from both March 14 and March 8, as well as independents, it appeared unable to slow the decline in the country's economic and security situation. Meanwhile, the ongoing trial in The Hague of those allegedly behind the 2005 assassination of Lebanese prime minister Rafik Hariri shed light on the activities of Hizbullah, Lebanon's most significant Shia militia during the period of Syrian occupation.

The country continued to experience serious threats to its security due to repercussions from the conflict in Syria. Groups such as Jabhat al-Nusra and ISIS made incursions into Lebanon, ostensibly in retaliation for Hizbullah's efforts to aid Syrian President Bashar al-Assad. In summer 2014, 27 Lebanese troops were kidnapped and held hostage by Jabhat al-Nusra and ISIS after the groups overran the town of Esral; several of the soldiers were later gruesomely executed. This exacerbated popular sentiments against Islamist militants and Syrian refugees; and while it generated support for the Lebanese military, it also raised questions about the capabilities of the force. To shore up the army, the United States provided Lebanon with weaponry and other forms of military assistance, while France started in mid-2015 to provide arms worth US$3 billion, financed by Saudi Arabia. There was public outcry in Lebanon in May 2015 after a former minister was sentenced to just four and a half years in prison for planning a massive bombing campaign against anti-Assad targets.

In an attempt to reduce sectarian tension within Lebanon, Saad Hariri's Future Movement entered into a dialogue with Hizbullah in late 2014. The small measures subsequently agreed upon by the parties combined with increased deployments of security personnel to reduce violence in country. Yet although the security forces curtailed the car bombings that had plagued the country in preceding years, they were unable to prevent Jabhat al-Nusra and ISIS from launching a series of deadly attacks on civilians and military personnel.

Hizbullah continued to play a major role in Syria, with its leader Hassan Nasrallah emphasising the need to fight the Sunni jihadist enemy on Syrian soil and pledging full support to the Syrian regime. Nasrallah stridently opposed Saudi policy and alleged that Gulf states had created and funded ISIS. However, his group suffered heavy losses in Syria, especially in the battle for control of the Qalamoun border area. Hizbullah's participation in the Syrian conflict was brought to light once more in January 2015, when an Israeli airstrike in the Golan Heights killed some of the group's top commanders, along with an Iranian general. The group was suspected of building security infrastructure in the region to place further pressure on Israel, a move that threatened to end containment of Israel–Hizbullah violence in Lebanon.

The Syrian refugee crisis placed a massive burden on Lebanese society. The cost of assisting the million or more people who sought shelter in Lebanon was not met by international aid, and exacerbated popular discontent with their presence. The predominantly Sunni refugees were unlikely to return home in the medium term and accordingly altered the country's demographics. Reflecting concerns about the threat this posed to Lebanon's social fabric, the government imposed strict requirements on the entry and movement of refugees.

Israel and Palestine: Hardline Politics and Resurgent Violence

The Israeli government and the Palestinian Authority (PA) seemed further apart than ever in the year to mid-2015, due to upheaval in their respective political arenas and renewed violence between Hamas and the Israel Defense Forces (IDF). Israel's politics became increasingly hardline, as the country experienced a heightened sense of threat from turmoil in the Middle East and grew more dissatisfied with US policy on both the Israeli peace process and the Iranian nuclear programme.

Relations between the Israelis and the Palestinians began to rapidly deteriorate on 12 June 2014, when three Israeli teenagers were kidnapped from an Israeli settlement in the West Bank. The Israeli government declared that they had been abducted by Hamas, although no evidence of this was made public and the allegation was denied by the group's leadership. After the IDF subsequently launched *Operation Brother's Keeper* to search for the teenagers and crack down on terrorism in the West Bank, there were clashes between Israeli forces, local residents and the border police. During the operation, which the PA denounced as a form of collective punishment, five Palestinians were killed and more than 350 arrested, including several members of Hamas. The bodies of the three teenagers were discovered near Hebron on 30 June, prompting the revenge killing of a Palestinian teenager, allegedly by anti-Arab supporters of the Beitar Jerusalem football team.

Seeking to punish Hamas, the IDF expanded *Operation Brother's Keeper* to include airstrikes against the group's facilities in the Gaza Strip. This was followed by retaliatory rocket attacks on Israel, launched from Gaza by Hamas and affiliated militant groups. The intensification of longer-range rocket fire led Israel to begin *Operation Protective Edge* on 8 July, conducting airstrikes in Gaza while Hamas and its affiliates responded with further rocket and mortar attacks. Although little initial progress was made in subsequent ceasefire talks mediated by Egypt, the discussions produced a brief humanitarian ceasefire on 17 July.

An attempted incursion into Israel by Hamas prompted the IDF to begin a ground offensive in Gaza, ostensibly to destroy tunnel networks near the Israeli border. That phase of the operation lasted until 3 August, and was followed one week later by a 72-hour ceasefire, which was extended until

18 August. After the agreement was reached, there continued to be intermittent Hamas rocket attacks on Israel and IDF airstrikes in Gaza until 26 August, when a final ceasefire was accepted. Both Israeli Prime Minister Benjamin Netanyahu and Ismail Haniya, a Hamas leader based in Gaza, declared victory for their side.

The fighting resulted in the deaths of around 2,500 Palestinians and approximately 80 Israelis; internally displaced many civilians; inflicted significant damage on infrastructure in Gaza and the tunnel networks; and destroyed entire neighbourhoods, including Beit Hanoun and Shijaiyah. While US$5.4 billion was pledged to reconstruction efforts at a conference held in Cairo the following October, much of the funding came from pre-existing projects, and by mid-2015 only one-quarter of that amount had been disbursed.

Residual tension over the conflict led to a so-called 'silent intifada', marked by an increase in violence, particularly attacks by lone individuals. Demonstrations in the West Bank and Arab-populated areas of Israel often resulted in bloody clashes between Israeli forces and protesters. In December, one such confrontation caused the death of senior PA official Ziad Abu Ein. Along with a rise in assaults on Israeli civilians by the drivers of vehicles – incidents of which occurred in August, October and November – Israeli troops were also targeted. One soldier was shot at a bus stop in Jerusalem in August; in November, another was stabbed at a train station in Tel Aviv and three more run over in Gush Etzion. An attack on a Jerusalem synagogue on 18 November resulted in the deaths of five people, including four rabbis and a Druze policeman. Some believed that the act had been motivated by the Israeli authorities' decision, made the preceding month, to deny access to Haram al-Sharif/Temple Mount as a security precaution for the first time in 14 years, a move that angered Muslim Palestinians and was described by the PA as a 'declaration of war'. The following January, a Palestinian from the West Bank carried out an indiscriminate knife assault in central Tel Aviv.

There was no evidence that these incidents were ordered or coordinated by Hamas, Fatah or any other group, making it difficult for Israel to curtail them. And the response by Israeli civilians stoked further hostility: Israeli vigilantes, most of them settlers, mounted a series of reprisal attacks, primarily in Jerusalem and near West Bank settlements. The Israeli authorities conducted widespread arrests, demolishing the houses of Palestinians accused of participating in the violence.

Drive for Palestinian statehood

Against this backdrop of instability, Palestinian politics grew more fractious as the Fatah–Hamas leadership failed to govern effectively and the PA reinvigorated its push to have Palestine recognised as a state, following the collapse of the US-brokered peace talks with Israel.

The 'unity government' established by Fatah and Hamas proved contentious from its early stages. Following *Operation Protective Edge*, the antagonism between the two was on public display, with PA President Mahmoud Abbas accusing Hamas of preventing the PA from taking over civil administration, as stipulated in the ceasefire agreement. Slow reconstruction efforts, seen as the PA's area of responsibility, bolstered the popularity of Hamas at the expense of Fatah and Abbas. Although efforts were made to signal improvements in the fraught relationship, as seen in the decision to hold their first cabinet meeting in Gaza, further divisions were created by violence targeted against Fatah leaders in Gaza and an alleged Hamas plot to undermine the unity government, uncovered by the Israeli domestic-security agency, Shin Bet. The unity government's failure to organise presidential elections scheduled for November 2014 led to further paralysis and brinkmanship by the sides.

In December, as part of Palestine's bid for international recognition, Jordan submitted a draft UN resolution setting a deadline for achieving Palestinian statehood, only for it to be rejected. The following month, Palestinian leaders applied to join the International Criminal Court, prompting punitive measures by Israel. These included withholding tax revenues collected on behalf of the PA, a move that forced it to suspend the payment of government salaries. Palestine's formal acceptance as a member of the International Criminal Court, on 1 April, was celebrated as a victory that would ostensibly allow the PA to prosecute Israel over alleged war crimes. And in June, the Vatican recognised Palestine as a state, adding considerable weight to the push for sovereignty. This followed a similar move by Sweden in late 2014, and an overwhelming vote by the European Parliament in favour of the recognition, 'in principle', of Palestinian statehood.

Yet combined with the moves towards Palestinian unity, these efforts hardened Israel's position towards the PA, diminishing the prospects for success in future peace talks. The Israeli leadership declared that it would not deal with a unity government that included Hamas. In an attempt to embarrass and undermine the PA, it withheld revenues and cut access to public utilities in the West Bank such as electricity. Coupled with the rising violence, these actions jeopardised already weak Israel–Palestinian security cooperation in the West Bank.

Volatile Israeli politics

In December 2014, debilitating infighting within Israel's coalition government prompted Netanyahu to dismiss prominent centrist ministers and call for early legislative elections, scheduled for the following March. Fissures between Netanyahu's Likud Party and its centrist rivals had intensified after the breakdown of the US-brokered peace negotiations with the Palestinians, leading to heated disagreements over the budget, economic policy and proposed legislation seeking to define Israel as a 'Jewish state'. Netanyahu also perceived the weakness of centrist and leftist parties as an opportunity to achieve a more decisive victory, and to thereby form a government with a larger majority.

The election campaign proved to be volatile, with 26 parties running and new alliances taking shape. The Labor Party and Hatnua, led by Isaac Herzog and former justice minister Tzipi Livni respectively, formed a centre-left joint electoral list entitled the Zionist Union. The Arab-dominated parties Balad, Hadash, Ta'al and the United Arab List formed their first political alliance, known as the Joint List, while the ultra-orthodox Agudat Israel and Degel Hatorah established United Torah Judaism. Some parties also reached surplus-vote agreements, which created a de facto joint list when leftover seats were distributed in the Knesset. On the right, Likud and Naftali Bennett's Habayit Hayehudi entered an agreement, while the ultra-nationalist Yisrael Beytenu, a party headed by Avigdor Lieberman that had aligned with Likud in the 2013 elections, partnered with the new, economics-focused Kulanu. The ultra-orthodox Shas then joined United Torah Judaism, and the Zionist Union entered into an agreement with the left-leaning Meretz.

In the event, Likud won 30 seats to the Zionist Union's 24, despite the fact that exit polls had predicted a tie between the two. Both nationalist and religious-right parties lost seats, including Habayit Hayehudi and Yisrael Beytenu. Yesh Atid, the centrist kingmaker of the 2013 elections, lost seats while the Zionist Union exceeded the combined total won by Labor and Hatnua in the previous elections. The Arab Joint List emerged as the third-largest parliamentary bloc thanks to a high turnout among Arab voters. While the results did not demonstrate a rightward shift among the electorate – as Likud gained seats at the expense of parties further to the right – they allowed Netanyahu to form a coalition that excluded centre-left parties. As such, the election created a more stable and conservative government.

As the leader of the largest parliamentary bloc, Netanyahu was due to form a government by 6 May. Kulanu, Shas and United Torah Judaism joined Netanyahu's coalition, bringing their total to 53 seats. In order to win the support of Kulanu, Netanyahu had agreed to appoint its leader, Moshe Kahlon, as finance minister, raise soldiers' salaries and pass a budget by October 2015. Kulanu also gained control of the housing ministry, the national zoning commission and the land commission – all key economic posts. Kahlon appeared to be the new kingmaker in the Knesset, as Kulanu's support was required to pass both the budget and any legislation. Several posts were reserved for the pro-settlement Shas, notably that of the construction ministry.

Two days before the 6 May deadline, the leader of Yisrael Beytenu made the surprise announcement that his party would not join the coalition. This forced Netanyahu to make major concessions to Habayit Hayehudi, which joined the coalition just hours before the deadline. These included an increase in the education budget, additional pay rises for soldiers and a budget increase for Ariel University, located on the West Bank. In a decision that generated public outrage, Ayelet Shaked, a hawkish politician who supported a one-state solution and the 'Jewish state' legislation, was given control of the justice ministry. Bennett received the education and diaspora-affairs portfolios.

Other key ministries were reserved for members of Likud. Moshe Ya'alon held on to the defence ministry, while control of the science and technology, intelligence, interior and energy ministries was also granted to the party. With only a one-seat majority in the Knesset, Netanyahu was compelled to offer the foreign ministry to Herzog, who rejected the proposal. As a result, Netanyahu took control of the portfolio himself and appointed a trusted Likud official as deputy foreign minister. Led by the Zionist Union, the opposition consisted of five parties that ranged from the left to the far right, and accordingly lacked cohesion.

Israel's efforts to counter Iran

The tense relationship between Netanyahu and US President Barack Obama, which in 2014 frayed over the former's uncompromising stance on the peace process, had by mid-2015 become openly antagonistic due to the nuclear talks between Iran and major powers. Substantive policy differences on the issue were exacerbated by personal mistrust between the leaders. Israel publicly opposed the nuclear negotiations and resulting framework agreement, alleging that US concessions would allow Tehran to acquire a nuclear weapon and that any final deal would come at the Israelis' expense.

Netanyahu's acceptance of a controversial invitation to address Congress on 3 March 2015, issued by Republican leaders, was regarded as a breach of diplomatic protocol by the White House, which had not been consulted, and as interference in US domestic politics. Netanyahu used the speech, which was boycotted by some senior Democratic senators, to warn that the nuclear negotiations would have dire strategic and security repercussions for Israel, the Middle East and the United States. Nevertheless, there remained widespread support in both countries for maintaining a strong bilateral relationship. This had been seen in December 2014, when Congress passed the United States–Israel Strategic Partnership Act, a law that designated Israel as a 'major strategic partner' of the US and expanded security cooperation between the two.

In addition to the perceived threat from Iran, Israel continued to deal with the repercussions of the four-year-old Syrian civil war, demonstrating greater willingness to intervene in Syria against Hizbullah and Iran. The Israeli authorities closely monitored fighting between regime forces and rebels across the Golan Heights, as well as the increased presence of Hizbullah and Iranian commanders there. Israel also conducted airstrikes against the Syrian government and Hizbullah, allegedly bombing targets near Damascus in December 2014, and a Hizbullah convoy carrying S-300 missiles through the Golan Heights in January 2015, an operation that killed several Hizbullah leaders and an Iranian general.

Iran: Nuclear Agreement Reached

Thirteen years after its nuclear programme became an open sore in its relations with much of the rest of the world, Iran in summer 2015 reached a landmark agreement with the six global powers to sharply cut back sensitive aspects of that programme in exchange for lifting of sanctions that had come to exact a stiff toll on its economy. If faithfully implemented, the agreement will remove for a decade or more the threat of both an Iranian nuclear weapon and a war designed to stop it. This would help Iran's pragmatic president, Hassan Rouhani, fulfil a key promise made when he was elected in 2013: to restore sustainable economic growth. Yet hardliners led by Supreme Leader Ayatollah Ali Khamenei were likely to continue to deny him scope for political reforms.

Nuclear negotiations

After 20 months of intense negotiations and six missed deadlines, on 14 July 2015 Iran and the European Union/E3+3 (the EU, France, Germany and the United Kingdom, plus China, Russia and the United States) came to an agreement to limit Iran's nuclear programme and to ease sanctions imposed on the Islamic Republic. The Joint Comprehensive Plan of Action (JCPOA), as the agreement was called, will not fully resolve international concerns nor completely restore Iran's access to international trade and investment, but it will provide sufficient confidence that for the duration of the deal Iran would not be able to produce fissile material for nuclear weapons without detection.

Under the terms of the initial interim agreement reached in November 2013, which prevented the imposition of further sanctions while placing a limit on the size of Iran's uranium-enrichment programme, a final deal was to have been completed by July 2014. That deadline was postponed to November 2014, and then again to 30 June 2015. The latter postponement set an intermediate deadline in March 2015 for reaching a political understanding on the contours of an agreement. The parties missed that target date, but after intense negotiations in Lausanne they announced on 2 April a framework for an agreement. A vague joint statement by EU foreign-policy chief Federica Mogherini and Iran's foreign minister, Javad Zarif, was supplemented by much more detailed national statements, including a four-page US 'parameters' document that went beyond what many observers had thought would be possible at that stage. Differences between the national statements – each side played up the advantages it had gained while soft-pedalling concessions – led to diplomatic tensions and public criticisms in the final three months of the talks.

The 30 June deadline was then extended by several days three more times until ministerial-level leaders from the eight parties finally concluded a deal, on Bastille Day. The agreement met Western goals in that it would block all potential paths to an Iranian nuclear weapon for at least ten years. Firstly, Iran accepted limits on its stockpile of low-enriched uranium (LEU), and on the number and type of centrifuges at the uranium-enrichment facility at Natanz, so that it would not be able to produce a bomb's worth of highly enriched uranium in less than 12 months (the so-called 'break-out' period). Iran's previous rejection of such limits had convinced many analysts that a deal was impossible. Although Israel had insisted that the break-out period should be two years and US Secretary of State John Kerry had earlier spoken vaguely of perhaps accepting six months, US President Barack Obama fixed on one year as the key criterion for an agreement. The 19,000 installed centrifuges are to be reduced to 6,104 for ten years; and only 5,060 of them will be used to enrich uranium. During this period, only first-generation (so-called IR-1) centrifuges will operate, and research and development on more advanced models will be limited. The LEU stockpile will be reduced from around 15,000 kilograms to 300kg for 15 years. The reduction will be accomplished via a combination of diluting the product to an unenriched level and through export.

Secondly, Natanz will be the only place in which Iran is allowed to enrich uranium for 15 years; the Fordow enrichment facility will only be used for other nuclear-research purposes. Thirdly, the Arak research reactor will be modified to make it unfit for producing weapons-grade plutonium, including by replacing the reactor core and by redesigning it to use LEU fuel. Finally, the potential for clandestine uranium enrichment or plutonium production will be reduced by the most intrusive monitoring regime applied by the International Atomic Energy Agency (IAEA) anywhere in the world. The Additional Protocol, which allows for IAEA access anywhere it has reasons to suspect nuclear activity, will be implemented in perpetuity. Going beyond the Additional Protocol, the IAEA will monitor Iran's uranium mines and milling plants, centrifuge-production and -assembly sites, and procurement supply chains for a defined period. A 'dispute resolution process' was established to resolve disagreements on implementation of IAEA access and other provisions.

The framework also met Iran's bottom line. Most of the economic sanctions imposed due to its nuclear activities will be lifted or suspended once the IAEA certifies that Iran has taken the required steps to remove centrifuges and the Arak reactor core, and to reduce the LEU stockpile. This may take until the first or second quarter of 2016. Sanctions relief will include the release of approximately US$120 billion of proceeds from oil sales, frozen in accounts abroad. Iran will not be required to close down any facilities nor to dismantle any equipment. Keeping in storage the 13,000 centrifuges that are to be removed from Natanz was a face-saving measure that will also give Iran the scope to restore enrichment production to previous levels in case the agreement breaks down.

Iran also kept intact its goal of expanding the Natanz enrichment facility to an industrial scale. In July 2014, Khamenei surprised his negotiators by announcing that Iran needed the equivalent of over 120,000 first-generation centrifuges (using technical language, he put this in terms of 190,000 separative work units). He said this would not be needed in the immediate future, although the head of the Atomic Energy Organisation of Iran, Ali Akbar Salehi, then explained that it would be needed by the time a Russian contract to fuel the Bushehr nuclear reactor expired, in 2021. In the ensuing negotiations, Iran agreed to postpone this goal until well past that date. In any case, most experts assessed that Iran would not be able to produce fuel for Bushehr on its own for many years.

Western nations similarly preserved their leverage because most of the economic penalties could be restored quickly, via so-called 'snapback' sanctions in the event of violations of the agreement. The six UN Security Council resolutions that hitherto placed restrictions on Iran will be replaced by a new Security Council resolution that will allow for restoration of sanctions by a majority vote of the council without a veto right by any member. The replacement resolution will continue restrictions on conventional arms and missile-related transfers for five and eight years respectively, and will contain provisions for monitoring legitimate procurement of nuclear-related goods and equipment consistent with the allowed size and function of the enrichment programme.

While most nations applauded the chance for an agreement, the prospect alarmed Saudi Arabia, some other Gulf Arab states and Israel. The latter countries worried that repatriation of the unfrozen oil-sale proceeds would enable Iran to expand its influence in the region at their expense. At a May summit meeting with members of the Gulf Cooperation Council, held at Camp David, Obama downplayed this possibility, saying that most of Iran's 'destabilising activity' is conducted at little cost and thus would not be significantly boosted by a bigger budget.

Of most concern to Israelis is that, once limits expire in 15 years, and with restrictions on centrifuge research and development gradually being lifted from year eight, Iran will be able to ramp up its enrichment capacity to an industrial scale, thereby reducing the break-out time to weeks. In their view, the prospective deal only postpones the danger, while legitimising nuclear activity that had been illicit and removing sanctions enforcement. They are also displeased that the nuclear deal places no limits on Iran's ballistic-missile programme, other than transfers of missile-related items. The agreement's proponents counter that 15 years of successful implementation will build trust that the nuclear programme is exclusively for peaceful purposes, and that Iran's missiles are less threatening in the absence of nuclear warheads.

Many members of the US Congress, sharing Israel's concerns, sought to impose new sanctions on Iran and tried in other ways to force the Obama administration to toughen its negotiating position. Some legislators wanted US sanctions to remain in place until Iran ended its missile-development programme, its support for groups employing terrorism and its refusal to recognise Israel. Tehran threatened to walk out of negotiations if such measures were added, and Obama cautioned that he would veto any legislation along these lines. The Obama administration also opposed an effort led by Republican Senator Bob Corker to require congressional approval of any nuclear agreement. When the so-called Corker bill was amended in ways that made it difficult for Republicans to block a deal, Obama reversed his opposition. The resulting measure, which was passed by near-unanimous majorities in both US houses in early May, gave Congress 30–52 days to review the JCPOA before it goes into effect, plus another 30 days if the review period did not start until after 10 July. The agreement would not be treated as a treaty that requires congressional ratification. A two-thirds vote of disapproval by both houses could kill the agreement, but more than one-third of the members of the House of Representatives signed a letter in May expressing their support for the diplomatic effort, thus effectively inoculating the prospective deal.

The congressional review period complicated the timing of the JCPOA. Sanctions relief will not start until Iran completes the actions required to remove centrifuges from Natanz, reduce the LEU stockpile and replace the Arak reactor core. This could take six months, and the process will not start until the congressional review period is finished. The resulting timetable means that Iran is unlikely to receive relief from sanctions until after February 2016 elections for the 290-member Majles (parliament) and the Assembly of Experts, the 86 Islamic theologians tasked with choosing the Supreme Leader.

In a speech delivered one week after the Lausanne framework was announced, Khamenei appeared to walk back from some of its provisions and to set contentious 'red lines' regarding some of the matters still to be resolved. He insisted that all economic sanctions must be totally lifted on the first day of implementation of the deal, that inspections would not be allowed at military bases and that Iranian scientists could not be interviewed. His foreign-ministry team creatively interpreted the first of these conditions to mean that 'day one' of the deal would follow the period of preparation. It was also understood that many US sanctions could only be suspended, not removed, and that it would take time to unravel the complex set of regulations relating to the measures. In addition, the ministry contended that while military sites would not be subject to regular IAEA inspections, the Additional Protocol allowed for 'managed access' to the bases under certain conditions. Given that the IAEA had already visited Iranian military bases at least 12 times and conducted several interviews of Iranian scientists, Iran could not prohibit them in the future.

This was not the first time that Khamenei's red lines concerning the negotiations were overcome. In February 2015, for example, he opposed the two-step process that had been agreed, with a political framework to be worked out by March, followed by a detailed agreement in June.

Negotiators got around this by announcing, but not signing, the 2 April framework. But his stipulations on inspections and interviews did make it more difficult to finalise the agreement, as military commanders echoed his prohibition.

Throughout the course of the negotiations, Iran abided by the Joint Plan of Action agreed in 2013. The number of centrifuges remained at approximately 19,000, of which about 9,000 were operating. Iran did not enrich uranium above the 5% agreed level and 'neutralised' its stockpile of near-20%-enriched uranium, blending roughly half of it down to less than 5% and putting the remainder into an oxide-powder conversion process for use in making fuel assemblies for the Tehran Research Reactor. More than four tonnes of uranium enriched up to 2% was also diluted to the level of natural uranium. Iran also began to convert newly produced 5%-enriched uranium hexafluoride to oxide form; however, much of this material remained in intermediate conversion stages, and the amount fed into the conversion process fell behind schedule. While this appeared to be due to technical difficulties, it allowed US opponents of the diplomatic process to claim that Iran was not complying with the interim deal.

A controversy also arose in November 2014 over Iran's feeding of an advanced IR-5 centrifuge with uranium-hexafluoride gas for the first time, a practice that some analysts considered to be inconsistent with the Joint Plan of Action. When the US government requested that Iran cease the practice, Iran complied. A new type of advanced centrifuge, IR-8, was also introduced, although it was not injected with uranium hexafluoride.

Tehran remained adamant that its missile programme would not be a part of the negotiations. Despite its claims that it had no intention of developing intercontinental ballistic missiles (ICBMs), this remained of concern to Western nations. It appeared, however, that Iran had not made significant strides in this direction. An ICBM capability, often predicted to exist by 2015, remained several years away. But Iran had made strides in related areas. In March 2015, a new long-range cruise missile, dubbed *Soumar*, was unveiled. It appeared to be based on Russia's Kh-55 missile, a dozen of which Ukraine sold to Iran in 2001. The Kh-55 has a range of 2,500 kilometres and can carry conventional or small nuclear warheads of up to 410kg, but it was not clear whether the *Soumar* engine was powerful enough for this range and payload.

Iran cooperated with the IAEA in accordance with most of the terms of its standard safeguards agreement and the Joint Plan of Action. The agency was granted daily access to the enrichment facilities at Natanz and Fordow, and monthly access to the unfinished Arak heavy-water reactor. Inspectors were also given access to centrifuge-assembly facilities, rotor-production workshops, and uranium mines and mills. Yet there was scant progress on the so-called possible military dimensions of Iran's nuclear programme. Of the five practical measures that Iran had agreed in May 2014 to implement to address concerns in this area, two remained outstanding: as of June 2015, it had yet to provide satisfactory information related to its alleged work on the initiation of high explosives and its studies of neutron transport. Iran also continued to deny the IAEA access to the Parchin military site, where work on nuclear weapons is alleged to have taken place, mostly prior to 2005. Landscaping work near the building in question at Parchin continued, potentially making it impossible for IAEA environmental samples to reveal any evidence of nuclear activity. Under the JCPOA, Iran agreed to address all outstanding IAEA questions by November, although doubts remained as to whether they would be answered to the agency's satisfaction.

Internal dynamics

It is generally assumed that an international agreement on the nuclear issue that relieves sanctions will strengthen Rouhani's hand politically, although views on this are not unanimous. What does seem clear is the obverse prediction that failure to meet the high expectations on the part of the Iranian public for sanctions relief would undermine his popularity. In public statements, Rouhani repeatedly reminded critics of the deleterious impact of Iran's economic isolation. In January 2015 he even threatened to call for a national referendum if political opponents blocked a nuclear deal. The success of the nuclear negotiations, however, will not necessarily translate into increased political power for Rouhani, especially if sanctions relief is not visible before the February 2016 elections. Hardliners continue to control most of the levers of power: the judiciary, internal security forces, the Iran Revolutionary Guard Corps (IRGC), parliament, the Guardian Council and, most importantly, the Supreme Leader's office. Rouhani has thus been unable to implement political and social reforms, or to steer Iran's foreign policy in a more conciliatory direction.

In August 2014, for example, Rouhani's reformist-inclined minister of science research and technology, Reza Faraji-Dana, was impeached for decisions that included allowing back into college students who had been expelled over their involvement in the 2009 Green Movement pro-democracy demonstrations. Contrary to Rouhani's wishes, the two 2009 presidential candidates associated with the Green Movement, Mehdi Karroubi and Mir Hossein Mousavi, continued to be held under extrajudicial house arrest. Prominent human-rights activists remained jailed and there was a spike in state executions, generally for drug trafficking and other criminal offences. According to the Iran Human Rights Documentation Center, the number of executions rose to 721 in 2014, compared to 665 the previous year, and by mid-April 2015 were on track to experience a further annual increase, of 50% (partly due to a backlog of execution orders dating from the previous administration). As of May 2015, Iran's jails held more than 900 political prisoners, including eight who received lashes and long sentences in 2014 for activity on Facebook. A critical US State Department report, released in June 2015, said there had been no discernible progress on Iran's record of human rights since Rouhani's 2013 election.

Khamenei seeks to maintain balance among Iran's political factions. Although he allowed the nuclear negotiations to remove sanctions, he remains intensely suspicious of the West and opposes rapprochement with the US. He has thus allowed *Washington Post* Tehran correspondent Jason Rezaian to be incarcerated in Evin Prison since July 2014, a move that seemed designed to embarrass Rouhani. In April 2015, the reporter, who holds both US and Iranian citizenship, was formally charged with espionage and 'collaborating with hostile governments', among other crimes that carry a maximum sentence of 10–20 years. The hardliners will be unwilling to cede power over such matters ahead of the 2016 elections. As an example of the continuing power of this group, the Assembly of Experts selected in March 2015 a conservative cleric, Ayatollah Mohammad Yazdi, to head the council on an interim basis after the death of Ayatollah Mohammad Reza Mahdavi Kani. Yazdi received twice as many votes as the runner-up, former president Akbar Hashemi Rafsanjani, who is considered to be moderate. In light of persistent rumours about the precarious health of the 75-year-old Khamenei, who underwent a routine prostate operation in September 2014, the make-up and leadership of the Assembly of Experts is of growing importance.

Yet Rouhani does have control over economic levers, which he has been able to manipulate to the nation's advantage. Inflation, which stood at 42% when he took office in August 2013, was reduced to 15% as of April 2015. Unemployment dropped to around 10%, according to government figures. Wild fluctuations in the exchange rate were steadied. The limited sanctions relief that resulted from the 2013 interim agreement, which released US$700 million in frozen assets per month, contributed to positive economic growth beginning in the second quarter of 2014, reversing a two-year decline. The economy remained constrained, however, by the continuing sanctions on the oil trade, banking and other sectors, and by the decline in oil prices in 2014, which some Iranians blamed on a Saudi–US conspiracy.

Conclusion of a nuclear deal that lifts sanctions will provide a significant boost. Some economists expect GDP to grow by as much as 7–8% annually in the years following an agreement. But popular expectations may not be entirely fulfilled, and the unfreezing of oil revenues will have to be carefully managed to avoid destabilising the domestic economy. Oil exports, which have been limited to around 1.3m barrels per day, can be increased rapidly through the release of up to 40m barrels of oil that reportedly have been stored at sea for the past two years. Oil production, which in the first quarter of 2015 was 3.3m b/d, could be increased by 400,000 b/d relatively quickly by reversing controlled reductions. The psychological boost created by a comprehensive deal will boost economic momentum. Non-oil trade, which was around US$100bn in the Iranian year that ended in mid-March, is likely to grow sharply, reflecting pent-up demand for foreign machinery and consumer goods. Western banks will be wary of servicing this trade, however, until they are sure that the agreement will not unravel and leave them exposed to US penalties: a dozen mostly European banks have been fined a total of US$14bn for breaking sanctions since 2009. Foreign investors will be similarly cautious about entering into long-term arrangements. And US sanctions unrelated to the nuclear issue will remain in place, such as those concerning human-rights violations.

External relations

Iran's most vocal antagonists in the region and in the US characterised the country's foreign policy as a march towards domination of the Arab world by a 'Shia crescent'. But the nature of Iran's external activities was often exaggerated, including by Iranians themselves. In autumn 2014, a member of the Iranian parliament close to Khamenei spoke of three Arab capitals (Beirut, Damascus and Baghdad) having 'fallen into Iran's hands', with a fourth (Sana'a) to follow. In fact, Iran does not control any of these capitals; it is involved in events in each of them and exerts influence, but each is an independent actor. Iran does not manipulate them so much as take advantage of opportunities offered by turmoil.

The most costly foreign endeavour is in Syria, Iran's only formal state ally. Helping defend the Alawite-led regime is deemed of supreme strategic importance for Iran, which has around 1,000 military personnel in the country. Approximately 150 Iranian troops have died in the fighting, including six or more generals. Most of them were slain in battles against Sunni rebels, but one IRGC brigadier-general was killed in January by an Israeli strike against a Hizbullah convoy on the Syrian side of the Golan Heights; the Israelis said they were unaware that he was with the targeted group. The amount of financial support Iran has provided to Assad is a state secret, but is estimated to have been between US$15bn and US$19bn cumulatively in 2013 and 2014. On the Arab Sunni streets where Iran once was heralded for its defiance of Washington, the country is now regarded as the enabler of Assad's chlorine and barrel-bomb attacks on Syrian civilians. On the positive side, in May 2015 Iran was for the first time invited to join UN-led consultations aimed at ending the bloodshed in Syria. Mogherini called on Tehran to play a 'major but positive' role to encourage the Assad regime to agree to a political transition.

In Iraq, where gains by ISIS presented an impending direct threat to its own borders, Iran supported Baghdad with money, munitions and advisers, as well as by mobilising pro-Iran Shia militias. Dozens of IRGC personnel were reportedly killed in the fighting. The militias were organised by IRGC Quds Force commander General Qassem Suleimani, who became a media star in Iran when photos of him with Iraqi fighters were widely circulated. In August 2014, after initially supporting the failing

Iraqi prime minister Nuri al-Maliki longer than many observers thought wise, Iran helped engineer his replacement by Haider al-Abadi.

The civil war in Yemen found Iran engaged in yet another sectarian conflict. While the Houthi rebels were not acting at Iran's behest, either before or after their takeover of Sana'a in September 2014, they received some Iranian funding, training and equipment. Iran's overall role, however, has been marginal. Iranian weapons shipments increased in 2015, but an Iranian cargo-ship convoy bound for Yemen in mid-April 2015 turned back after the US Navy deployed a dozen warships to the area. In May, an Iranian aid ship bound for Yemen agreed to a UN request to first stop at Djibouti, after Tehran initially refused to divert the vessel. In response to Saudi Arabia's military intervention in Yemen, Khamenei said the kingdom's foreign policy had been hijacked by 'inexperienced young people who want to show savagery instead of patience and self-restraint'. The Supreme Leader's outburst contrasted with Zarif's accommodating response to a request made by Kerry on the sidelines of nuclear negotiations: for Iran to use its influence with the Houthis to convince them to join talks on a ceasefire.

The first half of 2015 saw an escalation of aggressive Iranian behaviour in the Strait of Hormuz. On 25 February, the IRGC held a long-delayed naval exercise involving an attack on a mock-up of an American aircraft carrier off the coast of Larak Island. Shortly after the Yemen-bound Iranian cargo ships turned back, the IRGC harassed a US-flagged cargo ship and two other commercial vessels that were passing through the strait. One of them, the Marshall Islands-flagged *Maersk Tigris*, was seized on orders from an Iranian court over a commercial dispute. This prompted the US Navy to temporarily provide naval escorts to some US and British ships. The *Maersk Tigris* was released ten days later, after the company settled the case. In the third incident, on 14 May, IRGC naval forces fired across the bow of a Singapore-flagged commercial ship, *Alpine Eternity*, which weeks earlier had collided with an Iranian oil rig – an incident for which Iran claimed damages. When the United Arab Emirates deployed coastguard boats in response to the ship's call for help, the IRGC vessels withdrew.

Russia tried harder than any other state to improve its political and economic relations with Iran. In August 2014, the economic and energy ministers from the two nations signed a comprehensive agreement on economic relations that sought to increase the volume of trade tenfold, from a relatively low base of US$1.5bn. The next month, presidents Vladimir Putin and Rouhani met twice at summits of the Shanghai Cooperation Organisation and of the Caspian Sea littoral states. Russian Minister of Foreign Affairs Sergei Lavrov called Iran a 'natural ally' in the struggle against religious extremists in the Middle East.

Fleshing out the economic agreement, Russia contracted in November 2014 to build two more nuclear reactors at Bushehr, with the intention of constructing eight new units in total, for which Russia is to supply the fuel for the lifetime of the reactors. Further details emerged of a long-heralded oil-for-assets barter deal worth up to US$20bn, although the terms appeared to remain aspirational. A more concrete measure of cooperation emerged in early April 2015, when Putin announced the lifting of a ban on the transfer to Iran of Russia's S-300 air-defence system, imposed in 2010 as Moscow's unilateral contribution to international-sanctions pressure on Tehran. Coming less than two weeks after the 2 April framework for a JCPOA, the announcement annoyed Russia's Western negotiating partners, who wished Putin had waited to relax sanctions until after a comprehensive deal had been finalised. Worried that Western nations would benefit most from resumed trade relations with Iran, Russia wanted to be the first with its foot in the door of the Iranian market, and to demonstrate that it was Iran's most reliable partner. Russia later clarified that the S-300 would not be delivered until 2016.

China and India also sought to improve economic relations with Iran. China increased its oil imports from Iran by nearly 30% in 2014, following the interim nuclear deal. This was a sign that oil sanctions were beginning to crumble, giving Western nations another reason to seek a comprehensive agreement. Beijing also enhanced ties with Tehran in other ways, such as by sending ships to the Gulf for China's first-ever joint military exercise with the Iranian navy, which focused on rescue missions. India, for its part, announced in May 2015 that it was moving ahead with plans to develop a port at Chabahar, in southeast Iran near the border with Pakistan, as part of a plan to open up a route to western Afghanistan.

Despite the comprehensive nuclear deal, a broader rapprochement with the US is unlikely in the foreseeable future. There remain too many issues of division, including Iran's support for the Assad regime in Syria and its opposition to Israel. Khamenei sent a non-committal response to an October 2014 letter from Obama, which reportedly raised the possibility of more robust cooperation against the Iraq-based forces of ISIS if a nuclear deal was secured. Nevertheless, the tide has turned after decades of confrontation between the two countries. Kerry and Zarif speak frequently by telephone; the new communication channels seem likely to remain in place. Anti-American displays in Iran are less vitriolic, and American flags have been spotted at a hotel in Shiraz and at an international film festival in Tehran. Moreover, Khamenei's reply to Obama did not rule out the possibility of an accommodation. And in a speech delivered on 9 April 2015, Khamenei held out the possibility of negotiating other issues with the US if nuclear talks succeeded.

Prospects

Implementation of the comprehensive agreement on the nuclear issue will boost the Iranian economy and restore its global trade. The nation's 78m citizens are largely middle class and desire international engagement. Most nations are eager to tap into Iran's large consumer market and pent-up demand. They also look forward to reducing tension over the nuclear issue and the potential for Iran to consequently ease its internal repression and external interference. But key countries in the Middle East fear the opposite effect, and in the short term they may be proven right. However, there is reason to believe that the nuclear settlement will contribute to Iran eventually becoming less isolated in its neighbourhood, and in the world as a whole.

Saudi Arabia: Succession amid Regional Crises

There were significant and potentially profound changes within Saudi Arabia in the year to mid-2015, in terms of both foreign policy and the domestic balance of power. The accession to the throne of King Salman bin Abdulaziz coincided with growing Middle East crises and a heightening of Saudi threat perceptions. The country responded forcefully to the advance of Houthi rebels in Yemen, as well as to Iranian assertiveness in

Iraq and the Levant and the United States' apparent recalibration of its role in the region. Saudi foreign policy also reflected a determination to counter rising threats to the kingdom's stability, both external and domestic, in more visible ways. Despite the high risks associated with such assertiveness, the approach affirmed the authority of the new monarch while also stirring a sometimes strident nationalism among many Saudis.

King Salman

An apprehensive Saudi Arabia was shaken out of its lethargy on 23 January 2015, when the ailing King Abdullah bin Abdulaziz passed away and was succeeded by Crown Prince Salman. Apparently following the wishes of the late monarch, his youngest half-brother Prince Muqrin bin Abdulaziz was elevated to crown prince and Prince Muhammad bin Nayef, the powerful interior minister, to deputy crown prince. Salman proceeded to make important changes in the cabinet, appointing his 29-year-old son Muhammad as defence minister and replacing reformist officials, including the minister of education and the head of the religious police, with conservative figures – a move intended to mollify a clerical establishment that had been uncomfortable with some of Abdullah's reforms. Two senior sons of Abdullah, Turki and Mishaal, were replaced as the governors of Riyadh and Mecca respectively. Decision-making was also streamlined and centralised, with Muhammad bin Nayef and Muhammad bin Salman put in charge of the newly established Defence and National Security Affairs Council and the Economic and Development Affairs Council respectively.

In April, King Salman also dramatically reordered of the line of succession. Muhammad bin Nayef replaced Muqrin as crown prince, and Muhammad bin Salman was elevated to deputy crown prince; these decisions were rubber-stamped by the Allegiance Council, demonstrating the monarch's domination of family dynamics. Prince Saud al-Faisal resigned from his post as foreign minister, which he had held for 40 years, and died on 9 July. He was replaced by Adel al-Jubeir, a commoner who had served as ambassador to the US.

Salman's decisions heralded the long-awaited transition to the grandsons of the kingdom's founder, King Abdulaziz. They also concentrated power within a subset of the Sudairi clan, with many of Abdulaziz's surviving sons and grandsons effectively sidelined. The most significant development was the advancement of Muhammad bin Salman, the king's untested but clearly trusted youngest son, who also became chairman of Saudi Aramco's Supreme Council. Previous monarchs had avoided placing their own children in the line of succession.

Assertive foreign policy

The last years of Abdullah's reign saw the emergence of a complex and perhaps unparalleled array of regional threats to Saudi Arabia. The kingdom countered some of these, supporting the overthrow of the Muslim Brotherhood government in Egypt and sponsoring its successor, the regime of Abdel Fattah el-Sisi. But its efforts to unseat Syrian President Bashar al-Assad were frustrated and it failed to prevent the development of an increasingly sectarian conflict in Iraq, while the civil war in Yemen spiralled out of control. As a consequence, there was a prevailing sense that the kingdom's Middle East policy was adrift.

Salman sought to address this perception. His rapprochement with the clerical establishment served to placate Islamists across the region, and he gave lower priority to the fight against the Muslim Brotherhood outside Egypt.

The new king also built a large coalition of Sunni states and ordered in March an air campaign designed to roll back the Houthi advance in Yemen, perceived as a symbol of growing Iranian influence in the country. Overseen by his son, the Saudi intervention became closely associated with the monarch's approach and eventual legacy. The king's courting of Sunni clerics and an intensive media campaign produced overwhelming Sunni support for the Yemen operation, which also helped counter Islamist dissatisfaction with Saudi relative inaction in Iraq and membership of the US-led coalition conducting airstrikes against ISIS.

The intervention in Yemen was designed to demonstrate Saudi military dominance of the Arabian Peninsula. A degree of legitimacy was provided to the mission by the participation of all other Gulf states (except for Oman), as well as by calls for action from the exiled Yemeni government. The Saudi air force carried the bulk of the operational effort, while the country's national guard was deployed to secure the border and its navy imposed a blockade.

A few weeks into the operation, the Saudi strategy was shown to have several flaws. The air campaign failed to recover territory occupied by the Houthis or to break down their resistance; instead of disrupting the rebels' alliance with former president Ali Abdullah Saleh, the operation antagonised many Yemenis, who had to contend with dire living conditions. Outside the Arab world, the intervention attracted some scepticism and – from Iran – condemnation. Furthermore, Saudi Arabia faced a diplomatic challenge in keeping the coalition together. Egypt resisted the deployment of ground forces into Yemen, and the Pakistani parliament voted down a similar proposal. With the prospects for a direct ground intervention diminishing, Riyadh focused on training and deploying local allies, particularly tribal fighters, while providing political support to Yemeni President Abd Rabbo Mansour Hadi, who remained in Riyadh.

Tehran's heavy criticism of the Saudi operation intensified regional tension. Although Iran's contribution to the Houthi advance remained unclear, the country nevertheless benefited from Saudi Arabia's entanglement on a complex terrain of marginal importance to Iranian security, as well as from the perception that Riyadh was fighting a sectarian war against a popular resistance movement. In denouncing the Saudi intervention, Iranian officials and media contrasted the mission with Riyadh's alleged complacency or even complicity in the rise of ISIS. Iran also sought to test US and Saudi 'red lines', provocatively dispatching planes and ships ostensibly carrying humanitarian assistance to Yemen despite the blockade.

King Salman's foreign policy also gave new momentum to another major arena for Saudi–Iranian competition, the conflict in Syria, with Riyadh revising its approach to backing the Syrian rebels' campaign in tandem with Turkey and Qatar. After divisions between Riyadh, Ankara and Doha – which had damaged rebel cohesion and effectiveness since 2012 – were cast aside, Islamist factions in northern Syria were able to make significant gains, while Saudi-backed southern rebels increased their foothold along the Jordanian border.

Iranian nuclear deal and US policy

A key source of anxiety for Salman related to Washington's Middle East policy, under which President Barack Obama had prioritised negotiations that led in July 2015 to agreement over the Iranian nuclear programme.

The immediate Saudi concern was that such a deal would legitimise and reward Iran's nuclear pursuits while softening the US approach towards perceived Iranian aggressiveness in the Middle East. In the long term, Riyadh feared a rapprochement between Tehran and Washington that would create a new regional order. To signal their discontent, Saudi officials pledged to match Iran's nuclear and military capabilities. Prince Turki al-Faisal, a senior royal, declared that 'preserving our regional security requires that we, as a Gulf grouping, work to create a real balance of forces with [Iran], including in nuclear know-how, and to be ready for any possibility in relation to the Iranian nuclear file.'

To assuage such concerns, Obama called for a summit at Camp David with Gulf leaders. Salman declined to attend, sending Muhammad bin Nayef and Muhammad bin Salman in his place. This could have reflected Saudi dissatisfaction with the limits to the US offer, but equally could have resulted from the king's advanced age and poor health. Whatever the truth, the move was widely interpreted as a snub. Washington's apparent unwillingness to confront Iran in Syria and Iraq compounded Saudi misgivings, although the US provided intelligence and logistical support, as well as weapons resupply, to the Saudi intervention in Yemen.

Domestic security threats

Saudi Arabia's decision to join the coalition against ISIS stemmed in part from the concern that the country's young people – 3,000 of whom had joined the jihadist movement – were susceptible to radicalisation, and that the group would seek to target the kingdom in a future phase of expansion. The potency of ISIS was demonstrated in a string of attacks. Following low-level assaults on Western expatriates living in Saudi Arabia, in November 2014 three gunmen associated with ISIS killed seven Shi'ites in the village of Al-Dalwah, in Eastern Province. Abu Bakr al-Baghdadi, leader of ISIS, escalated his rhetorical attacks against the Saudi kingdom in 2015. In May 2015, the recently established ISIS unit 'Najd Province' claimed responsibility for a large-scale bombing at a mosque in Qatif that killed 24 Shia worshippers. In what was seen as a show of defiance against ISIS and a warning to the government, the largest demonstration of Shia mourners to date followed. One week later, a suicide bomber killed two men who stopped him as he attempted to enter a mosque in the same region.

While senior royals paid visits to the targeted sites and those who had been injured to demonstrate sympathy and solidarity, Saudi Shi'ites complained of growing anti-Shia sentiment in the Saudi media and persistent discrimination against them by the government. The planned execution of a senior Shia clerical dissident, Sheikh Nimr al-Nimr, was subsequently postponed, allegedly to forestall escalation. In a possible sign of distrust of the regular security forces, citizens across the Eastern Province formed unarmed self-defence units (in cooperation with the local police force).

Oil and the economy

Saudi Arabia's behaviour on the oil markets changed considerably in the year to mid-2015. While the country had previously acted to stabilise oil markets using its spare production capacity, the huge increase in US shale-oil production, over several years, increased the global supply of oil. Instead of tightening its own production to keep prices high, Saudi Arabia maintained production of over ten million barrels per day, in an effort to defend its market share and apply pressure to US shale producers, whose production costs were much higher. Partly as a result, oil prices dipped from US$115 per barrel in June 2014 to below US$46 in January 2015.

This decline in the oil price to its lowest levels came as King Salman sought to build legitimacy for his leadership. As part of this effort, a few weeks after his accession to the throne he announced the distribution of US$32 billion in stipends and bonuses to state employees, the security forces and other segments of society; additional funding for water and electricity projects; and grants to non-governmental organisations. This spending contributed to a drop of US$49bn in Saudi foreign reserves during the first four months of 2015, and to a projected 2015 fiscal deficit of 20% of GDP.

Despite such adverse conditions, Salman enacted two important reforms: the opening of the Saudi stock market – the largest in the Middle East, with a capitalisation value of US$590bn – to foreign investors, and the introduction of a real-estate tax to address his country's acute housing crisis, which resulted from a lack of land appropriate for development.

Gulf States: Tentative Integration

Faced with growing instability on the Arabian Peninsula, the terrorist threat from ISIS, continued Iranian provocations and doubts about Washington's reliability, the Gulf states moved towards regional military integration in the year to mid-2015. Under Saudi and Emirati guidance, they also demonstrated greater diplomatic and military assertiveness.

With the apparent defeat of the Muslim Brotherhood in Egypt and the strengthening of the Sisi regime there, the Gulf states turned their attention to Iran. Viewing the advance of Houthi rebels in Yemen as Iranian encroachment, they (aside from Oman) participated in a Saudi-led military intervention, which was launched in March 2015. After years of competition, Saudi Arabia and Qatar began to better coordinate their efforts to support the Syrian rebellion, seeing Assad's continued hold on power as an important driver in the appeal of ISIS.

As part of a wave of militarisation across the region, many Gulf countries purchased new weapons, built up their militaries, and increased recruitment in the security services and the armed forces. At their annual summit held in December 2014, the states of the Gulf Cooperation Council (GCC) pledged to form a joint military command, a regional police force and a navy.

After helping create a framework nuclear agreement with Iran in April 2015, the United States felt compelled to reassure its Gulf allies, pledging to strengthen defence ties with them at a summit held at Camp David in mid-May. Washington renewed its commitment to build a regional ballistic-missile-defence capability, including an early-warning system, to protect the Gulf from a potential Iranian attack.

The decline in the oil price – from US$115 per barrel in June 2014 to US$65 the following May – put pressure on Gulf governments, forcing them to dip into their reserves to maintain high public spending necessary for their national-development objectives.

Qatar: Rapprochement with neighbours

Following a sharp deterioration in relations during the first half of 2014, Qatar and its neighbours experienced a gradual rapprochement from late July onwards. Bahrain, Saudi Arabia and the United Arab Emirates returned their ambassadors to Doha in November, after an emergency meeting to end the diplomatic rift was held in Riyadh. The terms of the reconciliation remained unclear, but the sense was that Qatar's new leadership was compelled to adjust its position after suffering setbacks to its policies in the region. As a result, the GCC summit in December was used to project an image of unity, and to announce political and military initiatives.

Qatari foreign policy took on a less militant tone. Following the December summit, the GCC states announced their unanimous support for Egyptian President Abdel Fattah el-Sisi. Although Doha took small steps to loosen ties with the Muslim Brotherhood and sought Saudi mediation with Egypt and the UAE, both countries remained distrustful of Qatar's links with the organisation. Relations with Egypt were further damaged in February, when Doha recalled its ambassador after Cairo accused it of sponsoring terrorism during a row over an Egyptian attack in Libya. And Qatar's image continued to be tainted by the controversy over the conditions in which it had succeeded in its bid to host the 2022 football World Cup, as well as its treatment of foreign workers.

Qatar invested heavily in weapons, signing a deal to buy 24 French *Rafale* fighter jets, at a cost of US$7 billion. This came ten months after an US$11bn deal with Washington that included the purchase of air-defence systems and *Apache* attack helicopters.

Bahrain: Continued internal unrest

Bahrain's Crown Prince Salman bin Hamad bin Isa Al Khalifa attempted to restart the national dialogue with the country's main opposition groups in September 2014, ahead of parliamentary elections scheduled for November, but the effort rapidly faltered. Despite receiving foreign advice to participate in the vote, five opposition groups, including the Shia al-Wefaq party, boycotted the elections, accusing the government of failing to keep its promises. Prospects for reconciliation diminished further as the government launched a crackdown against dissidents after the elections. Ali Salman, leader of al-Wefaq, was arrested in December on charges relating to the incitement of violence, hate speech, contact with foreign groups and threats to use force against the state. His detention sparked demonstrations among his supporters on a near-weekly basis. A prominent human-rights activist, Nabeel Rajab, was sentenced to six months in jail in

January, after commenting on Twitter that the state's security institutions were the 'ideological incubator' for radicalised Bahrainis who joined ISIS.

The same month, Bahrain revoked the citizenship of 72 people accused of 'illegal acts', most of whom were charged with anti-government activity at home, but some of whom were fighting alongside ISIS. Several activists were also arrested for criticising the government's participation in the Saudi-led military campaign against Houthi rebels in Yemen. While sporadic demonstrations continued throughout the year, improved security practices helped the authorities contain the violence. Radical opposition groups, some allegedly linked to Iran and Iraqi Shia militias, continued to mount attacks against policemen, using home-made bombs. These assaults resulted in the deaths of two policemen and one civilian, as well as the injury of nine others. Three people were sentenced to death over their involvement in fatal bombings.

Relations with the US remained tense over Washington's insistence that Manama reach a domestic political compromise. In July 2014, Bahrain ordered visiting US diplomat Tom Malinowski to leave the country, after he met with members of al-Wefaq on a three-day trip to Bahrain – a move described by the foreign ministry as interference in domestic affairs. In contrast, relations between Manama and London improved, with the sides signing a £15-million (US$23m) deal to establish a permanent British naval facility in Mina Salman, the United Kingdom's first such agreement in the Gulf since its 1971 withdrawal. There was also a rise in UK arms sales to Bahrain. Designating the country as one of its 'priority markets' for weapons, London entered into discussions with Manama over Bahrain's potential purchase of 12 *Typhoon* fighter jets, at a cost of £1bn (US$1.5bn).

Overall, Bahrain appeared to be taking on a larger international role: the GCC announced at its December summit that the planned joint naval force would be based in the country, and Manama also deployed its small air force in support of the international coalition conducting airstrikes against ISIS in Syria and Iraq, and later in the intervention in Yemen.

Kuwait: Political discord

Kuwait was shaken by discord within the ruling elite and dissent outside it. Although former prime minister Sheikh Nasser al-Sabah and former parliament speaker Jassim al-Kharafi were cleared of allegations of graft and conducting a plot against the government, there remained significant public discontent over alleged corruption among the ruling family and senior officials. Meanwhile, a split between Sheikh Nasser and former oil minister Sheikh Ahmad al-Fahad al-Sabah revealed an ongoing power struggle within the ruling family.

In February 2015, an appeals court sentenced opposition leader Musallam al-Barrak to two years in jail over charges of insulting the emir. An anti-government protest held in March resulted in the arrest of another 18 activists, including prominent human-rights campaigner Nawaf al-Hendal. Kuwait stripped 32 people of their citizenship in the year to mid-2015, in an attempt to silence dissent.

The Kuwaiti government also took steps to discourage opponents of its role in the Saudi-led military operation against the Houthi rebels in Yemen. Khalid al-Shatti, a former lawyer and member of parliament, was detained after criticising Kuwait's involvement in the airstrikes, as was academic Salah al-Fadhli. The dispute had sectarian undertones, with Shia parliamentarians condemning the offensive against the Houthis and arguing that Kuwait's participation in the war broke its official ban on offensive warfare. A call by parliamentarian Abdul Hamid al-Dashti to question the foreign minister over the war was rebuffed by his counterparts in government. In light of these political and sectarian tensions, Kuwait joined the anti-ISIS coalition operating in Iraq and Syria, but refrained from military action.

UAE: Growing assertiveness

Enjoying stability at home, the UAE pursued a more assertive foreign policy against perceived external threats. In cooperation with Egypt, it carried out airstrikes in Libya in August 2014, aiming to prevent the takeover of Tripoli airport by Islamist militias. This initially covert intervention was revealed by the US, and reflected disagreements between allies over the best course of action to counter Libyan Islamist movements. Nonetheless, the UAE contributed more to the US-led campaign against ISIS than any other Arab country.

The UAE also continued to bankroll the Sisi regime and to invest heavily in the Egyptian economy. It played a key role in organising a

March 2015 economic-development conference in Sharm el-Sheikh, which was designed to boost investment in Egypt. At the event itself, the UAE pledged another US$4bn in aid to Cairo (as did Kuwait and Saudi Arabia).

The UAE's hardline position vis-à-vis political Islam was expressed by Minister of Foreign Affairs Abdullah bin Zayed Al Nahayan, who stated in November 2014 that 'our threshold is quite low when we talk about extremism'. The same month, the UAE listed 82 Islamist organisations as terrorist organisations, including extremist groups such as ISIS, Jabhat al-Nusra and the Taliban, as well as the Muslim Brotherhood and the UAE-based al-Islah. The UAE also sought to influence US policy in the Gulf, demanding that Washington provide assurances and key weapons systems in the aftermath of the nuclear talks with Iran.

Oman: Ongoing neutrality

Sultan Qaboos Al Said returned to Muscat in March 2015 after eight months of medical treatment in Germany. His long absence due to ill health exacerbated anxiety about Oman's stability and a possible succession crisis, due to the fact that Qaboos has neither children nor a publicly designated heir.

In line with its policy of neutrality and mediation over regional crises, Oman distinguished itself from other Gulf states, refusing to take part in the isolation of Qatar, the US-led coalition against ISIS or the Saudi intervention in Yemen. In April, it offered to mediate between Saudi Arabia and Iran, following the announcement of the framework nuclear agreement between Iran and major powers.

Yemen: From Political Transition to Civil War

Yemen's fragile political transition collapsed in the year to mid-2015, leading to a full-blown civil war and external intervention. Although President Abd Rabbo Mansour Hadi never seemed to be fully in control of the country, his tenuous hold on power broke down in a violent struggle with the Houthis (a movement formally known as Ansar Allah). After seizing territory and overrunning the capital in September 2014, the

Houthis sought to translate their military victories into political influence, directly confronting and undermining Hadi's rule. Following three precarious months of power-sharing in Sana'a, Hadi's authority started to implode under Houthi pressure. The power struggle escalated in January, deepening political divisions and inflaming regional tensions. At Hadi's request, a Saudi-led coalition intervened in late March to neutralise the Houthi threat in Yemen, imposing an aerial and naval blockade on the country, striking Houthi positions (especially airpower and missile capabilities), arming pro-Hadi militias in the south and providing military training to hundreds of Yemeni tribesmen. The Saudi intervention was motivated in large part by a desire to check perceived Iranian backing of the Houthi movement. With the political transition backed by the United Nations and the Gulf Cooperation Council (GCC) effectively disintegrating, Yemen has become a new proxy battlefield for the rivalry between Riyadh and Tehran.

Takeover of Sana'a

The Houthi takeover of Sana'a was preceded by months of expansion from their northern stronghold of Saada, southwards into Amran and eastwards into Al-Jawf. The advance triggered bloody clashes with armed groups along the way, including tribesmen, militias aligned with the Islamist al-Islah movement and several brigades of the Yemeni army. The Houthis had already reached the outskirts of Sana'a in early 2014, but their march on the capital in September was facilitated by an economic crisis. In order to meet conditions for a reform package from the IMF, Hadi withdrew energy subsidies in July 2014, a move that led to soaring fuel prices, severe fuel shortages and protests.

The Houthis presented themselves as supporters of the poor and as a populist alternative to the government, using the opening created by rising public discontent to enter Sana'a in mid-August. There, they set up protest camps and demanded the reinstatement of subsidies and the resignation of the government. After a month of sit-ins and skirmishes in Sana'a, clashes broke out between the Houthis and the army. In fighting during 16–22 September, Houthi operatives seized state institutions, including the central bank, the defence ministry and a major army base – facing little resistance. Although they stopped short of a *coup d'état* and signed a power-sharing agreement, they demanded a greater role in the government's decision-making process. The Houthis began dictating government policy, citing a duty to fight rampant corruption among the ruling elite. They thus investigated and controlled government finances, replaced provincial governors with loyalists and attacked political opponents, ranging from al-Islah to General Ali Mohsen al-Ahmar, an army commander who had led battles against them in the past.

In the meantime, Houthi militias continued to seize strategic political and military infrastructure in Sana'a and beyond. They spread across large areas of the country, moving from Sana'a into at least seven provinces. Demonstrations against such incursions were met with live fire, killing protesters. Elsewhere, Houthi deployments provoked armed resistance, the deadliest of which took place in Al-Bayda, where many tribesmen allied with al-Qaeda in the Arabian Peninsula (AQAP) against the Houthis. More than 800 people were killed in AQAP–Houthi clashes between October 2014 and mid-2015. AQAP used a sectarian discourse to appeal to Sunni tribes, while targeting Houthis in areas as varied as the coastal city of Hodeida, the oil-rich province of Ma'rib and the capital. AQAP thus exploited the upheaval and the collapse of counter-terrorism forces to expand its capacity, operating unhindered in places previously considered beyond its reach.

Houthi expansion into the south

Having coexisted, albeit uncomfortably, in Sana'a for months, Hadi and the Houthis entered into direct confrontation in January 2015. The main point of contention was a draft constitution that stipulated the division of Yemen into six regions, as suggested by the National Dialogue Conference in 2014 (a process that brought together Yemen's competing factions). The Houthis rejected the proposal, fearing it would marginalise them in the landlocked, resource-poor north. In light of a history of disenfranchisement at the hands of the state, they sought to secure a greater political role for themselves at any cost, increasingly relying on violence to achieve this end.

During 17–19 January, they apprehended Hadi's top aide, stormed the presidential palace and placed the president under house arrest. After initially agreeing to the Houthis' demands, Hadi later resigned, along with the entire government. Subsequent attempts to restart UN-led negotiations on a political transition proved fruitless. There was a rift between, on the one hand, the Houthis and the General People's Congress (GPC), which was led by former president Ali Abdullah Saleh, and, on the other hand, the rest of Yemen's political parties. It became clear that the Houthis and the GPC opposed the reinstatement of Hadi, especially after the Houthis released a unilateral constitutional declaration dissolving parliament and announcing the formation of a transitional council in its stead. Following the collapse of talks on 10 February 2015, Gulf and Western states shut their embassies and evacuated their personnel from Sana'a, citing heightened insecurity.

In a move that surprised many, Hadi fled in late February to his home town of Aden, in southern Yemen, where he withdrew his resignation. He established a parallel government and temporarily moved the capital from Sana'a to Aden, declaring Sana'a to be 'occupied' and the Houthis 'stooges of Iran'. In a sign of support for Hadi, several Gulf states reopened their embassies in Aden. Riyadh and its Arab allies were wary of the Houthis' alleged links to Iran and general anti-Saudi orientation, as indicated by Saudi Arabia's quiet suspension of aid to Yemen after the Houthis took over Sana'a.

The Houthis responded by advancing towards Aden in March. An alliance with Saleh enabled them to coordinate with divisions in the military that had remained loyal to the former president. These included the Special Security Forces, an autonomous paramilitary force that had been founded to combat AQAP and that retained large caches of weapons. Within days, the Houthis had reached Aden and seized its international airport, along with towns in the districts of Abyan, Al-Dhale, Lahij and Ta'izz. Hadi then went into exile in Saudi Arabia.

External intervention

Hadi called on the UN to allow 'willing states' to intervene in Yemen, thereby providing legal cover for a Saudi-led coalition to launch *Operation Decisive Storm*. Purportedly aiming to restore Hadi to the leadership and to defeat the Houthis, the Saudi intervention was also meant to demonstrate decisiveness in the face of Iran's gains in the region and to protect the security of the Arabian Peninsula. The coalition formed by Saudi Arabia included

Egypt, Jordan, Pakistan, Bahrain, Kuwait, Morocco, Qatar and the United Arab Emirates, and received diplomatic backing as well as logistical and intelligence support from the United States. The coalition was also endorsed by the Arab League at a summit held in Cairo. The UN Security Council imposed sanctions and an arms embargo against Houthi leaders and Saleh. In spite of Russian efforts to the contrary, the Security Council refrained from condemning the Saudi intervention or from imposing a ceasefire.

Like Hadi, the GCC and its allies portrayed the Houthi movement as an Iranian proxy, equating its rise with Iranian encroachment into their sphere of influence. However, although the Houthis have received political support from Tehran, their mobilisation seemed largely uncoordinated with the Iranian leadership and rather driven by local calculations. US sources even suggested that Iran had advised them against taking over Sana'a and later Aden. But the resulting situation benefited Tehran: Saudi Arabia is entangled in a complex conflict that is of only marginal importance to Iran, which described the intervention as a 'massacre' and condemned its humanitarian effects. Similarly, the Houthis continued to use revolutionary, nationalist and anti-elite rhetoric, suggesting that there had been collusion between Saudi Arabia and AQAP, which it views as sharing a similar ideology. Asserting their right to defend Yemen in the face of Saudi 'aggression', Houthi operatives launched deadly cross-border attacks against Saudi Arabia, drawing heavy retaliation from the coalition against the northern provinces of Hajjah and Saada.

The Saudi-led coalition announced the end of *Operation Decisive Storm* in April 2015, replacing it with *Operation Renewal of Hope*. However, airstrikes continued in the new phase of the campaign, which purports to incorporate humanitarian and political dimensions alongside military action.

Power vacuum

Houthi militias initially advanced in the south despite coalition airstrikes, but they suffered their first major setback on 25 May 2015, when they were pushed out of Al-Dhale. By mid-2015, they were still embroiled in fierce battles with militias and popular committees, which were backed by coalition airstrikes, in Aden and Ta'izz.

Southern militias led the ground battle against the Houthis and received arms from the coalition. Following the convergence of interest between these militias and Hadi in fending off a Houthi–Saleh attack, the anti-Houthi Southern Secessionist Movement (SSM) suspended a long-standing civil-disobedience campaign. Yet many southerners had disputed Hadi's legitimacy even before the Houthi takeover, and his position was further weakened when he chose exile in Saudi Arabia. The SSM leadership sought to exploit the power vacuum that resulted from the Houthi takeover of Sana'a, taking symbolic measures towards independence. While the SSM preferred Hadi to the Houthis in the short term, its ultimate goal of secession meant that its loyalty to the president was questionable – as was the notion that Aden was the government's last stronghold.

Capitalising on the power vacuum, AQAP also made gains on the ground. It regrouped after suffering setbacks in mid-2014 and opportunistically increased its attacks against the state and infrastructure following the start of *Operation Decisive Storm*, seizing the port city of Al-Mukalla, in Hadhramaut province, as well as critical infrastructure there, such as the Al-Riyan airport and the Al-Dhabah oil terminal. It staged a prison break in April 2015, releasing inmates who sympathised with the group. Facing little resistance as its two main adversaries battled one another, AQAP strengthened its control of Hadhramaut by broadening its support bases and co-opting local tribes, such as the Hadhramaut Tribal Alliance, while working alongside a local administrative body to govern Al-Mukalla. The group's operatives moved with growing confidence across the country following the departure of US forces from Yemen in March 2015, a move precipitated by growing insecurity.

The US continued to target AQAP, despite the departure of American forces from the Al-Anad air base in Lahij, and its officials from the embassy in Sana'a. Strikes by US unmanned aerial vehicles increased significantly following the Houthi takeover – nearly doubling between January and June 2015, owing to AQAP's more visible presence and greater activity against its foes.

Amid this chaos, a local faction of ISIS was established in Yemen, after its members defected from AQAP. A group of Yemeni mujahideen joined ISIS in November 2014, and ISIS claimed responsibility for large-scale attacks including a 20 March 2015 bombing that killed 147 people in two Houthi mosques, and the execution of 15 soldiers in Shabwa in mid-April.

Meanwhile, much of Yemen's oil infrastructure ceased to operate. A liquefied-natural-gas plant halted production in April 2015, citing *force majeure*, while the government forces responsible for protecting the Masila oilfields withdrew, handing responsibility to local tribes.

Limited prospects of reconciliation

In April 2015, Hadi appointed former prime minister Khaled Bahah as vice-president, in what seemed to be a conciliatory gesture. Nonetheless, there was little prospect of reconciliation in Yemen. Weeks of aerial bombardment under *Operation Decisive Storm* did not reverse the Houthis' territorial gains, expel them from Sana'a or other important cities, or force them to accept political compromise. *Operation Renewal of Hope* did not produce a ceasefire. No inclusive negotiations had been held by mid-2015, reflecting the sides' apparent preference for brinkmanship and theatrics over genuine engagement.

A four-point peace plan put forward by Iran's foreign minister in April was rejected by the Yemeni government and the Gulf countries. A conference was held in Riyadh during 17–19 May, bringing together a number of parties in an effort to find a political solution. But the meeting was boycotted by the Houthis. The attendance of many Yemeni political parties, including the GPC, enabled Hadi to regain some legitimacy as a unifying figure. At the conference, the coalition stated that it would persist with the intervention, reaffirming its support for the anti-Houthi fighters by pledging to supply them with weapons. Although UN-mediated talks were scheduled to take place in Geneva in May, they were postponed at the request of the government and various Yemeni factions.

Meanwhile, the humanitarian crisis grew worse. With many Yemenis dependent on imports, the blockade caused prices to soar and led to shortages of food, fuel, water and electricity. Houthi officials accused the coalition of using cluster munitions and targeting civilian infrastructure, including a refugee camp, a cement plant and a dairy factory, as well as humanitarian facilities storing food and other types of assistance. The airstrikes destroyed critical infrastructure such as airports, seaports, bridges, roads and petrol stations, as well as water and electricity facilities. More than 2,000 people were killed and around 550,000 displaced in just a few months, following the onset of the airstrikes. By mid-2015, it appeared that Yemen had become a failed state.

North Africa

The fates and political trajectories of the five countries of North Africa differed significantly throughout the year to mid-2015. While Libya sank into fully fledged civil war and political brinkmanship, nearby Tunisia completed its democratic, albeit still fragile, transition. The consolidation of power by Abdel Fattah el-Sisi in Egypt following his election as president was paralleled by the emergence of a mid-level Islamist insurgency. Simmering discontent in Algeria struggled to find political expression, while in Morocco the government was under political pressure ahead of elections in 2016. The arrival of ISIS as a militant group that was able to operate in most North African countries constituted the region's most notable security development.

Egypt: New Political Order

Egypt settled into a new, if familiar, pattern in the year to mid-2015, as President Abdel Fattah el-Sisi strengthened the military's control of politics, economics and security. The relative stability he brought, after the uprising in 2011 and the abortive rise to power of the Muslim Brotherhood, allowed for a gradual improvement in the economy, albeit one that fell short of the recovery needed to address the challenges that the country was facing. While there were some developments that could theoretically lead to greater political freedoms for ordinary Egyptians in the long term, such as constitutionally stipulated rights to freedom of assembly, it did not seem that they would gain such freedoms in the foreseeable future.

Sisi's election did little, however, to address or resolve the deep rifts in Egyptian society. While genuinely popular, he began to suffer from the gap between lofty rhetoric and the semblance of order, and the reality of political division and enduring Islamist activism, both peaceful and violent. By mid-2015, it had become clear that he was facing a spreading insurgency that targeted his regime and threatened his ambitious economic plans. Previously confined to the Sinai Peninsula, the insurgency turned into a broader armed movement operating in Cairo and other areas of the country. This spread was fuelled by young Islamist recruits who were disillusioned by the failed political engagement of the Muslim Brotherhood and inspired by the success of ISIS. Gulf states' support for Egypt was maintained even as questions emerged about Sisi's governance and foreign policy. Sisi's anti-Islamist agenda differed considerably from Saudi Arabia's new regional positioning under King Salman bin Abdulaziz, which emphasised Sunni cohesion and resistance to Iran.

Sisi, previously the armed-forces chief, had been elected to the presidency by a landslide in June 2014 – in a vote that was harshly criticised for its lack of freedom and openness – eleven months after leading a coup against his predecessor, Muhammad Morsi of the Muslim Brotherhood, whose authoritarian tendencies and incompetence prompted mass protests. Although it had strong public support, the Sisi government continued to implement policies that did not adequately address the need for widespread reform in the security sector, the judiciary and the political arena, among other areas. The negative effects of this approach have been exacerbated by competition between various centres of power in Egypt, the most significant of which are the presidency, the security services, the business elite and the Supreme Council of the Armed Forces (SCAF).

Delayed parliamentary elections

While the appointment of a new president was an important step in the army's post-Morsi road map, the government failed to build on this by holding parliamentary elections. Originally scheduled to occur before the presidential vote, the elections were postponed several times, and by mid-2015 seemed unlikely to take place before the end of the year. The delay raised concern about what to expect from any parliament that was elected, and also encouraged speculation about whether Sisi intended to concentrate legislative power in the presidency by foregoing the vote altogether.

Should a parliament be elected, it is unclear if it would provide any checks and balances to Egypt's political structure – particularly when, under the proposed parliamentary-elections law, individual candidates are favoured over party lists. With political parties underdeveloped and individual candidates backed by influential business elites and feudal families based in rural areas, the same networks that supported former president Hosni Mubarak's regime would have a prominent role in parliament. With the government having outlawed the Muslim Brotherhood and its allies, the law threatened to virtually wipe out the new political forces that had arisen following the revolution. Overall, parliament might be able to influence economic development in a limited fashion, but would be unlikely to push for reforms to governance or other areas of political life.

Assessments of Sisi's attitude towards pluralism remained largely negative. Prior to becoming president, his political experience amounted to a short stint as minister of defence. As such, he came to power as a military officer, and by mid-2015 did not seem to have changed his approach to engaging with political institutions. On more than one occasion, he displayed impatience with pluralism. Although he did not appear to oppose citizens electing representatives to speak on their behalf, he repeatedly urged all parties to run on a single list, as though Egypt's political system ought to resemble that of a one-party state. Indeed, he has said publicly that he would endorse such a list as one of 'national salvation'. The genuine differences between the visions of political factions seemed to strike Sisi as distractions or weaknesses, particularly at a time when the state had a growing array of problems.

Nonetheless, while Sisi appeared unperturbed by the delay in holding parliamentary elections, there were signs that he recognised the vote's importance to the post-Morsi road map from which his government derived its legitimacy. The president had wanted the elections to take place prior to an international investment conference held in Sharm el-Sheikh in spring 2015, so as to show other countries that Egypt was progressing along what he considered to be a democratic path. The failure to do so was therefore a source of frustration, albeit of a limited kind.

The investment conference went well politically, with strong participation from Arab and Western leaders. Although few business deals were finalised, the event appeared to strengthen the legitimacy of Sisi's presidency abroad. Having previously expressed reluctance to host bilateral talks with Sisi in Berlin before an Egyptian parliament was in place, Germany opted to invite him anyway after a series of judicial interventions relating to the proposed election law.

Competing centres of power

Meanwhile, the judicial branch asserted its power within the new political order. This reflected the emerging dynamics of the Egyptian state, in which the judiciary formed one of several centres of power rather than an impartial mechanism to oversee democratic processes. The tension between the power of the presidency and the power of the judiciary was also evident in the high-profile trial of three journalists employed by the Qatar-owned television network Al-Jazeera, who were arrested in June 2014 and charged with a variety of crimes relating to terrorism. The international community, human-rights organisations and civil-rights groups were almost unanimous in their opposition to the case, and lobbied heavily against it. Nevertheless, the public prosecutor brought the case forward, and the journalists were given prison sentences of between seven and ten years. There was confusion as to why Sisi did not pardon the journalists or order their release, particularly as he had declared his preference for them to be deported.

Following an order for a retrial from within the judiciary, Sisi did deport one of the journalists, Australian–Latvian national Peter Greste. But Mohamed Fahmy and Baher Mohamed – a Canadian national of Egyptian origin and an Egyptian national respectively – remained in Egypt and were released from jail pending the conclusion of the retrial. The differences in the ways that the journalists were treated appeared to shed light on the power dynamics within the country. After their initial conviction, Sisi issued a presidential decree allowing him to deport foreign nationals where this would be of 'national benefit', with the assumption that those deported would serve out their jail terms in their own countries. After a judge harshly criticised Greste's imprisonment in a subsequent retrial, Sisi used the decree to have him deported. At that point, the president had expended minimal political capital within the administration because he had not ridden roughshod over the judiciary by going against its recommendations. (In contrast, it appeared that deporting Fahmy would have required Sisi to expend greater political capital.) Moreover, given the outcry in the international press caused by Greste's imprisonment, there was no obvious benefit to continuing to detain him.

Another case that showed Sisi's reluctance to expend political capital by interfering with the judicial system was that involving Mohamed Soltan, an Egyptian–American national who had supported Morsi following the military takeover, and whose father was a senior figure in the Muslim Brotherhood. After his arrest in 2013, Soltan was detained for almost two years. In April 2015, he received a heavy jail sentence that drew growing attention from the international media, especially following a partial hunger strike that caused his health to rapidly deteriorate. Soltan was deported the following month, after renouncing his Egyptian citizenship. Although the US government had been lobbying Cairo to release him for some time, Sisi had been unwilling to become involved until the case had been completed. This was despite the fact that Soltan was a relatively minor figure, and it was therefore unlikely the judiciary would have been offended by such an intervention. Sisi's partial deference to the judiciary as a centre of power, rather than due to respect for the rule of law, contrasted with the approaches taken by Morsi and Mubarak before him.

Threats to state coherence

Compounding the effects of tension between the presidency and the judiciary, Egypt's economic problems posed a continued threat to the stability of the state. Due to the country's growing and increasingly young population, the government was under pressure to expand the economy and create new jobs. It responded by announcing a series of large-scale projects, such as that to expand the Suez Canal, but it remained to be seen whether these initiatives could be completed quickly and efficiently. As a consequence, discontent over the economy threatened to escalate into civil unrest – as it had in the 1970s, during Anwar Sadat's presidency – particularly if the government continued to cut subsidies on basic goods. This danger was especially apparent during summer: the June–August period is the most energy-intensive of the year due to high temperatures, and the economic pressure this creates is compounded by the rise in expenses linked to Ramadan. Economic reform is therefore vital to the overall health of the state.

Egypt also needed to adapt to changing internal and external security threats. Although the Egyptian security forces defied expectations by preventing any attacks from being carried out during the international investment conference, there was a sharp rise in violence in the Sinai Peninsula. Around 900 fatalities were reported in the area during 2014, up from approximately 175 the previous year, as Ansar Bayt al-Maqdis continued to carry out operations there and a faction of the jihadist group pledged allegiance to ISIS. Cairo also remained concerned about the western border, fearing that jihadists aligned with Ansar al-Sharia, ISIS or the Islamist-leaning parliament in Tripoli would cross into Egypt from Libya. In March 2015, this apprehension was heightened when ISIS forces based in Libya executed 21 Egyptian Coptic Christians. With no sign of an immediate resolution in the Libyan civil war, there was an increasing possibility that Egypt and other countries would carry out a military intervention in the conflict, perhaps in coordination with the non-Islamist parliament based in Tobruk.

Finally, the Egyptian state was threatened by the domestic political polarisation that had begun in 2012, which the government had made little effort to resolve, and which had subsequently sharpened dramatically. Due to its popularity at home and broad acceptance – if not open backing – abroad, the Sisi government had few incentives to initiate a national reconciliation that would bring supporters of the Muslim Brotherhood back into the political arena, and the crackdown continued to intensify. It appeared that a majority of Egyptians accepted Cairo's indifference on the issue, although this was difficult to confirm given the narrowed space for political discussion. For those aligned with the Muslim Brotherhood, the country's new political order was illegitimate on every level, and could not be accommodated in any way. The organisation was having difficulty maintaining its internal unity, as some factions advocated continuing its broadly non-violent approach, while others favoured vigilantism or a low-level insurgency. The trial of Morsi, who was sentenced to death in June 2015, remained a potential flashpoint, although it seemed unlikely that he would be executed in the short term, if at all. As of mid-2015, his conviction was being appealed.

Maghreb: Differing Political Trajectories

The differences between the Maghreb countries' political trajectories became ever more apparent in the year to mid-2015.

In Libya, there emerged a second parliament to challenge the elected government, effectively dividing the country in two and bringing civil war. The war reflected, if imperfectly, regional fault lines. An Islamist government, the General National Congress led by Abdullah al-Thinni, was based in Tripoli and had the backing of Turkey and Qatar, the two regional champions of the weakening Muslim Brotherhood. The government became a vehicle for Libya's Islamist factions, including the militias of the powerful Misrata Brigades. The rival, internationally recognised government was renamed the House of Representatives and relocated to the eastern town of Tobruk. It had political and military support from the United Arab Emirates and Egypt. The fighting between the sides caused considerable damage to institutions, public services and oil production, and had a significant humanitarian cost. (See map, *Strategic Geography* p. XV). Hopes for political reconciliation diminished in October 2014, when, having tried to be a genuinely independent political institution, the House of Representatives formed an alliance with former army general Khalifa Haftar in an effort to re-establish its authority.

Having installed a caretaker government in January 2014, Tunisia moved ahead with parliamentary elections in the second half of the year. It was expected that the vote would result in a victory for An-Nahda, the Islamist party that had won Tunisia's first democratic elections following the 2011 Jasmine Revolution. But in the event, Nidaa Tounes, a secular party alleged to be closely associated with ousted president Zine al-Abidine Ben Ali, gained 39% of the seats, with An-Nahda winning 31%. Anticipating victory, An-Nahda had announced prior to the vote that it would not put forward a candidate for the subsequent presidential election. The move was designed to assuage fears that it was attempting to dominate Tunisia's political institutions, and thereby head off public resentment and a possible counter-revolution. Despite its poor showing in the parliamentary elections, the party was unable to go back on its word. As a consequence, Nidaa Tounes's 87-year-old presidential candidate, Beji Caid Essebsi, easily won against representatives from a collection of smaller parties. With Nidaa Tounes in control of both parliament and the presidency, An-Nahda's influence was much diminished. The secular party promised compromise and, after parliament rejected its first minority government, formed a coalition. Prime Minister Habib Essid's cabinet included only one member of An-Nahda, the minister of employment, who held what was perhaps the most challenging and politically fraught portfolio of all, given that unemployment and underemployment had been important causes of the Jasmine Revolution.

Abdelilah Benkirane remained Morocco's prime minister despite coming under pressure from rivals in government as the country's parties positioned themselves for general elections in 2016. Benkirane was forced to deal with the withdrawal of the pro-monarchy Istiqlal, historically Morocco's largest party, from his government – an event that occurred shortly after the palace had brokered a deal for it to remain part of the ruling coalition. The withdrawal was likely made in the expectation that the coalition's leading party, the Islamist Party for Justice and Development (PJD), would be defeated in the legislative elections (as many incumbent majority parties had been in the past). Istiqlal therefore sought to distance itself from the leadership ahead of the polls. Benkirane repeatedly went out of his way to insist that his party, though Islamist, supported the monarchy and had no links with the international Muslim Brotherhood. These claims took on heightened importance in December 2014, following the strange death of Abdellah Baha, his long-time associate and fellow party founder. Although officials stated that Baha was hit by a train while inspecting the scene of another fatality, there were rumours that he was in fact murdered. Why and by whom was unclear, but his death could have been a way to signal to the PJD not to overstep the bounds set by the monarchy. At the very least, it considerably weakened support for the PJD. As a result, it appeared that Morocco's Islamists would be unable to remain in power after the elections, either becoming minority members of a future coalition or returning to the opposition.

In Algeria, President Abdelaziz Bouteflika was still immobilised by a stroke he had suffered in 2013, although he appeared to retain his mental acuity and knowledge of domestic and international affairs. Some disruption was caused by speculation about the president's well-being, but little changed in Algerian politics until May 2015, when Bouteflika reshuffled the cabinet, appointing new ministers of the interior, public works and energy. The latter appointment was perhaps the most significant, given the importance of hydrocarbons to the Algerian economy. While no official rationale was given, there seemed to be two possible motives for the reshuffle. Firstly, it may have indicated a realignment of priorities: the new minister of energy, Salah Khebri, is a specialist in shale gas, a resource that Algeria intends to exploit. Secondly, Bouteflika may have wanted to distance his administration from the corruption scandals that had plagued the country over the preceding five years – a theory suggested by the fact that most of the ministers who were replaced had connections with the graft investigations.

ISIS in North Africa

The appearance of ISIS in North Africa, while unsurprising given the group's expansionist nature and challenge to statehood, illustrated splits within the jihadist movement. Existing jihadist groups in the region, such as al-Qaeda in the Islamic Maghreb (AQIM) and Ansar al-Sharia, faced competition that heightened the complexity of already tangled political and security situations. While ISIS had already been attracting North African recruits in large numbers, the decision to step up attacks within the region itself – including through the beheading of Egyptian Christian workers in Libya, the killing of Western tourists in Tunisia and the targeting of senior regime figures in Egypt – was a qualitative escalation designed to provoke responses from governments.

In a sign that North Africa's jihadist movement was fragmenting, a group of fighters broke off from AQIM and allied themselves with ISIS. In September 2014, shortly after their defection, the fighters captured and decapitated a French tourist in Algeria, prompting a massive response from the country's military. Within three months, the group had been almost completely eliminated. The military maintained its offensive throughout spring 2015 and distributed pictures of dead terrorists to the media, apparently as a means to demonstrate its effective counter-terrorism capabilities and to discourage further attacks. Nonetheless, AQIM and a group led by one of its former members, al-Murabitoun, remained active in Algeria and the wider region.

Tunisia was also affected by the shifting loyalties of North African jihadists, and was threatened by both ISIS and al-Qaeda. A July 2014 attack on Tunisian security forces by the Uqba ibn Nafi Brigade, an ally of AQIM, left at least 14 soldiers dead. On 1 December, the body of a Tunisian police officer who had been beheaded by ISIS supporters was discovered 50 kilometres from the border with Algeria. This was followed by the attack on the Bardo Museum, which was claimed by ISIS but which the Tunisian government blamed on the Uqba ibn Nafi Brigade. Nonetheless, the former group was undoubtedly behind the killing of 38 tourists during an assault on a Sousse beach resort in June 2015, with the attacker, Seifeddine Rezgui, having trained in ISIS camps in Libya. This increase in terrorism served as a reminder that the Jasmine Revolution had created new space for jihadist groups in Tunisia by compelling the state security services to temporarily step back – disrupting their surveillance capabilities – and by broadening the spectrum for political expression to include jihadist ideology.

In Libya, ISIS capitalised on the frequent clashes between warring militias to capture and hold territory in the eastern and central parts of the country, creating yet another threat to the governments in Tripoli and Tobruk. The group had been quietly establishing itself in the eastern city of Derna, but in February 2015 announced its presence with a gruesome video showing the murder of 21 Egyptian Coptic Christians. This was followed by a video showing the execution of Eritrean Christians in three separate locations in Libya. The group subsequently began to publish videos of its enforcement of law in Derna, and of its flag flying over the central city of Sirte. Fighters allied with Tobruk and Tripoli made only occasional efforts to combat ISIS, although in one instance they coordinated their operations to drive back the group. As a consequence, by mid-2015 there were effectively two wars taking place in Libya: Tobruk against Tripoli, and Tobruk and Tripoli against ISIS.

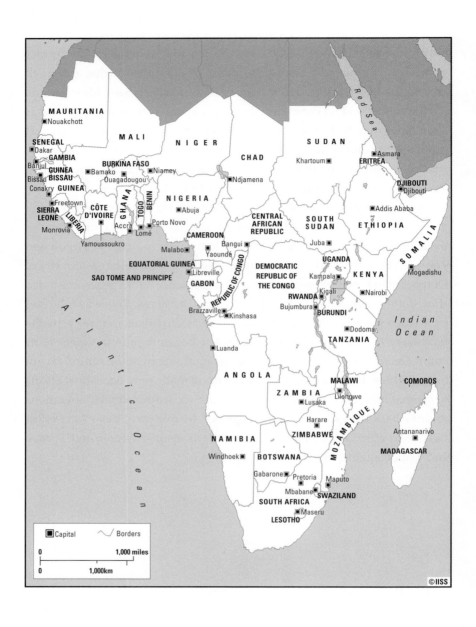

Chapter 9

Sub-Saharan Africa

Sub-Saharan Africa continued on its upward economic trajectory in the year to mid-2015. Yet the pace of growth slowed due to a range of local and international factors, such as continued insecurity and conflict on the continent, as well as the low price of oil and other commodities. As both external and intra-African trade remained relatively muted, domestic demand supported economic activity in many countries. Nevertheless, the World Bank predicted that Africa would remain one of the world's three fastest-growing regions, a forecast echoed by the African Development Bank, which projected that the continent's GDP would grow by 4.5% in 2015 and 5% in 2016.

But the situation was more nuanced than it appeared. Although there was greater investment in sectors such as extractive industries and telecommunications, the region's infrastructure as a whole required still higher levels of investment. And ensuring that the advance of Africa's economies benefited all sectors of society remained important to sustaining their progress, particularly because the population of the continent was both growing faster and increasingly young. Indeed, according to the United Nations Population Fund, in 2014 half the population in 15 Sub-Saharan countries was under the age of 18.

This meant that, in future, African governments and the private sector would have to create enough jobs to employ the growing number of young people. This challenge was starkly illustrated by the IMF in its 2015

'Regional Economic Outlook', which stated that 'by 2035, the number of Africans joining the working-age population (ages 15–64) will exceed that from the rest of the world combined'. Across the continent, the demographic transition was still only starting, and although mortality rates were falling, fertility rates remained high. Accordingly, the IMF concluded that the region would need to create an average of around 18 million jobs per year until 2035; but if enough jobs could be generated, these trends had the potential to increase per capita growth.

Investment in communications helped facilitate a rapid increase in mobile-phone use and, according to figures released by the International Telecommunications Union, online connectivity also rose. However, many of Africa's economies were still centred on agriculture, a sector particularly vulnerable to natural disasters and climate change. Improved agricultural productivity integrating informal economies and structural adjustment would help boost productivity. This was needed to ensure that the benefits of economic growth were distributed more evenly, especially given that, according to the UN, more than 40% of the population still lived in extreme poverty.

The Ebola outbreak that began in West Africa in early 2014 illustrated many of the problems facing the continent. The World Health Organization reported that by June 2015 there had been 27,443 confirmed, probable and suspected cases of Ebola in Sierra Leone, Liberia and Guinea, with 11,207 reported deaths. The disease had a direct impact on societies by forcing changes in established religious and cultural norms, as well as by disrupting local economies. For example, because of travel restrictions, some farmers could not bring goods to market or plant for the new growing season, the effect of which was compounded by the reduction in food imports caused by border closures. The UN World Food Programme estimated that in November 2014 around 200,000 people were affected by food shortages because of the outbreak.

Before 2014, West African countries had been attracting attention for the economic and social improvements they were making after decades of war. But the Ebola crisis exacerbated structural weaknesses in local health systems, which were not configured for the rapid response that was needed. This highlighted the capacity deficits that persisted in many states, which needed to boost the effectiveness and resilience of their institutions in the long term. Such shortfalls in capacity were also evident in the security domain.

Conflicts continued to display alarming transnational dimensions. The conflict with the extremist group Boko Haram in northern Nigeria spread to involve several neighbouring countries. Popular discontent at the government's lack of progress against the militants contributed to the election of President Muhammadu Buhari, who unseated Goodluck Jonathan in Nigeria's first democratic transfer of power from one party to another. Nigeria, Benin, Chad, Cameroon and Niger established a joint task force to tackle Boko Haram, which caused more casualties in 2014 than in any previous year. In Somalia, the Islamist group al-Shabaab continued to be a potent force and carried out further attacks in Kenya.

In August 2014, France, which had recently intervened in conflicts in Mali and Central African Republic, reshaped its anti-terrorism posture and deployments in Africa, deepening its military engagement and coordination with regional armed forces. *Operation Barkhane* repositioned many French forces, creating forward operating bases further north into the Sahel, in an effort presented as a strategic joint venture with Mauritania, Mali, Niger, Chad and Burkina Faso. The overall intent was to create a more unified force structure able to operate across the Sahel, within an environment in which national borders mattered less due to the relatively free movement of insurgent groups there. This was due in part to these groups' increasing effectiveness, but also to the capacity problems of the authorities.

Efforts continued to develop rapid-response capacities through the African Standby Force. But these have been delayed, and the pressing nature of security crises has led to ad hoc multinational responses, a change in approach by the UN – illustrated by its 'intervention brigade' in Democratic Republic of the Congo – and the French-led operation in Mali. This latter mission prompted the African Union to call for the establishment of an African Capacity for Immediate Response to Crises. With the African Standby Force due to be declared operational after exercise *Amani Africa II* in late 2015, the AU should subsequently be able to call on a rapid-deployment capacity. But even without this, the AU has increasingly tackled complex security crises, as seen in its activity in Darfur (UNAMID, a hybrid AU/UN deployment); the mission to counter al-

Shabaab, AMISOM; efforts such as the AU Regional Task Force targeting the Lord's Resistance Army; and its operations in the conflict in the Central African Republic (before it transferred control to the UN).

Overall, African states had begun to develop increasingly durable security initiatives and activities on a continental scale, to deal with difficult issues such as persistent security crises. But external support was still vital, with the European Union and UN particularly important partners for funding and logistical support. In a year in which an African health crisis dominated the headlines, and amid reminders of Africa's vulnerability to external economic shocks, these persistent, complex and often transnational security problems – along with the capacity deficits they revealed – significantly hampered the continent's progress.

Nigeria: Elections amid Growing Insurgency

The Nigerian presidential elections of March 2015 brought to an end 16 years of government by the People's Democratic Party (PDP), with former military ruler Muhammadu Buhari chosen to replace incumbent Goodluck Jonathan. The vote cleared the way for Nigeria's first democratic transfer of power to an opposition party – which occurred the following May – as Jonathan graciously accepted defeat. There were high expectations for the new leadership, both domestically and abroad, but the country still faced intractable economic and security problems.

The insurgency waged by Islamist group Boko Haram in the northeast reached new levels of violence in the year to mid-2015: the rebels pledged allegiance to the Islamic State of Iraq and al-Sham (ISIS) and expanded their activities well beyond Nigeria's borders, prompting combined military action by several countries in Lake Chad Basin. Militancy and other crime, especially oil bunkering and abductions, remained major concerns in the oil-rich Niger Delta region, where fighters vowed to renew their attacks under the Buhari administration and frequent oil spills heightened local resentment of the energy industry.

In the states of the Middle Belt, around 400 people were killed in inter-communal violence, as Fulani herdsmen battled local villagers in

Plateau, Benue, Kaduna, Taraba and Nasarawa states. The fighting, which also affected the northern state of Zamfara, resulted from ethno-religious tension between indigenous peoples and settlers, inflamed by the introduction of sharia law in northern states between 1999 and 2001.

Efforts to deal with these security threats were made more difficult by the 2014–15 fall in the price of oil, due to the government's disproportionate reliance on the product for revenue. The shift in the energy market also meant that Buhari had fewer resources with which to implement planned reforms such as the creation of 720,000 new jobs, infrastructure improvements, economic diversification away from the oil sector and an anti-corruption drive at the Nigeria National Petroleum Corporation. Upon taking office, he inherited a depleted treasury and a public sector in which some government workers had not been paid for several months.

Long-awaited political change

The Nigerian political scene continued to centre on identity politics, with parties built along ethnic, religious and regional lines rather than on clearly defined political goals designed to benefit the entire country. Such divides were particularly apparent in the rivalry between the PDP and Buhari's All Progressives Congress (APC), stemming partly from the split between the predominantly Muslim north and the mainly Christian south. Aside from the differing religious characters of the two regions, the north had long been home to a population mired in poverty and unemployment, while the south had driven Nigeria's economic growth (despite containing some marginalised areas of its own).

The presidential elections were the closest since Nigeria adopted democratic rule in 1999. This was partly due to new-found relative unity among the opposition. The APC was founded in February 2013 as a coalition designed to defeat the PDP, bringing together the Action Congress of Nigeria, the All Nigeria People's Party, the All Progressives Grand Alliance and Buhari's Congress for Progressive Change. The position of the PDP was severely weakened by Jonathan's ineffectual response to Boko Haram, particularly his vacillation over the April 2014 kidnapping of 276 girls in Chibok, which led to international criticism of his administration. The party was also hurt by the defection of some of its most prominent members to the APC, including highly influential former president Olusegun Obasanjo. Jonathan's supporters made a series of attempts to undermine Buhari, filing several lawsuits that sought to have the APC leader disqualified due to doubts about the authenticity of his birth certificate and academic qualifications.

Originally scheduled for 14 February, the elections were postponed in the early part of that month as the military began a major six-week offensive against Boko Haram. While the PDP and some small parties welcomed the delay, the APC and the US government, among others, expressed their frustration at the move. Many who opposed the move questioned the impartiality of the Independent National Electoral Commission, expressing fears that the democratic process had come under threat.

Nonetheless, the polls ran smoothly overall (barring some technical problems) and were more transparent than previous national elections owing to the introduction of biometric voter cards. Buhari won 15.4 million votes to Jonathan's 12.9m, a result credited to the former's strong support in both the north and the southwest.

The election results once again highlighted the identity-based divides in Nigerian politics. Led by Buhari, a northerner, and his running mate Yemi Osinbajo, from Lagos, the APC attracted votes in the north and the largely Yoruba southwest. Under Jonathan, a Christian, the PDP maintained its traditional support base in the Niger Delta despite losing ground in the southwest.

Buhari was a well-known figure in Nigerian politics, both as a former ruler and as a presidential hopeful during elections in 2003, 2007 and 2011. In December 1983 General Buhari, as he was then called, seized power by conducting a coup. He went on to rule Nigeria until August 1985, when he in turn was overthrown by General Ibrahim Babangida and jailed for 40 months. A devout Muslim, Buhari gained a reputation as an incorruptible and highly disciplined leader. Although his first presidential term was characterised by human-rights abuses, restrictions on press freedom and poor economic performance, it also led to the incarceration of hundreds of politicians and businessmen on corruption charges.

The high expectations for Buhari's return to office stemmed in large part from the electorate's deep frustration with the Jonathan administration and resulting desire for change, factors that arguably generated a large number of votes for the PDP. The key promises Buhari was expected to fulfil included ending the Boko Haram insurgency, addressing the marginalisation of the north, supporting economic growth beyond the oil sector and tackling corruption.

The General Assembly had not confirmed Buhari's cabinet by June 2015, but Nigeria's system of assigning ministerial posts on the basis of state representation meant that many other senior political figures could influence the country's direction. In the new administration, these included APC leader Bola Tinubu and President of the Senate Abubakar Bukola Saraki, as well as politicians from the PDP such as Rotimi Amaechi, once the governor of Rivers State, and former vice-president Atiku Abubakar.

The APC's dominance grew further with the April gubernatorial elections, in which the party won 20 out of 36 governorships, and in the polls for the Senate and the House of Representatives held the same month, in which it also won majorities. However, these votes were marred by violence, widespread fraud and low voter turnout, particularly in the Niger Delta. Rivers State experienced the highest incidence of result-sheets theft, destruction of card readers and other irregularities. A PDP stronghold in both April elections, the state was the only area to experience large-scale protests against APC's gains. A commission was subsequently established to investigate election-related killings and other disorder, with the APC accusing the PDP of interfering with the votes.

Evolution of Boko Haram

The insurgency waged by Boko Haram since 2009 showed no sign of abating, and in 2014 led to more casualties than in any preceding year. The group continued to carry out killings and abductions as it terrorised the inhabitants of northern and central Nigeria, leading to a larger-scale international response as well as the recruitment of private-security contractors by the Nigerian government.

Established as an isolated, non-violent sect in the early 2000s, Boko Haram has since adopted the aim of imposing strict Islamic law on Nigeria and increasingly operated in neighbouring Cameroon, Chad and Niger. The group's evolution in 2014 was reflected in its use of new tactics that hinted at a change in overall strategy. Five significant steps by the group marked its development: an advance that gave it control of more towns and villages in the northeast; the use of female suicide bombers; the targeting of neighbouring countries; the declaration of an 'Islamic state' by its leader, Abubakar Shekau; and the pledge of allegiance to Abu Bakr al-Baghdadi, self-styled caliph of ISIS.

Boko Haram displayed its intent to return to urban areas, after having been forced to retreat to the Mandara Mountains and the Sambisa Forest in 2013. In summer 2014, the group captured Gwoza, a Borno State town of 265,000 people that looked set to become a major stronghold for the militants – indeed, the 'capital' of Shekau's proclaimed Islamic state. Although the authorities argued that Nigeria's sovereignty remained intact, the group proceeded to take over several more towns in the state, including Bama and Michika. The offensive suggested an attempt to encircle Maiduguri, the capital of Borno State and occasionally Boko Haram's main stronghold (until autumn 2013). Aerial and ground assaults carried out by the security forces throughout autumn 2014 allowed the government to gradually retake most towns captured by the insurgents in Borno, Yobe and Adamawa states, and prevented the fall of Maiduguri. Boko Haram suffered high casualties during its advance on the latter town, particularly in Konduga, where an estimated 600 insurgents were killed by government forces. Yet the group was far from defeated: during a four-day attack in early January 2015, it seized Baga and a nearby base operated by the Multinational Joint Task Force (MNJTF). That assault led to hundreds of civilian fatalities, and was a major blow to the counter-insurgency effort.

Amid the ongoing fighting, there were uncorroborated reports that a deal had been struck between the government and Boko Haram, with the mediation of Chadian President Idriss Déby. The agreement was said to include a ceasefire and the release of the girls kidnapped in Chibok. Nonetheless, as with previously declared truces and ceasefires, the violence and smaller-scale abductions continued, while Shekau eventually denied that any such deal had been made.

By mid-2015, the whereabouts of the Chibok girls remained unknown, and there was growing speculation that some had either been killed along with other civilians abducted earlier in the year or else forced to carry out suicide bombings. The latter theory was partly based on the fact that Nigeria's first female suicide bomber struck in June 2014, around two months after the kidnapping in Chibok. This attack, which took place in Gombe, involved a tactic that would be reused across Boko Haram's areas of operation, and would at times involve children. Those coerced into carrying out such assaults included a ten-year-old girl who was stopped in Katsina State wearing a suicide vest in June 2014, and a seven-year-old girl who on 22 February 2015 carried out a bombing in Yobe State, killing several people. Boko Haram's tendency to use women and children for suicide missions has become firmly established. It appears likely that the group adopted the tactic due to the greater ease with which these victims escape detection by security personnel, and to the increased shock effect of such attacks. Yet Boko Haram's abduction of women and girls is also carried out with a view to their sexual enslavement, as well as to their serving as domestic workers in its camps, and as smugglers of weapons and supplies. Such kidnappings are sometimes designed to punish Christian women and those who receive Western education; intimidate communities and the government; retaliate against the authorities for detaining insurgents' wives and children; and provide captives for prisoner exchanges.

Since its early days, Boko Haram has sought refuge from attacks by Nigerian security forces in the borderlands of Niger, Chad and Cameroon. But sometime between late 2014 and early 2015, these countries for the first time became a battleground for the group. The sharp rise in Boko Haram violence outside Nigeria drew a new level of international attention. Its operations in Cameroon included a series of abductions: the wife of Vice-Prime Minister Amadou Ali was kidnapped in July 2014, only to be released the following October, as were a further 80 people, many of them children, in January 2015. These events caused outcry abroad and lent urgency to efforts to deploy a new MNJTF, which had been established in principle at a summit hosted by the United Kingdom in July 2014 (in the wake of the Chibok kidnapping). The mission would be led by Nigeria, Niger, Chad, Cameroon and Benin, who initially pledged to jointly deploy 2,800 troops.

Cameroon began to take on a particularly assertive military role as a result of Boko Haram's increasing activity in its territory. Cameroon President Paul Biya was verbally threatened by the group, and his country experienced a series of retaliatory attacks after stepping up its counter-terrorism efforts. The government in Yaoundé permitted the deployment of foreign troops in Cameroon for the first time in January 2015, after the Chadian parliament voted 150–0 in favour of sending forces to help its neighbour. Chad's contribution to the counter-insurgency campaign was especially significant due to the combat experience of its soldiers, who had gained a reputation as effective desert fighters in *Operation Serval*, the French-led intervention in Mali of 2013.

While Niger and Chad also came under attack in February 2015, by the end of that month the regional operation appeared to be becoming more cohesive, as representatives from Nigeria, Chad, Cameroon, Niger and Benin finalised their strategy for an 8,750-strong force to counter Boko Haram. In May 2015, the African Union established the MNJTF headquarters in the Chadian capital, N'djamena, while authorising a further increase in personnel to deploy 10,000 troops on an initial one-year mission.

Rumours began to circulate in January 2015 that the militaries of these countries were being supported by foreign mercenaries, possibly from Eastern Europe and South Africa. The involvement of these fighters – from which the South African government distanced itself – was thought to have been behind the increased success of the counter-insurgency campaign. In March, photographs were published showing white fighters alongside Nigerian soldiers in the northeast, forcing Jonathan to admit to employing mercenaries, although he claimed the fighters were primarily tasked with training. Having taken office, Buhari announced that he would end the use of foreign military contractors.

Shekau swore allegiance to Baghdadi in March, just as the Nigerian military seemed to have gained the upper hand in its pre-election offensive. The offer was later accepted by the ISIS leader, and created further international concern about Boko Haram. But the long-term implications of the groups' alliance were unclear, and it was possible that Shekau's pledge was little more than a cry for help or a publicity stunt, at a time when Boko Haram was losing ground and needed to reassert its status and relevance. In April 2015, the group rebranded itself as Islamic State's West Africa Province, a move that could cause internal discontent. Cooperation between ISIS and Boko Haram subsequently became more evident, with the Nigerian group benefiting from the more advanced technical skills of its new ally. Nonetheless, the partnership did not appear to affect Boko Haram's operations on the ground.

Although the group suffered some setbacks, the human cost of the insurgency was higher than ever in the year to mid-2015. The United Nations reported in March 2015 that 7,300 people had been killed in violence related to Boko Haram since January of the preceding year. Thousands of houses, schools and other buildings had been destroyed, and more than 1.5m Nigerians internally displaced, since the conflict began. By early 2015, there were growing reports of violence and other abuse at camps for displaced persons, which became ideal hunting grounds for human traffickers. The hundreds of thousands of civilians who fled into Niger, Chad and Cameroon placed additional strain on already stretched local resources. There were also continuing human-rights violations by the security forces. The UN Central Emergency Response Fund attempted to mitigate the damage in March 2015, allocating US$28m to support humanitarian efforts in the conflict.

Militancy and widespread corruption

The Niger Delta experienced a resurgence of criminal activity, particularly kidnapping, vandalism and oil theft. With the 2009 amnesty programme to combat militancy in the region scheduled to end in 2015, many fighters showed a renewed interest in attacking oil installations. Their theft of thousands of barrels of crude each day caused significant losses for energy companies and prompted Royal Dutch Shell to divest some its holdings in the region. Piracy also remained a problem in the Niger Delta, despite the launch of several military operations designed to address the threat.

Abductions were one of the most significant security challenges in the region. It became particularly evident that kidnappers were targeting middle-class Nigerians rather than foreign oil workers (who tended to be protected by stronger security measures). The rise in abductions has often been attributed to local communities' frustration with the environmental damage and unequal distribution of wealth associated with the Niger Delta's oil industry. Although Shell agreed in January 2015 to pay the Bodo community US$83m in damages relating to ruptures in the Trans-Niger Pipeline during 2008, a leak of around 3,800 barrels of oil the previous month had put further strain on the relationship between the energy giant and local communities. And this was hardly an isolated incident: Amnesty International reported that there were 550 oil spills in the region in 2014 alone. The December accident highlighted a perverse cycle long apparent in the Niger Delta. While at times leaks are caused by companies' negligence and inadequate maintenance of infrastructure, at others they result from the actions of disgruntled locals or environmental activists, who seek revenge against energy firms responsible for damage to pipelines. Such retaliation has targeted not only foreign-run infrastructure but also pipelines belonging to the Nigerian Petroleum Development Company. This was seen in April 2015, when militant group Urhobo Gbagbako – which opposes marginalisation of the ethnic Urhobo minority – declared a resumption of hostilities and threatened to carry out bombings on an unprecedented scale.

The oil sector also faced another long-term challenge: corruption. In an attempt to curb this endemic problem, Jonathan replaced in August 2014 the four top executives of the Nigeria National Petroleum Corporation. The industry generates around 80% of Nigeria's GDP, and large-scale, oil-enabled graft has long been an integral part of the Nigerian bureaucracy. The fall in the oil price that began in summer 2014 was therefore a major concern for both the legal economy and those who benefited from illicit oil revenues.

The eradication of corruption was also a keystone of Buhari's presidential campaign, and he was widely expected to focus on the Niger Delta in this effort, given the magnitude of the problem in the region. Nevertheless, voters in the Niger Delta largely supported Jonathan (who was born in the region) during the presidential elections, and the APC failed to secure a gubernatorial seat there. Despite the deployment of soldiers to the region in the run-up to the presidential elections, several members of the APC were killed during the period. Prior to the vote, militants in the Niger Delta had threatened to begin a war should Buhari become president, and although this had not transpired by mid-2015, there remained a possibility of large-scale violence leading to a regional crisis. The lack of support for the new president in the Niger Delta suggested that there would be an uneasy relationship between its state authorities and the central government, perhaps impeding Buhari's planned anti-corruption drive.

In laying out his economic plans, Buhari promised to bring to an end Nigeria's costly system of fuel subsidies. Some of his predecessors had attempted to remove the measures, only to be prevented from doing so by mass protests. A similar dilemma may await the new administration, as the removal of subsidies featured prominently among recommendations submitted to Buhari by the APC transition committee in June 2015. The new president also declared his intent to install a 'leaner' government, vowing to reform the oil-and-gas sector and thereby attract new investment.

West Africa's Ebola Crisis

Before the Ebola virus began to spread through West Africa, in March 2014, countries of the region had been attracting attention for the recovery of their economies and societies after decades of conflict. Yet by 2015, several of these states had become synonymous with the outbreak in the international press, as the focus of policymakers shifted to addressing its devastating human cost and the longer-term implications for states in the region.

According to the World Health Organization (WHO), the first recorded cases of Ebola haemorrhagic fever occurred in 1976 in Zaire, now Democratic Republic of the Congo, and Sudan. But the 2014 outbreak was far more serious than any that preceded it. As of 21 June 2015, the WHO reported that there had been a total of 27,443 confirmed, probable and suspected cases in Sierra Leone, Liberia and Guinea, with 11,207 reported deaths. By mid-2015, the virus had still not been eradicated (although Liberia prematurely declared itself Ebola-free in May).

The epidemic had a destructive impact on local communities, and affected local and national economies. Overtaxed state health-care systems buckled under the strain. The outbreak also presented formidable challenges for the international community, including the WHO. In September 2014, the United Nations undertook its first emergency health initiative, the Mission for Ebola Emergency Response (UNMEER). Foreign governments and other international agencies provided significant assistance.

Development of the outbreak

The first case was reported in March 2014 in Gueckedou, a town on a main road in southeastern Guinea, close to the borders with Sierra Leone and Liberia. It is unclear how the young boy judged to be 'patient zero' became infected; he is reported to have died in December 2013. But the case went unreported for three months, and Ebola was not suspected in that or other early deaths until after samples were sent abroad for analysis. By late March, the virus was spreading rapidly in Guinea, and there were the first reports of suspected cases in Sierra Leone and Liberia. Ebola was transmitted to urban as well as rural areas, and across porous borders; by early April, it had reached the Guinean capital, Conakry. Mali also began to report suspected cases.

The spread of the virus was aided by its pathogenesis, and by the nature of the affected societies. It is highly contagious, with human-to-human transmission taking place via direct contact '(through broken skin or mucous membranes) with the blood, secretions, organs or other bodily fluids of infected people, and with surfaces and materials (e.g. bedding, clothing) contaminated with these fluids', according to the WHO. Close family members were at high risk from those carrying the virus, as were health workers and those who handled the bodies of people who died of the disease. This increased the difficulty of isolating cases and quarantining environments, particularly in urban areas. A particular problem was that identifying the early stages of the virus was problematic; its initial symptoms, such as fever, were often associated with other illnesses. It could take anywhere between two and 21 days for symptoms to emerge, meaning that infected persons might wrongly consider themselves safe to travel.

The crisis exacerbated structural weaknesses in local health systems. These were too small and were not configured for the necessary rapid response. There were insufficient isolation rooms and protective equipment, testing laboratories were too few and had limited capacity, and medicines were in short supply. There was only a limited number of local medical personnel able to handle complex cases. Doctors and nurses themselves contracted Ebola: the WHO reported that, as of June 2015, there had been 872 confirmed cases of infection among health workers in Guinea, Liberia and Sierra Leone, 507 of which were fatal.

The virus spread fear in local communities. In the early days of the outbreak, they lacked accurate information about the symptoms of Ebola and the steps they could take to protect themselves. Although governments mobilised available resources once the virus had been identified, the large scale and rapid spread of the virus meant that the authorities were unable to assist all affected communities. According to reports by non-governmental organisations, many people died without samples being taken for diagnosis. This could have resulted from local customs and burial practices, or from a shortage of trained health-care workers. Due to this lack of verification, it is possible that overall statistics may not reflect the actual number of cases – as some fatalities could have been mistakenly attributed to Ebola or, conversely, been caused by the virus but linked to a different disease.

Burial practices were particularly difficult to address. In many parts of West Africa, families would traditionally take charge of the dead to prepare them for burial, a task that involved washing the bodies of the deceased. But people who had direct contact with the bodies of Ebola victims were at high risk of infection. Efforts by health authorities to remove corpses for safe burial could provoke a violent response and exacerbate mistrust of the authorities; it was reported that some local communities already suspected outside agencies of being the source of the virus. On occasion, these responses by locals – which included attempts to remove corpses from mortuaries – prompted the deployment of security forces. Communities had to be encouraged to alter their burial practices, in some cases by relocating burial grounds. Bodies had to be buried with impermeable coverings, and deeper graves had to be used (the WHO recommended two metres as the minimum safe depth). However, by November 2014, community sensitivities over safe burials were being addressed: the WHO released guidance emphasising the 'inclusion of family members and encouraging religious rites as an essential part of safe burials'.

Ebola therefore had to be countered with social-mobilisation and community-education programmes – which would encourage communities to participate in countering Ebola and persuade them to adopt infection-control measures that would minimise the risk of continued transmission, as well as helping ensure that those who survived the disease would not be ostracised. Affected communities were themselves crucial to defeating Ebola.

Civilian responses

Once the scale of the epidemic became apparent, emergency procedures were incrementally enacted across affected countries, Ebola task forces formed and existing healthcare legislation harnessed. Nonetheless, the virus continued to spread. Liberia declared a national public-health emergency in June 2014, Sierra Leone a state of emergency in July and Guinea a national health emergency in August.

In July, announcing the formation of a National Task Force, Liberian President Ellen Johnson-Sirleaf declared that Ebola could undermine her country's 'economic and social fabric'. She closed Liberia's borders, except for major entry points, launched a screening programme for international travellers and directed the security forces to provide support to technical and medical teams. In August, Johnson-Sirleaf declared a state of emergency in Liberia. She stated that 'the scope and scale of the epidemic, the virulence and deadliness of the virus now exceed the capacity and statutory responsibility of any one government agency or ministry.' All affected countries restricted internal movements, and several international air routes were suspended. However, responses were still hindered by a continuing lack of capacity, and were generally national in their scope and application despite the fact that the virus was spreading across borders.

On 8 August, the WHO declared the outbreak a 'Public Health Emergency of International Concern' and a 'health risk to other states through the international spread of the disease', drafting an Ebola Response Roadmap later that month. On 12 August 2014, UN Secretary-General Ban Ki-moon appointed David Nabarro, a British doctor and senior UN health official, as senior coordinator on Ebola – later making him a special envoy. The Security Council passed Resolution 2177, declaring the UN's first health-care emergency. In September, UNMEER was launched, along with the informal Global Ebola Response Coalition, to coordinate responses.

With UNMEER coordinating the response of UN agencies, the rapid increase in international assistance resulted in greater capacity on the ground, bolstering local responses in capabilities such as diagnostic facilities and forward-deployed treatment units. This included national and international non-governmental organisations, which were also mobilising substantial resources, leveraging existing ties with local communities. According to the WHO, by May 2015 there were more than 60 Ebola treatment units, with around 3,000 beds, in Guinea, Sierra Leone and Liberia. More than 63 Ebola community-care centres were established. Around 2,500 personnel were deployed within 58 foreign medical teams.

UNMEER recognised the importance of locally focused initiatives: its operating principles included 'adopting a regional approach; centrality of national ownership; [and complementing the] work of governments and partners'. The organisation said in June 2015 that 'more than 90% of the Ebola workforce has been national personnel from affected countries'.

Some countries donated substantial resources to the Ebola response. According to a document published by the UN in February 2015, the US committed US$939m, followed by the United Kingdom with US$553m, the European Union with US$503m, Germany with US$225m, Japan with US$155m, France with US$150m and China with US$120m.

Role of the military

Some countries also deployed elements of their armed forces to West Africa. Military responses consisted in the main of medical support and associated training, logistics (including airlift) and engineers, as well as – importantly – communications, and command and control. This support was aimed at delivering enabling capacities, for instance improving the number and effectiveness of diagnostics centres and treatment facilities, as well as delivering capacities that would improve coordination and rapid response.

Under *Operation United Assistance*, the US sent over 2,000 military personnel to Liberia, and under 200 to staff an air hub in Senegal. In Liberia, US personnel were based in Monrovia, building a 25-bed hospital there, as well as ten treatment centres across the country, while working in concert with the US Agency for International Development, among others. The UN reported in October that a US Navy laboratory in Liberia was providing test results in hours rather than days. The UK deployed the naval hospital ship *Argus* off the coast of Sierra Leone for six months, flying helicopter missions in support of international agencies and local authorities, as well as employing engineers to construct diagnostic and treatment facilities. Leveraging London's historical relationship with Sierra Leone (a former colony), the British military worked with the country's aid and foreign ministries to deliver a coordinated response. Cooperating with local authorities, and treating Freetown as the focal point of operations, they established a coordination centre to tackle the management of Ebola cases. Their subsequent activities included building six treatment facilities across the country, setting up command-and-coordination centres at a district level, and developing training programmes for local medical staff (4,000 of whom were trained before the programmes were handed over to a non-governmental organisation). British personnel were joined by medical staff from the Canadian armed forces. France, meanwhile, deployed personnel such as medical and logistics workers to Guinea, as well as troops trained for chemical, biological, radiological and nuclear warfare.

Long-term effects

While international support – both civilian and military – was vital in rapidly building capacity, it was apparent that Ebola could only be beaten on a local level. This meant that education in infection control and prevention was vital, as was ensuring that local health-care systems developed greater capacity and resilience, not only to tackle the current epidemic but to cope with future outbreaks of Ebola and other diseases.

Ebola had a direct impact on societies by forcing change on established religious and cultural norms, and by disrupting established patterns of behaviour. For example, because of travel restrictions, farmers could not bring goods to market or plant for the new growing season. Coupled with the reduction in food imports caused by border closures, this had a serious social and economic effect. The UN World Food Programme estimated that in November 2014, around 200,000 people were affected by food shortages because of Ebola.

Sierra Leone's government estimated that economic output was reduced by 30% due to the outbreak. Labour markets, travel and transportation all suffered across affected states; the IMF reported that 'current growth projections in [Liberia, Sierra Leone and Guinea] have been marked down substantially', and that financing needs for 2015 would be higher. Spending on health care increased the budgetary burden on governments, which had only limited resources with which to sustain high levels of investment in the area. Industrial activity was also affected, with mine owners relocating workers and slowing production.

By mid-2015, the threat from Ebola had receded considerably, and lessons were beginning to be drawn. These were no less important for the international community than for local actors. Amid criticism of its initial response, the WHO published in May 2015 a report stating that the outbreak constituted 'a defining moment for the work of [the organisation]'. The report continued, 'at present, WHO does not have the operational capacity or culture to deliver a full emergency public health response.' The review recommended investments 'so that the operational capacity of WHO for emergency response is fully in place' – in other words, that the organisation develop a rapid-response capability. Meanwhile, UNMEER chief Peter Graaff drew three lessons from the outbreak: there should be no shame in countries asking for help; national leadership was important during such crises; and, in shaping a response, communities were 'not only your primary [beneficiaries], but also your biggest allies'. Yet challenges remained. On the local level, while the facilities developed to combat the disease would be useful, the resilience of local health-care systems was still inadequate. Areas of weakness included a lack of health-care workers; poor pay and conditions for medical staff; shortfalls in flexible and scaleable rapid-response capacities; inadequate surveillance and contact tracing; and still-developing community-engagement and education schemes. It was vital that West African states improved governmental and community resilience, and maintained higher capacity to curb any future outbreaks of Ebola, as well as similarly destructive diseases.

Persistent Conflicts in Eastern and Central Africa

Conflicts in Eastern and Central Africa continued unabated in the year to mid-2015, and while there were some encouraging political developments, the overall situation in affected countries remained dire. Attempts at long-term economic and political reconstruction were hampered by failed peace talks, ongoing military operations and rebel activity, as well as by the displacement of people.

Sudan and South Sudan: Fragmented insurgency

The civil war in South Sudan, stemming from a power struggle between President Salva Kiir and his former deputy Riek Machar, displaced around 1.5 million civilians in 2014. Battles between the Dinka and Nuer factions of the presidential guard, which supported Kiir and Machar respectively, spread quickly into wider Juba and elsewhere in the country. As a consequence, the Sudan People's Liberation Movement split into Kiir's faction (SPLM–Juba) and Machar's in-opposition group (SPLM–IO).

The UN Security Council expressed its disappointment over the failure of Kiir and Machar to reach an agreement by the deadline of 5 March 2015. Kiir's representatives stated Machar was making impossible demands regarding the constitution, and the government rejected the creation of two separate armies. The year to mid-2015 was characterised by a series of broken agreements and delays, with ceasefires negotiated at a high level having little impact on the ground. In October 2014, Kiir agreed to Machar becoming prime minister in a transitional government. But both sides then sought exclusive executive powers for their leaders, indicating that there had been no resolution of the underlying struggle between Kiir and Machar. Meanwhile, many elements of society were excluded from the peace negotiations – led by regional body the Intergovernmental Authority on Development – and supported neither party. The presence of around 25 independent armed groups in South Sudan underlined the separation between the peace effort and the conflict itself.

Foreign involvement also complicated the situation: there were disagreements over the presence of the Ugandan army, which had been deployed to South Sudan at the start of the war to protect key government facilities, such as the airport and the state house. The SPLA–IO accused the Ugandan force of fighting alongside its opponents, as well as seeking to preserve its own interests. While Kiir agreed to a phased withdrawal of Ugandan troops in November 2014, the following month Ugandan President Yoweri Museveni declared that the force would only withdraw once Juba was 'stable and secure'. At the same time, the government of Sudan, from which South Sudan gained independence in 2011, maintained links with rebel groups in the latter country. The conflict also saw rebel activity spread across the border to Sudan, causing the violence in both countries to become increasingly intertwined. As soon as the war broke out in South Sudan, rebels from Sudan joined the fight on Machar's side. The hostilities caused major disruptions in South Sudan's energy industry, as much of the fighting between the government and the opposition occurred in oil-producing areas such as Unity, Upper Nile and Jonglei states.

There was also rising violence in Sudan's Darfur, South Kordofan and Blue Nile states. Much of the fighting stemmed from Khartoum's failure to implement the reforms these states had demanded for decades. In March 2015 alone, more than 20,000 people were displaced due to fighting between Sudanese troops and rebels in South Kordofan. The Sudan People's Liberation Army–North was particularly active in Blue Nile and South Kordofan, and joined forces with Darfur rebels to create an anti-government umbrella group known as the Sudan Revolutionary Front.

In Darfur, intensifying conflict led to the displacement of around 450,000 people in 2014, and another 100,000 in January 2015. Since 2003, when the fighting began, at least 2m people have been displaced. No progress was made in the last round of negotiations between the government and rebel groups, held in late 2014. Given the increase in clashes between the sides in the first half of 2015, it seemed unlikely that the parties would resume negotiations in the near future. The government remains committed to a military approach, and appears reluctant to pursue talks that would address all of Sudan's conflicts in one combined agreement.

Khartoum was also disinclined to negotiate with rebels in Darfur on any basis other than the 2011 Doha Document for Peace in Darfur (DDPD). However, the insurgent forces' fragmentation into a variety of armed groups with different agendas will make it increasingly difficult for the government to identify one party to negotiate with. On 4 January, the Sudanese parliament approved 18 amendments to the 2005 interim constitution. Parliament also incorporated the DDPD into the constitution, reinforcing the government's approach to the negotiations.

The United Nations Security Council discussed in March 2015 the possible departure, or drawdown, of the peacekeeping mission in Darfur jointly led by the UN and the African Union. It was expected that a full exit strategy would be developed following new talks between Khartoum, the UN and the AU.

Somalia: Cross-border terrorism

Against a background of persistent attacks by Islamist group al-Shabaab and international efforts to defeat the insurgency, the Somali political process was undermined by clan rivalry and political manoeuvring that reduced the efficiency of regional and federal authorities.

Violence also exacerbated the worrying humanitarian situation. According to the UN World Food Programme, 2.3m people in Somalia are 'struggling to meet their minimum daily food needs'. At least 1.1m people were internally displaced within Somalia, and the conflict had caused 1m Somalis to flee to neighbouring countries. Despite such challenges, the government continued to work on Vision 2016 – its plan for elections for constitutional revisions, regional-state formation and elections by October of that year.

After repeated delays due to disagreement between the offices of the president and the prime minister over the shape and composition of the administration, Prime Minister Omar Abdirashid Ali Sharmarke announced in February 2015 the formation of a 66-member administration. The government then pushed forward with the formation of regional authorities. The establishment of a federal system is meant to serve the dual purpose of bringing the government closer to the people, while safeguarding Somali unity. In line with the provisional constitution, the establishment and delimitation of federal states is intended to be a voluntary process based on political and economic viability, demographic composition and, as far as possible, respect for existing regional boundaries. But the process has proved difficult in most parts of Somalia because of the clan system and other divisions. While there was some progress in the effort, disagreements over boundaries of a new Interim South West Administration (ISWA) led to clan violence throughout 2014. Despite national and international recognition of the ISWA, tensions continued well into 2015.

A dispute over the planned boundaries of a new, central state damaged relations between Mogadishu and the autonomous state of Puntland. In October 2014, the central government and the Puntland authorities signed a 12-point agreement stipulating that the new central state would include southern Mudug and Galguduud, while northern Mudug would remain part of Puntland. The deal was welcomed by Maman Sidikou, the AU's special representative to Somalia, who declared that it could serve as a blueprint for resolving disputes in other areas of the country. Relations between the central government and Puntland subsequently improved, and in April 2015 Sharmarke and Puntland President Abdiweli Mohamed Ali Gaas signed a seven-point bilateral cooperation agreement. Puntland pledged around 3,000 troops to the Somali National Army, and agreed to respect the provisional constitution for regional-state formation.

The joint operations of the AU Mission in Somalia (AMISOM) and the Somali army put considerable pressure on al-Shabaab in 2014, particularly due to two major initiatives. The first of these, *Operation Eagle*, began in March 2014 and resulted in the liberation of ten towns. The second, *Operation Indian Ocean*, started in September 2014 and focused on Somalia's strategically important coastal towns. These settlements were targeted to disrupt the group's supply routes, and to locate, isolate and destroy pockets of resistance. On 5 October, after several months of preparation, around 1,000 AMISOM peacekeepers and Somali troops seized Barawe. This was a major victory: Barawe had been the nerve centre of al-Shabaab operations, and it was the most significant town to be captured since the group lost Mogadishu and Kismayo. In 2015, a joint AMISOM and Somali offensive also captured Kuday Island, near Kismayo, a key logistical base for al-Shabaab and one of the group's last strongholds in the region.

The US persistently targeted high-ranking members of the group in strikes using unmanned aerial vehicles. The group's leader, Ahmed Abdi Godane, was killed during such an operation, conducted in the Lower Shabelle region in September 2014. Two months later, Tahlil Abdishakur, the head of Amniyat – a unit believed to be responsible for suicide attacks in Mogadishu – was killed in another such operation in Middle Juba. Airstrikes in January and March then killed Yusuf Dheeg, the group's head of external operations, as well as Adan Garar, believed to be responsible for the 2013 attack on Kenya's Westgate shopping centre.

Despite these setbacks, al-Shabaab continued to carry out brutal attacks in Somalia, targeting civilians, government workers and infrastructure in Mogadishu and beyond. At least eight people were killed in an assault on a government compound in Baidoa housing both the ISWA and UN offices. Hotels and restaurants were often attacked. On 20 February 2015, at least 25 people were killed, including members of parliament, when al-Shabaab targeted Central Hotel in Mogadishu. Two months later, around ten people were murdered outside a restaurant near the same hotel. More than ten people, including Somalia's ambassador to the UN, were killed in

March by an improvised explosive device detonated at Mogadishu's Maka Al-Mukarama Hotel. Seven more people, including four UNICEF staff, were killed by another improvised explosive device on 20 April, during an attack in Garowe, in Puntland.

Al-Shabaab frequently threatened countries contributing to AMISOM, especially Kenya. In July 2014, the group killed around 29 people during gun attacks in the towns of Hindi and Gamba. On 22 November, it claimed responsibility for an attack in Mandera in which gunmen killed 28 non-Muslims travelling by bus, purportedly because they were unable to recite passages from the Koran. The following day, Kenyan security forces announced that they had pursued and killed more than 100 militants, destroying their camp in Somalia. Nevertheless, the group killed 142 students at Kenya's Garissa University in April 2015, its deadliest attack in the country since the 1998 US Embassy bombing.

The spread of violence from Somalia to Kenya was a major concern for the Kenyan government, and became a divisive, politicised issue. President Uhuru Kenyatta sometimes blamed his political rivals for the assaults, dismissing claims that the group was responsible, while opposition leaders such as Raila Odinga called for the withdrawal of Kenyan troops from Somalia. The response of the Kenyan security forces was denounced as heavy-handed, with some opposition figures suggesting that the government was using the fight against al-Shabaab as an excuse to silence its political opponents. This theory was lent credence in mid-December, when the government shut down more than 500 non-governmental organisations, including 15 groups it accused of financing terrorism.

Nairobi also asked the UN Refugee Agency to close the Dadaab refugee camp, located in northeast Kenya, which houses more than 335,000 Somali refugees. And it began construction on a 700-kilometre wall on the border with Somalia.

Weakened by AMISOM and Somali army operations, as well as by US airstrikes, al-Shabaab showed signs of internal divisions, as intelligence chief Mahad Karate and a number of foreign fighters reportedly considered declaring their loyalty to the Islamic State of Iraq and al-Sham. Although Ahmed Diriye, al-Shabaab's new leader, opposed the idea and pledged allegiance to al-Qaeda, many saw Karate as the de facto head of the group.

Central African Republic: Retaliatory violence

The conflict in Central African Republic grew more destructive in the year to mid-2015, with humanitarian organisation Médecins Sans Frontières describing the situation in the country as 'catastrophic' in December. More than 850,000 people – one-fifth of the country's population – had been displaced by late 2014, according to the UN Refugee Agency. At least 187,000 people fled to neighbouring countries in the year, bringing the total number of Central African refugees in the region to 423,000.

Although security improved in the capital, Bangui, Muslims there remained vulnerable. Those who had chosen not to flee during the conflict were isolated in their neighbourhoods and had limited mobility. Criminal violence was also high. Security was a major concern in parts of the country that received limited deployments of forces from the UN Multidimensional Integrated Stabilisation Mission in the Central African Republic (MINUSCA), particularly the east. After visiting the country in March 2015, US Ambassador to the UN Samantha Power reported that 417 of the country's 436 mosques had been destroyed in the fighting.

The country had descended into chaos in March 2013, when a rebel force mainly comprised of Muslim Séléka fighters marched on the capital and ousted President François Bozizé. The conflict quickly took on ethnic and sectarian undertones, with the United Nations warning that there was a high risk of genocide in the country. Séléka leader Michel Djotodia declared himself president in place of Bozizé, but subsequently failed to reign in his supporters, who carried out serious human-rights violations. In response, 'anti-balaka' (anti-machete) vigilante groups dominated by Christians and animists conducted attacks against Muslim civilians. Djotodia was put under pressure by regional powers to resign. Following his departure in January 2014, a transitional government led by Catherine Samba-Panza was installed.

A truce signed by representatives of the ex-Séléka and anti-balaka groups in Nairobi in January 2015 was rejected by the transitional government, which had not been invited to participate in the discussions. The terms of the agreement, which were also rejected by the Economic Community of Central African States and the UN, failed to improve the situation on the ground.

But there were high hopes for the Bangui Forum, a summit on national reconciliation and the political future of the country held the following

May. Regarded as a key event for Central African Republic, the meeting was attended by almost 700 leaders from a variety of groups, including the transitional government, national political parties, the main opposition armed groups, businesses, civil-society movements and religious organisations. As the forum concluded, armed groups and representatives of the transitional government signed an accord on the disarmament, demobilisation, reintegration and repatriation (DDRR) of combatants. In addition, the armed groups agreed to halt their recruitment of child soldiers, and to release all such fighters within their ranks.

Participants in the forum also agreed on a timeline for elections and an extension of the transitional government's mandate, as well as the structures for justice and reconciliation in the country, which included a national truth and reconciliation commission. Yet there were considerable challenges ahead, including funding discrepancies in the DDRR programme and problems with local reconciliation initiatives. Although the Bangui Forum was regarded as a success, Central African Republic has a history of national debates on peace that are followed by periods of crisis (at least five since 1980).

Regardless of whether its accords would endure, the forum was a step towards legislative and presidential elections scheduled for later in the year. However, there were rumours that members of the many transitional government bodies, including President Samba-Panza, might run in the election, a move that would contravene the 2010 N'Djamena Declaration.

The relationship between MINUSCA and former Séléka fighters worsened following clashes between them in the eastern town of Bria. Assisted by French forces, MINUSCA carried out an attack against Front Populaire pour la Renaissance de la Centrafrique (FPRC) in February 2015, after the group set up a parallel administration there by removing the local authorities. The operation succeeded in driving out the rebels and reinstating the authorities. But with the FPRC dislodged from its former stronghold and on the move, nearby villages became vulnerable to reprisal attacks.

Security gradually improved in the areas in which MINUSCA was deployed. The mandate of the European Union task force in Central African Republic expired on 15 March. After withdrawing the force, which had been deployed in 2014 to secure Bangui's airport and other areas of the capital, the EU authorised a military advisory mission centred on security-sector reforms and army-training programmes. Meanwhile, the 2,000-strong French mission, *Operation Sangaris* – deployed in December 2013 amid concerns about potential genocide and state collapse – was slowly withdrawing, and was expected to be reduced to 500 troops by the end of 2015.

Democratic Republic of the Congo: Rising political opposition

There was little respite in the series of conflicts that have long plagued Democratic Republic of the Congo. Fighting between Congolese forces and rebel groups in the east of the country displaced around 770,000 civilians in 2014, bringing the total number of internally displaced people to 2.7m. Military operations against rebel groups in the east had mixed success.

Congolese troops launched *Operation Sokola 2* against the Democratic Forces for the Liberation of Rwanda (FDLR) in late January 2015. The mission was prompted by the group's failure to disarm, despite being given an ultimatum to do so within six months of June 2014: by the end of the year, only around 200 of the estimated 1,500 rebels had given up their weapons.

The Congolese government stated that it was ready to launch military operations against the FDLR, and the UN Security Council backed an offensive to 'neutralise' the group. However, the UN Organization Stabilization Mission in the Democratic Republic of the Congo (MONUSCO) did not participate in the operation, after the government appointed General Bruno Mandevu as its head. This was due to the fact that he was on a MONUSCO 'red list' – comprising individuals the UN wanted to avoid working with – because of his alleged involvement in 121 human-rights violations, including summary executions and rapes. Government relations with MONUSCO became increasingly tense following the appointment, which the government refused to reverse.

Although the FDLR remained the most significant rebel militia, Congolese troops also focused on combating the Allied Democratic Force–National Army for the Liberation of Uganda (ADF–NALU) in Beni, in North Kivu. Composed of Ugandan opposition forces who set up bases in Democratic Republic of the Congo, the group became increasingly active in 2014, carrying out a series of attacks on civilians despite offensives against it by the military (which had also attempted to destroy it in 2005 and 2010). The ADF–NALU's campaign culminated in assaults on Beni in October and November 2014 that killed hundreds of people, leading the town's mayor to impose a curfew. The surge in violence prompted President Joseph Kabila to visit Beni in October 2014, while Martin Kobler, head of MONUSCO, stated in November that defeating the group had become a priority for the mission. The following March, the Congolese military launched large-scale operations against the ADF–NALU in several areas on the border between North Kivu and Orientale Province. Congolese forces declared that the goal of the operation was to force the surrender of all Ugandan rebel fighters opposed to voluntary disarmament.

Two months earlier, UN and Congolese troops had launched strikes against remnants of the National Liberation Forces, a Burundian rebel group based in eastern Democratic Republic of the Congo. A UN diplomat stated that the operation, which took place in South Kivu, was mainly aimed at clearing the way for an offensive against the FDLR.

Katanga Province experienced several outbreaks of fighting due to the growing insurgency campaign conducted by Mai Mai Kata Katanga. The group seeks independence for the region, which has the largest cobalt deposits in the world, as well as copper reserves that have allowed Democratic Republic of the Congo to become Africa's second-largest supplier of the product. Most of the violence associated with the insurgents occurred in the east of the province, between the towns of Pweto, Mitwaba and Manono.

Along with the violence, the Kabila administration was also forced to deal with significant political opposition. In August 2014, hundreds of opposition supporters attended a protest in Kinshasa against the government's attempts to change the constitution so as to allow him to serve a third term. They included members of the Union for Democracy and Social Progress, and the Union for the Congolese Nation – the two largest opposition parties – as well as those of several smaller groupings. In December, Kabila responded by announcing the formation of a unity government he hoped would broaden his political base. Augustin Matata Ponyo retained his post as prime minister within the new administration. But opposition party Movement for the Liberation of Congo fired its leader and two other senior officials after they agreed to join the new government. As a result, there was speculation that Kabila had intended to cause just such a split among his opponents, who were already divided.

Nationwide protests also took place in January, this time against a proposed amendment to the electoral law before parliament. The amendment included provisions for a census to be conducted before elections scheduled for 2016, which the protesters argued would delay the elections and be used as an excuse to prolong Kabila's term. Demonstrations and violence also broke out in Kinshasa, as well as in eastern cities such as Goma and Bukavu, and in the capital of Katanga province, Lubumbashi. In February, the senate adopted the legislation without the disputed clause, and presidential and legislative elections were scheduled for November 2016. Yet the continuing unrest in the east showed the government's inability to gain nationwide support or to exert control over the country as a whole.

Foreign Military Forces in Africa

The role played by foreign militaries in combating the Ebola virus has followed a trend towards their deepening involvement in sub-Saharan Africa. As part of a broad international response, troops deployed by several countries have played a substantial part in bolstering local infrastructure and in improving command and control to prevent the spread of the virus.

Deployment on UN missions remains central to foreign military activity in Africa, largely because of the persistence of some of the continent's conflicts. But there has been increasing international focus on opposing the growth of insurgent and terrorist groups. The number of counter-terrorist operations under way has increased, as has the use of military force by non-African states against such groups and support to African forces engaged in similar tasks.

External security engagement in Africa is not new. European nations maintained military forces on the continent during the colonial era, and some sent military forces and equipment even after that period ended. Cold War confrontation led to both East and West supplying military equipment and training to African states, and even to the deployments of troops, such as Cuba's to Angola in 1975.

The first large-scale peacekeeping mission carried out by the United Nations was the UN Operation in the Congo, which saw nearly 20,000 military personnel deployed by 30 countries between 1960 and 1964. Today, the highest numbers are still deployed on UN missions. For example, the UN mission in the Democratic Republic of the Congo, MONUSCO, has more than 19,000 troops deployed by around 50 states. All told, there are nine operations across Africa managed by the UN's Department of Peacekeeping Operations (DPKO). Some missions address new crises; most continue to tackle the continent's complex challenges and persistent conflicts. As of May 2015, these nine missions boasted a total of 76,000 troops, with the largest numbers from African and South Asian nations. China's troop contributions have grown in recent years, a trend that will likely continue as its armed forces develop and the country's commercial ties with Africa increase.

Operations by the UN are increasingly seen as 'multidimensional' in design, taking into account not only the need to improve security but also requirements such as that to 'facilitate the political process, protect civilians, [and] assist in the disarmament, demobilization and reintegration of former combatants', according to the organisation. These objectives are complicated by the increasingly transnational nature of security threats, which include pandemic disease, insurgency and terrorism, illegal migration, and organised crime. Concern over issues such as these increasingly drives military responses from Western countries.

The military engagements of Western nations still tend to be focused on those countries with which they already have established links. Decades after the end of the colonial era, outside powers still retain substantial military ties to their former dominions. Thus, following the Ebola outbreak, Sierra Leone was the focus of the United Kingdom's response and Guinea the focus of France's. The United States was particularly active in Liberia, where Washington has long-standing ties.

More broadly, the UK retains specific links with Sierra Leone, where its forces form part of the International Security Advisory Team, and with Kenya, which hosts a peace-support team for East Africa and a British army-training unit. France, which is running a number of active military operations in Africa, has military forces in the Central African Republic, Chad, Côte d'Ivoire, Djibouti, Gabon, Mali, Niger and Senegal. It has pre-positioned defence stocks in some of these countries.

Building local capacity

This pattern of foreign involvement persists even though African states are paying greater attention to regional security challenges, and some are more willing to deploy military force to deal with problems in other countries on their continent. However, African armed forces are hampered by lack of capacity in areas such as logistics, maintenance, airlift, surveillance, and command and control; often, they also lack sufficient funding to deploy on external operations.

As security dynamics in Africa evolved, the nature of foreign military involvement also started to change. Military training and capacity-building initiatives have grown in the past 20 years, in line with a desire by African states and institutions to do more themselves. Foreign governments understand that it is in their interest to help African countries develop security institutions so as to bolster stability and resilience. Improving the capability of military and security forces is one way to achieve this, and also gives these states greater ability to undertake peace and security operations.

France, for instance, engages in capacity-building sometimes as a national initiative and sometimes nested within broader efforts, such as gendarmerie training offered as part of the European Union's mission in Mali. A long-standing set of French capacity-building exercises transitioned in 2006 into the EURORECAMP series, designed to aid development of the African Standby Force concept of the African Union and Africa's Regional Economic Communities. Efforts are now focused on the *Amani Africa II* exercise due at the end of 2015, which, with substantial EU support, will be important to operationalising the Standby Force.

The US has been involved for many years in capacity-building initiatives. These include the African Contingency Operations Training and Assistance programme, intended to enhance the ability of African partners to take part in multinational operations across the world. Other activities include the Africa Partnership Station, designed to build capacity in maritime security, and the US Africa Command (AFRICOM), established in 2008 as Washington's Africa-focused geographic combatant command, managing US operations, exercises and security cooperation on the continent.

Military assistance ought not to take place in isolation. For example, having a stable military means ensuring that salaries are paid on time.

EU Missions in Africa, June 2015			
Name	Location	Start date	Type
EUTM Mali	Mali	2013	Military
EUCAP Sahel Mali	Mali	2014	Civilian
EUCAP Sahel Niger	Niger	2012	Civilian
EUMAM RCA	Central African Republic	2015	Military
EUSEC RD Congo	Democratic Republic of the Congo	2005	Civilian
EUCAP Nestor	Djibouti, Seychelles, Somalia, Tanzania	2012	Civilian
EUTM Somalia	Somalia	2010	Civilian /Military
EU NAVFOR	Gulf of Aden	2008	Civilian /Military

Source: European External Action Service

Therefore, finance-ministry procedures are as important as those of the defence ministry. There is increasing understanding of other government bodies' needs when assistance packages are being constructed, but putting this into practice is challenging. Such coordination is easier to design when military assistance is considered from the start as just one part of a solution to a wider problem: foreign counter-piracy activities off the Somali coast are a good example. Piracy has declined substantially in recent years, most importantly as a result of new practices by shipping firms, but also because of naval operations by NATO and the EU. Military action off the coast cannot address the root causes of the problem, which lie in long-term political and economic failures that the Somali government, with foreign assistance, is seeking to address.

As well as supporting the Somali government and providing humanitarian assistance, Brussels has established EU Training Mission–Somalia to help develop the country's armed forces, covering not only military training but also issues such as human rights. Meanwhile, another mission, EUCAP Nestor, is aimed at the development of maritime-security capacity in East Africa.

Counter-terrorism imperatives

The immediacy of the threat posed by groups such as al-Shabaab in Somalia and Boko Haram in Nigeria means that a substantial element of Western international military engagement in Africa is now focused on operations against terrorism and insurgency. Al-Shabaab poses a persistent threat to the nascent Somali government, and its attacks in Kenya, including that on the Garissa University in April 2015, show its growing international reach. The conflict with Boko Haram in northern Nigeria has spread into several neighbouring countries: a plan for a multinational task force involving Niger, Cameroon, Chad, Benin and Nigeria was approved by the AU in May 2015.

Longer-term development assistance and capacity-building are vital elements in foreign efforts to counter such groups, but military action has a higher profile.

For the US, countering violent extremism and enhancing stability in East and West Africa are the top two immediate priorities for AFRICOM, according to a 2015 posture statement. The US Trans-Sahara Counterterrorism Partnership has been in operation since 2005, a successor to the earlier Pan-Sahel Initiative. It is designed to bolster the ability of governments in the Sahel to counter violent extremism; the military element of this multi-agency activity is *Operation Enduring Freedom–Trans Sahara*. Meanwhile, the *Flintlock* series of special-forces capacity-building exercises have also been conducted for several years; the 2015 iteration was held in Chad.

From AFRICOM's long-term forward operating base at Camp Lemonnier in Djibouti – a training and deployment hub – the US mounts surveillance operations and strikes against militant groups, as do France and other countries. (Lemonnier is also used by other armed forces for various tasks, such as air operations in support of counter-piracy missions.)

However, the centre of gravity for France's involvement remains in the Francophone region to the west, where the country keeps most of its Africa-based forces. In recent years, France has reshaped its African anti-terrorism posture and deployments, deepening the level of military engagement with regional armed forces. The principal vehicle is *Operation Barkhane*, launched in August 2014 as a strategic 'joint venture' with Mauritania, Mali, Niger, Chad and Burkina Faso. In effect, *Barkhane* merged missions previously under way in Mali and Chad, altering the locations of bases. The intent was to create a more unified force structure able to operate across the Sahel, as insurgent groups increasingly moved across borders.

In 2013, France led *Operation Serval* to help government forces in Mali stem the advance of rebel militias towards the capital, Bamako, and to tackle Islamist groups in the north. Later in the same year, French forces were deployed to Central African Republic amid a violent sectarian conflict. Such missions require flexible assets capable of rapid despatch, substantial tactical and strategic airlift capacity, and the ability to mount persistent overwatch. But these missions also highlighted areas where the French lacked certain capacities: *Barkhane* saw the rapid entry into service of France's new *Reaper* unmanned aerial vehicles, augmenting its existing *Harfang*. *Serval* saw the UK's Royal Air Force deploy a *Sentinel* R1 surveillance aircraft, reportedly flying 66 missions in support of the French-led operation, while British and American C-17s flew airlift missions in its early stages.

Other militaries have provided assistance in specific situations: in May 2014, Washington sent an unmanned aerial vehicle to Chad to assist Nigeria's government in trying to find 276 schoolgirls kidnapped by Boko Haram. Responding to the conflict in Nigeria, the UK offered to provide training in counter-insurgency techniques.

There is growing understanding among Western states of the commonalities between security challenges in Africa: capacity deficits among state institutions and armed forces have the potential to make countries more fragile. Addressing these shortfalls requires enduring engagement from external partners, while responses to the continent's security challenges increasingly demand cross-border cooperation. It is important to look beyond immediate counter-terrorism imperatives, and to consider support that bolsters the capacity of broader state institutions as well as defence and security organisations. These longer-term agendas would also help in making Africa's security organisations more resilient, and in developing the broader capabilities needed to address the continent's complex security problems – at a time when African states and security institutions are looking to do more for, and by, themselves.

France: Selected Deployments in Africa – 2014 (Source: *The Military Balance 2015*)

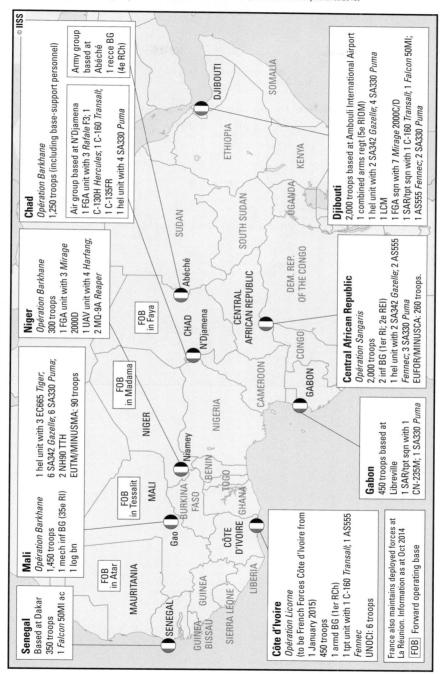

© IISS

Army group based at Abéché
1 recce BG (4e RCh)

Chad
Opération Barkhane
1,250 troops (including base-support personnel)

Air group based at N'Djamena
1 FGA unit with 3 *Rafale* F3; 1
C-130H *Hercules*; 1 C-160 *Transall*;
1 C-135FR
1 hel unit with 4 SA330 *Puma*

Djibouti
2,000 troops based at Ambouli International Airport
1 combined arms regt (5e RIOM)
1 hel unit with 2 SA342 *Gazelle*; 4 SA330 *Puma*
1 LCM
1 FGA sqn with 7 *Mirage* 2000C/D
1 SAR/tpt sqn with 1 C-160 *Transall*; 1 *Falcon* 50MI;
1 AS555 *Fennec*; 2 SA330 *Puma*

Niger
Opération Barkhane
300 troops
1 FGA unit with 3 *Mirage* 2000D
1 UAV unit with 4 *Harfang*;
2 MQ-9A *Reaper*

FOB in Faya

FOB in Madama

Central African Republic
Opération Sangaris
2,000 troops
2 inf BG (1er RI; 2e REI)
1 hel unit with 2 SA342 *Gazelle*; 2 AS555
Fennec; 3 SA330 *Puma*
EUFOR/MINUSCA: 260 troops.

Mali
Opération Barkhane
1,450 troops
1 mech inf BG (35e RI)
1 log bn

1 hel unit with 3 EC665 *Tiger*;
6 SA342 *Gazelle*; 6 SA330 *Puma*;
2 NH90 TTH
EUTM/MINUSMA: 90 troops

FOB in Tessalit

FOB in Atar

Gabon
450 troops based at
Libreville
1 SAR/tpt sqn with 1
CN-235M; 1 SA330 *Puma*

Senegal
Based at Dakar
350 troops
1 *Falcon* 50MI ac

Côte d'Ivoire
Opération Licorne
(to be French Forces Côte d'Ivoire from
1 January 2015)
450 troops
1 armd BG (1er RCh)
1 tpt unit with 1 C-160 *Transall*; 1 AS555
Fennec
UNOCI: 6 troops

France also maintains deployed forces at
La Réunion. Information as at Oct 2014

FOB Forward operating base

Abéché

CHAD

N'Djamena

Niamey

Gao

GABON

CÔTE D'IVOIRE

SENEGAL

DJIBOUTI

SOMALIA

ETHIOPIA

KENYA

UGANDA

SUDAN

SOUTH SUDAN

DEM. REP.
OF THE CONGO

CENTRAL
AFRICAN REPUBLIC

CONGO

CAMEROON

NIGERIA

NIGER

MALI

BURKINA
FASO

BENIN

TOGO

GHANA

LIBERIA

SIERRA LEONE

GUINEA

GUINEA
BISSAU

MAURITANIA

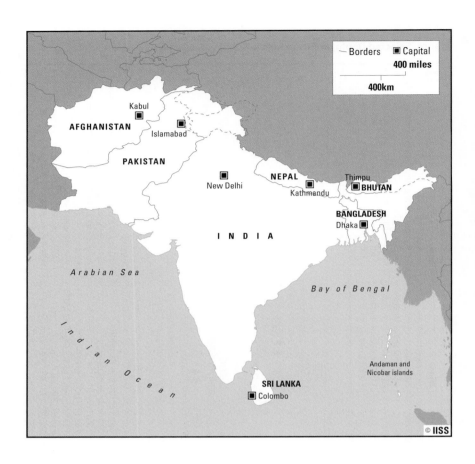

Chapter 10

South Asia and Afghanistan

Despite undergoing a series of political transitions that generated huge public expectation, the countries of South Asia failed to significantly strengthen their economies in the year to mid-2015. Narendra Modi, India's new prime minister, began to liberalise key sectors of the economy but was unable to implement his two most important legislative reforms, the Land Acquisition Bill and the Goods and Services Tax (GST) Bill, due to a lack of seats in the Rajya Sabha (upper house of parliament). In Pakistan, Prime Minister Nawaz Sharif's indecisiveness and differences with the army hampered his ability to tackle energy shortages and push forward desperately needed economic reforms and infrastructure investment. In Sri Lanka, having won a surprise victory in the presidential election of January 2015, Maithripala Sirisena became the head of a minority coalition government but was also unable to effectively implement a reform agenda. Meanwhile, Afghanistan suffered from divisions between President Ashraf Ghani and his chief executive, Abdullah Abdullah, whose unity government struggled to enact substantive economic reforms.

While the lack of such reforms had negative effects for growth and foreign investment across South Asia, the sudden decrease in the price of oil had tremendous benefits for the economies of the region, which have been hugely dependent on energy imports. In India, the drop in the oil price helped to lower inflation and interest rates, thereby strengthening economic recovery. In Pakistan, the fall-off helped stabilise foreign-exchange reserves and lower the fiscal deficit to 5% of GDP, down from 8% two years earlier.

For the most part, domestic political transitions did not lead to overhauls of foreign policy. But there were a few significant shifts. Modi aspired to India becoming a 'leading' rather than 'balancing' power, and made no reference to the non-alignment favoured by his predecessors. At the same time, he was keen to foster economic partnerships and growth across the region, and to that end emphasised the role of the South Asian Association for Regional Cooperation (SAARC). Yet this effort did not appear to include Pakistan, towards which India's policy had hardened after two and a half years without an official dialogue between the sides. The apparent attempt to isolate Islamabad seemed especially problematic given New Delhi's effort to galvanise SAARC, as well as Afghanistan's moves towards rapprochement with Pakistan, which included Ghani's visit to Pakistan's army headquarters and the resumption of military-to-military cooperation. There were also questions about the impact on India's aspirations of the improved relationship between Islamabad and Beijing, reflected in the establishment of the US$46-billion China–Pakistan Economic Corridor.

Relations between South Asian countries were also affected by several growing security threats. India and Pakistan increasingly accused each other of sponsoring terrorist attacks that they had suffered at home, while denying their own involvement in such acts. Similarly, both Afghanistan and Iran denounced Pakistan for its alleged involvement in terrorist activities on their territory. This prompted Islamabad to accuse both countries of sponsoring terrorist assaults on Pakistani targets. While it adopted a new counter-terrorism strategy in the aftermath of a brutal assault on a school in Peshawar in December 2014, Pakistan did not appear to have changed its attitude towards providing covert support to militant groups. Nonetheless, reports that the Islamic State of Iraq and al-Sham (ISIS) had established a limited presence in both Afghanistan and Pakistan raised concern in security establishments. While the countries' counter-terrorism strategies were not complementary, there seemed a chance that this new threat could force them to better align their approaches to dealing with religious extremism.

India: Stalled Reforms

In July 2014, a few weeks after taking office, Modi passed an interim budget that focused on pragmatic structural reforms designed to spur economic growth. As part of this, the cap on foreign direct investment in India's defence and insurance sectors was raised from 26% to 49%. In September, Modi launched a major 'Make in India' initiative that aimed to boost domestic manufacturing and employment in multiple sectors, including defence. This effort was later aided by the government's first full budget, in February 2015, which centred on measures to attract foreign investment and increases in spending on infrastructure. After reaching out to key regional political parties outside the National Democratic Alliance (NDA), the centre-right coalition led by Modi, the government passed the insurance bill in the Rajya Sabha in mid-March, its first major economic reform. This was followed by the Mines and Minerals (Development and Regulation) Amendment Bill, which sought to improve transparency in minerals allocation by allowing mines to be sold at auction; and the Coal Mines (Special Provisions) Bill, which enabled private companies to mine coal for sale on the open market. The government also indicated that it would permit 51% foreign investment in multi-brand retail businesses (a policy it had strongly opposed while in opposition). It also launched an ambitious set of low-cost pension and insurance schemes, as part of its campaign to provide financial services to a greater number of citizens.

But two of the government's most important reforms were blocked due to a lack of sufficient NDA seats in the Rajya Sabha. While Modi sought to amend the 2013 Land Acquisition Bill to make it easier for companies to acquire land for manufacturing purposes, Congress – the main opposition party – criticised the move as benefiting a few corporations at the expense of farmers, and threatened to conduct protests across India in response. Meanwhile, the GST bill sought to create a countrywide tax regime and a unified national market, thereby doing away with multiple federal and state levies. Although both bills were passed by the Lok Sabha (lower house of parliament), they were sent to parliamentary committees while the government attempted to generate enough political support to ensure that they were passed. This would be a difficult task for the government, with the Land Acquisition Bill requiring a majority and the GST a two-thirds majority in the Rajya Sabha, with the latter also requiring ratification by half of the country's state legislatures.

Yet despite these challenges, the government was able to raise business confidence in India among domestic and foreign companies, which remained upbeat about the prospects for major reforms. Modi also sought to improve India's business environment by streamlining bureaucratic procedures and countering corruption. The business-friendly 2015 budget included a phased reduction in corporate tax over four years and the replacement of the wealth tax with an additional surcharge on high earners. The government also clarified that it would not implement any retroactive changes in taxation that could lead to fresh tax liability.

The fall in oil price that began in mid-2014 came as welcome relief for India, which was the world's fourth-largest consumer of oil and petroleum products, and imported more than 70% of the oil it consumed. The resulting fall in inflation helped bring down interest rates just as the government worked to end state controls on fuel prices and lower the cost of fuel subsidies. Fiscal and current-account deficits were reduced. India's economic recovery looked more encouraging as a result of a change in the method used to calculate annual growth rates, which raised the figure to 6.9% in 2013–14, up from less than 5%, and to 7.5% in 2014–15. These new rates were accepted by both the IMF and the World Bank.

Rising religious intolerance

At the time of Modi's electoral victory, the NDA controlled nine of India's 29 state legislatures, and the Bharatiya Janata Party (BJP), which he led, only five. To strengthen BJP rule nationwide and implement his economic reforms, Modi needed to secure control over a majority of states, and therefore victory in successive state-assembly elections. This would not only provide greater political leverage to the BJP but would also increase the number of seats held by the party in the Rajya Sabha (whose members are indirectly elected by provincial assemblies).

In the first set of elections, held in Maharashtra and Haryana in October 2014, Modi wrested control of both states from the Congress party, resulting in a BJP-led coalition government in the former and a majority government in the latter. In the Jharkhand assembly elections, held in December, the BJP won against an alliance that included Congress. In the Jammu and Kashmir elections, which witnessed a record turnout, the BJP became part of a governing coalition led by the local People's Democratic Party. This was especially significant in light of the key ideological differences between the two parties over talks with the Kashmiri separatist group All Parties Hurriyat Conference; the withdrawal of the Armed Forces (Special Powers) Act; and Article 370, which gives Jammu and Kashmir a special status under the Indian constitution.

In February 2015, Modi suffered his first major electoral setback: the BJP lost the New Delhi assembly elections to the anti-corruption Aam Aadmi Party (AAP), winning only three of 70 seats. This was due largely to the BJP's nomination of an unpopular candidate for chief minister, as well as impatience for economic progress among the electorate.

Nonetheless, with Congress failing to recover lost ground in state elections, and Rahul Gandhi unable or unwilling to take over leadership of the party, the NDA did not face any serious political threats. Shortly after its victory in New Delhi, the AAP began to suffer from infighting that diminished its chances of gaining significant national support.

However, the political dominance of the BJP, a centre-right Hindu nationalist party, appeared to facilitate a rise in religious intolerance, as seen in provocative anti-Muslim rhetoric from parliamentarians and others affiliated with the party; a series of attacks on Christian churches and institutions; and a *ghar wapsi* (homecoming) campaign, in which Hindu hardliners attempted to convert Christians and Muslims. Modi's initial silence on these incidents finally ended in February 2015, when he publicly condemned religious violence. He later denounced religious discrimination of any kind in a parliamentary session. Yet somewhat awkwardly, Modi only adopted this conciliatory stance after a lecture given in New Delhi by Barack Obama, in which the US president argued that India's success would depend on it avoiding division along religious lines.

Although the Indian government was able to reassure itself that only a handful of Indians had travelled to Iraq and Syria to join ISIS, it remained concerned about the spread of violent extremism at home. Al-Qaeda established a new branch in the Indian subcontinent in September 2014, amid anxiety over its links with the locally based Indian Mujahideen terror group. Meanwhile, the Maoist Naxalite insurgent group suffered setbacks through the arrest of senior leaders and the mass desertion of fighters, although in April 2015 the guerrillas killed seven policemen during an attack in Chhattisgarh. In December 2014, 60 adivasis (indigenous people) were massacred by armed Bodo militants of the National Democratic Front of Bodoland's Songbijit faction in India's northeastern state of Assam. Five months later, militants from the National Socialist Council of Nagaland–Khaplang and the Manipuri Kanglei Yawol Kanna Lup carried out the worst assault on the Indian Army in decades, killing 18 soldiers in the northeastern state of Manipur and prompting a retaliatory strike against two operating bases in Myanmar.

Leading-power aspirations

While Modi largely focused on domestic issues in his first year as prime minister, his interactions with foreign leaders did much to raise India's global profile. The most obvious changes were in the style rather than the substance of diplomacy, even as important shifts in foreign policy were made. Modi's trips abroad made use of quite different visuals to those of his predecessor, Manmohan Singh, and bore a strong personal touch – whether through a welcome hug for Obama in New Delhi, or a 'selfie' with Chinese Prime Minister Li Keqiang in Beijing. He was received like a rock star by Indian diaspora communities in many of the states he visited. Modi ventured to countries that his predecessors had not visited bilaterally for several decades, including Canada and Australia. He made sure that India played an active role in rescuing its nationals and those of several other countries from conflict zones in Iraq and Yemen, as well as in the aftermath of the Nepal earthquake (in which it also played a major crisis-response role). There was a far greater emphasis on cultural diplomacy, as shown by the declaration of the first International Day of Yoga by the United Nations General Assembly on 21 June 2015.

More substantively, Modi's foreign policy had much in common with that of the previous administration, albeit with greater pragmatism. The prime minister was eager to use foreign policy as a means to gener-ate business and inward investment. His enthusiasm for engaging with other South Asian countries in this effort was demonstrated by his focus on SAARC. At the same time, he revised some of the foreign-policy positions that the BJP had taken while in opposition. Although the government worked closely with friendly countries on mutually beneficial initiatives, it made few attempts to deal with states with which it had difficult or adversarial relations. In just over a year, Modi visited all India's immediate neighbours other than Pakistan and the Maldives (a visit to the latter was cancelled).

Significantly, bilateral visits to Nepal and Sri Lanka were the first by an Indian prime minister in decades. Modi offered to renegotiate a 1950 treaty between India and Nepal, long considered unfair by the latter; and he signalled a new start in ties with Sri Lanka, dealing with a Sirisena government regarded as more responsive towards India than its predecessor. In Bangladesh, Modi signed a landmark boundary agreement, resolving an issue that had hampered bilateral relations for four decades (and reversing the policy on the issue that the BJP had adopted while in opposition). This involved the exchange of 198 tiny enclaves of foreign territory inside each country, a move that simplified India's longest border. The agreement also bolstered the July 2014 settlement of the India–Bangladesh maritime boundary, made through arbitration under the provisions of the UN Convention on the Law of the Sea. Regarding Afghanistan, India was concerned about Ghani's outreach to Islamabad but continued to pledge support to development projects including the much-delayed construction of the parliament building in Kabul and the Salma Dam.

There was also continuity in India's relations with China: Modi worked to establish strong bilateral ties, particularly trade and investment links. The sides maintained the mechanism of using special representatives to resolve border disputes, with India granting e-visas to Chinese nationals despite problems over the issue of Chinese visas to Indians living in territory claimed by Beijing. Yet when Chinese forces crossed the Line of Actual Control at Chumar in September 2014, during a trip to India by Chinese President Xi Jinping, Modi responded in a robust manner, sending reinforcements to the area and ensuring that Indian troops held their positions. He publicly expressed concern over the border dispute and raised Beijing's policies towards India's neighbours with the Chinese leadership. The joint statement issued at the end of Modi's May 2015 visit to China did not contain references to maritime cooperation or Asia-Pacific security, unlike a similar statement made eight months earlier. Nor did it refer to China's 'One Belt, One Road' initiative or its Maritime Silk Road, both of which India views with suspicion.

Modi visited the United States within weeks of becoming prime minister. The trip surprised many, as Modi had been denied a US visa for nine years due to his alleged complicity in sectarian riots that had taken place in Gujarat in 2002, when he was chief minister of the state. Reversing the BJP's previous position, Modi pushed hard for implementation of the stalled 2008 US–India nuclear deal. In January 2015, Obama made his second state visit to India, becoming the first American chief guest at India's Republic Day Parade and announcing a breakthrough on a controversial civil-nuclear liability issue, as well as a deal on administrative arrangements to track nuclear material passing through prospective US-made reactors in India. This made it more likely that such reactors would eventually be assembled in India, thereby improving the country's energy security. In June, during a visit to New Delhi by US Secretary of Defense Ashton Carter, a ten-year defence framework agreement was signed that envisaged joint development and manufacture of military equipment and technology, including jet engines and aircraft-carrier design and construction. Joint projects to develop mobile electric hybrid power sources and protective suits were also agreed.

Four shifts in foreign policy took place under Modi. Firstly, India now aspires to becoming a 'leading' rather than a 'balancing' power: instead of trying to limit Western or Chinese power, Modi now seeks to leverage India's growing national capabilities to take on a greater global role. Accordingly, New Delhi appears to have abandoned its position of non-alignment; indeed, Modi skipped the April 2015 Asia–Africa Summit held in Indonesia, which marked the 60th anniversary of the Bandung Conference that led to the Non-Aligned Movement. India also seeks a proactive role in the Indian Ocean: Modi unveiled in March 2015 a vision for the region, the first issued by an Indian prime minister in decades, which focused on defending India's maritime territory and interests; deepening economic and security cooperation with maritime neighbours; promoting collective action for peace and security; and integrating initiatives for sustainable development. To build security links with Indian Ocean island states, India launched a coastal-surveillance radar project in the Seychelles, provided an offshore patrol vessel to Mauritius and, perhaps most significantly, agreed on investment and infrastructure development in Assumption Island in the Seychelles and Agaléga Island in Mauritius – both of which could be used for surveillance purposes.

The second foreign-policy shift has been Modi's willingness to form a united front with the US on Asia-Pacific security. During Obama's visit to India in January 2015, the two countries published a document that outlined their joint strategic vision for the Asia-Pacific and the Indian Ocean. It included a paragraph affirming 'the importance of safeguarding maritime security and ensuring freedom of navigation and over flight throughout the region, especially in the South China Sea'. This was widely perceived as implying that the two parties had reached a consensus on the need to counter Beijing's assertive approach to territorial disputes in the region. In essence, the joint vision recognised the complementary nature of Modi's 'Act East' policy focusing on Japan and Australia, and the US 'rebalance' to Asia. While India and the US appear to be reaching a consensus on Asia-Pacific security, neither wants a confrontational relationship with China.

The third shift has been the hardening of India's position towards Pakistan, as relations between the two deteriorated. A meeting between the Pakistani high commissioner in New Delhi and the leadership of All Parties Hurriyat Conference in August 2014 led to India's sudden cancellation of scheduled talks between the countries' foreign secretaries – talks that were expected to have restarted the formal dialogue between the two countries that had been stalled since January 2013. The worst border clashes between the two in the last decade broke out two months later, as India deliberately intensified violence across the Line of Control and both sides blamed each other for ceasefire violations, as well as the deaths of civilians and troops. There was a distinct chill between Modi and Sharif at the SAARC summit held in Kathmandu the following month, and a visit by the new Indian foreign secretary to Islamabad in March (under the aegis of SAARC) did not result in preliminary talks. In April, New Delhi was angered by a Pakistani court's decision to release on bail Zaki-ur-Rehman Lakhvi, operations chief of the Lashkar-e-Taiba militant group – and the alleged mastermind of the 2008 Mumbai terror attacks – after he had spent six years in prison.

This discontent had been exacerbated by sharper rhetoric from both sides. In August 2014, Modi told Indian soldiers assembled on the heights of Leh in Jammu and Kashmir that Islamabad was 'continuing to engage in the proxy war of terrorism against India'. Pakistan described this as 'baseless rhetoric'. And India was surprised by Islamabad's criticism of Obama's visit to New Delhi in January 2015. The trip was followed by a flurry of accusations by Islamabad that India was involved in terrorism in Baluchistan, Karachi and Pakistan's tribal areas. In May, the Pakistani corps commanders' conference for the first time formally accused India's foreign-intelligence agency, the Research and Analysis Wing, of 'whipping up terrorism' in Pakistan (a charge denied by India). Later that month, the Indian defence minister argued that 'terrorists have to be neutralised only through terrorists', leading his Pakistani counterpart to assert that this confirmed India's involvement in terrorism on Pakistani soil. There were also unsubstantiated allegations that the Research and Analysis Wing was attempting to disrupt the China–Pakistan Economic Corridor, following the Indian foreign minister's statement in June 2015 that the project was 'unacceptable' to New Delhi as it would make use of infrastructure built in disputed territory. The Indian government did not appear to be interested in establishing a private channel for talks with Pakistan, a confidence-building mechanism that had been used by the previous administration.

Yet despite these tensions, the sides made some attempts to reach out to each other. Modi sent a conciliatory message to Sharif on 23 March, Pakistan's national day, and contacted him again shortly before Ramadan in mid-June 2015, prior to their scheduled meeting in Russia the following month. Pakistan rescued 11 Indian nationals from Yemen in April 2015. India and Pakistan each released fishermen arrested for fishing in the other's waters. India officially maintained that it was willing to resume a bilateral dialogue with Pakistan on 'all outstanding issues', although this depended on the establishment of an 'atmosphere free from terror and violence'. In contrast, Islamabad was keen to restart the dialogue without any preconditions.

The fourth shift in India's foreign policy was the abandonment of its traditional support for the Palestinian cause, in favour of Israel. New Delhi made clear that it would not take sides in the Gaza conflict that began in July 2014, urging peace talks between Israel and Palestine. Although the Indian government subsequently voted against Israel at the UN Human Rights Council, thereby condemning the country's 'disproportionate use of force', this was reportedly the decision of the foreign ministry rather than the prime minister's office, which would have preferred to abstain. Modi met Israeli Prime Minister Benjamin Netanyahu in New York in September 2014, on the sidelines of the UN General Assembly, and the first visit of an Israeli defence minister to India took place the following February, aiming to strengthen the countries' security ties. In May, India abstained from voting on an application by a Palestinian non-governmental organisation for special consultative status in a UN committee. A few days later, it was announced that Modi would become the first Indian prime minister to visit Israel.

Pakistan: New Counter-terrorism Efforts

Although Prime Minister Nawaz Sharif had a working majority in the National Assembly, Pakistan was shaken by political instability in the second half of 2014. This weakened Sharif and strengthened the army, which gained greater popularity by leading an extensive military operation in the tribal areas bordering Afghanistan, as well as by taking a leading role in the counter-terrorism effort launched in December, following a mass-casualty attack on an army-run school in Peshawar.

Sharif's problems were largely of his own making. Due to political indecisiveness and divisions among the people he trusted, the prime minister was unable to address Pakistan's energy shortages or implement much-needed economic reforms. Differences with the army made these tasks even more difficult, although a consensus did emerge between the army chief, General Raheel Sharif, and the prime minister (the two men are not related) on jointly fighting terrorism in the tribal areas, as well as on stopping hasty action in the trial of former president Pervez Musharraf. Although Sharif had ignored the army's mistrust of India by attending Modi's inauguration ceremony in New Delhi in May 2014, tensions across the Line of Control and a hardline Indian policy ensured that no talks with India had taken place by mid-2015.

More importantly, Sharif refused to address accusations of vote-rigging in the May 2013 general elections and ignored demands for electoral reform. On 14 August 2014, Pakistan's independence day, thousands of Pakistanis marched in Islamabad to challenge the legitimacy of Sharif's election and demand his resignation, after separate demonstrations were organised by political parties Pakistan Awami Tehreek and Pakistan Tehreek-e-Insaf, led respectively by Canada-based Pakistani cleric Tahirul Qadri and cricketer-turned-politician Imran Khan. Two days later, several people working for Pakistan Awami Tehreek were killed by police while attempting to clear barriers in front of the party's offices in Lahore (the capital of Punjab, where Sharif's brother was state governor). On 19 August, anger over delays in the investigation into the killings prompted thousands of protesters to camp in front of the parliament building, refusing to move until Sharif resigned. The protests later turned violent: three people were killed by police when some demonstrators tried to enter the prime minister's residence. It was widely believed that the rallies had been backed by elements of the military in an attempt to overthrow the civilian government, although the army denied involvement and called for the situation to be resolved quickly and peacefully. Demonstrations lasted for four months, and were only ended after Khan called for unity in the wake of the attack in Peshawar.

National Action Plan

On 15 June 2014, the army launched the operation *Zarb-e-Azb* (*Sword of the Prophet*) aimed at clearing out militant strongholds in the tribal areas of North and South Waziristan. The operation, which began one week after 28 people were killed during an assault on Karachi airport by Tehrik-e-Taliban Pakistan (TTP), ended failed attempts at engaging with the Islamist militant group. It began with airstrikes on militant camps in North Waziristan that reportedly killed Uzbek militant leader Abu Abdur Rehman Almani, who was linked to the assault on Karachi airport. This was followed by a sustained ground campaign.

In October, the armed forces launched the smaller-scale military campaign *Khyber One* – replaced in March 2015 by *Khyber Two* – against remnants of the TTP and affiliated groups, who had taken refuge in the remote Tirah Valley, between the Tora Bora mountains and the plains of Bara. By the end of April, the security forces had taken control of areas of Sipah and Akkakhel in Tirah Valley, a significant victory. The government reported in June that since the launch of *Zarb-e-Azb*, at least 2,763 militants had died in ground and air operations, with 837 hideouts destroyed, while 347 troops had been killed. Yet there were also media reports that a number of militant leaders had escaped into Afghanistan. The army stated that its activities in the tribal areas could be completed by end-2015, allowing an estimated one million internally displaced people to return to their homes. With elements of the TTP having declared their allegiance to the Islamic State of Iraq and al-Sham, however, there remained concern about the operation's success.

Although the TTP had been driven out of most parts of the tribal areas, the group did not appear to have lost its leadership or organisational capacities. On 16 December 2014, the TTP retaliated by killing 141 people, most of them children, during the assault on the school in Peshawar. Sharif condemned the attack as the worst act of terrorism in Pakistan's history and a 'national tragedy unleashed by savages'. He said there would no longer be any distinction between 'good' and 'bad' Taliban, alluding to the perception that Pakistan covertly supported the Afghan Taliban while fighting against the TTP. On 17 December, General Sharif, the army chief, met Ghani in Kabul to seek his cooperation in capturing TTP leader Mullah Fazlullah, who was believed to be based in borderlands of Afghanistan. A few days later, Pakistani jets and ground forces responded to the school attack by killing 67 militants in the tribal areas.

Nawaz Sharif revoked the ban on capital punishment in cases of terrorism, allowing those convicted of the Peshawar attack to be executed. The prime minister also established three special military courts in Peshawar, Lahore and Quetta to try those charged with the mass murder of civilians and soldiers. In January, the National Assembly and the Senate approved the Constitution (Twenty-First Amendment) Act, 2015, designed to provide constitutional protections to military courts trying civilian terrorism suspects. By April, the measures had led to the hanging of 64 convicts.

Facilitating the execution of convicted terrorists and the establishment of special courts were the top two priorities of the government's 20-point National Action Plan (NAP) against terrorism, which was unveiled on 24 December 2014 and backed by all major political parties. The government also sought to improve coordination and intelligence-sharing among the country's 33 intelligence agencies. According to officials, between December and May around 3,000 intelligence operations were carried out and 37,666 arrests made, leading to the detention of 725 people. Continuing operations in Karachi, Pakistan's largest city, against the influential Muttahida Qaumi Movement political party, also improved security there.

While the army chief vowed to apprehend all terrorists, their facilitators and financiers, this was a difficult task. There was no significant change in Pakistan's overall strategy on terrorism, which was plagued by contradictions in that it dealt with different types of militant groups in different ways. Core promises made in the NAP were ignored. For example, there was no attempt to implement its third objective: ensuring that 'no armed militias are allowed to function in the country'. Banned outfits such as Jaysh-e-Mohammad and Ahle Sunnat Wal Jamaat continued to exist. A formal proposal to outlaw the Haqqani terror network was still under consideration. There was no attempt to ban the Jamaat-ud-Dawa. led by alleged Mumbai attack mastermind Hafiz Saeed, on the basis that there was no evidence to link it with terrorism or the outlawed anti-India militant group Lashkar-e-Taiba. Meanwhile, moves to register religious seminaries (madrassas) remained bogged down at the provincial level due to a lack of political support for the effort.

Despite the NAP's 18th objective, 'dealing firmly with sectarian terrorists', there was a rise in sectarian attacks during the first half of 2015. On 30 January, a suicide bomber killed more than 60 Shi'ites in Shikarpur, Sindh Province, an attack for which the Baluchistan-based group Jundallah claimed responsibility. Two weeks later, suicide bombers stormed a Shia mosque in Peshawar, killing 22 people. In May, an attack on a bus in Karachi led to the deaths of 47 Shi'ites.

As a result, Sharif's political opponents were able to accuse him of implementing the NAP without sufficient speed or transparency, and called for the process to be monitored by a parliamentary committee. Nonetheless, in April, two men from the TTP were convicted of involvement in the attempted murder of human-rights campaigner Malala Yousafzai in October 2012, and were given 25-year jail terms.

Intervention dilemma

Pakistan's largest foreign-policy dilemma came from an unexpected source, Saudi Arabia. Riyadh was keen for Islamabad to contribute ground troops and aircraft to the multinational military coalition it was leading against Houthi rebels in Yemen. Pakistan had several reasons to do so. Riyadh was one of its greatest benefactors, and about 1.5m Pakistani nationals live in Saudi Arabia, providing valuable remittances. Pakistani security personnel are regularly stationed there.

Nonetheless, agreeing to the Saudi request would have required Islamabad to redeploy troops from overstretched military units conducting operations in the tribal areas, at a time of tension with India. More importantly, involvement in a conflict between Sunnis and Shi'ites in the Middle East had the potential to exacerbate Pakistan's own sectarian fissures, with Shi'ites accounting for an estimated one-fifth of Pakistan's population.

Given the high stakes involved, Sharif convened a joint parliamentary session to debate Pakistan's role in Yemen. After days of discussion, parliament voted in April 2015 against joining the coalition, while declaring that Islamabad would provide support should there be any threat to Saudi sovereignty or territorial integrity. Although this strained bilateral relations with Saudi Arabia and some of its coalition partners, such as the United Arab Emirates, Pakistan worked hard to offset any negative consequences by reassuring Riyadh that strong military and diplomatic relations would continue.

Meanwhile, Pakistan continued to experience border tensions with Iran. In April 2015, eight Iranian border guards were killed in a clash with Pakistani Sunni militant group Jaish al-Adl in Iran's Sistan and Balochistan province. Tehran threatened to cross the border to contain such rocket-propelled-grenade and gun attacks if Pakistan failed to protect its border. Iran was also becoming increasingly concerned about the vulnerability of Pakistan's Shia community, with which it has historically maintained strong political and cultural ties.

Meanwhile, Islamabad's relations with the US, China and Russia improved. Significantly, Washington provided almost US$1bn in additional funding for the counter-insurgency operations in Pakistan's tribal areas. Islamabad also completed its first arms deal with Moscow, reaching an agreement to buy Mi-35 multi-role attack helicopters. Chinese President Xi Jinping, during an April 2015 visit to Pakistan, signed 51 memoranda of understanding ranging from 'strategic cooperative partnership' to collaboration between educational institutions. Most related to cooperation on the ambitious China–Pakistan Economic Corridor linking the western Chinese city of Kashgar and the Pakistani port of Gwadar.

Sri Lanka: End of Rajapaksa's Presidency

In November 2014, Sri Lankan President Mahinda Rajapaksa confidently called a snap election, hoping to secure an unprecedented third term and a two-thirds majority in parliament. Although he had lost support due to his growing authoritarianism and alleged nepotism, Rajapaksa appeared to believe that he would win due to his record of defeating the Tamil Tiger insurgency in 2009 and securing an economic peace dividend. However, the election, dominated by reports of violence, intimidation and the misuse of government money by Rajapaksa, resulted in an unexpected win for Maithripala Sirisena, Rajapaksa's former health minister, who won 51.3% of the vote on a record turnout of 81.5%. Sirisena had campaigned on an anti-corruption, socially conservative platform, securing support from Sri Lanka's ethnic Sinhalese majority as well as the Tamil minority.

In January 2015, Sirisena formed a minority coalition government with his faction of the Sri Lanka Freedom Party, Ranil Wickremesinghe's United National Party and some parties belonging to the United People's Freedom Alliance. Wickremesinghe was appointed prime minister for the third time. Sirisena took steps to signal that the Rajapaksa era was over: a Tamil chief justice was appointed; restrictions on the media were lifted, with exiled journalists called back home and censored websites unblocked; and the security forces were ordered to cease intimidating civilians.

But rivalries and disloyalty weakened the cabinet. Sirisena began to struggle to introduce key legislation as members of parliament defied his authority. Nonetheless, on 28 April his government passed a constitutional amendment that restored checks and balances lost under Rajapaksa's rule. Key powers were given back to the prime minister and the cabinet; the two-term limit on presidencies was reintroduced; some presidential immunities were removed; rules were changed to allow the dissolution of parliament only after four and a half years rather than one; and an inclusive constitutional council was set up to oversee independent judiciary, civil-service and police appointments. Yet Sirisena was still unable to totally abolish the semi-presidential regime known as the 1978 Executive Presidency: a bill to ensure an executive fully in alignment with parliament was watered down by his own party.

Despite his defeat, Rajapaksa's power base remained largely intact, and he planned to stand in the next general election with the aim of becoming prime minister. Sirisena had promised to spare Rajapaksa from prosecution for wrongdoing while in office. Although the judiciary appeared unwilling to go along, uproar among his supporters inside and outside parliament had the effect of slowing down a bribery case. Rajapaksa was also accused of having conspired with his brother Gotabaya, the former defence secretary, and the chief justice to declare an emergency during the election and thereby impede vote counting. It was reported that the plan had failed because he had been overruled by the attorney general, the police chief and the army commander. The former president dismissed all allegations, claiming that they were part of a vendetta pursued by his successor.

Sirisena took small, pragmatic steps to address the expectations raised by both his agenda and the election. Rajapaksa had resisted three inter-linked processes: national reconciliation, addressing the marginalisation of Tamils and reducing the military's role in society. By contrast, Sirisena pledged inclusiveness and transparency to tackle Sri Lanka's largest problems – which his government blamed on Rajapaksa's divisive brand of nationalism, but whose causes lay as much in the legacy of the country's decades-long civil war.

The government focused on finding the right balance among its supporters and allies, looking to provide concessions to the Tamils without alienating the Sinhalese on the issue of releasing prisoners. A former civil servant was appointed to replace an obstructive military governor in the Tamil-dominated north, while another was chosen as governor in the east. Answering calls for political prisoners to be set free, a prominent Tamil activist was released on bail in March 2015. Nonetheless, according to one official estimate there were still more than 200 political detainees in jail.

Aware of the sensitivity of the subject, Sirisena indicated early on that he would not rush the process of reconciliation; he aimed to adopt a model similar to that used in South Africa by increasing accountability without sharpening confrontation. With no sign that the Tamil insurgency was reviving, former president Chandrika Kumaratunga was appointed to lead the Task Force on Reconciliation. On 19 May, Tamil politicians in the north and east were able to attend memorial events for the first time, after the government rebranded the sixth anniversary of the end of the war as a day of remembrance rather than of victory. On 5 June, Sirisena made good on his commitment to re-engage Sri Lanka with the United Nations Human Rights Council, pledging to attend its September session – although the government had not fulfilled its pledge to establish a domestic mechanism for investigating alleged war crimes, and had stated that the UN would play only an advisory role in the process.

Sirisena rehabilitated former army chief Sarath Fonseka – whom Rajapaksa had jailed for treason – by appointing him as Sri Lanka's first field marshal and calling on the army to clear his name. The military's influence on politics and the economy persisted, as the president gave it time to reform from the inside, thereby delaying the reduction of its role as guardian against any renewal of the insurgency. Sirisena announced that he would publish a new national security plan by the end of 2015 and would retain the Prevention of Terrorism Act, which granted the security services broad powers to search, arrest and detain suspects. By June, Sirisena had appointed new commanders of the army and the air force, as well as a new chief of the defence staff. Nonetheless, the military faced no immediate threat to its interests, which included lucrative commercial activities, and seemed uninterested in accelerating a resettlement programme for refugees or giving up the land it had acquired during the war.

Due to fierce opposition from both inside and outside the government, Sirisena and Wickremesinghe were unlikely to enact further major reforms before the next general election. As they were unable to ensure a two-thirds parliamentary majority needed to pass a constitutional amendment on electoral reform – creating a first-past-the-post system with some proportional representation – Sirisena dissolved parliament ten months early, paving the way for general elections in August 2015.

Continued non-alignment

Sirisena wished to reorient rather than radically change Sri Lanka's foreign policy, and described the country as 'absolutely non-aligned'. India was relieved by his election due to what it perceived as Rajapaksa's strengthening of ties between Sri Lanka and China, as suggested by the docking of two Chinese nuclear-powered submarines in Colombo in late 2014. Sirisena visited India for four days in February, in his first foreign trip as president; the following month, Narendra Modi made the first bilateral trip to Sri Lanka by an Indian prime minister since the 1980s. Several deals were signed, including Sri Lanka's first agreement on civil-nuclear cooperation and a currency swap worth US$1.5 billion (akin to that made by China in 2014). With an eye on the 2016 state elections in Tamil Nadu, where ethnic Tamils formed a large part of the electorate, Modi also visited northern Sri Lanka.

Western governments also welcomed Sirisena's victory, and attempted to engage with Sri Lanka through a mixture of diplomatic visits and inducements for the government to keep its election promises. They argued that improving respect for human rights and the rule of law would be the best way to increase political representation and ensure the country's future. In January, the government lifted travel restrictions for foreigners in the north. In February, the publication of a 2014 UN inquiry into war crimes in Sri Lanka was delayed until August 2015, a move supported by the United States and the European Union. In May, John Kerry made the first official trip to Sri Lanka by a US secretary of state in at least a decade, announcing that Washington and Colombo would start an annual bilateral dialogue.

Sirisena did not turn his back on China. Sri Lanka had borrowed heavily from Beijing under Rajapaksa, and in September 2014 Xi Jinping had promised to add to the US$6bn Chinese investment in the country. The terms of investments were scrutinised as part of the new government's anti-corruption drive, but this did not lead to the termination of any contracts. The authorities merely suspended, pending investigation, the China-funded Colombo Port City project, which involved an investment of US$1.4bn and aimed to reclaim land for use as a trade hub. The initiative was expected to eventually go ahead, along with many other Chinese-funded projects, and China remained Sri Lanka's largest creditor, as well as its second-largest trading partner, after India. In March 2015, after construction and private investment in Sri Lanka had slowed due to the investigations, Sirisena travelled to Beijing and attempted to reassure

Xi. Sirisena recognised that the Sri Lankan central bank's forecast of 7% growth for 2015, compared to 7.4% in 2014, would only be achievable with continuing Chinese investment in infrastructure and tourism.

Afghanistan: Critical Transitions

Afghanistan went through multiple transitions in the year to mid-2015 – in its politics, its security situation and its economy. The inauguration of a new president and government was the most critical shift, and the one on which everything else rested. The two bitterly fought rounds of the presidential election resulted in a power-sharing agreement to create a national unity government, which was installed on 29 September 2014. With Hamid Karzai ineligible to run having served two terms as elected president, there was – after electoral disputes were resolved – a peaceful and democratic transfer of power, the first in Afghanistan's history. The new administration of President Ashraf Ghani faced three main challenges: improving security amid conflict with the Taliban and tensions with Pakistan; stabilising the economy; and developing better governance, especially by reducing corruption.

Power shared

Held on 5 April 2014 following a highly charged campaign, the presidential election was the third such poll since the US-led military intervention of 2001. As no candidate obtained the majority required to win the vote outright, a run-off was conducted on 14 June between Abdullah Abdullah, former foreign minister and previously an anti-Soviet resistance fighter, and Ashraf Ghani, former finance minister and an academic expert on state-building. The preliminary uncertified results of the run-off, announced by the Independent Election Commission of Afghanistan (IEC) on 7 July, showed Ghani to be the winner. However, Abdullah claimed that widespread fraud had taken place, and refused to cooperate with the electoral bodies. The resulting deadlock precipitated a political crisis.

Following negotiations facilitated mainly by the United States and the United Nations, the two candidates agreed to an audit of all eight million ballots cast, and promised to respect its outcome. The audit – conducted by the IEC under UN supervision and involving hundreds of national and international observers – again put Ghani in the lead. But Abdullah's team, unhappy with the whole process, repeatedly boycotted the audit and threatened to establish a parallel government. US President Barack Obama spoke to the candidates, and Secretary of State John Kerry visited Kabul twice. After months of wrangling, protests and threats of military force by former warlords, Kerry brokered an agreement under which both candidates would form a national unity government. Nearly six months after the first round of the election, Ghani became president and Abdullah took on the newly created position of chief executive officer, holding powers similar to those of a prime minister in a presidential system. They also agreed to distribute key government posts between the two camps.

The government suffered at times from internal power struggles. There were concerns both at home and among foreign governments about the slow speed of appointments of cabinet members and provincial governors, as well as the quality of some appointees. On assuming office, Ghani promised to select the cabinet within 45 days, but this in fact took eight months. The last appointment to be made was that of the defence minister. Provincial governors, ambassadors and appointees for several other important posts were yet to be selected by mid-2015.

In addition to the creation of Abdullah's post, the power-sharing agreement stipulated the convening of a Loya Jirga (Grand Council) within two years to consider amending the constitution so as to create the position of an executive prime minister. As it stood, the president had delegated some powers to the chief executive officer through a presidential decree; the Loya Jirga would consider formalising the role in the constitution, although the president would retain top executive authority. The power-sharing deal also called for reform of the electoral system before the parliamentary election originally scheduled for mid-2015. Lack of progress in reforming the system caused that poll to be postponed.

These pending moves – as well as the inherent difficulties of power sharing – created the risk of future political instability. The formation of the national unity government and Abdullah's post meant that there were double the number of top positions. The president and his two vice-presidents worked alongside the chief executive officer and his two deputies

– all of whom had their own offices, budgets, staff and sets of advisers. The new government held both weekly meetings of the ministers' council headed by Abdullah and monthly meetings headed by Ghani. The formation of the new government had been seen as an opportunity for the two rivals to combine their different sets of skills and to build on progress made over the preceding 13 years. But the tensions between their teams often affected the workings of the government, prompting some Afghans to describe the leadership as 'two-headed'. This dysfunction was acknowledged by some high-ranking officials, especially members of Abdullah's team.

Pakistan policy shift

The most obvious change in the new government's foreign policy was in its approach towards Pakistan. Soon after taking office, Ghani took several steps aimed at improving bilateral relations and gaining Islamabad's trust. Aware of Pakistan's ability to influence the peace process under way within Afghanistan, Ghani sought to wipe the slate clean, and hoped that this would be reciprocated. The concessions he made to Pakistan would have been unimaginable under the Karzai administration.

After visiting Islamabad's close allies, Saudi Arabia and China, Ghani went to Pakistan in November and said he wanted to end the 'undeclared hostilities' between the two countries. His aim was to harness Pakistani influence to bring the Afghan Taliban to the negotiating table. Authorities in Kabul have long accused Pakistan of supporting the Taliban. While this was repeatedly denied by Pakistani officials, former president General Pervez Musharraf admitted in press interviews in 2015 that Inter-Services Intelligence (ISI), Pakistan's security agency, had established links with the Taliban because India and Pakistan were engaged in a long-running proxy war on Afghan soil.

Appreciating the role and influence of the Pakistan military establishment, Ghani's focus was on forging and maintaining close contacts with the generals. With a series of bold steps, he sought to lift their suspicion and mistrust. Firstly, as a symbolic gesture and in a notable departure from protocol, Ghani visited the Pakistani military's General Headquarters in Rawalpindi and called on the army chief, General Raheel Sharif. Meanwhile, responding to Pakistani concerns about increasing

Indian influence in Afghanistan, Ghani delayed his visit to India for seven months and put on hold a request for Indian weapons made by the Karzai government. When Ghani eventually visited India, in April 2015, his focus was mainly on trade and investment, and less on security cooperation.

Secondly, Afghanistan took steps to assist Pakistan in its own struggle against the Pakistani Taliban, Tehrik-e-Taliban Pakistan (TTP). Latif Mehsud, a senior TTP commander who was held in Afghanistan's Bagram jail, was handed over to the Pakistani authorities in December 2014. This was apparently done without any quid pro quo. In addition, after the December 2014 attack on a Peshawar school in which more than 140 people were killed, several suspected TTP members were arrested in Afghanistan at the request of Pakistani authorities, who claimed that the operation had been orchestrated by the TTP leader Mullah Fazlullah. It was reported that Pakistani interrogators were allowed to question them in Afghan detention before they were handed over to Pakistan. To prevent TTP infiltration across the Durand Line (the border between Afghanistan and Pakistan), the Afghan army strengthened its deployments in border provinces such as Kunar and Nuristan.

Thirdly, meetings between high-ranking military commanders from the two countries, aimed at coordinating efforts against militancy, resumed in January. Such contacts had been stopped by Karzai four years earlier in response to Pakistani shelling across the Durand Line which, according to Islamabad, was aimed at stopping TTP attacks in Pakistan. Fourthly, Ghani took up a long-standing Pakistani offer and, for the first time, sent six Afghan cadets for training at the Pakistan Military Academy at Abbottabad. Karzai had refused to do so, saying Afghan troops should not be sent 'for training in any of the neighbouring countries, particularly when they are sending us suicide bombers in return'.

There was outcry in Afghanistan over the change in relations with Pakistan when the countries' intelligence agencies agreed in May 2015 on a memorandum of understanding. Signed by the deputy heads of Afghanistan's National Directorate of Security (NDS) and Pakistan's ISI in Kabul, the document stated that the two agencies would share intelligence and conduct complementary operations. Afghan and Pakistani officials announced the deal without publishing the text of the memorandum, but some of its clauses were leaked to the media, generating strong opposition among Afghan civil-society activists, parliamentarians and members of the public. One of the most controversial aspects of the agreement was its stipulation that the two sides fight insurgents together, and that the ISI train and equip NDS personnel. This was seen as an astonishing reversal for the Afghan agency, which had long accused its Pakistani counterpart of supporting and directing the Afghan Taliban to carry out attacks inside Afghanistan. The deal was described as contrary to the country's national interest by several members of the Afghan parliament, including the speakers of Wolesi Jirga (Lower House) and Meshrano Jirga (Upper House), as well as by Karzai. Faced with this backlash, the Afghan leadership announced that the deal had not yet been finalised. In a meeting hastily convened at the presidential palace, Ghani tried to convince tribal elders, members of parliament and civil-society activists that the document would be carefully reviewed, and that Afghanistan's national interest would be taken into consideration.

Despite this controversy, Ghani appeared to have some success in the wider effort to improve bilateral relations with Islamabad. Pakistan's military and intelligence chiefs visited Kabul several times, indicating a clear shift in Islamabad's policy. Pakistan's interior minister, Chaudhry Nisar Ali Khan, said in February 2015 that the two neighbours were engaged in the 'most effective coordination that did not happen in history before'. Visiting Kabul in May with military and intelligence chiefs, Pakistani Prime Minister Nawaz Sharif stated: 'Afghanistan's enemies will be treated as Pakistan's enemies and Pakistan's enemies will be treated as Afghanistan's enemies.' Yet caution seemed in order about the prospects for a major shift in Pakistan's Afghan policy, in the absence of a significant improvement in Pakistan–India relations.

Continuing conflict

Ghani's first task upon taking office was to sign a Bilateral Security Agreement with Washington, allowing the US to keep 9,800 troops in Afghanistan after the end of NATO's International Security Assistance Force combat mission in December 2014. Karzai had refused to sign the agreement in part because Washington sought immunity from prosecution for its personnel. He also asked for additional assurances, including the stipulation that American forces not raid Afghan homes. Karzai's refusal to sign, although popular in some circles domestically, strained ties with the US and raised security fears in Afghanistan.

Obama initially announced that, provided the security agreement was signed, the US would leave 9,800 troops in Afghanistan, before halving the size of the deployment by the end of 2015 and withdrawing altogether by the end of 2016. But at Ghani's request and on the recommendation of US commanders, Obama decided to maintain the initial size of the force until at least the end of 2015. Pentagon officials announced that they would review the timetable for withdrawal. Under a separate Status of Forces Agreement, around 3,000 additional NATO troops remained in Afghanistan. Thus, at mid-2015, there were around 13,000 foreign troops deployed in Afghanistan, down from a high of around 140,000 in 2011. The new missions train, advise and assist the Afghan National Security Forces (ANSF), who have assumed the bulk of the fight against the Taliban and number around 350,000 soldiers and police. A contingent of reportedly around 1,800 US special-operations forces are involved in counter-terrorism operations against al-Qaeda and similar groups.

As foreign forces were drawn down during 2014, the Taliban became increasingly aggressive. The 2015 spring fighting season began with some of the bloodiest fighting since the US-led invasion, as the group opened new fronts and increased its focus on territorial battles. In an apparent attempt to scatter Afghan security forces, the Taliban launched heavy ground attacks in more than ten provinces, some of them simultaneously. The group also stepped up its complex series of coordinated suicide bombings and gun attacks in almost all major cities, particularly Kabul. Some insurgents had interpreted the NATO withdrawal as a victory for their side, reportedly leading thousands of fighters to move into Afghanistan from sanctuaries in Pakistan. The Taliban gained control of more Afghan territory, especially in rural areas. Hundreds, if not thousands, of militants, many of them foreigners, also moved into Afghanistan from the North Waziristan tribal region after the Pakistani military launched an operation against them in mid-2014. Although these militants travelled to different parts of Afghanistan, most reportedly went to the north.

As the fighting in Afghanistan intensified, civilian casualties reached a new peak. According to the United Nations, a total of 3,699 Afghan civilians were killed and 6,849 were injured in 2014. The summer of 2014 was also the deadliest for Afghan security forces since the start of the Taliban insurgency, with around 10,000 personnel reportedly killed or injured, most of them in ground warfare rather than by roadside bombs or suicide attacks. While suffering from high attrition as well as inadequate training and a lack of certain equipment – especially aircraft – the ANSF proved a force to be reckoned with by preventing Taliban advances in many parts of the country. Nevertheless, the Taliban made some of its largest territorial gains in years, and by mid-2015 threatened to overrun district headquarters in several provinces. After beginning its spring offensive in April 2015, the group captured at least three district centres, holding them for several days despite counter-offensives by government forces.

As Karzai had previously done, Ghani repeatedly invited the Taliban to take part in peace talks, saying that 'the grounds for peace have never been better in the last 36 years' – that is, since the Soviet invasion in 1979. However, the Taliban called him a puppet brought to power by the Americans and refused to recognise his legitimacy. It insisted on preconditions such as the withdrawal of all foreign troops before agreeing to negotiations with the government. Ghani sought the mediation of outside countries, including Saudi Arabia and China, both of which enjoy good relations with Pakistan. There was hope that China's mediation – perhaps playing the role of a guarantor to make sure all sides, including the US, kept their promises – could help towards a peace agreement. China offered to help in facilitating negotiations, and Taliban representatives visited Beijing for preliminary talks.

Meanwhile, back-channel contacts were being made and messages exchanged between the Taliban and the Ghani government, with the aim of ending the violence and reaching a political settlement. Among the ideas being floated, it was suggested that the Taliban stop fighting in exchange for positions in the central government and governorships in a few provinces, before holding elections and possibly enacting constitutional amendments. In this regard, an important meeting was held in May 2015 in Al-Khor, a beach resort near Doha, at which several Taliban representatives have resided for more than two years. The unofficial, off-the-record meeting, organised by the Pugwash Conferences on Science and World Affairs, was attended by eight Taliban representatives, as well as negotiators from the Afghan government's High Peace Council, members of civil society, and people linked to various groups and parties in Afghanistan. Although no deal on a ceasefire was reached, all participants agreed that foreign forces would have to leave Afghanistan soon, and that there should be further meetings so as to sustain the peace process.

The Taliban appeared to be at a crossroads. As it considered whether to make peace or keep fighting after the withdrawal of most foreign forces, its leaders were walking a tightrope. The peace process risked causing friction within the Taliban, as some fighters were willing to participate in a political settlement, while others wished to continue the campaign to reap the profits of war, or else for ideological reasons. The Taliban feared that the peace process might simply be an attempt to discredit and weaken it as an insurgency. Similarly, there were also divisions within the Afghan government about how to approach the peace process and the shape of any future political settlement. Several factions and figures within the government had serious reservations about making concessions to the Taliban and favoured continuing the conflict.

In the short term, the war seemed set to intensify as the insurgents tested the resilience and strength of government forces, seeking to gain as much territory as possible so as to increase their leverage in future talks. The Taliban was unlikely to disband its military forces before gaining concessions and guarantees as part of a political settlement. It was also possible that some elements would stay outside the process so as to exert extra pressure on government negotiators and to be able to carry on the fight if the talks failed.

The apparent improvement in relations between Afghanistan and Pakistan was another factor in the equation, adding to hopes that peace would be achieved in the region. However, substantial progress seemed unlikely in the near future unless the government made significant concessions to the Taliban.

ISIS in Afghanistan: Danger overstated?

The Taliban, which calls itself the Islamic Emirate of Afghanistan, remains the principal insurgency in the country and is responsible for most of the violent attacks against the government and its international backers. But it is facing a new challenge in the form of the Islamic State of Iraq and al-Sham (ISIS), which has gained a toehold in the Afghanistan–Pakistan region.

In response to repeated messages from several TTP commanders and disgruntled former Afghan Taliban members who had been expelled for unauthorised activities, ISIS officially announced in January 2015 its expansion into 'Khorasan', an old name for Afghanistan and the surrounding parts of Central Asia, Iran and Pakistan. This was the first time that ISIS had officially spread outside the Arab world. It named Hafiz Saeed Khan, a former TTP commander in Orakzai tribal agency, as the *wali*, or governor, of Khorasan and Abdul Rauf Khadem, a former Afghan Taliban commander, as his deputy. Khadem, an experienced Taliban commander from Helmand province, had spent six years in the US prison at Guantanamo Bay, where he came under the influence of Arab detainees and embraced Salafism. After his release in 2007, the Taliban appointed him as a senior military commander, but removed him after they found him promoting Salafism among his peers and subordinates. After a period in Pakistan, he moved back to his village in Helmand in 2014. ISIS found in him an ideal candidate to lead their mission in Afghanistan. Yet on 9 February 2015, just two weeks after his appointment, Khadem was killed in a US drone strike. A few days later, his successor was also killed in Helmand in another drone strike.

The group has attracted small numbers of followers and sympathisers in both Afghanistan and Pakistan, including some TTP commanders. The Islamic Movement of Uzbekistan, a group operating in Central Asian countries as well as in northern provinces of Afghanistan, declared its allegiance to ISIS in March 2015 on the grounds that it had neither seen nor heard from Mullah Omar, the Taliban leader to whom it had previously sworn loyalty, for 13 years.

Addressing the Munich Security Conference in February 2015, Ghani warned of the threat that ISIS would establish itself in Afghanistan. He later told the US Congress that the group 'is already sending advance guards to southern and western Afghanistan to test our vulnerabilities'. General John Campbell, commander of the remaining US–NATO forces in Afghanistan, stated ISIS had a 'nascent' presence in Afghanistan and was recruiting both there and in Pakistan. But he added that the group was not yet 'operational' in Afghanistan.

Judging by the available evidence, Afghan officials appeared to be exaggerating the ISIS threat. Reports from local officials about ISIS followers in their regions seemed to be aimed at drawing resources or fighting forces to their areas. In some cases, local Afghan officials simply mistook foreign militants entering Afghanistan from Pakistan for members of ISIS. In fact, there are significant obstacles to the group in Afghanistan. Firstly, the Taliban, which is highly territorial, decided not to allow it to set up a base in Afghanistan, and ordered field commanders to prevent its development. The Taliban sees statements on ISIS gains in Afghanistan as part of a conspiracy to weaken and divide its insurgency. Previously, it could not tolerate the existence of an older and comparatively minor Afghan insurgent group, Hizb-e-Islami, led by a former mujahideen leader Gulbuddin Hekmatyar. While the Taliban was in power in Kabul in the 1990s, al-Qaeda's foreign fighters had to obey its rules and accept its authority, and the al-Qaeda leadership pledged its allegiance to Mullah Omar. From the Taliban's perspective, by establishing a so-called caliphate and declaring Abu Bakr al-Baghdadi the leader of all Muslims, ISIS was challenging the authority and leadership of Mullah Omar, who is regarded by the Taliban as Amir-ul-Momineen (leader of the faithful) of the Islamic Emirate of Afghanistan.

The Taliban and ISIS are ideologically and culturally dissimilar. The Taliban is a conservative clerical movement whose members are generally loyal to the puritanical version of the Hanafi school of Sunni Islam, believe in Sufism and have so far avoided sectarian violence. In contrast, ISIS embraces borderless Salafi jihadism and incorporates *takfir*, branding opponents including Shia Muslims as *kufar* (non-believers) and *mushrek* (polytheists). Thus, the Taliban, the Afghan government and the US are all its enemies – indeed, ISIS evokes a rare consensus between all three. According to the report released at the end of the May 2015 meeting in Al-Khor, all participants in the discussion agreed that 'the model of the so-called Islamic State … is alien to the tradition and the desires of the Afghan people'. The same month, there were reports of conflict between the Taliban and self-proclaimed followers of ISIS in the south, east and west of Afghanistan, resulting in the deaths or flight of the newer groups.

As of mid-2015, the Afghan Taliban had not publicly criticised ISIS, but had warned it against recruiting in Afghanistan and 'creating parallel Jihadist front' in the country. In an open letter to Baghdadi dated 16 June 2015, Mullah Akhtar Muhammad Mansour, interim head of the Taliban's leadership council, wrote that 'any mobilisation and activities under different flags is detrimental to jihad, Islam and Muslims'. He went on to say that if ISIS continued to interfere in Afghanistan, the Taliban would be 'forced to react to defend our achievements'.

One week later, ISIS spokesman Abu Muhammad al-Adnani announced the creation of a 'province' in Russia's North Caucasus, calling on rival jihadists to 'repent' and join the caliphate. He specifically mentioned ISIS opponents in Khorasan, Libya and Syria, accusing them of committing a religious crime. He also demanded that competing groups in Khorasan abandon their battle against ISIS, and encouraged fighters loyal to Baghdadi to have 'no mercy or compassion' for their enemies. Although Adnani did not present his message as a direct response to the Afghan Taliban, it appeared that ISIS would continue its activities in Afghanistan and that fighting between the two groups would increase.

There was a general hostility to the emergence of ISIS among Afghanistan's neighbours, particularly the Shia-majority Iran. The Iranian ambassador in Kabul stated in May 2015 that his country would be willing to assist with attempts to counter ISIS in Afghanistan. Animosity towards the group also helped offset the rivalry between Tehran and the Taliban; the Taliban confirmed that a delegation of its Qatar-based representatives had visited Iran to discuss 'the current situation in Afghanistan, regional and Islamic world issues, and the condition of Afghan refugees in Iran'. Although it would therefore be very hard for ISIS to establish itself as a major force in Afghanistan, the group became a new, if small, actor in the country's already complex political and security situation.

Economy and governance

Afghanistan's fragile economy shrank dramatically in the year to mid-2015, due to the deteriorating security situation, political uncertainty relating to the presidential election, delays in the signing of the Bilateral Security Agreement and the slow formation of the new government. With the withdrawal of foreign forces, there was a drastic reduction in activity by the international aid organisations that had spent billions of dollars there over more than a decade. Key sectors of the economy lacked investment and struggled for funds, and the economy was also affected by the closure of large military bases. There was a drop in the construction business, one of the few industries that offered employment outside aid projects, as rents fell sharply in major cities. Mining, long touted as the economic bedrock of development, has yet to draw substantial amounts of foreign investment.

Ghani's focus was on boosting trade and investment, with a view to transforming Afghanistan into a regional trade hub. But political tensions and security problems looked set to deal another heavy blow to the economy, at least in the short term, before any improvements occurred. According to the World Bank, economic growth declined to 2% in 2014, down from 3.7% in 2013 and an average of 9% during 2003–12. Domestic revenues also fell, from a peak of 11.6% of GDP in 2011 to 8.4% in 2014. Growth in 2015 was projected to be 2.5%, below the forecast of 4% made at the end of the preceding year. The value of the Afghan currency, the Afghani, reached in late May 2015 its lowest point since 2003 (when currency reforms were completed and the new currency printed). Afghanistan still depends on foreign assistance for two-thirds of its nearly US$7.6bn annual budget, and its economy will continue to depend on international aid in the short to medium term.

As in the past, the drugs trade has an important distorting effect on the economy. In 2013 and 2014, cultivation of poppies for opium hit record levels. Drug production is expected to rise further because of the decline in foreign aid to other sectors of agriculture and the wider economy. In addition, the Taliban's reliance on taxing drug cultivation and trafficking is increasing as other sources of funding, including donations from the Middle East, are in decline.

The government nevertheless continued to pursue its reform agenda, emphasising development and efforts to tackle corruption. In his first week in office, Ghani appointed Ahmad Zia Massoud, who was a first vice-president under Karzai, as his 'special envoy for reform and good governance'. The government also established the National Procurement Commission, which meets every week to evaluate large-scale projects and major contracts. From May 2015, each ministry was required to publicly deliver its action plan for the next 100 days, with the Afghan media and public invited to monitor and evaluate their progress.

As the conflict against the Taliban continued, economic progress would continue to be faltering at best. With the foreign military presence so much reduced, it was more vital than ever to achieve progress in peace efforts.

However, the war appeared to have reached a stalemate, with neither the government nor the Taliban able to achieve overall victory in the immediate future. There were also fears that the departure of NATO forces would lead to increased interference in Afghanistan by its neighbours, resulting in the intensification of proxy battles between regional players, especially India and Pakistan. Afghanistan remained unfinished business for the international community, and the country would continue to need outside help for years to come.

Chapter 11
Asia-Pacific

Significant tensions remained between the major powers involved in Asia-Pacific security in the year to mid-2015, posing risks to peace and stability. Underlying these frictions were the increased assertiveness and strategic extroversion of China and Japan, under the relatively new leaderships of Xi Jinping and Shinzo Abe respectively, as well as Washington's reassertion of its role as a leading actor in regional security, a policy that found widespread support among the Asia-Pacific's increasingly insecure lesser powers. While inter-state tensions remained high, many governments in the region also faced serious challenges at home from political opponents and economic difficulties.

In China, it was clearer than ever that President Xi had brought to an end the system of 'collective leadership' practised by his predecessors since the 1970s. Having established control of all major policy areas, Xi displayed his power more visibly than any Chinese leader since Mao Zedong, in both the domestic and international spheres. At home, his rhetoric emphasised the rule of law, but in practice he used the most ferocious anti-corruption drive in the history of the People's Republic to crush potential challengers within the party-rule system and to reassure the middle class – whose acquiescence the party needed – that corrupt officials would not be able to threaten their new-found wealth with impunity. However, several challenges proved less tractable and remained major irritants to Xi and his administration: separatism inspired by ethnicity and religion in Xinjiang and Tibet; popular resistance in Hong Kong to Beijing's impulse to dominate the territory politically; and Taiwan's continuing determination to remain separate.

Under Xi's leadership, China has exercised a more confident foreign policy. Beijing's relations with Washington and Tokyo have remained competitive, but in both cases there was a degree of détente from mid-2014 onwards. Nonetheless, China did not cease to press its maritime claims, particularly in the South China Sea, where it undertook extensive construction activities on numerous features it had occupied in the Spratly group, rapidly turning some of them into military outposts. This further undermined confidence in Beijing's trustworthiness among some Southeast Asian governments. While China's relations with Europe remained positive and focused on economic cooperation, those with India and Russia were considerably more complex: in both cases, strategic competition and distrust cast a shadow over successes in economic partnership.

In Japan, despite the mixed record of 'Abenomics', Prime Minister Abe used his relatively strong domestic position, reinforced by his election victory in December 2014, as a platform for implementing more assertive defence and security policies. Most importantly, a cabinet resolution allowed Japan to exercise collective self-defence in support of the United States and other countries, under certain conditions; a related development was the preparation of new laws to support the expanded role of the Japan Self-Defense Forces. Tokyo strengthened relations with the US, particularly through a revised set of Guidelines for US–Japan Defense Cooperation, released in April 2015. The 'US–Japan Joint Vision Statement' announced by Abe and President Barack Obama noted the synergy between Japan's aim to contribute actively to peace and the US rebalance to the Asia-Pacific. Nevertheless, there were still irritants in bilateral relations, notably Tokyo's continuing failure to relocate US Marine Corps Air Station Futenma within Okinawa, difficulties over the Trans-Pacific Partnership, and Abe's obduracy over historical issues. The latter also continued to undermine Japan's relations with China and South Korea, thereby contributing to regional tensions.

Meanwhile, North Korea's continuing pursuit of improved ballistic-missile and nuclear-weapons capabilities directly threatened South Korea

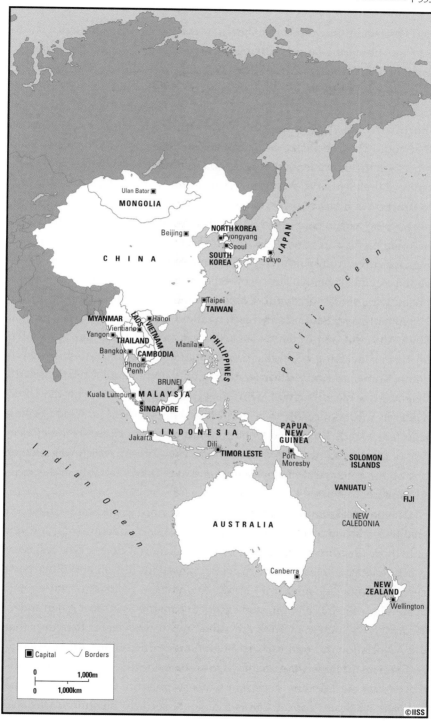

and Japan, and showed clearer signs of targeting the US. Although a North Korean submarine-launched ballistic-missile (SLBM) capability probably remained many years away, the surprising test launch of a prototype SLBM gave particular cause for concern. The continuing expansion of Pyongyang's nuclear-weapons stock was also significant, and there was much speculation regarding the North's ability to miniaturise weapons that could then be mated with ballistic missiles. North Korea has been more isolated than ever, although China continued to provide a vital international lifeline that allowed the regime to survive and the North's society to function at a basic level. Russia became more heavily involved in supporting the North, particularly through the supply of crude oil. Relations between North and South Korea remained frozen, with Pyongyang rejecting overtures from President Park Geun-hye's administration in Seoul aimed at bilateral talks. However, other aspects of South Korean foreign policy were more successful. Challenges remained in relations with the US, notably over Seoul's reluctance to allow the US to deploy a Terminal High Altitude Area Defense (THAAD) battery, but there was agreement on further delaying the transfer of operational control of joint forces to South Korea, and on nuclear-energy cooperation. Seoul's relations with Beijing grew steadily closer, which complicated relations with the US to a degree, most noticeably over the THAAD deployment (to which Beijing objected). South Korea and Beijing found common cause in their rejection of the Abe administration's historical revisionism, which was a major obstacle to better relations between Seoul and Tokyo, notably in the security sphere.

The physical reinforcement of China's presence in the South China Sea resulted in rising anxiety among Southeast Asian governments, and not only those that directly contested Beijing's territorial claims. One response was to enter into closer security cooperation with the US and other partners, including Japan. Yet a variety of domestic political obstacles and bilateral constraints complicated efforts to develop Southeast Asian states' security links with the US. At the same time, it was clearer than ever that the Association of Southeast Asian Nations (ASEAN) and other existing regional institutions were unable to formulate effective common positions that would significantly constrain Chinese pressure in the South China Sea. The weakness of ASEAN as a regional security institution was also clear in its inability to respond to the human-security crisis created by the exodus of refugees and migrants from Myanmar.

Uncertainty was the watchword in the domestic politics of Southeast Asian states. A landmark national election was due in Myanmar in November 2015: while it was widely expected that Aung San Suu Kyi's National League for Democracy (NLD) would do well, a range of possible outcomes was conceivable – not least in terms of the armed forces' reaction, the role played by the NLD leader in the next government, and the implications of a new administration for the long-running conflict between the central political authority and ethnic-minority rebels. In Thailand, the military regime led by General Prayuth Chan-ocha oversaw the drafting of a new constitution ostensibly intended to bring stability after a decade of political conflict, but in reality also aimed at weakening the power of the electorate, as well as former prime minister Thaksin Shinawatra and his proxies. It was by no means clear that an upcoming referendum would approve this constitution, and there was significant potential for further conflict. In Thailand's south, Prayuth's administration attempted to set up new talks with Malay insurgents, but pervasive distrust and the rebels' disunity were major impediments. In Malaysia, Prime Minister Najib Tun Razak faced growing opposition from factions within his own party, supported by former prime minister Mahathir Mohamad, particularly over the mismanagement of the 1Malaysia Development Berhad state investment fund. But the country's opposition coalition fractured after its de facto leader, Anwar Ibrahim, was jailed again and two of its constituent parties broke off relations with each other. In Indonesia, disillusionment quickly set in regarding the leadership of newly elected president Joko Widodo: his support for the appointment of a senior police officer facing graft allegations indicated both political weakness and a lack of commitment to anti-corruption measures that had been central to his electoral campaign. Concerns over Indonesians pledging allegiance to the Islamic State of Iraq and al-Sham, and travelling to the Middle East to fight, spurred new counter-terrorism measures, but also led to a turf war between the country's police and its armed forces, as the latter sought to revive their internal-security role.

In Australia, Prime Minister Tony Abbott's efforts at economic and social reform encountered opposition from a hostile Senate, and from ordinary people who saw them as unfair. Another challenge for the government was the impact of China's economic deceleration on the Australian economy, dependent as it was on commodity exports. One important area of success was in foreign policy. Canberra's 'stop the boats' policy, aimed at preventing seaborne asylum seekers from reaching Australia, was popular with the public. Abbott also developed the Australia–Japan strategic relationship, hosted successful state visits by Xi and Indian Prime Minister Narendra Modi, and further intensified Australian security cooperation with the US. In Southeast Asia, Australia entered into a 'comprehensive strategic partnership' with Singapore. Relations with Indonesia, however, remained complex and difficult to manage, and were damaged – even if only temporarily – when Widodo's government executed two Australian convicted drug smugglers despite appeals for clemency from Canberra.

China: Assertive Leadership

Since taking over as general secretary of the Chinese Communist Party in November 2012, Xi Jinping has not only moved faster to secure his position than any other leader since Deng Xiaoping, but has also flaunted his power more visibly than any of his predecessors. President Xi has taken control of all vital areas of policymaking, effectively bringing to an end the system of 'collective leadership' that had been in place since the start of China's 'reform and opening' in the late 1970s. Xi's grip has been strengthened by the most sustained and wide-ranging campaign against official corruption in the party's history. On the world stage, China has shown further evidence of more active foreign policies and of greater willingness to assume the role of a major power. Relations with the United States are characterised by growing strategic competition as China seeks to expand its influence through initiatives such as the 'One Belt, One Road' policy to spur regional development and the establishment of a new bank to finance development of Asian infrastructure.

Economic slowdown
In the year to mid-2015, however, signs of trouble began to emerge in China's economy that could overshadow the remaining years of Xi's lead-

ership (precedent suggests he will step down in 2022). Growth, at 7.4% in 2014, slipped to its lowest rate in nearly a quarter-century. In 2015 it will struggle to meet the official target of 7%. China's economy still has plenty of life, but will require careful management to sustain growth of 6–7%. That is the pace Chinese officials believe must be maintained to keep employment levels high enough to avoid unrest, and to prevent a collapse of the middle-class confidence that the party regards as a crucial bulwark of social stability. The country's stock market belied such anxieties: share indices more than doubled in value between July 2014 and April 2015, though they dropped back amid financial-market turbulence around mid-year. But many feared that this was a bubble waiting to burst, with potentially damaging consequences for some middle-class households.

The president will be anxious to ensure that the economy provides a buoyant mood for the party's centenary in 2021 – by then, he says, China will have become a 'moderately well-off society', with a GDP per capita double that of 2010. The threats to this goal include a huge build-up of local-government debt, the ageing of the population, diminishing returns on investment in infrastructure and sluggish growth in overseas markets. But the economy still has a tailwind. The private sector is growing strongly enough to keep urban unemployment low: 3.6 million private firms were set up in 2014, nearly double the number in the previous year. In September 2014, Chinese e-commerce firm Alibaba launched the largest initial public offering in stock-market history. Worth around US$25 billion, it surpassed the previous record of US$22.1bn, set by the state-owned Agricultural Bank of China in 2010. The economy is also rebalancing to rely more on consumption rather than investment. Economic reforms are gradually unfolding, especially in the financial sector, which in the long run should help prevent the economy from sliding into the kind of long-term malaise experienced by Japan.

Zhou Xiaochuan, the governor of China's central bank, has stated that full liberalisation of interest rates is possible by the end of 2015. This would encourage state-owned banks to price credit more effectively and ensure that it flows to the businesses that are best able to repay. It may be mainly for reasons of status that China is lobbying for the yuan to be accepted as one of a handful used by the IMF to underpin its own quasi-currency, the Special Drawing Right. The Chinese leadership remains nervous about exposing the yuan to the uncertainties of global demand, and the possibility that doing so might result in a crippling outflow of cash. But the push for the yuan's inclusion in the IMF basket will have a positive side effect if – as is expected – it helps to build political support for China's financial and capital-account liberalisation.

Against an uncertain economic background, Xi appears mindful that the middle class may not draw much inspiration from his talk of a 'Chinese Dream' unless it includes guarantees that the wealth that households have accumulated in recent years can be protected from the predations of corrupt officials. This is an important motive for his anti-corruption campaign, which in 2014 involved investigations by state prosecutors into nearly 600 senior officials – more than twice as many as in the previous year (the number investigated by the party's own investigators, before being handed over to the prosecutors, was much higher). Xi's popularity among the general public has undoubtedly been strengthened by these efforts. In 2014 state media began using the nickname 'Xi Dada' (Uncle Xi) to refer to the president. This was part of a deliberate effort to build up his image as a solicitous protector of ordinary people, and may have been the first stirrings of the kind of personality cult generally avoided by Chinese leaders who came after Mao Zedong.

Rule of law

Yet by targeting the anti-corruption drive at so many senior officials – including those in the military – and by taking over so many policy portfolios, Xi has also taken a political risk. Some figures caught in Xi's dragnet have close ties with influential, if retired, party elders who might chafe at his apparent hubris. By mid-2014 it was clear that Xi believed he could overwhelm any resistance. The government stated on 29 July that an investigation had been launched into Zhou Yongkang, former head of China's domestic-security apparatus and a retired member of the party's most powerful body, the Politburo Standing Committee. In June 2015, Zhou was sentenced to life in prison after being tried in camera for accepting bribes, abuse of power and leaking state secrets. This was a remarkable display of Xi's political strength; serving or retired members of the Standing Committee had hitherto been regarded as untouchable in anti-corruption campaigns.

Xi's efforts to catch 'tigers', as he described such high-level targets, appeared partly aimed at neutering political opposition. Zhou had been a supporter of Bo Xilai, a Politburo member who had once been thought likely to join the Standing Committee when Xi became general secretary, but was arrested for corruption and abuse of power, before being sentenced to life in prison in 2013. It was believed that Xi saw Bo as a political rival. It seemed that by going after Zhou, as well as many of Zhou's relatives and associates, Xi wanted to demonstrate his resolve to any potential challenger.

Beyond instilling fear among rivals, Xi was perhaps making a broader point: no one in the party is immune from prosecution. Party leaders have long spoken of the importance of the rule of law, but Xi has done so with particular relish since becoming general secretary (and state president in 2013). His aim is not to foster an independent judiciary – the law, in the party's view, must still serve the goal of keeping it in power – but to make the application of the law fairer and more transparent. Xi wants to ease concerns, especially among the emergent middle class, about officials' arbitrary use of the law to further their own corrupt interests.

Hence the centrality of the rule of law to the annual plenum of the party's 370-member Central Committee, held in October 2014. The conclave's declaration on the issue was intended by Xi as a manifesto for political reform. (Xi's economic manifesto had been unveiled at the previous plenum; its resolution called for market forces to play a 'decisive role' in guiding the economy.) The term 'political reform' is now rarely used for fear of giving too much encouragement to supporters of Western-style liberalism, but strengthening the rule of law could potentially involve considerable changes to the way the party exercises power. In his early days as China's leader, Xi spoke of 'putting power in the cage of systems and institutions'. The 2014 plenum was intended as a starting point for this. Officials would henceforth be punished for interfering in court decisions, it ruled (although politically sensitive cases were likely to be exempt). The leadership structure of lower-level courts would be changed to make such interference more difficult.

The plenum provided more evidence of Xi's growing confidence. It revived the idea that the state constitution should be treated as the country's supreme law, a notion he had raised soon after taking power. In theory that was already the case, but in practice officials usually avoided emphasising the constitution's importance. Xi's discussion of the concept in late 2012 inspired small-scale protests in the southern city of Guangzhou early the following year, as demonstrators called for the implementation of wide-ranging political freedoms nominally guaranteed by the constitution. State media then fell largely silent on the topic, apparently to avoid fuelling such demands. Xi's renewed attention to the constitution in 2014 suggested that he believed he was succeeding in his tough campaign against dissent, which involved the jailing of numerous activists: liberals would no longer dare to take advantage of his call for constitutional restraints on party rule to press for an end to the one-party system.

Democracy and dissent

The limits of Xi's willingness to reform the country's politics were made clear in May 2015, when formal charges of 'troublemaking' and support for terrorism were levelled at prominent lawyer Pu Zhiqiang, an outspoken participant in a grassroots movement to protect the legal rights of ordinary citizens. Despite his emphasis on the rule of law, Xi clearly does not want ordinary people to use the law to challenge the party. Pu's indictment was a sign of his determination to prevent the growth of an independent civil society. In line with this, restrictions on NGOs grew even tighter in the year to mid-2015. A new law that would likely make it harder for foreign NGOs to register and work in China stood to be passed by the end of 2015.

Xi's efforts to silence demands for democracy, however, did little to dissuade activists in Hong Kong from taking up the cause. In September 2014, one month before the plenum, students in the territory began class boycotts that evolved into large-scale protests and round-the-clock sit-ins on several major roads. The trigger was an August decision by the Chinese leadership to restrict democratic development in the territory. The national legislature ruled that Hong Kong would be granted 'universal suffrage' in the choice of its next leader, known as the chief executive, in 2017. But there would be a maximum of three candidates, each of whom would require the backing of at least half of the members of a committee stacked with party supporters. Pro-democracy politicians in Hong Kong said this would mean, in effect, that the choice of chief executive would be just as much controlled by Beijing as it had been since Hong Kong was handed back to China by Britain in 1997.

The 'Occupy Central' protests persisted until mid-December, constituting the longest street campaign for democracy in the territory's history. The authorities tried to disperse demonstrators using tear gas and batons, but abandoned such tactics when they appeared to encourage more people to join. In the end, they used court injunctions to clear out the protesters. By that time, the number of demonstrators had dwindled dramatically, and those who remained did not want to risk automatic prosecution for ignoring the court's order to leave.

The protests were described by some Chinese officials as an attempted 'colour revolution', a term often used by the party to denounce upheavals in authoritarian states elsewhere. Yet the Hong Kong government's handling of the demonstrations, exercising patience and avoiding extreme violence, was a tribute to Xi's political skill. Confronted with a high-profile challenge to the party's authority, Xi seemed to resist the temptation to instruct the chief executive, Leung Chun-ying, to respond with much greater force, or even to request the help of the army. Although Hong Kong notionally had control over its own internal security, Xi would certainly have played a role behind the scenes. As chairman of the National Security Commission, which he established in 2013 mainly to facilitate coordination between domestic-security agencies, Xi had oversight of responses to all perceived challenges to party rule. This included those arising in Hong Kong.

The protesters in the city drew inspiration from an outbreak of student-led unrest in Taipei in March and April 2014. That episode, which formed a new challenge for the Communist Party, was known as the Sunflower Movement because of the symbol adopted by demonstrators calling for more transparency in their government's trade negotiations with mainland China. Like the protests in Hong Kong, the Sunflower Movement was fuelled by the younger generation's distrust of China's growing economic power and the impact on its own wealthy, but much smaller, economy. In Hong Kong, high property prices are commonly blamed at least partly on demand from mainlanders; many in Taiwan fear that the territory will undergo 'Hong Kong-isation': a gradual loss of independent status as a result of Beijing's growing influence over the local business elite. The Communist Party had hoped that China's economic growth would help it win over public opinion in Hong Kong and Taiwan. Instead, it became evident in 2014 that closer economic interaction had created destabilising rifts in both societies, as well as growing hostility, particularly among the young and the poor, to China's perceived cultural and political encroachment.

Both Hong Kong and Taiwan will loom large in Xi's mind over the coming year. In June 2015, pro-democracy legislators in Hong Kong delivered a snub to the central leadership by vetoing their government's Beijing-backed plan for the next chief-executive elections. This means that the same method for choosing the chief executive will be used as before: a committee of 1,200 Hong Kong residents, most of them sympathetic to Beijing, will endorse whichever candidate the Communist Party appears to favour, without a popular vote. Pro-democracy politicians argue that this method has the advantage of being blatantly undemocratic: no one will be deceived into thinking the territory has made political progress.

However, public opinion in Hong Kong was deeply divided on the issue. There was a strong possibility that more large-scale pro-democracy demonstrations would follow, accompanied by counter-protests from supporters of the government. Elections for the Legislative Council scheduled for September 2016 stood to be a fierce contest between the rival camps. There was a chance that student radicals disillusioned by the ineffectual Occupy Central movement would adopt more confrontational tactics. Chinese officials worried that a rise of nativist sentiment in Hong Kong, marked by contempt for mainlanders and their culture, would evolve into outright demands for secession. Although there was little sign of support for Hong Kong independence, Leung attacked what he called the 'fallacies' of 'self-reliance and self-determination' in a speech to the Legislative Council in January 2015. The territory, he argued, had to stay on alert.

In Taiwan, presidential elections due to be held in January 2016 were likely to end eight years of rule by the Kuomintang (KMT). It seemed that the vote would result in a victory for the Democratic Progressive Party (DPP), the main opposition party, which supports Taiwan's *de jure* independence. China shunned the previous DPP government, which ruled from 2000 to 2008, and put pressure on the US to follow suit. The DPP's presidential candidate, Tsai Ing-wen, is more of a pragmatist – and therefore less likely to take steps towards independence – than the last DPP president, Chen Shui-bian (who was released from jail on medical parole in January 2015, after serving six years of a 20-year sentence for corruption). Elections for the legislature will be held at the same time as that for the presidency. Should the KMT and its allies maintain control of the legislature, Tsai would find it difficult to make bold moves such as constitutional revisions to assert independence, even if she wanted to. And Xi is a more forceful leader than his predecessor, Hu Jintao, who was in power during Chen's presidency. He may be tempted to warn the DPP using China's economic leverage, or even a demonstration of military might.

Repression in Xinjiang

Xi showed characteristic toughness when dealing with separatist challenges on the mainland. Tight security measures remained in place in Tibet, where some observers had speculated that Xi might adopt a more flexible strategy to win over the Dalai Lama (who knew the president's late father, Xi Zhongxun). The authorities' response to self-immolations by Tibetans in protest against Chinese rule, of which there have been around 140 since 2011, has been to intensify surveillance in monasteries and impose harsh punishment on friends and relatives of those involved.

In the western region of Xinjiang, there were numerous outbreaks of violence that the authorities blamed on ethnic Uighur separatists allegedly linked to foreign jihadist organisations. More than 400 people were killed in such incidents in 2014, a sharp increase over the previous year. Three people died and dozens were injured in April 2014, when there was an explosion at a railway station in Urumqi, the regional capital, at the end of a visit to Xinjiang by Xi. Uighur separatists were also blamed for a knife attack the previous month, which took place at a railway station in the southwestern city of Kunming, in Yunnan Province. More than 30 people were killed in that assault, making it the bloodiest act of terrorism outside Xinjiang in the history of the People's Republic, and prompting the Chinese media to refer to the incident as 'China's 9/11'.

The Kunming attack appeared to stiffen Xi's resolve to crack down on separatism. Restrictions on Islamic dress and on the growing of beards by Muslim men were stepped up across Xinjiang. A 'strike hard' campaign against the separatists, involving speedy trials and mass sentencings, was launched in 2014 and extended until the end of 2015. Ilham Tohti, a prominent Uighur academic who had argued publicly against repressive measures, was sentenced to life in jail in September 2014, one of the stiffest punishments for peaceful dissent in China in recent years.

New laws are being prepared to reinforce the party's message that it will not compromise with separatist demands. One is a counter-terrorism law, a draft of which was published in November 2014. It has alarmed human-rights groups because of its ill-defined terms, which could give the party a legal justification for labelling critics of the government as terrorists. Beijing is also drafting a new national-security law, which covers a wider range of perceived threats, including 'harmful moral standards' online. It calls for the protection of 'core socialist values' and the protection of 'cultural security'.

The proposed legislation does not necessarily herald tighter political controls, as the party has never felt restrained by law in its efforts to silence dissent. But it does suggest that Xi wants a clearer legal justification for the crackdown, in keeping with his emphasis on the rule of law. The praise heaped by Chinese officials and state media on Singapore's elder statesman, Lee Kuan Yew, after his death in March 2015 suggested that Xi admired that country's 'soft authoritarian' form of governance underpinned by law. Given the scale of the threats to party rule that he perceives at home, however, Xi has shown little inclination to experiment with softer methods of handling dissidents.

Social upheaval

The Chinese leadership worries about the emergence in recent years of social forces rooted in a new middle class and of an equally large underclass of people migrating to cities from the countryside, as well as a huge and potentially destabilising divide between them. It also worries about the proliferation of social media that can connect citizens with shared grievances, including people who are unhappy with the party. Widespread use of smartphones has enabled demonstrators to spread news of their protests in real time. By the end of 2014, China had nearly 650m internet users, 80% of whom used mobile devices to go online. Despite increased controls on the internet, including efforts to censor the hugely popular WeChat messaging service, social media continue to play an important role in staging many of the tens of thousands of protests that occur in China every year. The potential for these demonstrations to turn violent was shown in May 2015 in the southwestern town of Linshui, in Sichuan Province, where thousands of residents clashed with police in protest against plans to divert a high-speed rail line away from the area.

Xi will become all the more focused on internal stability in 2016, as he prepares for the party's crucial 19th Congress the following year. That event, and a meeting of the party's Central Committee immediately afterwards, will mark the end of Xi's fifth year in power and will involve sweeping changes in the leadership: the retirement of five out of seven members of the Standing Committee (the other two being Xi and the prime minister, Li Keqiang). Xi and his colleagues often speak of the country's economy having begun a 'new normal' of slower growth. That description may prove apt for the remaining years of his rule. Yet it is unclear whether a parallel 'new normal' has taken hold in the country's politics. Strains on the party's unity caused by the anti-corruption campaign and Xi's autocratic style will be compounded by pressure from the reshuffle of the leadership.

External affairs: 'Big-country diplomacy'

In November 2014, Xi sketched out his foreign-policy vision in a speech to the Communist Party's Central Conference on Work Relating to Foreign Affairs, the first such meeting to be held since 2006. While providing reassurances that China would not deviate from the path of 'peaceful development', Xi called for the adoption of 'big country diplomacy with Chinese characteristics' and declared that China would never 'relinquish our legitimate rights and interests' or allow 'core interests' to be undermined. The speech provided further evidence of China's movement away from Deng's guideline of 'keeping a low profile' in foreign affairs, in favour of a more active policy.

Competition with Washington

The relationship between the US and China took a positive turn in mid-2014, following a period of heightened friction in the first half of the year. At the sixth round of the US–China Strategic and Economic Dialogue (SED), held in July 2014, the two sides agreed to intensify their negotiations on a Bilateral Investment Treaty (BIT), and to launch talks in early 2015 on China's negative list, which details sectors in the country that are barred to foreign investment. Both sides were critical of the other's negative lists, which were exchanged in May 2015, and at the June 2015 SED they agreed to exchange revised negative lists and speed up talks on the BIT. Finalising a BIT before the end of US President Barack Obama's term, in 2016, remains a goal, although this may require another year or two of negotiations. Bilateral ties were also strengthened at the Xi–Obama summit held in November 2014, which generated joint statements on deals to extend business and tourist visas to ten years; increase trade liberalisation by expanding the World Trade Organisation's 1997 Information Technology Agreement; implement confidence-building measures between the US and Chinese militaries; and combat global warming. The two leaders also agreed to deepen cooperation on five global and regional challenges: Ebola, terrorism, proliferation threats, Afghanistan and the trade in illegal wildlife products.

Nevertheless, the overall relationship was fraught and increasingly competitive. Allegations that China was persistently using cyber capabilities to steal trade secrets from US companies and information on federal employees from the US government were a major irritant. At the June 2015 SED, the US and China agreed to work together to develop a code of conduct regarding cyber activities. Another source of tension was Beijing's criticism of US military alliances in Asia, which at times was accompanied by a call for the creation of a new regional security architecture that would be run 'by Asians, for Asians' – possibly to the exclusion of Washington. First announced by Xi at the Conference on Interaction and Confidence Building Measures in Asia meeting in May 2014, this proposal was reiterated by Vice-Foreign Minister Liu Zhenmin at the Chinese military's Xiangshan Forum the following November. Since then, however, Chinese officials have attempted to reassure Washington that China is not seeking to push the US out of Asia. For example, Foreign Minister Wang Yi stated in a speech to the fourth World Peace Forum, held in June 2015, that 'we do not seek dominance or sphere of influence in the region, nor do we intend to form military alliances or drive any country out of the Asia-Pacific.'

Tension between Washington and Beijing was exacerbated by disputes in the South China Sea, where China engaged in construction projects at a frenetic pace, expanding seven reefs into artificial islands with ports, fuel-storage depots, radar sites and an airstrip. Despite agreeing to avoid conflict in the air and at sea, in August 2014 a Chinese J-11 fighter jet intercepted a US P-8A *Poseidon* maritime-patrol aircraft close to Hainan Island. However, progress was made in late 2014, when the US and China signed two memoranda of understanding on 'rules of behaviour for safety of air and maritime encounters' and 'notification of major military activities'.

An additional point of contention was the writing of trade rules for the twenty-first century. Washington pushed for the conclusion of the Trans-Pacific Partnership, which did not include China; Beijing countered by promoting the Regional Comprehensive Economic Partnership and the Free Trade Area of the Asia-Pacific, as well as an initiative dubbed 'One Belt, One Road', which aimed to fund development projects in countries extending from Asia to Europe. To Washington's consternation, Beijing set up the Asian Infrastructure Investment Bank (AIIB), which the Obama administration feared would be used to challenge long-established Western governance standards for lending. In his February 2015 State of the Union address, Obama was adamant that the US – not China – would determine trade rules in Asia.

Obama agreed to work towards Xi's proposed goal of creating a 'new type of great power relations', but the two sides continued to differ on the content and configuration of the concept. The US approach emphasised cooperation where interests coincided, while effectively managing and controlling differences where they diverged. Xi repeatedly called for 'no conflict and no confrontation', mutually beneficial cooperation and respect for each other's core interests and major concerns. In this context, the emphasis on respecting core interests has long been considered unacceptable by the US because China's definition of them is unclear and at odds with Washington's commitments to its ally, Japan.

Economic partnership with Europe

Relations between the European Union and China continued to be defined primarily by attempts to enhance economic opportunities, with Beijing seeking to acquire advanced technology from Europe and the EU hoping to improve European companies' access to Chinese markets. Visits by Chinese Prime Minister Li to several European countries in autumn 2014 highlighted Beijing's enthusiasm for the economic benefits of the relationship, and confirmed the EU as one of China's most important 'strategic partners', a label that Beijing has used to describe its ties with almost 50 countries, the Association of Southeast Asian Nations (ASEAN) and the African Union. The Hamburg Summit held during Li's tour produced a framework for further development of China–EU economic relations.

It was unclear how changes in the EU's leadership in November 2014 would affect its interaction with Beijing. Cecilia Malmström, the EU trade commissioner, appears to have a more conciliatory attitude towards China than her predecessor, Karel De Gucht, who was perceived as aggressive in trade disputes with the Chinese. Federica Mogherini, the foreign-policy chief, celebrated 40 years of EU–China relations during a meeting with Li and several high-ranking party and government officials in May 2015, at the fifth round of a high-level strategic dialogue. They discussed possible areas for enhanced cooperation ahead of the EU–China summit in June 2015, and the Paris climate-change conference to be held in December.

Yet the numerous interactions between high-ranking Chinese officials and their EU counterparts have produced few concrete outcomes. Since the adoption of the 'EU–China 2020 Strategic Agenda for Cooperation' in 2013, the most notable success has been the joint proclamation in May 2015 of plans to reach a 'mutual recognition agreement' that seeks to boost customs cooperation and step up the fight against illegal trade. The second EU–China High-Level People-to-People Dialogue, held in September 2014, focused on expanding academic and youth exchanges, and deepening cultural ties. The EU–China Dialogue on Security and Defence convened the following month, but failed to create momentum on security cooperation. The EU urged Beijing to pressure Moscow after its annexation of Crimea in March 2014, but China carefully avoided taking sides in the escalating Ukraine conflict in order to avoid alienating either Russia or the West. Little was achieved in the EU–China Dialogue on Human Rights in December 2014, primarily due to China's insistence that it had 'its own model of human rights' and saw no need to reform internal policies at the behest of the EU.

In the economic realm, the sides placed an emphasis on investment. The third round of negotiations for a proposed EU–China bilateral investment treaty took place in June 2014, following rounds in January and March. According to the European Council on Foreign Relations' 'Foreign Policy Scorecard' for 2015, the EU seeks to negotiate a new agreement that includes investment protection, 'market access, rules on the role of state-owned enterprises, and sustainable development'. Both parties aim to conclude the treaty by June 2016. Negotiations are complicated by a business climate that is unfavourable to foreign firms operating in China. In its statement on the WTO's 5th Trade Policy Review of China in July 2014, the EU called for easier access to the judicial system for foreign operators, as well as market opening and the removal of discriminatory barriers to foreign direct investment. Foreign firms have also been targets of anti-monopoly investigations, seemingly to advance China's industrial policy and boost major domestic firms. Although the EU Chamber of Commerce has condemned such practices as discriminatory, no punitive actions have been taken by the organisation or individual member states.

On 12 March 2015, the United Kingdom went against the wishes of the US and announced its intention to become a founding member of the AIIB. The UK was soon joined by a cascade of countries, including 15 other European nations, bringing the total number of founding members to 57.

Contested territorial claims

China removed in July 2014 the oil rig it had deployed to waters near the Paracel Islands, within Vietnam's 200-nautical-mile exclusive economic zone. The move came one month sooner than expected, and while Beijing stated that the rig had completed its operations, the more likely reasons for the withdrawal were the threat of legal action from Hanoi and concern that worsening relations would cause Vietnam to align itself more closely with the US.

At the ASEAN Post Ministerial Conference 'plus one' session held with China in August 2014, Beijing's proposal for a 'dual track' approach to the South China Sea received a lukewarm response. That approach insists that territorial disputes be addressed by the claimants, while issues regarding peace and stability in the South China Sea be jointly dealt with by China and ASEAN, not countries outside the region.

Tensions rose in the South China Sea as it became apparent that China was undertaking large-scale land-reclamation projects there, building new islands on the land features it occupies in the Spratly archipelago despite protest from claimants Vietnam and the Philippines. Beijing dismissed these complaints, arguing that its actions were 'lawful, justified and reasonable'. Concern about China's building of artificial islands and potential militarisation of these outposts was a major focus of the 2015 IISS Shangri-La Dialogue, held in Singapore at the end of May, and of the SED, held the following month. The reclamation activities served several Chinese objectives, including boosting Beijing's ability to enforce its sovereignty claims through interference with fishing and energy exploration conducted by its rivals, and helping the Chinese military to project power in the South China Sea. There was speculation that once China completed its construction of ports and airstrips in the area, it would declare an Air Defence Identification Zone over the South China Sea similar to the one it established in the East China Sea in November 2013.

In the East China Sea, China continued to periodically conduct patrols in the 12-mile territorial waters and contiguous zone around the Senkaku/ Diaoyu Islands, whose ownership it disputes with Japan. Scrambles by Japanese and Chinese aircraft in the skies above the East China Sea surged, increasing the risk of an accidental conflict. Talks between Chinese and Japanese defence authorities on establishing a maritime crisis-management mechanism to prevent unwanted clashes in the air and at sea around the disputed islands resumed in January 2015, but by mid-year had not yielded an agreement.

Growing influence in East Asia

Beijing's desire to advance its economic influence and soft power in the Asia-Pacific was reflected in its relations with other countries in the region. In October 2014, one year after convening an unprecedented Communist Party work conference on diplomacy between China and neighbouring states, Xi stressed the importance of ties with these countries at the Central Conference on Work Relating to Foreign Affairs. He reiterated China's goal of creating a 'community of common destiny', and promoting the ideals of amity, sincerity, mutual benefit and inclusiveness in conducting neighbourly relations. Beijing created the 'One Belt, One Road' strategy by combining two major foreign-policy initiatives put forward in 2013: the Silk Road Economic Belt and the Twenty-First Century Maritime Silk

Road. Xi committed US$40bn to a new Maritime Silk Road fund designed to connect Asian and European economies through investment in infra-structure and resource development, as well as industrial and financial cooperation.

Relations between China and North Korea remained strained, with no high-level exchanges in the year to mid-2015. The spillover of political tensions into the economic relationship was exemplified by the announce-ment on 31 October 2014 of a delay to the opening of the Dandong–Sinuiju bridge, which Chinese state media blamed on North Korea's failure to com-plete its share of construction on schedule. Under Xi, China is somewhat more firm in opposing Pyongyang's nuclear programme and destabilis-ing behaviour. Beijing sees these activities as helping to strengthen the US–South Korea alliance, raising the risk of conflict in the region and increasing the international community's criticism of Chinese assistance to North Korea. At the same time, however, Beijing continues to seek stability in North Korea and maintains its support for the two nations' 'traditional friendship', as Xi put it.

The trend in China's relationship with North Korea stood in stark in contrast to that with Seoul. Xi held a July 2014 summit with South Korean President Park Geun-hye, marking the first time that a Chinese head of state had made an official visit to Seoul but not Pyongyang. The two met again on the sidelines of the Asia-Pacific Economic Cooperation (APEC) leaders' meeting in November 2014. The following February, China and South Korea completed a draft bilateral free-trade agreement, which covered 17 areas, including trade in goods and services, investment and trade rules, e-commerce and government procurement. The deal was designed to eliminate tariffs on 90% of all products traded between the two countries within 20 years. At the fourth Defense Strategic Dialogue between China and South Korea, held in July 2014, the parties signed a memorandum of understanding establishing a direct telephone line between their defence ministers, intended to enable more effective com-munication in the event of a crisis and to promote their bilateral military cooperation.

After a period of protracted tension between Beijing and Tokyo, trig-gered in September 2012 by the Japanese government's purchase from private owners of several of the disputed Senkaku/Diaoyu Islands, relations between the two showed signs of improvement. Xi and Japanese Prime Minister Shinzo Abe met for the first time, in Beijing, shortly before the APEC summit. The encounter took place after the two governments negotiated a carefully crafted, four-point consensus, which acknowledged their differing views on the source of recent tensions in the East China Sea and committed the sides to gradually resuming their political, diplomatic and security dialogue. Long-suspended talks between the Japanese and Chinese defence ministries on establishing a maritime crisis-management mechanism resumed in January 2015, and further progress was achieved at a meeting held four months later. The Japan–China Parliamentary Exchange Commission also held discussions in March, the first such gathering in almost three years. Xi and Abe then met in late April on the sidelines of the Asian–African Conference in Jakarta. Sino-Japanese trade was flat in 2014, after experiencing a 6.5% drop in 2013. Japan's direct investment in China plunged in 2014 to US$4.33bn, a drop of 38.8% from the previous year. This reflected the cool political relationship, as well as rising labour costs in China.

Beijing redoubled its efforts to persuade ASEAN member states that China's rise benefited both them and the region as a whole, with mixed results. China offered economic benefits via the Maritime Silk Road, the AIIB, loans for regional infrastructure development, the China–ASEAN Investment Cooperation Fund and the promise of preferential treatment to ASEAN investors under an expanded China–ASEAN free-trade agreement. Politically, China pushed for a bilateral treaty on what Li described as 'good-neighbourliness, friendship and cooperation'. At the 17th ASEAN–China Summit, held in November 2014 in Myanmar, ASEAN agreed to explore this proposal and designate 2015 the 'ASEAN–China Year of Maritime Cooperation'.

But even as ASEAN–China cooperation expanded, most Southeast Asian countries became more anxious about Beijing's construction of artificial islands in the South China Sea, which was accompanied by increased paramilitary patrols and naval exercises. At the 26th ASEAN Summit, held in April 2015, ASEAN expressed concerns that China's land-reclamation activities threatened 'peace, security and stability', drawing Beijing's ire. There seemed to be no progress towards establishing a China–ASEAN code of conduct for the South China Sea.

Concern in New Delhi

Relations between China and India improved on the economic front in the year to mid-2015, but were persistently troubled by competition for regional influence, a dispute along their shared border and overall mistrust. Xi's visit to India in September 2014 yielded some positive results, including a Chinese commitment to invest US$20bn in India's infrastructure, industrial parks and energy sector, as well as greater market access for Indian exports to China, including fruit, vegetables, pharmaceuticals and jewellery. However, the visit was marred by Chinese troops' incursion across the Line of Actual Control into the disputed Ladakh region.

Beijing was undoubtedly irritated by the higher degree of US–India strategic convergence and cooperation, signalled by Indian Prime Minister Narendra Modi's willingness to sign a 'Joint Strategic Vision for the Asia-Pacific and Indian Ocean Region' during Obama's visit to New Delhi in January 2015.

In September 2014, a Chinese Type-039 *Song*-class diesel-powered submarine conducted a patrol in the Indian Ocean for the first time, visiting Colombo. The following April, China deployed a nuclear-powered submarine as part of its anti-piracy patrols off the Gulf of Aden. New Delhi was increasingly concerned about China's operation of submarines in the Indian Ocean, along with the increasing pace of Chinese investment in India's immediate neighbourhood as part of its Maritime Silk Road strategy.

Nevertheless, China and India had a shared interest in promoting bilateral ties and managing their differences, as was demonstrated during Modi's return visit to China in May 2015. During that trip, a record 24 agreements were signed, covering areas such as railways, mining and outer space, as well as business deals worth US$22bn. Modi and Xi agreed to start annual visits between their militaries and establish a hotline linking army commanders on either side of their disputed Himalayan border, in an effort to build mutual trust. They also consented to the creation of a high-level task force to investigate the US$48bn trade deficit that India has with China. Despite these accomplishments, Modi stated that there was a need for China to reconsider its approach on some of the issues hindering the partnership between the countries.

Agreements with a weakened Russia

Relations between Beijing and Moscow gained new impetus following Russia's invasion of Ukraine and annexation of Crimea, due to the resulting sanctions imposed on Russia by the US and its allies. Plagued by a net capital outflow of US$151.5bn in 2014, Moscow looked to the Chinese leadership to help alleviate its economic distress. As a result, Russia and China agreed to improve bilateral financial coordination to facilitate the settling of transactions in their national currencies, potentially insulating their business dealings from the US-dominated global financial system. The net result of this intensified economic interaction was a surge in Sino-Russian diplomacy and trade.

All bilateral discussions between Xi and Russian President Vladimir Putin focused on strengthening their countries' strategic partnership. The two leaders discussed energy cooperation and Ukraine when they met in September 2014, on the margins of the 14th Shanghai Cooperation Organisation (SCO) Summit, held in Dushanbe. In November 2014, six months after Russia reached a US$400bn deal to supply 38bn cubic metres of gas to China annually for 30 years, Gazprom announced a framework agreement to deliver an additional 1bcm of gas to Xinjiang from western Siberia for 30 years, via another new pipeline. Yet since 2010 China has repeatedly expressed its reservations about the pipeline, citing security concerns in the territory and the belief that the project would do little to diversify its gas supply.

At the APEC and G20 summits held in November 2014, Putin and Xi agreed to implement a series of major projects, including the construction of pipelines, railways and satellite-navigation systems. One month earlier, Li visited Russia to sign 38 agreements, including a deal to open a yuan–rouble swap line worth US$24.5bn, in an apparent bid to reduce dependence on the US dollar. The two nations set a target of US$100bn for bilateral trade in 2015, which was likely to be met. Minister of Foreign Affairs Wang expressed a willingness to counter the adverse effects of Western sanctions on the Russian economy 'within our capacity'. Russia also joined the AIIB as a founding member on 31 March 2015, after hesitating to do so because of fears that the bank would clash with its vision of a Eurasian Economic Union. While in Moscow in May 2015 to commemorate the 70th anniversary of the end of the Second World War, Xi signed another 32 bilateral agreements, including a cyber 'non-aggression pact'.

China, Russia and the other members of the SCO carried out *Peace Mission 2014* in China's Inner Mongolia autonomous region in late August, their biggest military drill to date. In May 2015, the Russian and Chinese militaries conducted joint naval exercises in the Pacific and the Mediterranean, the fourth and fifth such drills by the sides (the first of which took place in 2012). Putin allowed China to purchase the S-400, Russia's most advanced air-defence system. Moscow also appears willing to sell Beijing its newest jet, the Su-35 multi-role fighter. This resurgence in the defence sector was particularly significant given Moscow's curtailment of sales of advanced weapons to Beijing in the preceding decade or more, after China was accused of reverse engineering Russian technology, before marketing knock-offs at lower prices.

Even as the Sino-Russian strategic partnership deepened, there was persistent friction on a number of issues. Mongolia, which both powers considered part of their strategic 'near abroad', increasingly sought greater connectivity with Russia rather than China. This caused worry in Beijing that the benefits of partnership with Mongolia would accrue to Russia's east, to the detriment of China's resources supply and border security. Russia also expanded its ties with Vietnam to gain greater access to naval ports, while Beijing's growing influence in Central Asia posed a challenge to Moscow's long-standing economic and political supremacy in that region. Although China did not support the West's policy of isolating and punishing Russia, the Chinese leadership was uneasy about the continuing conflict and referendum on self-rule in eastern Ukraine. Moscow, for its part, was anxious that it would become the junior partner in its relationship with Beijing, being overly dependent on the Chinese lifeline.

China's diplomacy is likely to sustain the trend of being increasingly proactive, as Beijing seeks to shape its external environment to better serve Chinese interests. Relying on projects such as the 'One Belt, One Road' and the AIIB, China will seek to leverage its economic power for political ends. Beijing's overarching objective is an external environment that serves the domestic interests of preserving political stability, sustaining economic development, and maintaining the legitimacy and rule of the Chinese Communist Party.

Japan: Defence Reforms and Faltering Recovery

Japanese Prime Minister Shinzo Abe continued to move ahead with his radical economic and security agenda in the year to mid-2015, encountering few challenges to his reforms. Abe strengthened his grip on power by winning a landslide victory in a snap general election held in December. While implementing the programme of monetary easing, fiscal stimulus and structural reform nicknamed 'Abenomics', the prime minister used his relatively strong domestic position to adopt a more assertive defence and security policy. The most important security-related developments were the removal of a ban on Japan exercising the right to 'collective self-defence' in support of the United States and other countries, and the preparation of a range of new legislation to support the military's expanded role. The Abe administration expended most of its diplomatic energy on bolstering the alliance with Washington by securing revisions to the Guidelines for US–Japan Defense Cooperation and pushing for a final deal on the Trans-Pacific Partnership (TPP). Tokyo and Beijing made some progress in improving their bilateral ties, and there were signs of rapprochement between Japan and South Korea. But Abe struggled against the sense that Japan was in decline relative to China and, even worse, at risk of isolation in East Asia and further afield.

Abe's strengthened position

The government persistently staked much of its credibility on ending deflation in Japan and improving the country's long-term economic dynamism through Abenomics. The Bank of Japan showed no sign of reducing quantitative easing – monetary stimulus achieved through large purchases of government securities, following the example of the US – even as the US Federal Reserve moved away from the policy. In fact, in October 2014 the Bank of Japan announced that it would increase the size of the programme: under the plan to purchase Japanese government bonds worth ¥80 trillion (US$670 billion) each year, the bank would by 2017 own securities worth more than Japan's GDP. In addition, further fiscal stimulus was announced in December, with a ¥3.5trn (US$29bn) package to support regional economies. This came six months after Abe set out a comprehensive agenda for structural reform, which included reductions in corporation tax, agricultural initiatives and liberalisation of the energy and health-care markets.

Yet there remained doubts about the success of Abenomics. Monetary expansion pushed down interest rates and the value of the yen, thereby helping large, export-oriented corporations and, for the first time since 2000, raising the Nikkei stock-market index above 20,000. There were also signs in 2014 of an end to deflation – the long decline in prices, which discourages consumption as buyers put off purchases in the hope of still-lower prices – as the consumer price index exceeded the Bank of Japan's 2% target to reach around 3%, its fastest rise since the early 1990s.

However, the rises in the stock market and corporate profits appeared to have limited benefits for Japan's wider economy. Japanese corporations and banks were content to sit on the cash assets they had generated due to the Bank of Japan's policies, rather than to increase employees' wages or invest. Although the unemployment rate fell throughout 2014, there was little sense of increased financial security among most households and thus no significant boost to consumer spending. While wages rose in nominal terms, they fell in real terms as a result of inflation, and living standards were also affected by an increase in domestic energy prices that stemmed from the 2011 Fukushima nuclear disaster. The tendency for households to save rather than spend had been reinforced by successive Japanese administrations' failure to improve social-security benefits. Most importantly, the Abe government's decision to raise consumption tax to 8% in April 2014 choked off household spending and retail sales.

The result was that in 2015 inflation began to dip well below the Bank of Japan's target, once again raising the spectre of deflation. Indeed, there were suggestions that inflation may not have been generated by the bank's policies but simply by rises in energy prices after the Fukushima disaster and up until early 2014, as well as the hike in consumption tax. Japanese economic growth was also affected by the impact on exports of weaker growth in key markets such as the US and China. Due to a series of fluctuations in 2014, including negative growth in some quarters, the Japanese economy technically slipped back into recession. Economic growth recovered to around 1% in the first quarter of 2015, helped by falling energy costs and renewal of consumer demand.

The longer-term prospects for Abenomics were equally mixed. Although Abe's structural-reform package required time to work, few commentators believed that the measures went far or fast enough to tackle Japan's economic malaise. And many were unconvinced that he had the political capital to enact all of the reforms, in the face of vested interests. Japan's monetary and fiscal position also appeared to carry significant risk. There remained concern that the markets would eventually lose confidence in the central bank, forcing an increase in bond yields and accordingly in the interest on the government's debt burden. The fear was that this would result in a financial and fiscal crisis that would reverberate through not just Japan but the entire global economy.

Even if Abe's radical policies were not a panacea for Japan's economic problems, they were sufficient to maintain his domestic support. The Japanese public appeared willing to give the administration the benefit of the doubt, and Abe decided to suspend for 18 months a further 2% rise in consumption tax scheduled for autumn 2014, and to use this window of opportunity to call the snap general election. Despite having won an overwhelming victory in the Lower House just two years earlier, Abe decided to strike early for a renewed mandate, while economic conditions were relatively favourable and the opposition was still in disarray. In the subsequent victory for his Liberal Democratic Party (LDP) and its coalition partner Komeito, Abe's party lost just three seats while Komeito gained three, allowing the coalition to retain a two-thirds majority in the Lower House. While voter turnout was at a record low, suggesting growing disaffection with the administration and politics in general, the win was secured by the coalition's powerful electoral machine combined with widespread distrust of main opponent the Democratic Party of Japan, whose leader lost his seat.

As a result of winning a new four-year term in the Lower House, as well as victory in the 2013 Upper House election, Abe would not face another national vote until 2016, when the next Upper House election would be held. He was also likely to be re-elected to another three-year term as president of the LDP, and thus prime minister, in September 2015, having sidelined party rivals such as former agriculture minister Shigeru Ishiba. Furthermore, the LDP was largely successful in local elections in April 2015. Hence, Abe, who took office in December 2012, had secured at least a further 18 months, and possibly until 2018, in power – a marked contrast from the short tenures of the previous five prime ministers, or six including his own first term in 2006–07.

New roles for the military

Throughout the year, the administration maintained the scale, ambition and pace of changes to Japanese security policy. Abe achieved in July 2014 his primary objective of lifting the ban on collective self-defence, as agreed by the LDP and Komeito earlier in the year. The cabinet passed a resolution allowing Japan to exercise a 'limited' form of collective self-defence under 'three new conditions': where an attack on another state in a 'close relationship' with Japan posed a clear danger to the Japanese people's right to life, liberty and the pursuit of happiness; where there was no other appropriate means to repel the attack; and where the use of force was restricted to the minimum necessary to repel the attack.

The LDP–Komeito coalition waited until after the Lower House and local elections to implement the legislation necessary to enable collective self-defence, and to bolster Japan's overall defence posture. In line with its traditionally dovish stance, Komeito held out for more *hadome* (brakes) on the LDP's ambitions, but by summer 2015 there had been enough progress in intra-coalition negotiations on concessions to Komeito concerns for the new legislation to be brought before the Diet.

Among the key bills prepared by the coalition was the Law on Response to Contingencies, which enabled the exercise of the right of collective self-defence. Japan had previously stretched its interpretation of the constitution to permit a form of de facto collective self-defence – by providing non-combat assistance to US-led military operations in Afghanistan and Iraq – but this was the first official reinterpretation and *de jure* repeal of the ban. While the right of individual self-defence had only allowed the country to employ force in the event that it was directly attacked, the new legislation permitted Japan to defend other states, where doing so would be in the interests of its own security.

The coalition also drafted the Law to Ensure Security in Contingencies Significantly Affecting Japan, which was intended to replace the 1999 Regional Contingencies Law. The older legislation undergirded the Guidelines for US–Japan Defense Cooperation, specifying Japanese logistical support for the US in peacetime, during armed attacks on Japan and in dealing with threats to regional security. The new law removed the rigid geographical divisions between security scenarios and enabled cooperation with the US and other states anywhere in the world, where this conformed with Japan's security interests.

The coalition's new International Peace Support Law was designed to remove the need for Japan to enact separate laws for each deployment of the Japan Self-Defense Forces (JSDF) aimed at providing logistical support to multinational forces. The LDP and Komeito also revised the International Peace Cooperation Law to enable the JSDF to use force when performing certain duties as part of UN peacekeeping operations, rather than solely in the defence of Japanese military personnel. The changes enabled the exercise of collective self-defence in specific situations, including the protection of other countries' militaries and the rescue of Japanese nationals overseas. Finally, the coalition's revisions to the Act on Ship Inspection Operations in Situations in Areas Surrounding Japan enabled Japanese forces to participate with other states in the interdiction of vessels, where such missions were carried out in pursuit of international peace.

Among the *hadome* insisted on by Komeito were the requirement that JSDF deployments receive prior approval by the Diet within seven days of the decision to carry out the mission, and the stipulation that deployments occur only with international consent, in the form of a UN resolution, and with due regard for the safety of Japanese military personnel.

However, many Japanese questioned the effectiveness of Komeito's measures as constraints on the use of force. The first of the government's three new conditions contained no objective criteria for identifying an existential threat to Japan. Concern about loose interpretation of the new laws was compounded by Abe's remarks that the JSDF might be deployed as far afield as the Persian Gulf, as part of missions to protect freedom of navigation along shipping lanes used to bring in vital energy supplies. It was unclear how the government would determine that there was no alternative to the use of military power, especially if the US were to call for Japanese support. As a consequence, Tokyo might be compelled to deploy the JSDF simply to preserve its alliance with Washington. Moreover, the requirement to keep the use of force to a minimum was an obvious consideration that applied to most militaries, and thus in practice had little power as a new constraint.

There was also concern about the requirement for prior Diet approval, as it was unclear whether the government could in a seven-day window provide enough information for an informed debate on deploying the JSDF. Given these considerations, there seemed to have been a significant lowering of the barriers to military deployment and the use of force overseas.

The Japanese public appeared to be anxious about the exercise of collective self-defence: following the July 2014 cabinet decision and the announcement of new security legislation, there were dips in the government's support ratings. Nonetheless, the public seemed willing to tolerate collective self-defence to assist the US, and to accept grudgingly that Japan needed to strengthen its national defences against China and contribute to global security.

It was expected that the January 2015 execution of two Japanese nationals by the Islamic State of Iraq and al-Sham (ISIS) might spur domestic opposition to expanding Japan's international role. This was particularly true given the group's claim to have acted in retaliation for Abe's pledge of non-military financial support for Middle East countries fighting ISIS. Yet Abe's firm stance, refusal to pay a ransom and measured handling of the crisis led to an increase in his domestic support.

Ties with the US

Japan's push on security legislation was closely synchronised with attempts to strengthen its alliance with the US. Both efforts were intended to counter a rise in the perceived threat from China resulting from disputes over the Senkaku/Diaoyu Islands and freedom of navigation, as well as the growing Chinese military presence in the Asia-Pacific, particularly the South China Sea. Abe's main opportunity to deepen the alliance came with his state visit to the US between 26 April and 2 May 2015, the first such visit by a Japanese premier since 2006. Abe was also awarded a unique honour on 29 April, becoming the only Japanese prime minister to address both houses of Congress.

The US–Japan Security Consultative Committee – a '2+2' grouping of foreign and defence ministers – met in New York on 27 April to release a revised version of the Guidelines for US–Japan Defense Cooperation. As the first revision of the document in 18 years, the move reflected a significant step forward in bilateral defence cooperation. The 2015 revisions expanded the range of functional support provided to Japan, specifying cooperation on intelligence, surveillance and reconnaissance; ballistic-missile defence; maritime security; ship-asset protection; joint facilities; peacekeeping operations; humanitarian assistance and disaster relief; and defence activities in space and cyberspace.

The revised guidelines stressed a 'seamless' and 'whole-of-govern-ment' approach, abandoning the previous version's rigid separation of US–Japan cooperation in peacetime, Japan contingencies and regional con-tingencies. The revisions were intended to ensure that bilateral military cooperation operated more smoothly in all potential scenarios and at every level of an escalating conflict. The revisions also emphasised that coopera-tion would no longer be constrained to Japan and the surrounding region, emphasising the global aspect of the relationship. Even more significantly, the revised document outlined the areas in which Japan could use armed force in defence of the US and its own security, a guideline closely linked with the new right to collective self-defence and the Abe administration's accompanying security legislation. Under the new agreement Japan could, for example, protect US shipping, interdict other ships, intercept ballistic missiles and provide logistical support in conflicts.

A meeting between Abe and US President Barack Obama on 28 April culminated in the 'US–Japan Joint Vision Statement', emphasising 70 years of friendship and the importance of the alliance to sustaining the US-led international order. The allies also noted the synergy between their respective strategies: Japan's stated aim to be a 'proactive contributor to peace' and the US 'rebalance' to the Asia-Pacific. They stressed the need for an international order undergirded by the principles of democracy, human rights and the rule of law; open markets, free trade and transpar-ent economic rules; and respect for sovereignty and territorial integrity. The statement also noted the importance of US–Japan negotiations to the finalisation of the TPP, which would in turn set the rules of the Asia-Pacific economic system. Abe therefore positioned Japan as heavily invested in continued US dominance of the Asia-Pacific and the strengthened bilateral alliance, tacitly contrasting this solidarity with China's frustrated attempts to create an alternative regional order.

But there remained problems with Abe's mission to strengthen the US–Japan alliance as insurance against a rising China. The 2+2 meeting statement confirmed that US Marine Corps Air Station Futenma would be relocated within Okinawa to Henoko; despite facing significant public opposition in Japan, the move was presented as the 'only alternative'. That issue threatened to weaken bilateral ties throughout 2014. In November, Takeshi Onaga was elected as the new governor of Okinawa, after running on a promise to prevent the base from being maintained or relocated within the prefecture. Abe continued preparations for the construction of the replacement facility regardless, before eventually meeting Onaga the following April in the hope of quelling local opposition prior to his visit to the US. Abe's failure to do so suggested that Onaga would attempt to withdraw prefectural permission for the construction project, preventing the prime minister from fulfilling a key promise to Washington.

The bilateral TPP negotiations also proved challenging, with Washington and Tokyo unable to reach a final agreement in time for Abe's state visit and the looming threat that Congress would block the initiative outright due to pressure from anti-Japanese groups. The latter problem was exacerbated by the suspicion with which American policymakers viewed Abe's historical revisionism and apparent interest in overturning Japan's apologies on 'comfort women' – sex slaves used by Japanese forces during the Second World War – which were included in the 1993 Kono Statement and the 1995 Murayama Statement. During his visit to the US, Abe meticulously avoided making any comments at odds with these statements. Nonetheless, while discussing the history of US–Japan conflict at length and expressing remorse for any suffering his country had caused, Abe did not use the terms 'aggression' or 'apology' in his speech before Congress. This suggested that he still had reservations about actively promoting the Kono and Murayama statements, a stance that potentially exacerbated tensions with the US and Japan's East Asian neighbours.

Relations with other East Asian states

Japan and China attempted in late 2014 to improve their bilateral ties, apparently realising that the Senkaku/Diaoyu Islands dispute could develop into a high-risk military confrontation if left unaddressed. They would also have been motivated by the effect of political tensions on economic activity, given the 40% fall in Japanese foreign direct investment in China during the first half of the year.

The opportunity for the first direct bilateral summit meeting between Abe and Chinese President Xi Jinping came on 10 November, around two years after they had assumed office, when Abe attended the Asia-Pacific Economic Cooperation summit in Beijing. Diplomatic protocol demanded that, as host, Xi meet with all national leaders in attendance. Prior to the meeting between their leaders, Japan and China simultaneously released 'joint' statements that overlapped in content and phrasing but differed in many senses, reflecting persistent bilateral tensions.

The sides came up with an ingenious formula for discussing the Senkaku/Diaoyu row. Prior to the summit, China insisted that Tokyo drop its position of denying there was a territorial dispute, in return for which Beijing would potentially be prepared to shelve the issue. Japan would not accede to this demand, as it maintained that the islands were its sovereign territory and thus there was no discussion to be had. Tokyo also demanded that the summit be held without any preconditions. Chinese and Japanese diplomats therefore agreed to use differing wordings for the joint statements, so as to facilitate a meeting. China stated that tensions had developed over the islands because of differing 'positions' between the two states, retaining room to argue that it had not foregone any official stance of asserting its sovereignty over the islands. Japan, meanwhile, announced that tensions had arisen due to differing 'views' on the islands, obviating the need for it to recognise that there was a dispute. This diplomatic hair-splitting allowed the sides to acknowledge that the islands were the cause of differences and tensions, and that a continuing dialogue was needed to manage the issue. As a consequence, Abe and Xi agreed to move forward long-mooted attempts to create bilateral crisis-management mechanisms in the East China Sea, with a view to avoiding inadvertent conflicts over the islands.

A similar face-saving formula was devised for dealing with historical tensions and Abe's December 2013 visit to the Yasukuni Shrine, a move some regarded as honouring Japanese war criminals. Abe refused to rule out further visits to the shrine as a precondition for a meeting with Xi, but agreed to reiterate Japan's past stance, alongside China, that both sides would work to squarely address historical legacies.

The meeting between the leaders appeared to have an important stabilising effect on ties, leading in 2015 to a limited reduction in Chinese incursions into Japanese territorial waters; improved economic ties and booming Chinese consumer tourism in Tokyo; the renewal of diplomatic contact in areas such as environmental cooperation; and the first bilateral security talks in four years, held by the countries' deputy foreign ministers in March. Abe and Xi also met again at the Asian–African Conference in Jakarta, shortly before Abe's visit to the US.

However, overall relations between Japan and China remained testy. Beijing condemned Abe's decision to send a ritual offering to the Yasukuni Shrine in April, while underlining the Japanese leader's reluctance to repeat historical apologies, and denounced the revisions to the Guidelines for US–Japan Defense Cooperation as a Cold War throwback aimed at China. Tokyo remained suspicious that the new Asian Infrastructure Investment Bank being set up under a Chinese proposal would be used by Beijing to marginalise Japanese influence in the Asia-Pacific – traditionally exerted through the Asian Development Bank – and to challenge the US-led global financial order. Both Japan and the US initially refused to join the new bank, claiming that its operational rules lacked transparency. Moreover, Japan continued to hedge its bets against China's rise, with a renewed effort to deepen economic ties with the members of the Association of Southeast Asian Nations, and an agreement in 2014 to transfer to Vietnam six vessels for use as naval patrol boats, bolstering maritime-security efforts in the South China Sea.

Japan's relations with South Korea improved at an even slower pace. South Korean President Park Geun-hye remained suspicious of Japan's attitude towards its imperial past, contributing to Seoul's drift towards Beijing on many strategic issues. Abe and Park had still not held a direct bilateral summit, despite both leaders having been in power for more than two years. The main improvements in relations between Japan and South Korea came when the sides signed in late 2014 a trilateral agreement to share defence information, along with the US; held in March 2015 their first trilateral meeting between foreign ministers, along with China; and the following month held high-level bilateral security talks for the first time in five years.

Despite Japan's often contentious relations with its neighbours, Abe appeared to have secured his domestic position for several years to come (barring political scandals, or any disasters caused by his economic programme). The major challenges he faced continued to be in foreign and security policy. The new security legislation drawn up by the LDP–Komeito coalition looked set to significantly expand the potential scope of Japan's exercise of military power, along with the operational effectiveness of its alliance with the US. Abe's next great problem was to navigate the perils of history in marking the 70th anniversary of the end of the Pacific War. His administration was preparing a new statement on Japan's history for release in August, to coincide with the event. Abe was almost certain not to revise the Kono and Murayama statements for fear of a backlash from the US, which had repeatedly expressed frustration at Japan's inability to improve cooperation with South Korea or reduce tensions with China due to its stance on history. Nonetheless, it was likely that, while maintaining these statements, Abe would seek to marginalise their importance, focusing instead on Japan's post-war achievements and future direction. It was unclear whether such an approach would be sufficient to reassure other East Asian states. The risk was that Japan would once again become embroiled in historical controversies, isolating the country not only from China, but also from South Korea and even the US.

Korean Peninsula: Diplomatic Stasis

The Korean Peninsula remains a tinderbox. North Korea's growing nuclear arsenal and ballistic-missile capabilities threaten both South Korea and Japan, and are progressing along a path towards targeting the United States through the development of land- and sea-based systems. In the year to mid-2015, denuclearisation talks remained lifeless, as did dialogue between Pyongyang and Seoul. The Democratic People's Republic of Korea (DPRK) turned to Russia to offset a cooling of relations with China, but young leader Kim Jong-un's cancellation of plans to visit Moscow in May 2015 diminished North Korean diplomacy. Only on the home front could he claim success: a strengthening of his leadership and small economic gains. US President Barack Obama's prediction of regime collapse may eventually prove true, but in the meantime the challenges Pyongyang poses are growing significantly more serious.

Expanding North Korean weapons programmes

North Korea's announcement on 9 May 2015 of a test of a submarine-launched ballistic missile (SLBM) heightened concerns about the increasing strategic challenge posed by the country. Although the declaration exaggerated the significance of what was a short-duration ejection launch of a prototype SLBM from a submerged testing platform, South Korean newspaper editorials called the event a '*Sputnik* moment' and a 'nightmare come true'. A full SLBM capability, which is still many years away, would give North Korea a second-strike option and an ability to hit US cities. It would also undercut South Korean missile defences, which are designed to protect against land-launched missiles. The missile shown in North Korean photos appeared to be modelled after the Soviet R-27 *Zyb*, which has a range of 2,400 kilometres.

The test launch took observers by surprise, although the submarine associated with the missile had been observed the previous year. An in-depth study published in March 2015 by the US–Korea Institute at the Johns Hopkins School of Advanced International Studies in Washington warned that the North's strategic capabilities may be on the verge of a dramatic expansion. In addition to SLBM development, the study noted the development of new road-mobile *Musudan* (BM-25) intermediate-range ballistic missiles and *Hwasong*-13 (KN-08) intercontinental ballistic missiles (ICBMs), as well as upgrades to the nation's main rocket-launch site to handle missiles significantly larger than the *Unha*-3 space-launch vehicle that was successfully tested in December 2012. Other developments include an acceleration in the pace of testing of shorter-range systems; the recent appearance of ship-launched cruise missiles; advances in solid-fuel rocket technology; and the modernisation of the missile-development testing and production infrastructure. North Korea's current force of 1,000 ballistic missiles is primarily comprised of short-range *Scud* and medium-range *Nodong* missiles capable of reaching all of South Korea and key portions of Japan. The *Musudan* and *Hwasong*-13 systems would be able to strike targets in Okinawa and the US. Submarine-launched ballistic missiles would also give North Korea a long-range capability.

The report by the US–Korea Institute also focused on North Korea's growing nuclear-weapons programme. Presenting three growth scenarios, the institute estimated that the country had 10–16 nuclear weapons at the beginning of 2015, and that this number would grow to 20–100 by 2020. The worst-case scenario would put North Korea on a par with current estimates for Israel, India and Pakistan, although the institute viewed 50 bombs by 2020 as the most likely scenario.

One month after the publication of the study, it was reported that Chinese non-governmental nuclear experts believed North Korea already had fissile material sufficient for 20 warheads, and the capacity to double this within a year. The estimate was revealed to a group of US nuclear specialists at an off-the-record meeting in Beijing in February. According to one of them, the estimate by the Chinese experts was based on open-source data and was higher than US estimates due to the significant uncertainty of conclusions drawn from assessments of covert uranium-enrichment facilities. Production of plutonium, which until recently was North Korea's primary path to a bomb, is easier to estimate because the activity of the reactors where it is produced is generally observable using satellites. The five-megawatt (electric) reactor at Yongbyon that has produced most of North Korea's plutonium was shut down for parts of autumn 2014, but appeared in the first quarter of 2015 to be operating again at low power or intermittently.

Judging by the intervals of three to four years between its previous three nuclear tests, North Korea might be expected to conduct a fourth test in 2016 or 2017, although it often threatens to do so in response to perceived threats – as it did when the UN General Assembly voted in late 2014 to condemn its human-rights record. Another nuclear test may prove whether the North has uranium- as well as plutonium-based weapons. It may also provide clues as to whether the North has miniaturised a device to fit in the nose cone of its ballistic missiles. Many US analysts, including those at the US–Korea Institute and the Defense Intelligence Agency, believe North Korea can already make bombs small enough for this purpose. In April 2015, Admiral William Gortney, head of the US–Canadian North American Aerospace Defense Command (NORAD), told reporters his agency also believed the road-mobile KN-08 to be operational, although he indicated that only in the worst-case analysis might North Korea be able to target the US with a nuclear-armed ICBM (of questionable effectiveness). In the Republic of Korea (ROK), the Ministry of National Defense distanced itself from both of these assessments (bomb miniaturisation and KN-08 operational capability), emphasising the absence of testing and other verifiable evidence. Analysts noted that emphasising the threat from DPRK ballistic missiles reinforced Washington's case for integrating missile-defence systems, which South Korea has been resisting. It seemed prudent, however, for the US and its allies to take heed of North Korea's strategic advances – and to prepare for more to come.

Kim's strengthened hold on power

The rule of Kim Jong-un has proven to be a smooth transition from that of his father, Kim Jong-il, who died in December 2011. The state seems stable and the leader's authority appears unchallenged, although he has carried out some brutal acts designed to enforce loyalty. While the country as a whole remains impoverished, Pyongyang's two million residents have increasing access to middle-class consumer products from kiosks, restaurants and grey markets selling Chinese-made goods. The economy grew at a sluggish rate of 1.1% in 2013, according to estimates by the ROK's Bank of Korea (the DPRK does not publish any economic figures). There is increasing evidence that Kim Jong-un has introduced reforms to move away from central planning and towards a more market-based economy. The so-called 'May 30' measures, introduced on that day in 2014, followed on from pilot reforms promulgated two years earlier. In the agricultural sector, work units are being reduced in size to four to six members (two households) from the previous 10–25 persons, while farmers are to till the same plots every year and, supposedly, be allowed to keep 60% of their harvest. The resulting incentives probably helped keep the autumn 2014 harvest from dropping below that of the previous year, despite severe drought. In the industrial and mining sectors, where all enterprises are state-owned, managers are to be given responsibility for procuring production materials, hiring and firing workers, and selling products, although this reform has not yet been implemented nationwide.

Many observers doubt that the reforms will be implemented throughout the country and that they can overcome structural impediments such as the lack of accountability and transparency, the misallocation of resources under the military-first system, and the international sanctions imposed on North Korea because of its nuclear-weapons programme. Underlining the contradictions of the leadership in Pyongyang, North Korea established in July 2014 six more free-trade special economic zones, bringing the total number to 19, yet refused to allow the few foreign firms that had invested in the country to repatriate earnings. It also created new obstacles for the Kaesong Industrial Complex, the only active special economic zone to attract South Korean capital.

Kim Jong-un's 40-day absence from public view in autumn 2014 drew more foreign speculation than any other North Korean event in the year, but turned out to be nothing more than a period of recuperation following ankle and foot surgery. Rumours of his sister, Kim Yo-jong, taking control and of a military coup proved to be groundless. Strengthening his hold on power, Kim Jong-un continued to shuffle the roles of senior officials. According to the South Korean National Intelligence Service, he also ordered the executions of more than a dozen of them for speaking against him. The highest-profile purge was that of Defence Minister Hyon Yong-chol, who was condemned for his alleged disloyalty and for dozing during a military rally in the presence of the leader. In April 2015, an anti-aircraft gun was reportedly used to execute Hyon as hundreds of officials watched, a method used in earlier public executions, according to satellite evidence. South Korean President Park Geun-hye said it signalled a 'reign of terror' in the North.

For the outside world, human rights remained a dominant issue regarding North Korea. The damning UN Commission of Inquiry report on atrocities there, released in February 2014, drew the attention of the UN General Assembly, which voted 116–20, with 53 abstentions, to condemn 'the long-standing and ongoing systematic widespread and gross violations of human rights in the DPRK', and to refer the issue to the Security Council. Pyongyang sought to head off UN action by allowing Marzuki Darusman, UN Special Rapporteur for North Korean Human Rights, to visit the DPRK for the first time, but the proffered deal was not accepted. By releasing a 75-page rebuttal, meeting with foreign press and joining UN debates, North Korea fought back against the affront to the dignity of its leader. Pyongyang's only success was to persuade Moscow and Beijing to block action by the Security Council to refer the DPRK to the International Criminal Court. Having called in February 2015 for North Korea's 'cult leadership system' to be dismantled and the Kim family deposed, Darusman ensured that he would remain persona non grata in the country.

Pyongyang's isolation

Concerned nations have long failed to find a formula for stopping North Korea's nuclear and missile programmes. To the extent that systems for ballistic-missile defence are effective, they provide deterrence by denial – and in the Asia-Pacific form part of the strong deterrence capabilities possessed by the US and its allies. But deterrence postures also incentivise North Korea to keep expanding its nuclear and missile systems.

Diplomatic engagement with Pyongyang remains stalled. Although the US, Japan and the ROK, along with China and Russia, still talk about reviving the multilateral Six-Party Talks, which have been on hold since 2008, there is little expectation that this will happen. As part of a policy sometimes called 'strategic patience', Washington is waiting for North Korea to take tangible steps towards discontinuing its nuclear programme, and hopes China can use its leverage to that effect. But Pyongyang refuses to accept the denuclearisation premise of the talks. The *'byungjin* line' of parallel commitment to nuclear weapons and economic development is Kim Jong-un's signature doctrine.

The US attempted informal discussions during winter 2014–15. North Korea initially expressed an interest, but did not follow through. The North conveyed in Track II forums that it would hold off on another nuclear test in exchange for the suspension of US–ROK military exercises, but this was deemed an implicit threat. Although Pyongyang's would-be interlocutors in the Six-Party Talks nevertheless agreed in May 2015 to seek exploratory talks without conditions, this was again met with indifference by North Korea.

Observers noted with irony that, rather than North Korea's nuclear programme, it was an alleged non-kinetic provocation by Pyongyang that elicited an energetic White House response. In late November 2014, hackers accessed Sony Pictures' computer network in California, stealing 11 terabytes of data, including several unreleased films. Initial circumstantial evidence pointed to North Korea, which had threatened 'merciless retaliation' over Sony's planned Christmas release of *The Interview*, a lowbrow comedy film in which two American talk-show journalists are tasked by the CIA with assassinating Kim Jong-un. Pyongyang denied the cyber attack but called it a 'righteous act'. By mid-December, US authorities had collected enough evidence to ascertain North Korea's guilt; in an unusual move, Obama publicly accused the country of an attack on freedom of speech and promised a 'proportional' response. Two weeks later, the US imposed new sanctions on North Korea, blacklisting 13 entities and individuals associated with the defence industry and the arms trade, and expanding the president's authority to target anybody in the DPRK government or the Korean Workers' Party – not just those involved in weapons programmes, as had been the case with previous US sanctions. North Korea's human-rights abuses and the Sony hack were explicitly cited as reasons for the new measures.

Adding insult to injury, Obama stated in January 2015 that '[North Korea is] brutal and it's oppressive and as a consequence, the country can't really even feed its own people'. He also predicted that over time the regime would collapse. The DPRK interpreted this as a threat to try to 'stamp out its ideology and bring down its social system'. A US State Department official subsequently clarified that, like Myanmar, the DPRK could reform itself without the need for regime change. Unsurprisingly, this did not mollify Pyongyang, which returned the insult the following March, praising a knife attack on US Ambassador to the ROK Mark Lippert by a lone extremist protester in Seoul.

Six months earlier, North Korea had sought to improve relations with the US by releasing three American tourists, one of whom, Kenneth Bae, had been held for two years for proselytising Christianity. As with previous cases of hapless American detainees, Pyongyang pressed for Washington to send a senior official or former president to plead for their release. This time, the US chose Director of National Intelligence James Clapper as the emissary. Because Clapper is not a policymaker per se, his selection signalled that the visit would not involve policy talks. North Korea interpreted the move differently, however, and portrayed his role as confirming its propaganda that the detained Americans were spies.

Although Washington remained frustrated by Beijing's unwillingness (or inability, as the Chinese contend) to force Pyongyang to denuclearise, China became ever more disenchanted with its supposed ally. To demonstrate its displeasure, President Xi Jinping shunned Kim Jong-un while strengthening relations with President Park, visiting Seoul in July 2014. Chinese state media ignored the 65th anniversary of China–DPRK diplomatic relations in October 2014, and Chinese commentators debated whether abandonment might be the best policy. In addition to a freeze on high-level exchanges, Chinese trade figures showed that there were no exports of crude oil to North Korea for the entirety of 2014 and the first half of 2015. Given that the North had been totally reliant on China for oil, foreign analysts found these statistics hard to believe, and assumed the flow continued as aid or in some other fashion. Indeed, Chinese officials claimed that trade with the DPRK remained normal.

Seeking to reduce its dependence on China, North Korea began to import crude oil from Russia on the basis of 'favourable loans', returning to a balancing policy with Moscow often practised during the Soviet era. Russia was an eager partner as it looked to balance its own deteriorating relations with the West. Pyongyang and Moscow designated 2015 as a 'friendship year', pledging to deepen their economic and political ties. Other projects in this vein included negotiations for a natural-gas pipeline between Vladivostok and the North Korean seaport of Rajin. A top Russian military official indicated that joint military exercises were being planned. This followed several visits to Moscow by North Korean senior party officials and cabinet ministers, including the later-executed Hyon, in the year to mid-2014.

Yet Kim Jong-un did not visit Russia, despite accepting an invitation to attend the 70th anniversary of the Soviet Union victory over Nazi Germany, on 9 May 2015. In the months leading up to the event, Russian officials repeatedly confirmed that the North Korean leader would be coming, and the ROK National Intelligence Service told a parliamentary committee on 29 April that the visit was 'highly likely'. It would have been the first time since assuming power that he had journeyed abroad, or had met with any foreign leader. On 30 April, however, the Kremlin announced that Kim Jong-un would not be visiting after all, due to unspecified 'internal Korean affairs'. Initial speculation as to what these might be ran the gamut from a coup to anger at Russia for refusing Hyon's request to sell the North the S-300 missile-based air-defence system. One reasonable guess was that Kim Jong-un had initially responded impulsively to the invitation and later had second thoughts when he considered the difficulty of stage managing meetings far from home in a crowded field of other leaders, some of whom might not hide their contempt for him. Whatever the reason, his failure to attend did not strengthen DPRK diplomacy. Similarly, North Korea in late May 2015 abruptly cancelled an agreement for UN Secretary-General Ban Ki-moon (a South Korean national) to visit the Kaesong Industrial Complex.

North Korea also stood up to Japan. Pyongyang agreed in May 2014 to conduct a new investigation into its abduction of Japanese citizens during the 1970s and 1980s, in exchange for which Japan would lift some uni-lateral sanctions. A year later, however, North Korea had yet to follow up with the promised initial report of its findings. Tokyo responded by extending a series of sanctions scheduled to end in May 2015. In addi-tion, Japanese police raided the premises of Chongryon (the General Association of Korean Residents in Japan), North Korea's de facto repre-sentative in Tokyo, over its alleged smuggling of high-value mushrooms.

Frozen North–South relations

Several false starts notwithstanding, there was no improvement in frozen North–South relations in the year to mid-2015. Expectations were height-ened in early October 2014 when, on short notice, three top North Korean officials – including second-in-command Hwang Pyong-so – visited Incheon for the closing ceremony of the Asian Games. But their purpose was strictly domestic: to honour the North Korean athletes who had exceeded expectations by finishing in seventh place. The trio rejected an offer to meet with President Park, and although they did agree to follow-up talks scheduled for several weeks later, North Korea found a reason not to attend when the time came.

The excuse given was that Seoul would not stop South Korean citizens' groups from sending balloons carrying anti-regime leaflets into North Korea. The long-running verbal dispute over the issue took a dangerous turn in October, when bullets fired at the balloons by North Korean forces landed in South Korea. The Park government argued that the distribution of the leaflets was an expression of free speech that it had no legal grounds to stop. It was not until several months later that a court ruling provided such a legal basis, although some balloon leafleting continued.

Despite issuing threats of nuclear war against the South, Pyongyang engaged in few kinetic provocations of its neighbour during the year. In December 2014 and March 2015, repeated cyber attacks were launched against the Korea Hydro & Nuclear Power company, which manages South Korea's nuclear power plants. Tracing back the IP addresses to an area in northeast China near the DPRK border, ROK authorities concluded that a North Korean hacker group was responsible.

Hopes for detente glimmered when Park suggested at the end of 2014 that North–South ministerial talks be held without preconditions, and Kim Jong-un used his 2015 New Year's address to hint at the possibility of a summit 'if the atmosphere and environment for it are created'. By this, he meant a halt to ROK–US joint military exercises, which the North claims are a prelude to invasion. His offer was ignored, and the spring exercises *Key Resolve* and *Foal Eagle* went ahead as planned.

The North insisted that ministerial talks could only begin after Seoul lifted the so-called 'May 24' sanctions, imposed on that day in 2010 after it concluded Pyongyang was responsible for the sinking of the naval ship *Cheonan*, which caused the deaths of 46 crew members. Seoul demanded an apology before those sanctions could be lifted, although it granted some limited exceptions. The unification ministry announced, for example, that to mark the 70th anniversary of liberation from Japan in August, it would encourage civilian exchanges in areas such as culture, sports and history. Several provincial governments quickly declared the resumption of discontinued aid and commercial projects involving North Korea. Pyongyang accepted the aid, but not the political intention behind it. It views with great scepticism Park's emphasis on preparations for unification, which it sees as premised on its absorption by the South. In arguing against her policies, the North resumed ad hominem attacks.

Caught up in the typical fluctuation of inter-Korea relations, the Kaesong Industrial Complex experienced new trouble. During winter 2014–15, the North unilaterally rewrote personnel and management rules for the facility, demanding an increase in wages for the 53,000 workers there above the 5% cap on annual rises agreed by the two governments. While the amount in question was modest, the South refused on principle. There were also several other disputes, including one over the rent to be paid for land used by the 123 South Korean small- and medium-sized enterprises operating in the North, after the initial period of grace lapsed. Pyongyang sought, by comparison, nearly four times the amount that Vietnam charged foreign investors.

Declining support for Park

By January 2015, Park was already being characterised by pundits as a lame duck, despite having served less than two years of her five-year, single-term presidency. Her popularity fell to a low not reached by any of her predecessors in the preceding 25 years: opinion polls found that less than 30% of the electorate supported her, while 63% disapproved of her performance. The immediate cause of the decline was a bungled tax-code reform that deprived middle-class households of an expected rebate. Troubled personnel choices added to the disenchantment. Two prime ministerial nominees withdrew in 2014; Park finally settled in early 2015 on a third – Lee Wan-koo, floor leader of the ruling conservative Saenuri Party – only to see him fall to a corruption scandal two months later. He and seven other of Park's associates were named in a suicide note left by the head of a construction firm, who had been under investigation for bribery.

Critics also faulted Park's management of the economy. The Ministry of Finance's prediction of 3.8% growth for 2015 seemed overly optimistic; given the sluggish performance of the economy in winter 2014–15, some private-sector analysts believed that growth might not reach 3%. A three-year shortfall in tax revenue prevented the president's promised expansion of welfare benefits, while a proposal to overhaul the universal health-insurance system was rescinded, after three years' planning. This all came in stark contrast to Park's claim that 2015 would be a 'golden year' for the implementation of her economic policy.

To Park's benefit, however, her political opponents on the left fared even worse. The main opposition, New Politics Alliance for Democracy, lost all four National Assembly by-elections held in late April, and faced internal divisions that threatened to split the party. Three of the contested seats had seemed likely to go to the liberals, having previously been occupied by the far-left Unified Progressive Party, until its pro-North Korea stance and dalliance with armed rebellion led to its dissolution by the Constitutional Court. Saenuri emerged with a secure parliamentary majority of 160 of 300 seats. Park's popularity rose in May 2015 to 39%, but was still far from the 61% she had enjoyed a little over a year earlier.

Seoul's balancing of Washington and Beijing

The ROK's relations with the US have rarely been better, both at the official and the popular level. Opinion polls in South Korea found support for the alliance at more than 93% as of mid-2015. One contentious issue was taken off the table in October 2014, when the two sides agreed to postpone indefinitely the transfer of wartime operational control over joint forces to South Korea, which had been scheduled to take place in 2015. Seoul pressed for the postponement in light of the North Korean nuclear threat, so as to avoid signalling any reduction in the US security commitment. This was the third such delay of the transfer.

Another thorny issue was resolved in April 2015; after five years of negotiations, the US and South Korea produced a new nuclear-cooperation agreement that was cast as a success for both sides. Holding to non-proliferation principles against the spread of technologies that could be used for nuclear weapons, Washington refused Seoul's request for advance consent for uranium enrichment and a form of plutonium recycling called pyroprocessing. South Korea had sought these technologies both on economic grounds and because Japan is allowed enrichment and reprocessing. A joint US–ROK study will continue into whether pyroprocessing is technically feasible and can be carried out without proliferation risk. As a further incentive for cooperation, the agreement allows for ROK participation in a multilateral enrichment consortium in Europe or North America, and for South Korea's spent fuel to be sent to France for reprocessing.

The ROK's relations with China are also good, as highlighted by Xi's warm visit of July 2014, which reciprocated Park's visit to Beijing one year earlier. The symbolism of the visit and personal rapport between the two was all the more pronounced in that Xi has neither visited nor hosted his North Korean counterpart. Xi's trip to Seoul went beyond symbolism; a large business delegation that accompanied him sought to expand economic ties with the South. The visit also accelerated the negotiation of a free-trade agreement between the two countries, which was concluded in November 2014 and initialled in February 2015. Once ratified, it would eliminate tariffs on more than 70% of two-way trade. Annual two-way trade reached US$229 billion in 2013 – 30 times greater than China–DPRK trade. China is South Korea's largest trading partner by far, as well as its biggest source of foreign investment.

Beyond economics, Xi sought to build on shared historical grievances vis-à-vis Japan so as to dissuade South Korea from participating in what it saw as a US-led strategy to contain China. Beijing's growing influence creates a dilemma for Seoul, which for the first time must balance ties between its largest trading partner and its security guarantor.

Seoul delayed for as long as possible answering Beijing's invitation to join the China-led Asian Infrastructure Investment Bank, in deference to Washington's opposition to the move. Only after the United Kingdom and other European states opted to become founding members of the bank did the ROK follow suit, narrowly making the April 2015 deadline. North Korea also expressed interest in joining, but was rebuffed.

South Korea also put off a decision on whether to allow the US to deploy a Terminal High Altitude Area Defense (THAAD) battery on its territory, in order to counter growing North Korean missile capabilities. Officials in Seoul were able to say that Washington had not yet asked them to deploy the system, although its intention to do so is clear. The ROK's position on THAAD has been lukewarm because Beijing warned that any such deployment would hurt its relations with China. Beijing argues that the THAAD radar system could monitor Chinese military facilities and thus weaken its own defences. Leftist groups and newspapers were sympathetic to this argument, fearing that the deployment could draw the ROK into a US conflict with China over Taiwan or the Senkaku/Diaoyu Islands. Without reconfiguration of its tracking mode, however, THAAD is not useful for offensive targeting.

Given the technical holes in Beijing's argument and its inability to restrain North Korea's missile threat, most South Koreans were irritated by what they saw as an imperious demand from China. In March 2015, after Chinese Assistant Minister for Foreign Affairs Liu Jianchao asked publicly for Seoul to heed China's concerns about THAAD, the ROK Ministry of National Defense warned Beijing against intervening in an issue that would be decided based on South Korea's own military interests. Even if THAAD would only marginally improve South Korean defence against low-altitude rocket attacks, it would contribute to alliance deterrence by denial against North Korean development of an ICBM. Yet the ROK feels a need to placate China, whose cooperation is vital both to rein in North Korean provocations and, it hopes, eventually to help manage the process of reunification.

One other reason for Seoul's ambivalence is that the deployment would tie South Korea into a system for ballistic-missile defence also involving Japan, which is consulting with the US on introducing THAAD there. Military cooperation with Japan is politically fraught in South Korea. Although 2015 marks the 50th year since bilateral relations were normalised, there is no plan to celebrate a golden jubilee. Park has refused a summit meeting until Tokyo shows a greater degree of atonement for the Japanese military's sexual exploitation of Korean women during the Second World War.

Nevertheless, there has been some progress in relations between Seoul and Tokyo. The two countries signed in December 2014 a long-delayed memorandum of understanding to share military intelligence on North Korea, albeit only indirectly, via the US. South Korean Minister of Foreign Affairs Yun Byung-se hosted in March 2015 the first trilateral meeting with his Japanese and Chinese counterparts in three years. The agenda included North Korea and Park's signature 'Northeast Asia Peace and Cooperation Initiative', designed to promote cooperation in security areas such as counter-terrorism and cyber policy.

Peninsular prospects

Kim Jong-un's interest in economic reform did not mean that political reforms were also in store. To the contrary, tight social controls will be deemed necessary to ensure that North Koreans' growing access to outside information does not spark aspirations that could challenge the authorities, as occurred with communist regimes in Eastern Europe. As Russian scholar and Korea expert Andrei Lankov put it, 'while filling the people's bellies with food, the government will have to continue to fill their people's hearts with fear.'

Similarly, market liberalisation showed little sign of carrying over to foreign and defence policy, aside from the faltering outreach to Moscow. The SLBM launch and Chinese warnings about enrichment capacity were stark reminders that North Korea presented an ever-growing security challenge to its antagonists, and that it had no intention of trading away its nuclear arsenal. Keeping tensions high, and thereby reinforcing the perception of an external threat, also helped to keep the population united. The danger of miscalculation argued for energised policy initiatives to reduce the risks, but none of the players appeared keen to make that gamble.

Australia: Political Rows and Regional Hedging

The conservative coalition government of Prime Minister Tony Abbott won Australia's national election of October 2013 on a promise to end political instability, revive the economy and return to a budget surplus. Yet less than a year later, the leadership was under mounting political pressure and had suffered a fall in its approval rating to new lows after announcing a highly unpopular budget that included cuts in foreign aid, health care, education, public-sector jobs and military salaries. Hoping to reverse the trend, the government proceeded to implement some key election promises. It stepped up *Operation Sovereign Borders*, a military-led effort to prevent asylum seekers from entering the country by sea, nick-named the 'stop the boats' campaign. The coalition also made good on its pledge to repeal the controversial carbon tax in July 2014, and two months later abolished the mining tax, which it saw as inhibiting businesses and therefore economic growth.

Yet, while *Operation Sovereign Borders* prevented the arrival of boats carrying asylum seekers and was popular with most Australians, Abbott's economic and social reforms increasingly ran into difficulties. The administration not only faced an increasingly hostile Senate willing and able to veto reforms, but also a public that largely viewed the budgetary measures as unfair. Calls to adjust the government's approach grew louder still after Treasurer Joe Hockey announced in September 2014 a record budget deficit of A$48.5 billion (US$37.3bn), making the goal of returning to surplus by 2018 seem even more difficult to achieve.

Over the following months, diminishing support for Abbott among the electorate and government ministers increased the pressure for change. According to polls in November, the leader of the opposition Australian Labor Party (ALP), Bill Shorten, was level with Abbott as a choice for prime minister. Moreover, in the face of broken promises and deadlocked budget measures, the electorate was unconvinced by Abbott's declarations in December about a 'year of achievement'. As the prime minister's personal approval rating fell, opinion polls showed a preference for the ALP (52%) over the coalition (48%).

The negative national trend for Abbott's Liberal Party also had an impact on state elections held in Victoria at the end of November, in which the party lost its lead over the ALP. In an attempt to break the downward spiral in public opinion and appease increasingly dissatisfied government backbenchers, the prime minister reshuffled his cabinet. Minister for Defence David Johnston, who had caused controversy by remarking that he would not trust the Australian Submarine Corporation to 'build a canoe', was sacked. However, hopes for a policy 'reset' were short-lived. On 15 January, Minister for Health Sussan Ley announced that the government would scrap contentious plans to cut the rebate for short visits to doctors, just one day after the prime minister had expressed his support for the measure. Criticism of Abbott's leadership was fuelled by his 'captain's call' to award a knighthood to Prince Philip, husband of Queen Elizabeth. The decision was widely interpreted as revealing a prime minister out of touch with the Australian people.

His problems were deepened by the coalition's massive defeat in the Queensland state elections of 31 January 2015. The prime minister fought for his political survival as backbenchers called for a change in leadership with a view to avoiding further damage to the party's re-election prospects. In an effort to shore up support among frustrated backbenchers, Abbott decided to dump a scheme for paid parental leave. Yet this failed to prevent a motion to depose him from the party leadership on 9 February. While this was defeated by 61 to 39 votes, Abbott described it as a 'near-death experience' and sought to steer the government into calmer waters by abolishing or adjusting unpopular proposals. But the coalition continued to have difficult relations with the Senate, which in mid-March prevented the passage of an unpopular higher-education bill designed to deregulate university fees.

The victory of the incumbent Liberal government in the New South Wales state elections, held in late March 2015, provided the coalition with some breathing space. Nonetheless, significant challenges remained. The slowing of China's economy and the related drop in the price of iron ore had a negative impact on Australia. In May, on the eve of the coalition's announcement of its second budget, the Reserve Bank of Australia cut interest rates to a record low of 2%, in an effort to stimulate growth. Hockey's assurances that the May 2015 federal budget would contain no surprises did little to dispel most voters' perception that the government favoured rich Australians – a view that most likely contributed to the drop in support for the coalition to 46.5%. The Abbott administration therefore struggled to balance the need for economic recovery with public opposition to further cuts to education, health care and other social services. Moreover, it faced the prospect of further political instability resulting from its diminished popularity.

Tackling the terrorist threat

The fight against both domestic terrorism and, in the Middle East, the Islamic State of Iraq and al-Sham (ISIS) became a major focus of the Abbott government in the year to mid-2015. In August 2014, the administration provided A\$630 million (US\$484m) in extra funding, over four years, to security agencies. The following month, the terrorism threat level was raised from 'medium' to 'high'. The growing risk created by terrorists in Australia was reflected in a series of counter-terrorism raids conducted across Sydney and Brisbane, in which 800 police officers foiled an alleged plot to commit violent acts in the country by ISIS sympathisers. Police also shot dead 18-year-old Abdul Numan Haider on 23 September after he attacked members of a counter-terrorism team in Melbourne.

In a speech to the United Nations two days later, Abbott affirmed his country's commitment to combating what he termed the ISIS 'death cult'. He also revealed that an estimated 60 Australians had joined terrorist groups in the Middle East, and that the passports of more than 60 others had been suspended to prevent them from travelling to the region. On 3 October, the Australian government authorised airstrikes against ISIS in Iraq, joining a US-led coalition. After initially contributing a task force of six F/A-18E/F *Super Hornets*, a KC-30A multi-role tanker and an E-7A *Wedgetail* airborne early-warning-and-control aircraft, Australia by the end of the month also committed around 200 special-forces personnel to the fight.

Furthermore, the Abbott government introduced extensive national-security legislation, strengthening the powers of the Australian Federal Police, the Australian Signals Directorate and the Australian Secret Intelligence Service to deal with domestic terrorism and foreign fighters returning to Australia. On 15 December, Man Haron Monis, an Iranian-born 'lone wolf', took 18 hostages in the Lindt Café at Sydney's central Martin Place, resulting in the deaths of three people, including the gunman.

The 'Sydney Siege' heightened public perceptions that the terrorist threat was growing.

The government further strengthened Australia's institutional and legislative counter-terrorism framework in the first half of 2015. Delivering his 'National Security Statement' on 23 February, Abbott announced the appointment of a counter-terrorism coordinator; in May, former ambassador to Iran and Indonesia Greg Moriarty took up this position. In his statement, Abbott also referred to intelligence assessments that at least 90 Australians were fighting with terrorist groups in Iraq and Syria; that as many as 30 others had returned to the country; and that around 140 Australians were actively supporting extremist groups. Crossbenchers, journalists and civil-rights activists voiced concerns over freedom of the press and the rights of whistle-blowers in relation to penalties under proposed legislation for disclosing information on intelligence operations. In response, the bill was amended to require police and intelligence agencies to obtain a warrant before accessing journalists' telecommunications data. The law reflected the delicate balance that the Australian leadership and parliament were attempting to strike between civil rights and security. In the May 2015 federal budget, the administration committed a further A$296m (US$227m) in funding for the Australian Secret Intelligence Service over the 2015–16 period.

Challenges for foreign and defence policy

In a speech to the National Press Club on 2 February 2015, Abbott described 2014 as a 'tumultuous year that's reminded us to expect the unexpected'. This view was borne out in demands on the government to navigate foreign relations in an increasingly complex and dynamic Asia-Pacific. Moreover, crises further afield increasingly required Abbott's attention.

In July 2014, the prime minister hosted a visit by his Japanese counterpart, Shinzo Abe, who addressed a joint sitting of parliament. This rare honour reflected the growing closeness of an Australia–Japan strategic relationship based on common values and interests, as well as the rapport between the two leaders. Abbott and Abe not only signed a new economic-partnership agreement but also announced a new 'special strategic partnership' and concluded an agreement on the transfer of defence equipment and technology. In combination with Japan's relaxation of its policies on arms-export control, the agreement paved the way for bilateral negotiations, which began the following October, on a possible deal to replace Australia's *Collins*-class submarines. Abbott's preference for the Japanese *Soryu*-class vessel was widely reported, fuelling speculation about a 'secret agreement' with Japan. With the prime minister's political future under threat in February 2015, however, the bilateral security relationship became a hostage to domestic politics. As he faced the vote on his leadership, Abbott promised wavering South Australian members of parliament that the local Australian Shipbuilding Company would be invited to make a bid for the submarine project. Kevin Andrews, the new defence minister, also announced a 'competitive evaluation process' for the submarine tender. As a consequence, German and French manufacturers were invited to make bids.

The government was faced with a significant international problem when Malaysia Airlines flight MH17 was shot down on 17 July 2014 over eastern Ukraine, an attack blamed on Russian-backed separatists. With 28 Australians and nine permanent residents of Australia among the 298 victims, Canberra issued a strong response. Minister for Foreign Affairs Julie Bishop utilised Australia's non-permanent seat on the UN Security Council to lead the push for the adoption of Resolution 2166, which established an independent international investigation into the crash. Australia's relations with Russia deteriorated in subsequent months over Moscow's refusal to accept responsibility. As a result, Abbott declared his intention to 'shirt-front' Russian President Vladimir Putin at the G20 summit in Brisbane in November 2014. Moscow responded by deploying four warships to the Coral Sea, north of Australia, in a show of force ahead of the meeting.

The summit and its aftermath proved a mixed success for the Abbott government. While the meeting produced some tangible results regarding reforms to the global economy, Australia found itself rather isolated in its attempts to downplay climate change and to defend the coal and fuel industry. German Chancellor Angela Merkel and US President Barack Obama used public speeches on the edges of the summit to indirectly criticise the Australian government's dismissal of climate change. Abbott delivered an address that was criticised for being domestically motivated.

Immediately after the G20 meeting, Abbott hosted a state visit by Chinese President Xi Jinping. In a speech before the Australian parliament,

Xi flagged the potential for a strategic partnership between the two countries, which signed a free-trade agreement. The next day, Abbott welcomed Indian Prime Minister Narendra Modi, marking the first visit by an Indian leader in 20 years. During the trip, Abbott announced the ambitious goal of negotiating a bilateral free-trade agreement within a year, even though experts cautioned against overly high expectations. The Australian government also lent its support to the Chinese-led Asian Infrastructure Investment Bank in March 2015, overriding opposition to the move from Washington.

These developments demonstrated Australia's continuing strategy to 'engage and hedge' – in the words of a government policy document – in the face of Indo-Pacific power shifts. On the one hand, the Abbott government forged closer ties with the emerging Asian giants, China and India, in order to be part of a new regional web of bilateral and multilateral economic relationships. On the other, Canberra remained concerned about China's strategic trajectory and its attempts to change the Asia-Pacific status quo through coercion and intimidation. Indeed, Abbott reportedly identified 'fear and greed' as the two factors driving Australia's approach to China in bilateral talks with Merkel at the G20 summit. As a consequence, the Australian government remained a strong supporter of the US 'rebalance' to Asia, despite the somewhat frosty personal relationship between Abbott and Obama. For instance, during the annual Australia–United States Ministerial Consultations held in Sydney in August 2014, the sides signed a legally binding Force Posture Agreement that provided a policy and legal framework for an enhanced US military presence in northern Australia, including enlarged deployments of US marines. This was complemented by an agreement to strengthen military interoperability and joint contingency planning for missions in the region.

The Australian government also aimed to increase its strategic relationships with several Southeast Asian nations, including Singapore – in many ways, Australia's most developed and trustworthy partner in Southeast Asia. At the eighth meeting of the Singapore–Australia Joint Ministerial Committee, held in Singapore in August 2014, the two countries agreed to further enhance their defence cooperation. Abbott and Singapore Prime Minister Lee Hsien Loong also planned to sign a joint bilateral declaration with a view to a 'comprehensive strategic partnership' in the second half of 2015. Moreover, Australia and Vietnam concluded in March 2015

an 'enhanced comprehensive partnership', which encompassed cooperation on defence and security matters; navigation and aviation security
and safety in the region; and law enforcement and transnational crime.
Canberra was clearly seeking to increase its strategic engagement with
Southeast Asia in the face of Beijing's growing influence.

Closer to home, hopes for improved relations with Indonesia faded
quickly after the election of President Joko Widodo in October 2014. Two
months earlier, Bishop and her Indonesian counterpart Marty Natalegawa
had signed a 'joint understanding of a code of conduct', which committed
their nations to avoiding the use of intelligence assets in ways that would
harm the interests of the other party. The deal was an attempt to repair the
damage done by revelations in November 2013 that, four years earlier, the
Australian intelligence services had tapped the phone calls of Indonesian
President Susilo Bambang Yudhoyono, his wife and political allies.

Shortly after taking office, Widodo pushed for the execution of several
convicted drug smugglers. These included Andrew Chan and Myuran
Sukumaran, Australian nationals who led the 'Bali Nine' group of traffickers. The Abbott government launched a concerted campaign to save
the two men, who had been on death row for almost ten years and had
undertaken extensive rehabilitation efforts. But protests from Australia
and other countries were dismissed by the Indonesian leadership; Chan
and Sukumaran were killed by firing squad on 29 March 2014, alongside
six other prisoners. Abbott, calling it a 'dark moment' in bilateral relations,
recalled the Australian ambassador to Indonesia and suspended ministerial contacts. Canberra also cut almost half of its A$600m (US$460m)
foreign-aid budget to Indonesia. Abbott's promise of an Australian foreign
policy that was 'more Jakarta, less Geneva' had been fulfilled, though not
at all in the way that he had intended.

Abbott's defence policy faced challenges. In light of his leadership
problems and the replacement of Johnston as defence minister, the publication of a defence White Paper was delayed to the second half of 2015.
Moreover, the government did not make significant progress towards
a final decision on three major programmes to replace ageing defence
equipment: *Collins*-class submarines, *Anzac*-class frigates and the army's
armoured fighting vehicles. However, Andrews announced on 1 April
the results of the government's First Principles Review of the defence

organisation, which recommended abolition of the procurement body and streamlining departmental responsibilities. The May 2015 budget increased annual defence spending by 4.2%, from A$30.1bn (US$23.1bn) to A$32.1bn (US$24.6) in 2015–16. This would bring defence spending up to 1.92% of GDP, closer to the government's promise to spend 2% of GDP on defence by 2023. Yet independent analysts pointed out that the extra funding was largely the result of a A$750m (US$575m) rise in spending on military operations and another A$700m (US$536m) to compensate for foreign-exchange fluctuation and the depreciation of the Australian dollar.

Overall, however, the budget was widely interpreted as having turned the political mood in the coalition's favour. The electorate approved of increased spending on childcare and tax cuts for small business: immediately after the announcement, the prime minister and the coalition gained a lead in public-opinion polls. Yet the government had done little to speed the process of deficit repair, and faced the perennial structural problems of an uncooperative Upper House and an economy overly dependent on commodity prices.

Southeast Asia: Major Security Challenges, Political Uncertainties

After an apparent lull during the second half of 2014, China continued to exert pressure on Southeast Asian states' claims to features in the South China Sea, particularly through its rapid construction activities, since early 2015, on some reefs and islets it occupied and the establishment on them of military as well as civilian facilities. This caused varying degrees of consternation among Southeast Asian governments that had a stake in maritime security, and they responded with a range of diplomatic and military measures, including closer security cooperation with the United States and other partners, notably Japan. However, there was little sign of a strong, unified riposte from the Association of Southeast Asian Nations (ASEAN). The association also failed to galvanise a coherent regional response to the crisis provoked by the outflow of Rohingya refugees from Myanmar in early 2015.

Meanwhile, a sense of uncertainty and widespread popular frustration characterised the domestic politics of several Southeast Asian countries. In Myanmar, the still-powerful armed forces' posture towards constitutional amendments, the government's tough responses to internal critics and its uncompromisingly hostile attitude towards Rohingyas, all raised concerns that it was not truly committed to the country's reform process, which did not bode well for the conduct or consequences of national elections scheduled for late 2015. In Thailand, the armed forces consolidated their control of politics and wider society following the coup of 22 May 2014. Against a background of stringent and largely successful efforts to stifle dissent, the military leadership attempted to create a new constitution that would limit the sway of the electorate and thereby help prevent the return to power of political forces controlled by, or allied with, exiled former prime minister Thaksin Shinawatra.

In Malaysia, Prime Minister Najib Tun Razak faced serious criticism from within as well as outside his own party, particularly over the disastrous performance of the 1Malaysia Development Berhad (1MDB) state investment fund. By mid-2015, reports directly implicated Najib in the misuse of 1MDB finances, and it was conceivable, if somewhat unlikely, that he might soon be unseated as party leader and prime minister. However, problems within and among Malaysia's opposition parties suggested that the ruling Barisan Nasional coalition would not face a major challenge before the general election, due by 2018. In Indonesia, Joko Widodo became president in October 2014 on a wave of optimism about his potential as a dynamic leader. But he was challenged by a legislature in which the factionalised Indonesian Democratic Party–Struggle that had backed his candidacy was in a minority, and he soon came under attack for indecisiveness and poor leadership, especially in economics and anti-corruption policy. A new terrorist threat, in the form of Indonesians recruited by the Islamic State of Iraq and al-Sham (ISIS), became prominent, but the reaction of Widodo's administration and its security forces appeared insufficiently firm and coherent to deal with the challenge effectively.

Growing tensions in the South China Sea

During the second half of 2014, it appeared that Beijing might be scaling back its assertiveness in the South China Sea following an international furore over the positioning of a major Chinese oil-drilling platform in waters that Vietnam claimed as part of its exclusive economic zone. In mid-July 2014, the state-owned China National Offshore Oil Corporation announced that the rig had 'completed its work', and it was withdrawn from the disputed area one month earlier than expected.

In 2015, however, the acceleration of China's construction activities on features that it occupied in the South China Sea led to a dramatic escalation of tensions, accentuating concern on the part of the US and other states with security interests in the region, as well as the Southeast Asian countries that contested or were concerned by Beijing's territorial claims there. While China was not alone in enlarging and building on South China Sea features – Malaysia, Taiwan and Vietnam made similar moves – its evidently determined policy focus and mastery of modern dredging technology meant that its land-reclamation activities and building of infrastructure proceeded much faster and on a considerably larger scale than those of other claimants. In the Spratly Islands, China expanded the existing Cuarteron, Fiery Cross, Gaven, Hughes, Johnson South, Mischief and Subi reefs – some of which were originally little more than coral outcrops – into islands, while also enlarging Woody Island in the Paracels group to the north. In total, it was estimated that between early 2014 and mid-2015 China added 2,000 acres (8 square kilometres) to existing features under its control, with most of this activity occurring during the first half of 2015.

Crucially, it also became clear that there was an important military dimension to China's South China Sea construction activities. Beijing established a 3km-long runway capable of supporting military air operations on Fiery Cross Reef; by mid-2015, an apron and taxiway had been added to this airfield, and helipads, satellite-communications antennae and, possibly, a radar tower were also visible in satellite imagery. Another airstrip was under construction on Johnson South Reef, together with a port and surveillance towers, and possibly another runway on Subi Reef. It was widely anticipated among Western and Asian analysts that these facilities would be used to bolster China's claims to features in the South China Sea and control over its waters. There was widespread speculation that the airfields and radars would be used to enforce an eventual Air Defence Identification Zone over at least part of the South China Sea. Some analysts viewed the construction effort as part of a broader strategy in support of long-term strategic purposes that went beyond strengthening Beijing's territorial claims: protecting China's sea lines of communication (and particularly its seaborne energy supplies), as well as deployment areas for its ballistic-missile submarines as the country develops a credible second-strike nuclear deterrent.

While China claimed that the facilities it was building were for peaceful purposes, criticism of its construction activities mounted, particularly from the US. Speaking at a naval conference in Australia in March, Admiral Harry Harris, then commander of the US Pacific Fleet, said that China was 'creating a great wall of sand' in the South China Sea and thereby provoking serious concerns over its intentions. At a change-of-command ceremony in Hawaii in May 2015, Secretary of Defense Ashton Carter emphasised that the US opposed 'any further militarization of disputed features' and would 'fly, sail and operate wherever international law allows'. Earlier in the month, it was reported that Carter had requested that the Pentagon consider expanding US Navy 'freedom of navigation' patrols in the South China Sea, in order to challenge assertions of sovereignty that were not recognised in international law. The US was already using aircraft to challenge China's attempts to control airspace over features that it occupied and had recently enlarged and militarised: in a well-publicised incident the previous week, the Chinese navy had ordered away a US Navy P-8A *Poseidon* maritime-patrol aircraft carrying a television crew as it flew over Fiery Cross Reef at 15,000 feet. In his plenary address to the IISS Shangri-La Dialogue in Singapore at the end of May, Carter said the US was 'deeply concerned about the pace and scope of land reclamation in the South China Sea', as well as about the prospect of further militarisation, and would 'continue to protect freedom of navigation and overflight'.

In an apparent effort to calm such criticism, in June 2015 China's foreign ministry claimed it had almost completed construction on some features. However, this left Beijing leeway to continue – or even to scale up – construction on other reefs or islets, and reports indicated that it was persisting with the establishment of military facilities on Fiery Cross, Johnson South and Subi reefs.

Washington's strengthened security relations

Meanwhile, the US attempted to maintain the momentum of its 'rebalance' to the Asia-Pacific, although some in Southeast Asia and the wider region questioned America's long-term commitment to the task. Implicitly addressing these doubts, Carter told the IISS Shangri-La Dialogue that the 'entire Obama administration and many others in Washington, both Republican and Democrat, are devoted to the rebalance'. As Carter pointed out, as well as bringing some of its newest and best military platforms to the Asia-Pacific, the US was making substantial efforts to develop its alliances and security partnerships throughout the region. However, in reality, complexities at the national political level and in bilateral relations sometimes impeded these efforts. In Southeast Asia, the US was working with the Philippines and Thailand to 'address the evolving threat environment', according to Carter. Yet in the Philippine case, bilateral defence relations were slow to develop. The US had signed a ten-year Enhanced Defense Cooperation Agreement with Manila in April 2014, providing US forces with much wider access to Philippine military facilities, but the following month a challenge to the agreement's legality in the Philippine Supreme Court meant that its implementation was still frozen at mid-2015. Nevertheless, the annual bilateral *Balikatan* military exercise of April 2015 was the largest for 15 years, and – in a clear response to China's pressure in the South China Sea – had a distinct maritime focus. The US also provided support to the National Coast Watch System, intended to improve the Philippines' awareness of the maritime domain.

America's defence relations with Thailand were also less than straightforward. The US was doubtlessly keen to retain the important benefits of its long-standing alliance with Bangkok, including access to Thai facilities for its ships and aircraft. However, following the Thai armed forces' coup in May 2014, Washington cut its military-aid programme and reduced its participation in the annual *Cobra Gold* multinational military exercise, held in February 2015. The US further signalled its discontent with the Thai junta by indefinitely postponing a planning meeting for the 2016 iteration of *Cobra Gold*. Apparently in response to these sanctions, the Thai junta brandished its ostensible openness to closer defence and security relations with China. In November 2014, Deputy Prime Minister Prawit Wongsuwan (who was also defence minister) visited Beijing and agreed that the two countries' armed forces should pursue bilateral air-force cooperation and joint-service exercises. In February, China's defence minister, Chang Wanquan, visited Bangkok and reached agreement with Prawit on defence-technology cooperation and the potential sale of Chinese arms at discounted prices. In April, Xu Qiliang, a vice-chair of China's Central Military Commission, met Thai Prime Minister Prayuth Chan-ocha and discussed intelligence exchanges. In July, Prawit announced that Thailand's navy had approved a plan to purchase three Chinese-built submarines, although this would need cabinet approval. While these developments provoked speculation among regional and international observers that Thailand might be changing its strategic orientation, the more likely reality was that, although Beijing hoped to benefit from the new frostiness in US–Thai relations, Bangkok's flirtation with China represented a gambit by the junta intended to mute Washington's criticism of the suspension of Thailand's democracy.

In June, Carter and his Vietnamese counterpart, General Phung Quang Thanh, signed a Joint Vision Statement on Defense Relations that reinforced an existing 2011 memorandum and called for, among other things, expanded defence-trade and defence-industrial cooperation 'where possible under existing law and policy restrictions'. The statement followed an October 2014 executive order from the US administration that eased restrictions on US defence-equipment sales to Vietnam in order to 'allow for the future transfer of maritime security-related defense articles' in support of Vietnam's 'efforts to improve its maritime domain awareness and maritime security capabilities'. Prior to this, only non-lethal equipment could be supplied.

Nguyen Phu Trong, secretary-general of the Communist Party of Vietnam, visited Washington amid much fanfare in July 2015 to mark the 20th anniversary of normalised ties between Hanoi and Washington, representing a new high point in bilateral relations. However, the optimistic statements on bilateral relations made in Washington by him and his host, Vice President Joe Biden, papered over significant constraints on expanded security cooperation. In the defence sphere, Vietnam wanted above all the benefit of US military equipment and technology as it reinforced its maritime deterrent capabilities, in the face of a long-term challenge from Beijing to Vietnamese claims in the South China Sea. Hanoi particularly needed to bolster its capabilities in long-range maritime air patrol, and was evidently interested in acquiring ex-US Navy P-3 *Orion* or perhaps even the new-build P-8 *Poseidon* aircraft. But even the revised US policy on arms sales to Vietnam essentially allowed only the transfer of defensive systems: although the US was assisting the development of Vietnam's coastguard, it had not been able to significantly enhance the capacity of the armed forces. Hanoi had lobbied at a high level in Washington for the removal of International Traffic in Arms Regulations restrictions on US arms transfers, but the Obama administration's decision to couple a lifting of these rules with improvements in Vietnam's respect for human rights and religious freedom remained a significant obstacle. One important consequence of the continuing embargo was that it seemed unlikely Hanoi would grant US forces wider access to the Cam Ranh Bay naval base and other Vietnamese facilities, as sought by the Pentagon.

Largely because of their concerns over Chinese activities in the South China Sea, Indonesia and Malaysia were willing to acquiesce in incrementally closer defence and security relations with the US, but these links were still constrained in both cases by long-established habits of non-alignment, suspicion of American motives and domestic political sensitivities, as well as the need to maintain important political and economic relations with China. In January 2015, the US and the new Indonesian administration led by Joko Widodo agreed on an 'action plan' to expand bilateral military cooperation, which already involved more than 500 exchanges, exercises and other joint activities annually. Yet apart from Widodo's announcement of a rather vague 'Global Maritime Nexus' doctrine in November 2014, Jakarta's strategic direction remained unclear, and it was evident that foreign relations were no longer being prioritised to the extent that they had been under the previous president, Susilo Bambang Yudhoyono. A visit by Widodo to Washington, originally planned for June 2015, was postponed for unknown reasons.

The US made more progress in its defence and security relations with Malaysia, whose concern over Beijing's operations in the South China Sea had been heightened by several major incursions into the Malaysian exclusive economic zone by Chinese naval and maritime-surveillance vessels. In June 2015, Malaysia's government confirmed that a ship from the Chinese coastguard had anchored only 135km off the coast of the Malaysian state of Sarawak. As well as developing its maritime capabilities and working with other Southeast Asian claimants to coordinate positions in relation to the South China Sea, Malaysia intensified its military cooperation with the US.

Most visibly, in June 2014 the US Air Force deployed F-22 stealth fighters to Southeast Asia for the first time, to take part in an exercise with Malaysia's air force, and in May 2015 a US Navy carrier strike group joined Malaysian navy and air-force units for a bilateral exercise in the South China Sea.

Meanwhile, US defence and security relations with Singapore continued to intensify. Crucially, the city state provided an increasingly important US Navy forward operating location (effectively a base, although this term was not used due to Singapore's concerns over its potentially adverse impact on relations with neighbouring countries and with China). As well as hosting a major US Navy logistics command and accommodating visiting carrier strike groups, Singapore provided facilities for the 'rotational deployment' of littoral combat ships such as the USS *Fort Worth*, which arrived at Changi naval base in December 2014 to begin a 16-month tour of duty in the region. According to the US Navy, by 2017 as many as four such vessels might be operating out of Singapore simultaneously.

While seeking to develop its bilateral security relations with Southeast Asian allies and partners, the US simultaneously attempted to foster greater unity of purpose among its regional interlocutors through multilateral initiatives. More than ever, the US recognised the potential of ASEAN as a platform for brokering common responses to regional security challenges. Carter announced that the US would add a 'defense advisor' to its diplomatic mission to the ASEAN Secretariat in Jakarta, and would step up its commitment to the ASEAN Defence Ministers' Meeting–Plus series of discussions. The US also attempted to foster cooperation among its regional partners through multinational military exercises such as the annual RIMPAC event. In addition, Carter said the US would launch a new initiative aimed at building maritime capacity in Southeast Asia.

Japan as a security partner

As concerned Southeast Asian states sought appropriate responses to Beijing's escalating assertiveness in the South China Sea, some were also willing to develop their security relations with Japan, which, facing its own challenge from China, sought to make common cause with them. A major concern for Tokyo – deriving particularly from its dependence on seaborne energy supplies – was to ensure that Southeast Asian waters, including the South China Sea, remained open to international shipping.

The most important avenues for Tokyo's efforts to bolster its relations with Southeast Asian countries have been the promotion of Japanese investment and aid: by 2014, more than 10% of Japan's foreign direct investment was going to Indonesia, Malaysia, the Philippines, Thailand and Vietnam; and at a December 2013 summit meeting to mark 40 years of Japan–ASEAN relations, Prime Minister Shinzo Abe promised US$19.4 billion in aid and loans to Southeast Asia over the following five years. In the security sphere, Japan focused on boosting the paramilitary maritime capabilities of the Philippines and Vietnam and, to a lesser extent, Indonesia and Malaysia. Ten new patrol boats, the purchase of which was supported by a soft loan from the Japan International Cooperation Agency, were due to be delivered to the Philippine Coast Guard from late 2015, boosting its limited capacity for operations in the South China Sea. The agency also provided a grant to modernise communications between the coastguard's headquarters, regional offices and vessels. In August 2014, Tokyo agreed to supply six vessels and radars as part of an aid package for Vietnam's coastguard and fishery-protection force. In February 2015, Japan announced a new Development Cooperation Charter, which will make it possible for the country to supply foreign armed forces with military aid for non-combat purposes. It was expected that Tokyo would view Southeast Asia as a key destination for such assistance.

The relaxation of Japan's long-standing, self-imposed ban on arms exports in April 2014 opened up new possibilities for Tokyo in its efforts to broaden security cooperation with Southeast Asian partners. In November 2014, Toru Hotchi, director of the Japanese defence ministry's new equipment-policy division, agreed with Indonesian defence officials to expand cooperation on equipment procurement. Visiting a Philippine naval base in January 2015, Hotchi said that bilateral collaboration on military equipment was 'highly important'. It seemed likely that Japan might begin making significant equipment transfers to Southeast Asian armed forces within the next few years, perhaps starting with second-hand ships or aircraft from its own forces.

Regional crises challenge ASEAN

Even as several ASEAN members perceived increasing challenges from China's behaviour in the South China Sea, and despite the fact that 2015 was the year in which the association was due to establish an 'ASEAN Community' including an important politico-security component, the organisation continued to have difficulty asserting a strong and united position on this and other important security matters. A typically bland chairman's statement was issued by the ASEAN leaders' summit in November 2014, under Myanmar's chairmanship; the document focused on the process rather than the substance of regional cooperation. On the South China Sea, it only mentioned that ASEAN leaders 'remained concerned', while welcoming both 'positive progress' towards implementing the Declaration on the Conduct of Parties in the South China Sea (DoC) agreed by China and ASEAN in 2002, and an agreement to work towards early conclusion of the Code of Conduct itself. There was also ASEAN consensus on the need to 'intensify consultations with China' on implementing the DoC and concluding the Code of Conduct.

However, as China stepped up its island-building activities in early 2015, there were signs of an incremental strengthening of resolve within ASEAN. With Malaysia chairing, the ASEAN summit of April 2015 issued a stronger statement, mentioning 'the serious concerns expressed by some leaders on the land reclamation ... in the South China Sea, which has eroded trust and confidence and may undermine peace, security and stability'. While not directly accusing China, the statement mentioned that ASEAN leaders had 'instructed our foreign ministers to urgently address this matter', including through ASEAN–China mechanisms. It also indicated impatience over the slow progress towards implementing the Code of Conduct, urging that 'consultations be intensified' to ensure its 'expeditious establishment', while reiterating the importance of freedom of navigation and overflight. This statement brought a rebuke from Beijing's foreign ministry, which claimed to be 'gravely concerned', and stated that there was no need for ASEAN to uphold peace and security because China's actions posed no threat to these principles. In an apparent attempt to divide the grouping, China's response alleged that 'a few countries [were] taking hostage the entire ASEAN and China–ASEAN relations'.

A new challenge arose for ASEAN's security role in early 2015, in relation to the outflow by sea of Rohingya refugees and Bangladeshi economic migrants from Myanmar. Discrimination and violence directed at the Rohingya ethnic minority in Myanmar's Rakhine State – where more than

800,000 people had been denied citizenship and approximately 140,000 were housed in government-designated camps following inter-communal attacks in 2012 – led the United Nations to report in August 2014 that more than 310,000 people in the state needed humanitarian assistance. These severe conditions led an estimated 58,000 refugees to depart the Myanmar–Bangladesh borderlands by sea during 2014. It was reported that Myanmar's security forces took payments from criminals involved in trafficking Rohingyas and even escorted refugee boats out to sea.

The trafficking network, which had existed for several years and had been partially exposed by journalists and non-governmental organisations as early as 2013, included camps in Thailand and Malaysia. There, thousands of Rohingyas had been held for ransom, used as forced labour, beaten, starved, raped and sometimes murdered, all with the complicity of local officials and security personnel in both countries. In June 2014, after the US government downgraded Thailand to the lowest category (Tier 3) in its annual *Trafficking in Persons Report*, which highlighted 'reports that corrupt Thai civilian and military officials profited from the smuggling of Rohingya asylum seekers', the newly installed military regime in Bangkok radically changed Thailand's policy on the matter. In January, Thai police stopped a convoy of trucks carrying around 100 malnourished Rohingyas, some of whom were dying. This incident led the Thai police to telephone records that allowed them to gain a better understanding of the trafficking network. In April, police arrested an alleged key figure in the network, along with three complicit local officials; in May, they uncovered a camp where as many as 400 Rohingyas and Bangladeshis had been held captive. While the traffickers had already evacuated the site, the police found more than 30 bodies in shallow graves nearby. During May and June, police arrested suspects connected to the network, including a three-star army general who had commanded a military operation aimed at disrupting the flow of refugees and migrants.

Most Rohingya refugees – and Bangladeshi economic migrants, who were trafficked using the same routes and means of transport – sought to reach Malaysia, where the authorities had for many years effectively accommodated this unregulated migration as it helped to address the country's labour shortage. However, in May Malaysia's most senior police officer revealed that his force had discovered approximately 30 abandoned traffickers' camps on the Malaysian side of the border, as well as at least 139 nearby grave sites.

The Thai and Malaysian clampdowns on trafficking inadvertently provoked a major regional human-security crisis. With trafficking routes across the land border between Thailand and Malaysia disrupted, around 7,000 Rohingyas and Bangladeshis were stranded on boats at sea, some being held hostage and others abandoned. International attention to their plight increased in May 2015: as Indonesia, Malaysia and Thailand initially refused to allow the crowded refugee boats to make landfall, the countries' security forces repeatedly pushed them out to sea in what Human Rights Watch Asia termed a 'three-way game of human ping pong'. Nevertheless, in mid-May, around 3,000 of the migrants reached the shores of Indonesia (many of them due to assistance from Acehnese fishermen) and Malaysia. The role of ASEAN in mitigating the unfolding crisis was notable by its absence, despite the association's rhetorical emphasis on human-security concerns in the context of the soon-to-be-established ASEAN Community.

Nevertheless, under immense international pressure, there was eventually a flurry of diplomatic activity in the region – if not under the auspices of ASEAN – and, on 20 May, the Indonesian, Malaysian and Thai foreign ministers met in Malaysia to discuss the crisis. As a result, Indonesia and Malaysia abandoned their policies of turning away boats carrying Rohingyas and Bangladeshis. The level of tension among Southeast Asian governments was evident in the failure of General Tanasak Patimapragorn, Thai minister of foreign affairs, to join his two counterparts for a press conference. But, on 29 May, Thailand convened an international Special Meeting on Irregular Migration in the Indian Ocean, which involved 17 regional states together with representatives from international organisations, including the UN High Commissioner for Refugees, and Japan and the US as observers. Crucially, Indonesia and Malaysia agreed at this conference to continue providing humanitarian assistance and, in due course, temporary shelter to the 7,000 migrants still believed to be at sea, 'provided that the resettlement and repatriation process will be done in one year by the international community'.

The special meeting provided only an inconclusive response to the challenge presented by Rohingya refugees. As long as the poor conditions in Rakhine State and camps across the border in Bangladesh persisted, it seemed almost certain that the Rohingyas would attempt to flee to the relative safety of other Southeast Asian countries. The recommendations of the special meeting included an attempt to address 'root causes' of the exodus, 'capacity building of local communities' and other socio-economic measures in the 'areas of origin', as well as 'full respect for human rights' there. But they carefully avoided any direct mention of Myanmar or use of the term 'Rohingyas', which Myanmar's government did not recognise. Naypyidaw's position was that the great majority of the seaborne migrants were Bangladeshis, and that criminal trafficking rather than conditions in Myanmar was the root cause. Some Southeast Asian governments were willing to disagree openly with this view. In May, Singaporean Foreign Minister K. Shanmugam stated that ASEAN needed not only to play a more active role in responding to the problem, but also to deal with conditions inside Myanmar and the criminal organisations involved in trafficking. Wan Junaidi Tuanku Jaafar, Malaysia's deputy home affairs minister, said the rest of Southeast Asia should send a 'very strong message' to Myanmar's leaders that 'they need to treat their people with humanity', arguing that the refugee problem was due in large part to Naypyidaw's mistreatment of Rohingyas. The issue was set to be an important topic for discussion, and possibly a cause of division, at future ASEAN meetings.

Myanmar: Uncertain future

The Rohingya crisis was only one of several adverse developments involving Myanmar, indicating that the country's reform process was not proceeding as smoothly towards democracy as many had expected in 2010–12. During that period, opposition leader Aung San Suu Kyi was released from house arrest, a nominally civilian government led by former general Thein Sein took office, and Aung San Suu Kyi's National League for Democracy (NLD) was allowed to contest by-elections, which it won decisively.

Concerns over media freedom came to the fore, particularly in July 2014, when four journalists and their chief executive were sent to jail over a report they had published on an alleged chemical-weapons factory. Moreover, the violent dispersal in March 2015 of a month-long protest by students in Letpadan, in Bago Region – who were angered by the new National Education Law, which they claimed imposed limits on academic

freedom – also appeared to indicate that President Thein Sein's government was less than wholeheartedly committed to the reform process. More
than 100 protesters faced criminal charges for 'unlawful assembly', and the
authorities intimidated those who spoke out in support of the students, as
well as journalists who attempted to report on the demonstration.

There were also looming questions about amendments to the constitution. In June 2015, Myanmar's parliament voted to reject five of six proposed
major amendments that the previous, overtly military, regime had put in
place in 2008. The only amendment that was accepted was a requirement
for presidential and vice-presidential candidates to be well acquainted
with 'defence' rather than 'military' matters. Among the amendments
that the legislature blocked was a measure that would have removed the
armed forces' effective veto over future constitutional changes by reducing the minimum necessary level of parliamentary approval from 75% to
70%. The parliament also failed to amend the constitution's Clause 59(f),
which disbars anyone who has or has had a foreign spouse or children
from becoming the country's president – a device intended to prevent
Aung San Suu Kyi (whose late husband was British, as are her two sons)
from leading the country. This obstacle raised the possibility that the NLD
might boycott the national election in November, thereby depriving the
party of credibility both within the country and internationally. However,
in mid-July Aung San Suu Kyi confirmed that the NLD would contest
the election in order to 'continue the unfinished democratisation process
for the country', with national reconciliation the first priority. The NLD's
de facto leader said that if the party won the election, it would 'make an
arrangement for [a] presidency which the people can accept'.

Yet the extent of the NLD's success in the elections was inherently
unpredictable: while the opposition movement had huge support (in
large part because of Aung San Suu Kyi's charisma and popularity), the
military-backed Union Solidarity and Development Party seemed likely
to receive considerable backing from those employed by the state, while
numerous ethnic-minority parties around Myanmar's periphery appeared
almost certain to win in their own regions. Even in the event of a landslide victory by the NLD, negotiations between the main political forces
would be necessary following the election. In particular, it was unclear
how the Tatmadaw (Myanmar's armed forces) might play their hand in

these negotiations: it remained to be seen whether they would be willing to relinquish their role as the country's political arbiter.

Nevertheless, it was clear that the November 2015 elections would be a turning point for Myanmar's politics. A decisive NLD victory might lead the armed forces to facilitate a rapid constitutional amendment that would, after all, allow Aung San Suu Kyi to become president. In any scenario, it seemed likely that she would have an important role to play in the formation of a new government, even if she could not become president immediately. For this reason, it was not altogether surprising that in June 2015 she was invited to Beijing, where she had a meeting with Chinese President Xi Jinping in which they spoke positively about their countries' bilateral relationship.

If the Tatmadaw allowed the formation of a new government over which it had less direct influence, any subsequent effort at national reconciliation would need to prioritise the relationship between the central political authority and the regions dominated by ethnic minorities, mainly in Myanmar's east and southeast. Since late 2013, the government and ethnic armed groups (EAGs), which had mounted long-running insurgencies in these areas, had been negotiating a nationwide ceasefire agreement (NCA). In February 2015, they made an important step towards this objective when Thein Sein signed a 'deed of commitment for peace and national reconciliation', initially with four EAGs representing the Karen and Shan minorities, committing the government to 'a union based on democratic and federal principles'. At the end of March, 16 EAGs signed a draft NCA with the government, but only after the points that had previously impeded progress had been deferred to the planned 'political dialogue' of the peace process. However, in June the leaders of the EAGs rejected the draft NCA agreed by their negotiators. The leaders proposed 12 amendments that would need to be negotiated with the government, and decided that none of their groups should accede to an eventual NCA unless there was unanimity among them. They also concluded that additional EAGs, including those still fighting the government, should be allowed to join the agreement. Furthermore, they proposed that the current group of observers at the talks (China, Japan and the UN) should be joined by ASEAN, India, Norway, Thailand, the United Kingdom and the US. This development virtually ensured that the NCA could not be signed before the

November election; increased the likelihood of conflict before, during and after the polls; and raised the prospect that the government might prohibit voting in some areas due to security concerns.

There was sporadic fighting between EAGs and the Tatmadaw, which carried on offensive operations in violation of existing ceasefire arrangements. The Tatmadaw used artillery against a Kachin Independence Army (KIA) camp in November 2014, killing 23 trainees from various EAGs, leading to the postponement of peace talks and to the KIA temporarily reducing its participation in them. In December, at least seven Tatmadaw soldiers were killed in a clash with the Myanmar National Democratic Alliance Army (MNDAA), which comprised mainly ethnic-Chinese insurgents, in northern Shan State. Apparently due to the build-up of government troops in areas nominally controlled by the insurgents, the heaviest fighting for two years broke out in February 2015, when the MNDAA, supported by the Ta'ang National Liberation Army and the Arakan Army, attacked the Tatmadaw in the Kokang Special Region of northeastern Shan State, close to the Chinese border. The Tatmadaw used ground-attack aircraft during this fighting, and in mid-March accidentally bombed Chinese territory, killing four people. Myanmar's ambassador was summoned for a reprimand from the Chinese government, and Beijing deployed fighter aircraft to protect China's airspace against further incursions. Clashes involving the KIA also increased and, in June, there was heavy fighting in northern Kachin State.

Thailand: Military rule

Led by army commander-in-chief General Prayuth Chan-ocha, the military junta that came to power in Thailand following a May 2014 coup seemed unlikely to effect a quick return to democracy. Known as the National Council for Peace and Order (NCPO), the junta had by mid-2015 tightened its control of the country by employing a degree of authoritarianism unseen since the 1970s. In July 2014, an interim constitution came into force. This charter broadly reflected the demands on the previous government made by the 'Yellow Shirt' protesters, who had called for an unelected council of 'good people' to enact reforms that would erase the influence of former prime minister Thaksin Shinawatra and his proxies (including his sister, Yingluck Shinawatra, who had been prime minister from 2011 until two weeks before the coup). Among the document's main points were the establishment of: an appointed parliament, the National Legislative Assembly (NLA); a provisional cabinet to run the country on a day-to-day basis; a National Reform Council to oversee extensive reforms and approve the draft of a new permanent constitution; and a 'constituent committee' – later known as the Constitution Drafting Committee (CDC) – to draw up a new permanent constitution.

Through its Article 44, the interim constitution gave the NCPO a vast remit and draconian powers, empowering its leader to issue any order for the sake of the reforms in any field, the promotion of love and harmony amongst the people in the nation, or the prevention, abatement or suppression of any act detrimental to national order or security, royal throne, national economy or public administration, whether the act occurs inside or outside the kingdom.

It deemed all such NCPO orders 'lawful, constitutional and final', and pre-emptively granted amnesty for all acts – past or future – linked to the military regime. The interim constitution had no time limitation, and public discussion of it was banned.

At the end of July 2014, Thailand's king approved the NCPO's nominations of the 200 members of the NLA, who included 106 active and retired senior military officers, 32 senior civil servants and ten senior police officers, with the remainder comprising former senators, academics and business leaders who had opposed Yingluck's government. Then, in a development that had been widely anticipated despite his earlier disavowals of interest in the post, in late August 2014 the NLA unanimously voted in Prayuth as prime minister; he assumed the position several days later. In this wider role, Prayuth – who explained NCPO policies in a folksy and direct manner during lengthy appearances on his own television programme every Friday evening – boosted his popularity with the minority of the population that had backed the anti-Yingluck protests and the subsequent coup, particularly the middle class and lower-middle class in the capital, Bangkok, and surrounding areas. With opposition forces cowed by a series of repressive measures, including selective arrests of political-party leaders and activists in the weeks following the coup, there was little overt resistance to military rule. Although the NCPO ended martial law in April 2015, it immediately introduced Order No. 3/2558, which invoked Article 44 of the interim constitution to impose even harsher restrictions on civil liberties and media freedom.

The evident reluctance of Thaksin (who lived in exile in Dubai) to mobilise the 'Red Shirt' forces still loyal to him, particularly in the north and northeast of the country, provoked much speculation inside Thailand and internationally. Possible explanations ranged from his concern not to avoid irredeemably losing the massive assets that a Thai court confiscated from him in 2010 to concern over the well-being of Yingluck and other family members who remained in Thailand. In March, the Supreme Court ordered Yingluck to stand trial for negligence in relation to her government's poorly conceived rice-subsidy scheme, which cost it billions of dollars, and for which she had been retroactively impeached in January. Yingluck's trial began in May, and she pleaded not guilty. The next hearing was originally due to take place in July, but after the former prime minister appealed for more time to submit evidence, the court set 31 August as the resumption date. Despite Thaksin's avoidance of confrontation, there was no evidence that the junta was able to win significant support from the majority of the population, which would evidently lose substantial political influence if the NCPO's essentially anti-democratic reform agenda became the basis for a new permanent constitution.

The NCPO initially indicated that the new constitution would take effect from July 2015, with elections following approximately three months later. However, in December 2014 Deputy Prime Minister Wissanu Kreangam said that the election could not be held until February 2016 at the earliest, as the draft of the new constitution would not be finalised until September, following which the NLA would take three months to formulate the necessary constitutional laws, and the Election Commission would subsequently need 60–90 days to prepare for the poll. If there was to be a popular referendum on the constitution, the election would be further delayed to May 2016. In the event, the CDC completed its first constitutional draft in mid-April 2015, declaring that the new charter was intended to lead Thailand 'out of cycles of conflicts, disunity and undemocratic fights'. But in reality, it appeared to be designed above all to prevent any group loyal to Thaksin from taking power, and included provisions for an unelected prime minister; the application of proportional representation, which would dilute the strength of major parties; a lower house of parliament that would only be partially directly elected; the appointment rather than election of most Senate members; and the creation of new institutions to promote 'reform and reconciliation' on a continuing basis. This draft met with much criticism and, in total, the National Reform Council, the cabinet and the NCPO proposed more than 100 changes to the draft, which was returned to the CDC for revision. But it seemed likely that the CDC would accept only some of the proposed amendments, and that the final draft – due to be completed by the end of August – would still attempt to reduce substantially the power of the electorate.

In May, Wissanu announced a further delay to the election schedule. So as to allow a referendum on the draft constitution, possibly in January 2016, he said that the election could not be held until August 2016 at the earliest. Yet with no guarantee that the referendum would approve the new constitution – which, if rejected, would need to be revised and submitted to a new referendum, thereby further delaying the election – there were prospects of continuing political uncertainty, and possibly renewed conflict amid growing frustration with the military dictatorship. In response, the NCPO clamped down hard on even minor expressions of dissent – for example, by detaining 14 protesters from the New Democracy Group, most of them students, whom the leadership said would be tried in a military court. Although they were released on bail in early July, the charges of sedition made against them were not dropped.

The imposition of military rule in Thailand did little to quell the long-running insurgency by ethnic-Malay nationalists in the far south of the country, despite concerted efforts by the new regime to resolve the problem. There was a fall in the number of casualties resulting from the insurgency in the year to mid-2015, largely because of intensified counter-insurgency operations by the government, but drive-by shootings and improvised explosive devices continued to claim lives and cause injuries. Following the suspension of peace negotiations between late 2013 and July 2014 due to Thailand's political disarray, the NCPO moved to restart its talks with representatives of the insurgents. In August, Prayuth issued orders for the talks to be broadened to include insurgent groups other than Barisan Revolusi Nasional (BRN), theretofore the only participant from the rebel side. In October, General Aksara Kerdphol was confirmed as the government's chief negotiator, and the NCPO announced that it would look again at five key demands – including granting sovereignty to the southernmost provinces – that the BRN had made in 2013. Prawit Wongsuwan, deputy prime minister and minister of defence, stated in November that the government would 'try to bring peace within a year' to southern Thailand. In December, Malaysia was confirmed as the mediator for the next round of talks, but the Thai and Malaysian prime ministers jointly stipulated that the negotiations could only resume if rebel groups agreed to a ceasefire. During early 2015, Thailand and Malaysia pooled their intelligence on insurgent groups, with a view to deciding which groups to invite to the next round of talks. In March, Thailand's Internal Security Operations Command announced that the talks would resume in April or May with three factions of the Pattani United Liberation Organisation (PULO), as well as the BRN. By the end of June 2015, however, dialogue between Bangkok and the southern insurgents had still not resumed. Thai security sources complained of persistent difficulties in bringing the rebels back into the talks, despite conducting a meeting in Kuala Lumpur earlier that month with representatives of MARA Patani, an umbrella organisation for six insurgent groups, which focused on a proposed truce during Ramadan. While there was no agreement on this, more than 470 insurgents stated that they would participate in a programme that granted them temporary immunity from arrest so that they could join their families during Ramadan.

Malaysia: Politics of disarray

Malaysia's politics appeared to enter a less stable era. In early 2015, the country's economic growth slowed due to low oil prices and reduced exports to China, necessitating unpopular measures such as spending cuts. Reflecting a relationship that had become increasingly acrimonious since the poor performance of the ruling United Malays National Organisation (UMNO) in the 2013 general election, Mahathir Mohamad, the 89-year-old former prime minister who had helped Najib Tun Razak become the country's premier in 2009, attacked his former protégé. In a blog post published in April, Mahathir called for the reopening of investigations into the 2006 killing of a Mongolian woman, an incident in which Najib's police bodyguards had been implicated. Mahathir also raised questions about the troubled state investment fund set up and chaired by Najib, 1MDB, which had accumulated debts of US$11bn; and criticised the government's purchase of a new luxury aircraft for use by the prime minister. According to Mahathir, Malaysians no longer trusted Najib, and the UMNO-led coalition government would lose the next general election if he remained prime minister.

During May, Najib used his own blog to hit back at Mahathir and other critics. But his troubles worsened in early July, when the *Wall Street Journal* released documents online, supposedly from a Malaysian government probe into 1MDB. These included a diagram that illustrated alleged transfers of funds into a bank account in Najib's name prior to the 2013 general election. The newspaper reported an unnamed investigator as claiming that almost US$700 million in 1MDB funds had been transferred into Najib's personal accounts. Najib denied the allegations, pledged to continue shouldering his responsibilities as prime minister and began legal moves against the *Wall Street Journal*. But a 'special task force' was quickly formed to investigate the allegations, and Singapore – where a branch of a private Swiss bank had allegedly facilitated the transfers – agreed to cooperate in the probe. The accusations were sufficiently serious that, if found to be accurate, they might lead to Najib's political downfall, and there was speculation about who might replace him as prime minister. However, it seemed more likely that Najib would survive the scandal, as he had others in the past, albeit with his standing further undermined. Despite having Mahathir's backing, Najib's opponents within the UMNO probably lacked sufficient support within the party to oust him, and it was possible that even the investigation into the affair was being stage-managed.

The Malaysian opposition also faced internal challenges. In February, Anwar Ibrahim, the former deputy prime minister who had created a broad-based opposition party, the Parti Keadilan Rakyat (PKR), was jailed once again on charges of sodomy. The case appeared to result from proceedings initiated by the Najib government to cripple the Pakatan Rakyat opposition coalition, which included the Democratic Action Party (DAP) and Parti Islam Se-Malaysia (PAS), as well as the PKR, which had won the majority of the popular vote in the 2013 general election. As well as serving a five-year sentence, the 67-year-old Anwar would also be barred from politics until 2025. He had previously been imprisoned on similar charges for six years, but that conviction was eventually overturned. His daughter, Nurul Izzah Anwar, a member of parliament and the PKR vice-president, assumed a leading role in protests against his new conviction. In March, Anwar's wife, Wan Azizah Wan Ismail, who led the Pakatan Rakyat coalition, easily won a by-election for Anwar's vacated parliamentary seat. But while it remained possible that, even in jail, Anwar would remain a unifying force for the opposition, his absence from politics came as a setback at a time when the tensions among Pakatan Rakyat's disparate constituent parties were more obvious than ever.

The largest dispute among the parties was between the DAP, a liberal party supported mainly by ethnic-Chinese Malaysians, and the PAS, a conservative Islamist organisation primarily representing the interests of rural Malays. The two parties differed greatly on a range of issues, but most importantly the aim of the PAS to enact *hudud* law (the criminal dimension of sharia), initially in Kelantan, where it controlled the state government, but potentially throughout Malaysia. The death, only days after Anwar was jailed, of Nik Abdul Aziz Nik Mat, the PAS spiritual leader and the most prominent advocate of the coalition within his party, diminished its will to compromise with the DAP. In mid-June, after the PAS congress voted to sever ties with the DAP, the DAP reciprocated and the coalition formally disbanded. Nevertheless, there were still links between the three opposition parties, particularly at a grassroots level, and it seemed likely that a new opposition grouping, excluding the PAS but perhaps including other parties, might form before the next general election.

Indonesia: Disappointment sets in

Following his election victory in October 2014, Joko Widodo, widely known as 'Jokowi' – a former furniture maker who had been mayor of the provincial Javanese city of Solo, and then mayor of the capital, Jakarta – was sworn in as Indonesia's seventh president, riding on a wave of popularity and optimism that his leadership would be transformative. Widodo was Indonesia's first president from a humble background, and his simple, straight-talking campaign approach had endeared him to tens of millions of ordinary people who expected him to promote their interests. Yet his initial performance as president was widely viewed as unimpressive, and by March 2015 polling indicated that his popularity had quickly slumped, with almost three-quarters of respondents indicating their dissatisfaction with his leadership. During his first weeks in power, Widodo appeared decisive. In November, his administration rapidly implemented some of his campaign promises, including an education- and healthcare-subsidy programme to assist poor Indonesians; simultaneously, the new president fulfilled his commitment to reduce fuel subsidies, thereby releasing government funds.

The main cause of the decline in Widodo's popularity was a controversy over his nomination of General Budi Gunawan to lead Indonesia's national police force. The move was widely interpreted as an effort to please the president's political patron, former president Megawati Sukarnoputri, who led the Indonesian Democratic Party–Struggle and with whom Gunawan was known to be close. The widely trusted Corruption Eradication Commission (KPK) revealed that it was investigating Gunawan for graft, and asked Widodo to withdraw his support for the general. In retaliation for its attempt to prevent Gunawan's appointment, the police arrested three of the five KPK commissioners on suspicion of offences including perjury and graft, leading Widodo to suspend them. Although the KPK investigation continued and Gunawan was charged with corruption, a district court ruled that the KPK lacked jurisdiction, and temporary commissioners installed by the president decided to abandon the case against the general, clearing the way for his appointment as deputy national police chief in late April. The episode created deep unease among Indonesians who had voted for Widodo, as it revealed not only his lack of commitment to anti-corruption measures (one of the key elements of his campaign) but also his apparent political weakness and, more specifically, his dependence on Megawati's support. If Widodo did not perform more effectively, there was a danger that he might be abandoned by the civil-society activists who had helped bring him to power.

Since the Bali bombings of 2002, Indonesia's authorities had mounted a broadly successful campaign, with considerable international support, against terrorist groups in the country, particularly the pan-Southeast Asian Jemaah Islamiah. Nevertheless, during 2014 it became increasingly evident that Indonesia was an important recruiting ground for ISIS, and that significant numbers of Indonesians had travelled or were planning to travel to the Middle East to fight with the group. In July 2014,

Abu Bakar Bashir, the Indonesian cleric who inspired the earlier generation of Southeast Asians to join Jemaah Islamiah, joined other imprisoned
jihadists in pledging allegiance to ISIS, and it was reported that thousands
had participated in oath-taking ceremonies across Indonesia. Estimates
of the number of Indonesians who had gone to fight with ISIS ranged
from the 202 documented by the Institute for Policy Analysis of Conflict,
an independent organisation based in Jakarta, to the Indonesian government's figure of more than 500. It was estimated that 35–40 Indonesians
had been killed while fighting with ISIS. Around 30 Malaysians and five
Singaporeans were thought to have also joined ISIS. In March 2015, it
was reported that Indonesians and other Southeast Asians with ISIS had
formed their own unit based in Ar-Raqqa, in Syria. A smaller number of
Indonesians, perhaps 20, had joined Jabhat al-Nusra, a rival armed group
affiliated with al-Qaeda.

In the short term, ISIS did not pose a major direct threat to Indonesia's
security. But a serious problem might develop in several years' time if
Indonesian and other Southeast Asian fighters returned home, having
acquired extensive combat experience as well as bomb-making knowledge and other technical skills. In the meantime, while the Indonesian
authorities demonstrated their awareness of the threat from ISIS, the implementation of counter-terrorism policy seemed somewhat convoluted. In
his final State of the Union address, delivered in August 2014, then-presi-
dent Yudhoyono spoke of the need to defend pluralistic 'Indonesian-ness'
against the 'misguided concept' of ISIS. Yet as Coordinating Minister for
Political, Legal and Security Affairs Tedjo Edhy Purdijatno stated in March
2015, after the authorities arrested five people who had allegedly intended
to join the group, the government had 'not explicitly declared [ISIS] as
illegal'. Therefore, it was impossible to charge people who wanted to
join it. In March and April, Indonesia's armed forces supported a police
counter-terrorism operation in Poso, in central Sulawesi, an area known to
contain jihadist training camps. However, the operation failed to achieve
one of its main objectives, capturing Santoso, a local terrorist-cell leader
who was believed to be affiliated with ISIS. Institutional rivalries between
Indonesia's security forces probably detracted from the operation's effectiveness: the police were concerned that the army intended to take back
the internal security role that it had relinquished in 1999, when the police

was separated from the armed forces. In June, the armed forces established a new joint-service counter-terrorism unit, thereby exacerbating concerns over competition between the military and the police in dealing with a terrorist threat that seemed likely to grow in the future.

Chapter 12

Prospectives

Strategic unease is the defining feature of the international security climate. Western leaders cling to the 'rules-based order' their predecessors created and on which they consider global stability to rest. Yet that order is being challenged. 'Rule breaking' is not being effectively deterred. Facts on the ground, sea, air and in cyberspace are being created that confront, rather than reinforce, established norms. The European security order has been rocked by a self-confident Russian leadership that, despite being subjected to heavy international sanctions, has asserted its regional national interests with vigour. Europeans previously safely tethered to the US superpower are now being invited to take up more responsibility for their own security given the American rebalance to Asia and residual firefighting tasks in the Middle East. China has methodically asserted its claims in the South China Sea (as have other claimant states), and backed these up with the development, in some cases, of militarily relevant installations. Unconvinced of the competence or fairness of Western financial institutions, China's creation of the Asian Infrastructure Investment Bank (AIIB) points to a desire to design some of its own architecture, with its own rules. An altogether new challenge has come in the shape of the Islamic State of Iraq and al-Sham (ISIS), which has been able to seize and hold territory as well as minds in the Middle East and way beyond. Wielding the promise of a 'caliphate', this neo-state with organised conventional war-fighting capacities needs to be aggressively contained, yet mustering a common and effective response between states with competing interests and approaches has proved elusive. Strategic unease in Europe, the Middle East and Asia is at the same time taxing the international system intensely. Deterrence, containment, balance of power are all high-maintenance strategies, and the United States, having managed these in the past, is pressed to conduct them simultaneously across three theatres. In a fragmenting world order, the quality of regional leadership is being tested, and generally found wanting.

Perhaps this sense of strategic unease is most pervasive in the Middle East. Political resolution of the wars in Yemen, Libya and Syria is highly unlikely. Battle fatigue may be a more important factor in limiting the effects of these conflicts. The international coalition against ISIS is frail, ensuring that the group will remain an enduring feature of the Middle East strategic landscape. The ideational and security challenges it poses may be most important in the neighbourhood, but extend beyond it. Leaders in Southeast Asia openly express their concern that 'ungoverned' spaces could fall under the control of ISIS-inspired groups. The organisation has, finally, no state allies, yet it is able to attract many adherents to its idea of an Islamic state. While the group may not sustainably expand, and could suffer setbacks on the periphery of its so-called caliphate, it will be able to retain a strong presence in the Sunni hinterlands of Syria and Iraq. Severing its lines of communication and supply, limiting the foreign-fighter flow and choking off its financial support, attacking with precision its commanders and fighters, and training local forces to confront it more effectively are all rightly part of the strategic mix. But the campaign is naturally hampered by the absence of political solutions to the wars flaring in the region and the limitations, both professional and otherwise, of local forces. The coalition depends heavily on Kurdish forces who will focus on defence in their areas and are unlikely to take the fight forward to Sunni front-lines. Iraqi Shia militias and Iran are important actors in the overall struggle, and they make most uncomfortable allies for the US and regional Sunni states. The reality is that the most that can be expected is persistent and repeated containment of the territorial reach of ISIS, waiting upon a more deliberate defeat of its theocratic message and more effective governance in areas liberated from its control. A strategic grand bargain is theoretically there to be struck between a Western group of nations willing to provide substantial training and forces to help contain the threat, and regional states willing to drop any support for extremist groups and work to establish a post-Assad regime and a future Iraqi state that each have a place for all sects. The distrust among key players in the region and between the region and outsiders makes such a grand bargain unlikely, so muddling through and containment seem the most likely direction of travel in the year to come.

The nuclear agreement with Iran concluded on 14 July will lead to complex hedging and even more strategic unease. The deal will be invested by many in the international community with a strategic importance that far exceeds its specific frame of reference. Properly implemented, the accord will ensure that there is no risk of Iran developing a nuclear weapon for 15 years, and in that period, assuming satisfactory compliance, the Iranian economy will be progressively freed of the constraints imposed by UN and other sanctions. This is a technical agreement on a specific subject, yet the economic renaissance of Iran that the deal makes possible will also provide increased funds to its government, which those in the neighbourhood warn could be used to support its strategic objectives in the region.

The Israeli government immediately judged the deal a bad mistake. For a number of Gulf Arab states, the readmission of Iran into the international community opens the door for the Revolutionary Guards and other forces in Iran to invest in regional destabilisation. They fear that Iran might have a freer and better-financed hand to continue a policy of interference in the region, and that there will be more pressure to cede to Iran a larger regional role. That perception alone will cause important strains. Iran's regional activities will inevitably come under even more careful scrutiny. Efforts to win a wider detente with Iran will be exceptionally hard, as will attempts to ensure its constructive engagement on conflict resolution in the region. Perhaps the deal offers a chance to settle other issues too, but Arab states will look closely at what price Iran may seek to extract as part of a wider regional-security arrangement. The jockeying for strategic position will be considerable, and the relationship between the West and its regional partners fraught with uncertainty as the 'post-nuclear-deal' environment is monitored. On balance, the time bought from this agreement needs to be used intelligently to engage Iran on issues in which it can be helpful, while holding Iran to account on activities that drain regional trust and endanger wider stability. Diplomatically, Iran will seek closer relations with the Gulf Cooperation Council (GCC) states as an endorsement of its regional position. That relationship can only improve if those same states can be convinced that other parts of the Iranian government apparatus are not being used to foment instability. In the next year, the evolution of GCC–Iran relations will be a key indicator of how much strategic unease persists.

The sense of strategic unease in Asia is also palpable, as the region absorbs the truth of China's strategic arrival as a self-confident and increasingly extrovert power. Australia's strategic bipolarity – an economic relationship that is biggest with China and a security relationship that is principally with the United States – is one increasingly shared by others in the region. There is a natural 'win–win', to use China's most deployed slogan, in the economic growth of China and the corresponding economic growth that most other countries in the Asia-Pacific are positioned to enjoy as part of China's extraordinary development. Yet on the sensitive issues of territorial claims and the manner in which these are asserted and discussed, the win–win paradigm seems much less evident. Territorial rivalries have more of a 'zero-sum' character to them, and the previous tendency to put disputes to one side while cooperation continued has been replaced by a desire to assert not just rights but control over disputed territory that runs against the ethos of cooperation. The Chinese defence White Paper released in May 2015 can be read as a foundational text for a China now more willing and able to defend its security interests in the Asia-Pacific, including on territorial questions. Regional states will also wish to defend their interests, including those that come into contact with China's, in order to show their own populations that they are not ceding ground or water in ways that compromise claims to legal title. How they can do this without relying implicitly or directly on the balancing role of the US is hard to imagine. The way in which the US engages in the region strategically and on a day-to-day basis will be acutely important in 2016. China, the US, Japan, the Republic of Korea, India, Australia, New Zealand and the Association of Southeast Asian Nations (ASEAN) states have not yet found a way to shape the boundaries of competition in Asia so as to alleviate the sense of strategic unease that is felt when so many powers rise at the same time, and when so many states have nationalist impulses both to satisfy and contain. Strategic friction will remain a problem. Even as China, India and others concentrate on domestic economic growth as a principal priority, their international commercial interests and unsettled territorial issues will engender concerns.

Moreover, a number of countries in the region are being consumed by domestic political questions that limit their engagement on international issues or hamper their ability to play a constructive regional role. The ability of ASEAN in particular to act as a coherent foreign-policy actor has been hobbled by the internal fissures in a number of member states. Continued conflict and unsettled governance in Myanmar, instability in the Philippines, civil–military governance challenges in Thailand, internal political wrangling in Malaysia, protectionist and nationalist sentiment in Indonesia all make it difficult for ASEAN to fulfil its core aim of driving regional cooperation. Until Indonesia, in particular, develops a self-confident and imaginative regional role, ASEAN's potential as a force for healthy cooperation will be stalled. In 2016 Asian states will be simultaneously seized by strategic introspection and strategic unease. Domestic politics are volatile, and the weakness of regional cooperation mechanisms will become ever more apparent. It will be statesmanship, rather than structures, that will be necessary to keep regional disputes comfortably and consistently below boiling point.

Doubts about whether Europe can recreate the structures for effective cooperation with Russia while deterring Russian provocation are the principal cause of strategic unease on the continent, especially its eastern half. The eurozone crisis sapped lots of energy in 2015, and in 2016 many efforts will still be concentrated on European finance and monetary questions. It will be necessary for political leaders to think strategically again on how a measure of predictability can return to the European security landscape. The Russian leadership has operated opportunistically, at speed, using all instruments of state power to assert its interests in Ukraine and to indicate its support for Russians living in others countries. Russian military activity close to the borders of NATO states, as well as evolving military doctrine that places more emphasis on nuclear weapons at the core of national strategy, requires NATO to take measures to reassure allies and show determination to defend NATO territory. Long accustomed to living with a post-Cold War 'peace dividend', Europeans will again be hearing their leaders speak of the need to offer a robust response to Russian assertiveness. As the machinery of NATO gets tuned up again, and re-oiled, it will be necessary to avoid simply repeating the containment policies of the past.

Europe is not divided into two camps. Though Russia is seeking to gain more influence in countries that have nationalist agendas and are uncomfortable with a 'Brussels-led' Europe, and while Russia is trying to insinuate itself in weaker states and wherever pro-Russian sentiment can be marshalled, it remains the case that the country does not command a great alliance system. It may wish to create stronger links with 'like-minded' states in the South Caucasus and Central Asia, but it is starting from a low base. For the West, the stakes of principle are high: the integrity of a rules-based order in Europe, the freedom of countries to choose their alliances, the preservation of sovereignty and non-interference in the internal affairs of other states. Yet the Russian challenge to these principles has not been so overpowering as to touch Western interests in a direct fashion – and there is the rub. Western countries will not be able to accept or reverse the annexation of the Crimea, and will wish to avoid any additional adverse changes to the European strategic order. That said, military rollback is not an option, and a war to recover Ukraine's full sovereignty would not command public support. It does not appear that the West is in a position to win back the status quo and defeat Russia on this issue. Yet it also appears that the West does not want to negotiate a political compromise. A new settlement in Europe that limits Russian influence and also avoids armed conflict but appears to sacrifice an element of these principles to those ends is unpalatable. A weak containment policy unconnected to a political strategy towards Russia seems the net result. That cannot for long be satisfactory. The risks of an action–reaction vicious cycle seem high, as do the risks of accidental flare-ups. The 'new normal' in European security is strategic unease, but it should not be allowed to become strategic unease on a high wire. As a containment policy is rolled out, NATO states in 2016 will need to develop the techniques to deter low-intensity provocation. Their leaders should also find a way to manage the crisis with Russia with firmness, but in a way that invites genuine discussion of a new political settlement in the eastern half of Europe that can calm tensions. There is a robust sanctions system in place, a revived NATO commitment to Article 5 defence and an appreciation of the new types of threats Europe may face, but not yet a political strategy to ease European strategic friction in the east.

At the same time as European states are having to rethink continental European security threats, the landscape to the south, in Africa, is turning more challenging as violent Islamic extremism continues to spread. The two most prominent and deadliest groups – Boko Haram and al-Shabaab – have both suffered losses but neither is a spent force. Territorial expansion beyond their countries of origin (Nigeria and Somalia respectively) is under way, and is likely to continue in the course of 2016 with serious regional economic and security repercussions. Kenya has seen a steep decline in its tourism and hospitality sectors as a result of terrorist attacks, as has Tunisia following the attack on tourists at Sousse. Cross-border trade between Nigeria and its neighbours has been curtailed. Groups such as Boko Haram in Nigeria and al-Murabitoun in Mali, alongside others active in the Sahel, have been exploiting local grievances but have also lived off the support and influence of foreign jihadists, in the form of first al-Qaeda and then ISIS. The growing presence of ISIS in North Africa will continue to provide inspiration for African groups, and the possible transfer of knowledge and weapons is a tangible threat for the year ahead. The United Kingdom and France are bound to become more engaged in challenges in Africa: cooperation between these two European powers in Africa, and their leadership of a coherent EU strategy for the region, will be important to contain and limit the terrorist challenge from the south.

Given this level of generalised strategic unease, strategic surprise is to be expected. In Asia, strategic surprise is most likely from an angry North Korea that may suddenly, to grab attention, launch a missile or even test a nuclear device. A strong dialogue between the US, the Republic of Korea, Japan, China and Russia is essential to ensure that the Korean Peninsula remains a managed problem. China's international geo-economic policy and in particular its 'One Belt, One Road' ambitions will have it increasingly engaged in many parts of the world, often as a result shaping national and regional politics. That has long been the case in Africa; it is also becoming more the case in Latin America. China will have a progressively larger voice on global governance structures, and the fact that it is interested in setting up its own instruments, such as the AIIB, is broadly to be welcomed. Japan is still struggling to gain regional acceptance of its attempted return to 'normal power' status, and India is tending to its neighbourhood as it prepares to take, in time, a 'leading power' role. Increasingly, what these Asian powers think will be a point of reference for others. They will become as important economic and political counterparts for many states in Africa and Latin America, as North American and European states have been. Yet they will not be important guarantors of security extra-regionally for a long time, nor leading organisers of effective collective-security endeavours.

As this edition of *Strategic Survey: The Annual Review of World Affairs* has shown, few conflicts in the world have decisively abated, and new ones have emerged. As conflicts multiply, sometimes freeze, but rarely get solved, the sense of strategic unease is only reinforced. Coping with strategic surprise requires the virtues of resilience, strategic purpose, flexibility and maintenance of the aim that are among the characteristics of sound military forces, and must be the virtues of political leaderships too in this fast-paced age. The world needs more exporters of security but is producing more exporters of insecurity. States and their enemies know that, in these circumstances, selectivity is imposed. Strategic unease is here to stay; too many things are in transition to think otherwise. The corollary is that there is still a lot to play for, if the right strategic leadership can be exercised.

Index